ESSAYS ON SHAKESPEARE
AND ELIZABETHAN DRAMA

Hardin Craig

ESSAYS ON SHAKESPEARE
AND ELIZABETHAN DRAMA

IN HONOR OF HARDIN CRAIG

edited by Richard Hosley

UNIVERSITY OF MISSOURI PRESS

COLUMBIA

1962

CONTENTS

PLATES

HARDIN CRAIG

by Richard Hosley

HARDIN CRAIG was born on his father's farm near Owensboro, Kentucky, on 29 June 1875. His father, Robert Craig, a native of Ayrshire, Scotland, had migrated to Kentucky in 1850, and his mother, Mary Jane McHenry Craig, came of a Colonial family which included a member of Washington's staff, Colonel John Hardin. In 1906 Craig married Miss Gertrude Carr of Ashby, Massachusetts. Their son, Hardin Craig, Jr., was born in 1907 and is now a professor of history and the librarian at Rice University. Through him, Craig has two grandsons.

In 1897 Craig received his A.B. degree from Centre College, Kentucky, and in 1898 he began graduate study at Princeton University. In the summers of 1899 and 1900 he studied also at the University of Chicago, where he came under the influence of John Matthews Manly. At Princeton he worked under Thomas Marc Parrott, taking his Ph.D. degree in 1901. He then taught successively at Princeton (1901-10, with a year of study at Exeter College, Oxford, in 1902-3), the University of Minnesota (1910-19, with service as a U.S. Army officer in 1917-18), the State University of Iowa (1919-28, as Head of the English Department), and Stanford University (1928-42, with an interval as Visiting Professor of English at the University of North Carolina in the winter of 1935). A detailed account of Craig's career down to 1940 may be found in the biographical essay by Rudolf Kirk in *Renaissance Studies in Honor of Hardin Craig* (Stanford University Press, 1941).

In 1940 Professor Craig was asked to continue teaching at Stanford beyond the customary retirement age of sixty-five. Thus began his second career, which this second Festschrift especially honors. It has been as rich in teaching and scholarship as the first, but more lonely, for Mrs. Craig died in 1941. The following year Craig accepted an appointment as Professor of English at the University of North Carolina, where he remained until 1949, except for the spring of 1944 which he spent as Walker-Ames Visiting Professor of English at the University of Washington. During the North Carolina period Craig produced several works in the field of the Renaissance: his edition of an Elizabethan manuscript translation of *The Prince* (1944), *An Interpretation of Shakespeare* (1948), and his literary history of the English Renaissance (1950). But, characteristically, he brought out also works of more general intellectual and academic interest: *Literary Study and the Scholarly Profession* (1944) and *Freedom and Renaissance* (1949). During this period he continued to edit the annual Renaissance bibliography for *Studies in Philology,* as he had done since 1925 and was to do until 1950; and in 1944, in collaboration with Allan Gilbert of Duke University, he founded the Southeastern Renaissance Conference. In 1947 he spoke at the International Shakespeare Conference sponsored by the Shakespeare Institute of the University of Birmingham; and in 1948 he was elected a Fellow of the Royal Society of Literature and gave a talk on Shakespeare over the BBC. In the following year he gave a series of lectures at the Shakespeare Institute Summer School in Stratford-upon-Avon.

In 1949 Hardin Craig accepted the position of Visiting Professor of English at the University of Missouri, where he taught until 1960. Early in this period he finished his edition of the complete works of Shakespeare (1951), and then, stimulated by his popular graduate course in the medieval drama, he returned to his scholarly interests of thirty years earlier and wrote *English Religious Drama of the Middle Ages* (1955). In 1957 he brought out a second edition of *Two Coventry Corpus Christi Plays,* which he had edited originally for the Early English Text Society in 1902. And toward the end of the Missouri period he wrote three books that amply testify to his continuing keen interest in a variety of special fields: *Woodrow Wilson at Princeton* (1960), *New Lamps for Old: A Sequel to The Enchanted Glass* (1960), and *A New Look at Shakespeare's Quartos* (1961).

In 1960 Craig became Scholar in Residence at Stephens College, where he now teaches and writes while retaining his association with the University of Missouri as Professor Emeritus of English. Thus he is still, as in earlier periods, an active participant in the thoughtful life both of his community and of the wider world beyond the immediate horizon. The authors of the following essays, and his colleagues at the University of Missouri, here pay tribute to Hardin Craig's enduring achievement and to the spirit of inquiry that has animated it from the beginning.

THE CONTRIBUTION OF
THE INTERLUDES
TO ELIZABETHAN STAGING

by Richard Southern

Two things about the Tudor interludes have perhaps hindered investigators from making full use of them as sources of the technique for staging Elizabethan plays. The first is the uncertainty of their dates, and the second the uncertainty of their place or places of performance. Upon examination, however, neither of these difficulties proves to be a final bar for at any rate some preliminary study of the subject.

In the matter of uncertainty of date we can make some progress even with an arbitrary chronology, for there exist at least between seventy and eighty interludes from the period c. 1510 to 1590. If, in arranging these eighty interludes, our ordering is somewhat provisional this does not alter the fact that a general picture of significant development can be seen.

The second uncertainty is the place of performance. Perhaps our chief guide here is that the early interludes, unlike the medieval mysteries and moralities, have several references to 'doors' in their directions. The first tentative deduction from this is that the interludes were played under a roof. Going further, there are other references to a meal at table and to lights. A meal indoors at night in the Tudor period suggests a gentleman's hall. Now it is to be stated emphatically that there is no proof that all interludes were always played in halls and nowhere else; nor even that all Tudor halls were of identical pattern. But in this very

3

doubt there lies an explanation of what emerges as one of the most interesting points about the staging of interludes, and that is that the directions in the scripts are often of a noticeably unspecific nature.

This lack of specific directions may be the result not of carelessness (we are too apt to label as careless a theatrical technique which we do not grasp), but of a clear realization in the playwright that the conditions under which the performance would be given were not themselves specific—that, in short, the conditions of playing had not yet become regularized. A simple deduction, but one that is of some assistance to what follows.

Content then with a provisional system of dating (based mainly on the list in T. W. Craik, *The Tudor Interlude*, 1958), and supposing the performances to have been in halls, we may make the following notes of development.

Medwall's *Nature* (printed c. 1525 but undoubtedly written at least a decade earlier) initiates the subject of technicalities in its opening stage-direction: *"Fyrst cometh in Mundus and syttyth down and sayth nothynge. . . . Than cometh in Nature / Man / Reason / and Innocencye / and Nature syttyth down. . . ."* Here is clear evidence of some form of entrance and of the setting of chairs or stools. If the performance took place in a hall the only entrances that would seem practicable are those in the screen at the far end opposite the high table, near which the crowd of general retainers would gather (thus justifying the frequent opening request of interlude characters for 'room').

Further, the performance is specified, in line 91, as taking place "thys nyght." And upon Pride's entrance a character observes that "a gentyl-man comys in at the dorys." Perhaps the term 'doors' is in the plural because the openings in the screen were hung with a pair of leaves, forming double doors; thus its use would be comparable to that in our modern phrase 'to come in through the swing-*doors*.' But if this were so, such a term would seem to me to bear a specific quality not really ascribable to early directions. Further, I am not satisfied that double doors were used in every screen opening. I would be happier to read the plural as signifying 'by one of the doors—whichever you please.'

So far, then, only the simplest technical means are called for: the screen doors, and certain seats placed. No more is needed.

In *Fulgens and Lucrece* (sometime before 1516), also by Medwall, there is a similar picture of technical simplicity. A note of interest is in the direction at line 833—*"Avoyde the place A"* ('A' being the designation

THE GREAT HALL (1531-6) OF HAMPTON COURT PALACE
(by gracious permission of Her Majesty the Queen)

given to one of the characters). This recalls the wide use of the term 'Place' in medieval mysteries and moralities. The word is also found in the interludes, and sometimes with a clearly similar implication, but its use gradually declines through the century as another technique begins to grow—one in which the actor mingles less and less with the audience and begins more and more to perform his play upon a particular area, as will be shown. Further, at line 631 in the first part of *Fulgens*, A says "I haue no more acqueyntaunce within this hall"; and in the concluding speech of Part 1 he refers to "these folke that sitt here in the halle," confirming that the performance was in fact indoors, and in a 'hall' at that; and confirming also, therefore, that the Place, an outdoor conception in medieval plays, has now been adapted to an indoor situation.

Skelton's *Magnyfycence* (c. 1516), as befits an early play, uses several directions about the Place such as *"and so they go out of the place,"* but also contains an order from one character to another to "go out of the dores fast!" (line 1725). Our two early references to 'doors,' then, are in the plural; this may strengthen the idea of the use of the screen.

John Heywood's *Love* (c. 1525) contains the well-known reference to the Vice *"ronnynge sodenly aboute the place among the audyens"* with a fire on his head. But we should not let the firework effect blind us to the firm proof in this direction that the 'Place' was an area which *both* audience and players could use—the floor, presumably, of the hall.

In Heywood's *Weather* (c. 1527) comes a problem that might be of considerable use to us could we but solve it. Merry Report, the Vice, refers to torches and to his having to "thrust" among the audience, but the problem is connected with the character of Jupiter who *"hath a song played in his trone."* The setting-up of some sort of throne is thus implied, and Jupiter is pictured as sitting in it to hear the song. Merry Report now appoints himself Jupiter's doorman, and a Gentleman comes in to see Jupiter. Merry Report's line is then curious; he says to Jupiter, "My lord there standeth a sewter euen here behynde a Gentylman in yonder corner. . . ." There is a marked suggestion that such visitors cannot be seen by Jupiter at first—or that Jupiter pretends he cannot see them. There is further suggestion of this remoteness later, in Merry Report's line to the Miller to whom he points out Jupiter "in yonder throne," before allowing him to approach. Again there is much play between Merry Report and several visitors which the audience see and hear but which Jupiter does not. The problem is: How could all this be made effective? Some sort of accepted technique seems to be growing. Either the whole thing could be done by miming, or the throne might be curtained like a medieval scaffold, or the effect might be gained by raising the throne up a couple of steps, on exactly the same lines as the throne at the back of the stage in Van de Venne's print of the Hague Fair (see the reproduction in *Theatre Notebook*, 9, 1954). But there is nothing so far to inform us.

Fig. 1. A sketch of the arrangements at the screen end of a Tudor hall during performance of an interlude, based on the Great Hall of Hampton Court Palace (see plate facing p. 4).

There may be added one reference to *Calisto and Melebea* (c. 1527) before breaking off to review the situation so far. At least twice in this play there are simultaneous directions for exit and entrance; for example, *"hic exeat Parmeno et intret Melebea."* One is disinclined, for technical reasons, to suppose that such examples of simultaneous exit and entrance would be confined to a single door; it would be clumsy. If, then, two doors are in fact implied, then again a reference to the screen of a Tudor hall is suggested.

So far, it is possible to compose the following picture of the staging of early interludes. It is strongly probable that they were written for performance indoors; at night; during or after a meal; on the same floor as was used by the ordinary people; that the players came in by doors, and

Fig. 2. A reproduction of the De Witt sketch of the Swan Theater from the same point of view as Fig. 1, showing the essential similarity of tiring-house facade and hall screen. The posts and stage-cover have been omitted.

since references to 'doors' suggest the plural then two screen doors *may* be implied; that furniture can be set and presumably removed; that sometimes this furniture represents a throne; and finally there is the ghost of a suggestion that some kind of means existed for concealing a character on a throne—though perhaps the means was, in fact, nothing more than a convention of the acting. The situation is summed up in

Fig. 1 (p. 6), which depicts the screen end of a Tudor hall, based on the Great Hall (1531-6) of Hampton Court Palace. The plate facing p. 4 shows the appearance today of this hall where so many royal performances of both plays and masques have been given. The screen is 40 ft. long and about 17½ ft. high; and each of the screen doors is about 7½ ft. wide and 12½ ft. tall.

With the anonymous *Godly Queen Hester* (c. 1527) we see the beginning of a second phase in the technique. In it all the previous devices are employed, but there is more. The opening direction, immediately following the prologue and without any instruction to any player to enter, reads *"The Kyng sitting in a chaire speaketh to his counsell."* Thus furniture is again used, but that this should be in effect an entrance-direction is remarkable. No word exists to indicate how the King (or the Council) came in. We seem to have here a foreshadowing of the Elizabethan direction *"Enter So-and-so in his Study."* Is this a 'discovery'? We do not know.

The King now discusses with his gentlemen "which is [the] most worthy honoure to attayne." They reply variously. The King sums up. But he concludes his speech with the unexpected question addressed (it seems) to no one in particular: "Sir, what is your name and progeny?" (line 103). Here a marginal note directs: *"One of the gentyllmen must answere whyche you will."* This is, by the way, a good example of the unspecific quality in a direction; but despite the air of *laissez faire* the text says that Aman is to reply, and this he does with the words "I am Aman sonne of Amadathy. . . ." The problems are growing and a greater one follows.

At line 130 King Assewerus calls Aman, and *"Here entrith Aman with Many men awaiting on hym."* The King gives them instructions to go and find him a bride. Then at line 140 the very remarkable marginal direction occurs: *"Here the Kynge entryth the trauers & aman goeth out."* Presumably this elaborate direction would not exist if all that was meant was 'The King and Aman exeunt.' It is only Aman who 'goeth out' (and his 'many men' together with the King's 'gentlemen' have also to be disposed of); but the King 'entereth *the traverse*' (with a particularizing article, as if it could only apply to one thing). But we do not know what this 'traverse' was. It might perhaps be the screen (but in that case how does the King's action differ from Aman's?), or it might have been a curtain slung a little in front of the screen between the two doors. (Or it might have been something quite different, which escapes me.) Leaving the problem for a moment and turning to the rest of the play:

There next come in Mardocheus and a maiden (Hester). A Pursuivant enters to them *"with manye maydens"* but does not see Mardocheus and Hester, for he remarks that he still "muste speake for Hester" (line 194). Thus presumably he entered at a different door from Hester. Then Mardocheus interposes, introduces Hester, and the Pursuivant summons her to the King. Next, *"Here Aman metythe them in the place."* The technique now is getting as involved as in an Elizabethan script. Eventually Aman's line comes, "Plesyth it youre grace . . . ," and he introduces Hester to the King *without there being any direction for the King to enter.* Thus the King would appear to have been hidden till then behind the 'traverse' and to be now discovered.

The scene of the selection of Hester as queen follows and concludes with the King's saying, "and we for a season thys busynesse will cease And oure selfe repose for our pleasure and ease." The supposition is that the Place is now left empty.

There follow great complications of plot and subplots, with much developing technique implied. Finally, *"Here must bee prepared a banket in the place,"* and at the banquet Aman is unmasked by Hester. There is already, in one or two decades, a clear expansion beyond the simplicities of *Nature.*

Passing now to Redford's *Wit and Science* (c. 1540), there are examples again of most of the previous technicalities such as 'doors' (*"Wyt spekyth at the doore"*) and 'the Place' (*". . . standing in the myddell of the place, Wyt sayth as foloweth: . . ."*), but also one notable innovation. Near the end, the hero Wit has to fight with the devil Tediousness; and his mentor Instruction tells him, "turne on your right hand Vp that mount before ye shall see stand" (*sic*). What is this "mount"? Wit fights Tediousness and then kills him off-stage and brings in the head on his sword as a gift to Science, his sweetheart. Confidence now comes running in and says that Science has seen all this from "vpon yonder mowntayne on hye," so Wit dispatches him to her with the head, but she anticipates with her entrance. Why all these references to a high place, unless one existed? Is this an ancestor of action 'above'?

The anonymous *Jacob and Esau* (c. 1550) is a highly developed play. Its plot is well devised, its characterization is alive, its lines can be apt and vivid. Already there is every sign that the playwright is using all efforts to exploit his medium of players and their exits and entrances; and to enable those players to make, with the means at their disposal, some effectual fiction that they are among the tents of Israel. "Tents" are often alluded to in the dialogue. But were these make-believe tents, represented by the doors in the screen? Or were they shown in actuality as tented scaffolds in the Place? The very fact that the text is so tantalizingly undecided on this matter may well be because so shrewd a playwright was aware that sometimes 'tents' would be available and that sometimes the players would have to make do with screen doors. One supposes from his allusions that it had not escaped him that *tenti* was one of the names formerly given to the 'scaffolds' or *sedes* of characters in fifteenth-century moralities; and the fact is that *Jacob and Esau* could be played with tents or mansions set up in the Place, or just as well by employing the screen doors only.

One of the great interests in Phillip's *Patient Grissell* (c. 1559) is its revolutionary handling of the 'unities' of time and place. To study the devices by which several years and many localities are crammed into a single evening's show on a hall floor, is to learn much of the broadness of approach which made the Elizabethan play-form so flexible. Here is a passage in illustration:

Grissell enters by one door (from her father's house) to go to the well to fetch water, for which she exits presumably by the other door. Through this second door Gautier now enters. She, having filled her pitcher outside, follows him in. Upon her re-entrance, however, she *does not see him,* but soliloquizes about obedience. He now interrupts her and talks. She says her father is in his cottage. Gautier says he wants to speak to him. She agrees and then *immediately* addresses her father and gives him the message; he replies that they both will "repaire to his [i.e. Gautier's] presence." And in two lines they are speaking with the Marquis.

Here, obviously, are advanced conventions. A character can be present in the Place but be understood to be quite separate from other characters also in the Place. They do not form a realistic picture, but groups of pawns in whom the interest is to see one detach himself and move to another group, take a further pawn, and bring him to the first. So *place* is handled.

Now as for *time*. Gautier asks the father for Grissell, is refused, says he thinks not of Venus's "bestiall playes," is then accepted but told he must not take Grissell's virgin flower; and on that condition he carries her off. He sends her away with his ladies and remains to talk with her father who says, If you have children (!) bring them up well. Grissell re-enters dressed as a bride and bids farewell; she must *"singe and then go out."* The Vice now sneers at it all for twelve lines and says she's big with child. Reason and Sobriety enter and say how good Grissell is. Then Dilligence enters to summon all to the Marquis because Grissell has had her child.

This child is taken away from her. Then the birth of a second child is similarly condensed. Subsequently Grissell is banished back to her father's house. Gautier proposes (or affects to propose in order to test her) to marry again. His messenger Dilligence comes in *solus* and explains: "From my Lord Marquis euen now I am sent" to fetch a new bride; but he will advise Grissell first. Then this remarkable sequence (line 1831):

> Harke me thinks I here hyr voice delectable,
> Suerly to vertue, this Lady was tractable,
> Now God be here, who resteth in this place.

> *Grisill* My poore Father and I this is a plaine case.

> *Go once or twice about the Staige, let Grissill singe some songe, and set Spinninge*

>> *A songe for Grissill, when the Messinger commeth to hir.*

Not only is this sequence a notable example of condensation, but the text also includes a word of particular importance to investigators—the word *stage*. Presumably we are now no longer entitled to picture an interlude as all taking place on the hall floor. Now part of it at least is on a 'stage.' Maybe not all the play is raised; maybe part is still performed on the floor and part only on a "*Staige*." But from now on (c. 1559) a stage is possible.

There may be some question asked whether this "*Staige*" indicates necessarily a raised platform or can be limited to mean an acting-area on the floor—in other words a part of the Place. Not only is tradition, however, against this but in the next interlude, *Apius and Virginia* (c. 1560), we have proof. Here at line 854 is the direction, "*Here let Virginius go about the scaffold.*" A 'scaffold' cannot be part of the floor. A raised platform, for at least some of the acting, is now certain.

To review, then, the developments in the second phase: There is far more complicated use of the act of entrance through doors as an essential means of telling the story (not merely of getting the actors on), and this is a considerable technical advance. There is the introduction of a 'traverse.' There is the expansion of 'effects' scenes needing props, such as banquets. There is the suggestion of action 'above.' There is the possibility that doors were used to represent tents or that actual tents were built; or that these were alternatives depending on the occasion. And there is undoubtedly use of some sort of raised stage.

Turning now to the last phase of development. In 1567 was published one of the most ambitious, advanced, and least quoted of the interludes, Pickering's *Horestes* (usually identified with the *Orestes* performed at Court in 1567-8). Here are the fullest examples of the technique. References to the Place are very slight and there are only two, but references to the 'stage' are important; and there is clear indication at last of action 'above.'

Horestes is a jumbled play, with a Vice changing into other characters, such as Revenge; some small interposed scenes of subplot; many Greek characters mixed with several typical English rustics; and a complete division of the play in the middle (as in *Fulgens and Lucrece*). It has very full stage-directions, some of them couched in the second person directly to the actor.

After rustic arguments to begin, Horestes enters and debates whether to avenge his father's murder by killing his own mother. He sees that "Idumeus, that worthy Kinge, doth come into this place." Idumeus at first does not see him and soliloquizes in ranting speech. Horestes kneels and begs his assistance; eventually a pact is made. Later: *"Let the drum play and enter Horestis with his band: marche a bout the stage."* There is much battle-talk, then a general exit.

Next, *"enter Egistus and Clytemnestra singinge"* (and all the lyrics in this play are good); it is an 'Antony and Cleopatra' atmosphere. News of battle comes. They part and go.

Now follows a strange episode: *"Enter a woman like a begger, rounning before they [sic] sodier; but let the sodier speke first; but let the woman crye first pitifully."* Here is typical Elizabethan episode-technique; the soldier bullies her and tells her to yield and follow; then he must *"Go a fore her, & let her fal downe upon the [sodier] and al to beate him. . . . take his weapons & let him ryse up and then go out both."*

Soon *"Horestis entrith with his bande and marcheth about the stage"* once again, but now he tells his soldiers he will storm "yonder citite" [sic]. Then, *"Let the trumpet go towards the Citie and blowe."* What was this 'city'? It was actually represented in some form (however conventionally), and with its defenses, for in a short time: *"Let the trumpet leaue soundyng and let Harrauld speake and Clytemnestra speake ouer the wal."* The last four words are of great significance—whether Clytemnestra merely spoke over a curtain from a ladder-top in the booth-stage fashion, or whether she ascended a hall gallery and threw down defiance from there. In any case this is action 'above.' After parley the besiegers attack; and the following classic direction describes how:

Go & make your liuely battel & let it be longe, eare you can win the
Citie, and when you have won it, let Horestis bringe out his mother
by the armes, & let the droum sease playing & the trumpet also, when
she is taken, let her knele downe and speake. . . .

She begs clemency. He sends her to captivity. *"Go out with on of the*
sodiares." The Vice exults and during his speech occurs the direction,
"Let Orestes syth [sigh?] *hard."* The Vice continues to mock—"Jesu god,
how styll he syttes"—and then: *"let Horestes ryse & bid him pease."*
Horestes is shattered, and at this moment Egistus comes in to the rescue:
"set hys men in a raye & let the drom playe tyll Horestes speaketh." There
is fighting talk, then: *"Stryke vp your drum & fyght a good whil, & then*
let sum of Egistus men flye, & then take hym & let Horestes drau him
vyolentlye, & let the drums sease." Horestes gloats and decides to hang
Egistus; the soldiers must hurry—*"fling him of the lader & then let on*
bringe in his mother Clytemnestra but let her loke wher Egistus hangeth."
She begs mercy of Horestes; then, *"Take downe Egistus and bear him*
out. . . ." And so the action proceeds.

By now sufficient has been quoted to serve as evidence of the pitch of
development of the interlude from the time of Medwall's *Nature* and
Fulgens and Lucrece near the beginning of the century. It is time to
summarize the findings of the last phase (ending well before construction of the first regular playhouse, the Theater, in 1576). I would suggest
that these findings are: considerable complication of plot, both in action
and in psychology; the development of military displays and battles; the
introduction of stage tricks such as scenes showing a hanging; the use of
detailed inset scenes, apart from the true plot, to give an atmosphere; and
specifically and without any doubt the achievement of means for portraying action 'above.' In fact, it would be true to say that our review of
progress has brought us to the threshold of Elizabethan play-technique
complete, that is to say that not only in matters of pure staging alone but
in the whole construction of plays, the way for the Elizabethan period
was fully prepared by the groundwork laid down during the growth of
the Tudor interlude.

There are three further observations to be made. It would appear from
the present study that we are perhaps wrong in seeing the origin of
English drama in the *quem quaeritis* element of the church liturgy; instead, it may well lie in the interludes which were interspersed with, or
which rose alongside, the performances that derived from *quem quaeritis*
—that is, the performances of the mysteries. Not only would it seem

that Elizabethan and subsequent plays are not indebted to the mysteries in respect of plot and the particular exposition of a plot by means of figures entering by doors and moving in a pattern on a Place or stage; but that above all, in their use of a stage with the particular technical resources such as we know them, our plays are again indebted to the interludes and not to the mysteries. Again, the interludes were presumably for performance by professional players; the mysteries were performed by ordinary working people who spent most of their year at other jobs and thus could not found a true professional technique of playing. With the interludes, however, all concentration could be given (and indeed *had* to be given) to the task of developing the technique so as to be effective on an audience and to ensure the living of the entertainers.

The second observation is that, despite the emphasis laid above on the performance in a hall before a screen, there is another type of performance into which these interludes, precisely with their technicalities of presentation, would fit with equal exactness. And that is the traveling booth-stage set up in the market place or on a village green, and possibly sometimes in a town hall or guild hall. This too provided the two entrances, either side its back curtain; its raised stage; its steps to allow descents to the Place; the thrusting on of furniture; the central traverse for special occasions; and the ladder inside by which a player could lean over the back curtain and play a scene from 'above.'

The final observation is that there is such a marked resemblance between the screen of a Tudor hall and the tiring-house facade shown in the De Witt sketch of the Swan Theater that we may well be justified in supposing the one to be a prototype of the other. Fig. 2 (on p. 7 above) is a reproduction of the Swan drawing designed to show, in conjunction with Fig. 1, the essential similarity of the two structures. Both have two large doorways, an upper-level gallery, and the same general proportions; and both stand in the same relation to an acting-area which is surrounded by audience on three sides.

TRISSINO'S *ART OF POETRY*

by Marvin T. Herrick

G IANGIORGIO TRISSINO (1478-1550), poet, dramatist, critic, grammarian, courtier, was one of the most distinguished *letterati* of his time. Born in Vicenza, he studied in most of the cities of northern Italy, applying himself to Latin and Greek and then to the Italian language and literature. In 1513-15 he wrote the first 'regular' tragedy of the Renaissance, *Sofonisba,* in which he tried to arrange Livy's historical narrative within the framework of a classical Greek play. Into his tragedy he introduced Italian 'blank' verse, that is, *versi sciolti* or verses 'freed' from rhyme. In 1547 he completed *L'Italia liberata dai Goti,* the first heroic poem of the Renaissance that was composed in the classical manner. His source was Procopius's history of the Gothic War in Italy, his guide Aristotle's *Poetics,* his model Homer, and his medium *verso sciolto.*

Although Trissino was not the inventor of unrhymed Italian verse he was the most important early advocate and practitioner of this form. Later on, in his *Poetica* (fols. 25-25v), first published in 1529, he explained why he chose blank verse for drama and epic poetry. Dante, he remarked, had found *terza rima* suitable for the heroic poem. Then Boccaccio, in his long narrative of Arcita and Palemone *(La Teseide),* had used the *ottava-rima* stanza, which was adopted by Boiardo, Ariosto, and others. Trissino, however, had decided that rhyme was not the best medium for the 'matter of arms' and therefore chose unrhymed eleven-syllable lines, *versi sciolti,* which he considered best for heroic poems and for dramatic poems.

In 1548 Trissino completed a comedy called *I Simillimi,* a 'Grecian' adaptation of the *Menaechmi* in which he followed Plautus's plot but changed the names of the characters and added a chorus. He produced other works, among which was *La Poetica,* the first complete 'art of poetry' of the Renaissance in a vernacular tongue.

The first four divisions of Trissino's *Poetica* were published at Vicenza in 1529. Publication of Parts 5 and 6 was delayed until after the author's death in 1550, those parts not appearing until 1562 at Venice. Trissino himself accounted for this delay by his preoccupation with the *Italia liberata,* which was twenty years in the writing. Although he did not say so, there may have been another reason, namely his discovery of important material on the art of poetry that had not been available to him before 1529. This important material, I suspect, consisted of better versions of Aristotle's *Poetics* and Francesco Robortello's great commentary on that work.

Although there was a Latin translation of the Greek *Poetics* by Giorgio Valla as early as 1498, this version was not much used by scholars. Trissino could read Greek and he might well have seen the good Aldine text of 1508; but the *Poetics* is difficult and few Renaissance critics ventured to use it until after the Latin translation by Paccius appeared in 1536. Paccius's version was a good one and reappeared time and again; Robortello used it in 1548 and so did Madius in 1550. Actually, few Renaissance critics ventured very far in interpreting Aristotle on poetry until after the commentaries of Robortello, Madius, Victorius, Castelvetro, and other scholars had taught them how to do so.

Since Trissino was noted for his command of Greek, he may have been the exception among contemporary critics, but he had two years before his death in which to examine Robortello's *Explicationes,* which first appeared in 1548. He also had an opportunity to examine Bernardo Segni's Italian translation of the *Poetics,* which came out in 1549. An inventory of Trissino's effects, dated 9 December 1550, listed among other books the following: "volumeni Robortelli, Petrarca, Retorica et Poetica de Aristotile vulgare, Catullo, Properzio, Virgilio, [etc.]."[1] This entry is no proof, to be sure, that the volume of Robortello was the commentary on the *Poetics,* but Robortello's *Explicationes* was his most important work, and it was just the sort of work that Trissino would have wanted to own and to study. It seems that he was going over the manuscript of Part 5 of his *Poetica* on the very day that his final illness struck him (Morsolin, p. 527).

2.

As it stands today, the *Poetica* (1529, 1562) epitomizes the development of literary criticism in the Renaissance, not only in Italy but in France,

---

[1] Bernardo Morsolin, *Giangiorgio Trissino* (1878), p. 524.

England, and other countries of western Europe. The first four divisions of 1529 constitute a handbook on versification, similar to other technical handbooks that had been appearing since the Middle Ages. The last two divisions of 1562 are philosophical discussions of poetry as a fine art; they are essentially a summary or paraphrase of Aristotle's *Poetics* with modern illustrations. These are mostly drawn from Dante and Petrarch and from the author's *Sofonisba, Italia liberata,* and the *Simillimi.* The rediscovery of Aristotle's *Poetics* revolutionized literary criticism in the Renaissance, and no document better illustrates this revolution than do the 1529 and 1562 printings of Trissino's *Poetica.*

Since the sixteenth-century *Poetica* is now a rare book and there is no reprinting of it beyond its inclusion in the *Opere* of 1729 at Verona, a brief summary of its contents may be enlightening.

Trissino begins with praise of the ancient Greeks and Romans and of Dante and Petrarch. Actually there is very little reliance on the ancients in the first four parts, but he does refer to Aristotle's definition of poetry as an "imitation of the actions of man . . . with words, rhythms, and harmony, like the imitation of the painter, which is made with design and colors" (2.5). Such a reference is pretty general and hardly positive assurance of a first-hand knowledge of the *Poetics;* but there is outside evidence that Trissino was familiar with the treatise before 1529. He dedicated his tragedy *Sofonisba,* first published in 1524, to Pope Leo X, and in his dedication he referred several times to Aristotle's theory of tragedy. One of these references is parallel to the statement already quoted from the *Poetica:* "Tragedy, according to Aristotle, is preferred to all other poems for imitating with comely speech a virtuous and perfect action which has magnitude; and, as the ancient painter Polygnotus in his works imitated personages who were better than the average and Pauson worse, so tragedy imitates better characters and comedy worse." There is no questioning that this pronouncement came straight from the *Poetics,* in particular from the early part of the second chapter.

In Part 1 of the *Poetica,* Trissino discusses the choice of words and phrases, such qualities as clarity, grandeur, sweetness, swiftness, character, sincerity, and artifice. He illustrates generously from Dante and Petrarch and occasionally from other Italian poets.

In Part 2 he discusses *rima* ("which the Greeks call rhythm"), letters, syllables, poetic feet, meters, caesura. *Rima* in the *Poetica* usually means rhythm; when Trissino means rhyme he says 'agreement of terminations' ("l'accordar le desinenzie").

In Part 3 he examines rhymes and rhyme-schemes: couplets, triplets (abc, aba, abb, aab, aaa), four-line stanzas (*quadernarii*—abba, abab, etc.), six-line stanzas *(senarii),* and various combinations of these.

In Part 4 there is a fairly elaborate discussion of the various kinds of lyric poems: sonnet, canzone, *ballata,* madrigal, and *serventese* (ditty). The whole character of the *Poetica* changes in Parts 5 and 6, which treat of the origin of poetry and its three major forms, tragedy, heroic poem, and comedy. Here the author displays an intimate knowledge of both the *Poetics* and *Rhetoric* of Aristotle. "I shall not depart," he says, "from the rules and precepts of the ancients, and especially of Aristotle, who wrote divinely of the art" (fol. 5). He did not betray his promise; he proceeded to summarize, actually to paraphrase, the *Poetics* chapter by chapter throughout his discussion of tragedy and the epic poem. When he came to comedy, in Part 6, he adapted Aristotle's scheme of analyzing tragedy to the comic form, thus filling in the omissions in the *Poetics.* Robortello had already done this in 1548 in his *Explicatio eorum omnium quae ad comoediae artificium pertinent,* an essay appended to his commentary; but it must be said that Trissino's treatment of comedy is more detailed than Robortello's and far richer in illustrations.

Trissino did not depend entirely on the authority of Aristotle, but made use of Plato and Horace and, on matters of style, of Dionysius of Halicarnassus. Nor did he confine his illustrations of ancient dramatic and epic poetry to Aristotle's favorites, Homer, Sophocles, and Euripides, but often turned to Virgil, Plautus, and Terence. Curiously enough, he all but ignored Seneca, the polestar of tragic writers in the Renaissance, for he did not share the contemporary admiration for the Roman tragedian: "Those [tragedies] of Seneca that have survived are for the most part fragments of Greek matter, put together with very little art" (fol. 13v). Trissino was a 'Grecian.'

Most of the illustrations in Parts 5 and 6, as in the earlier divisions, are from Italian writers, principally from Dante, Petrarch, Boccaccio, and Trissino. There are numerous references to other Italians, such as Pulci, Boiardo, Ariosto, Sannazaro, even to writers of farces like Ruzzante (Angelo Beolco) and Strascino (Niccolò Campani). The illustrations may not always be happy, but they must have brought home to his readers Aristotle's sometimes cryptic remarks, and they constitute one of the principal merits of the *Poetica.*

Towards the close of Part 6 Trissino added a section on rhetorical and grammatical figures that owed virtually nothing to Aristotle. It was the fashion in the sixteenth century to emphasize figures, and Trissino was doubtless as much interested in them as were most poets and critics. He did not attempt any extensive catalogue, however, but contented himself with defining and illustrating ten tropes and seventeen figures of speech.

Finally he added a brief section on a form of poetry that Aristotle had left untouched, the eclogue, "which is of the same genus of poetry that comedy is, that is, of the lower and worse sort. Moreover, the characters that are introduced in it are humbler and lower than those, because as comedy is about ordinary citizens so the eclogue is about peasants, plowmen, shepherds, goatherds, and other rustic characters" (fol. 45). Trissino did not like the rustic language of the eclogue, but he was aware of its important contribution to pastoral romance and drama, for he mentions Sannazaro, author of the famous *Arcadia*, Ruzzante, master of the peasant farce, and Strascino, who had delighted Siena with his rustic comedies.

3.

The *Poetica*, then, was a worthy representative of Renaissance criticism, and it was the readiest way in the sixteenth century to an understanding of Aristotelian criticism. Was it known and used in Elizabethan England?

The answer to this question is even more difficult than the answer to the question of how much did Italian drama influence Elizabethan drama. Every competent student of Elizabethan literature is aware of the Italianate flavor of English tragedy, comedy, tragicomedy, and pastoral from the time of Gascoigne through Greene, Marlowe, Shakespeare, Jonson, Chapman, Marston, Webster, Fletcher, Massinger, and Ford; but unless the English play is a translation or adaptation of an Italian one, it is extremely difficult to pinpoint the sources of the many Italian plots, characters, scenes, and verbal echoes that appear over and over again in Elizabethan drama. One may argue that English critics would have done well to examine Trissino's *Poetica* and that there must be echoes of his theories in Elizabethan criticism, but to demonstrate that Trissino provided the direct source for statements in Gascoigne, Sidney, Puttenham, or Jonson is another matter.

For over half a century now most scholars have accepted Spingarn's contention that Sidney was probably indebted to Trissino for his remarks on comedy. Compared with Trissino's clear analysis of the ridiculous, Sidney's discussion is fuzzy and sometimes contradictory, but it does seem that he had either read the *Poetica* or heard it talked about.

Trissino argued that comedy is "not to move laughter by every means possible, but only by the means proper to censuring, reprehending, and scoffing at matters that are ugly and vicious" (fol. 32v). There is delight in laughter, but it is a special kind of delight that comes from what is ugly: "If any one sees a fair woman or a beautiful jewel, or something that pleases him, he does not laugh . . . ; but if the object that is presented to the senses has some mixture of ugliness it moves laughter, as an ugly and distorted face, an inept movement, a silly word, a mispronunciation [etc.]" (fol. 37).

The argument in the *Apology for Poetry* is similar and at the same time different: "Delight hath a joy in it, either permanent or present. Laughter hath only a scornful tickling. For example, we are ravished with delight to see a fair woman, and yet are far from being moved to laughter. We laugh at deformed creatures, wherein certainly we cannot delight." If Sidney was following Trissino, and it looks as though he was, he took the liberty of sharply differing in the concept of comic delight. Sidney's interpretation was moral in a way that the Italian's was not; Sidney believed that the all-important didactic function of poetry could be defeated by laughter: "And the great fault even in that point of laughter, and forbidden plainly by Aristotle, is that they stir laughter in sinful things, which is rather execrable than ridiculous, or in miserable, which are rather to be pitied than scorned."

The Aristotle that Sidney referred to here was the author of the *Ethics* rather than the author of the *Poetics*. "Now they who exceed the proper limit in ridicule," Aristotle had said (*Ethics*, 4.8), "seem to be buffoons and vulgar people, as their heart is set upon exciting ridicule at any cost, and they aim rather at raising a laugh than at using decorous language and not giving pain to their butt." Cicero (*De oratore*, 2.61-6), whom Sidney revered as much as he did Aristotle and understood much better, repeatedly warned the would-be orator against the dangers of lapsing into bad taste and losing dignity when dealing with the laughable. Cicero did not favor buffoonery. Nor did Sidney.

If it were certain, as it is not, that Sidney had a first-hand acquaintance with Aristotle's *Poetics,* one would suspect that his moral distortion of Aristotle on the ridiculous stemmed in part from the usual sixteenth-century Latin translation of a famous passage in Chapter 5. The literal sense of this passage is: "The ridiculous is a fault or deformity free from pain and not pernicious." The key word is ἁμάρτημα, which means fault or failure but does not mean intentional wrong. This, Paccius (1536) translated as *peccatum,* which may mean a fault or crime in classical Latin but in Christian times certainly carried a more serious connotation of sin and guilt. It is easy to see that some people could have read Aristotle's statement as 'the ridiculous is a sin' or 'laughter is a sin.'

The commentators Robortello (1548) and Madius (1550) retained *peccatum*. Robortello, however, did not interpret the term as meaning something sinful or shameful, and Madius sensibly observed that *peccatum* is "truly a loose enough term." Victorius, who made his own Latin translation of the *Poetics* in 1560, kept *peccatum*. Later on, the Dutch scholar Daniel Heinsius added more confusion and led Ben Jonson astray when Jonson had already been led astray (perhaps) by Sidney. In his essay *Ad Horatii de Plauto et Terentio judicium,* Heinsius observed that nearly all of the ancient philosophers wisely considered laughter shameful and that the moving of laughter is not the proper function of comedy; "nam ridiculum, ut recte Aristoteles, 'vitium est et foeditas, doloris expers, quae partem in homine aliquem corrumpit absque morbo.'" Jonson, in his *Discoveries*, turned the passage into the following English: "For, as Aristotle says rightly, the moving of laughter is a fault in comedy, a kind of turpitude that depraves some part of man's nature without a disease."

Although Trissino did not approve of the clowns and jugglers that appeared in many between-the-acts entertainments (the *intermedi* or *intermezzi*), he understood that laughter is essential to comedy; he correctly interpreted Aristotle's brief remarks on the ridiculous.

There are other parallels between Sidney and Trissino, but since these embody critical ideas that were more or less commonplaces in the Renaissance they offer no proof that the English critic was following this particular Italian. Two examples will suffice.

The definition of poetry in the *Apology for Poetry* runs as follows: "Poesy, therefore, is an art of imitation, for so Aristotle termeth it in his word *mimesis,* that is to say, a representing, counterfeiting, or figuring forth: to speak metaphorically, a speaking picture, with this end, to teach and delight." The definition of poetry in the *Poetica* of 1529 runs as follows: "Poesy (as Aristotle first said) is an imitation of the actions of man, and it makes such an imitation with words, rhythms, and harmony, like the imitation of the painter, which is made with design and colors" (2.5).

Sidney's definition is a fusion of Aristotle, Plutarch, and Horace, though not necessarily at first-hand. *Mimesis* goes back to Aristotle and Plato. The speaking picture comes from Plutarch's aphorism, "A poem is a speaking picture and a picture a silent poem." The "to teach and delight" comes from Horace. Trissino was thoroughly familiar with the *Ars poetica* of Horace and doubtless knew Plutarch as well, but his definition, as has been shown earlier, was based directly on the *Poetics*.

In his praise of 'heroical' poetry Sidney argued that the examples of the great heroes in epic poems, such as Achilles, Cyrus, Aeneas, Turnus, and Rinaldo, teach and move to the highest and most excellent truth. This heroic poetry, said Sidney, makes magnanimity and justice shine; by dressing virtue in holiday apparel it makes her more lovely; for, "if the saying of Plato and Tully be true, . . . who could see Virtue would be wonderfully ravished of her beauty."[2] In Trissino's discussion of poetic characters (and he cites Achilles, Agamemnon, Menelaus, Odysseus, Hector, Nestor, and others), he gives special praise to Homer and the ancient poets, in whose pages "one can examine all human life as if he were in a most spacious theater, and thus appears what Plato confirms when he says that the poetry which ornaments many works of the ancients teaches posterity, because the study of characters [costumi] is the instruction of our life, and this attention to universal characters will suffice for our fleeing vice and following virtue" (fol. 33v).

There is little or no positive evidence, then, that Sidney or other Elizabethan critics read Trissino's Poetica. The documentary evidence, in fact, rather points the other way; if they had read Trissino with any care, English critics would have incorporated Aristotle's theory of poetry much earlier than they did. Sidney and his fellow critics would have fared better if they had studied Trissino instead of Julius Caesar Scaliger, whom they did know. The leading sixteenth-century commentators on the Poetics, Robortello, Madius, Victorius, Castelvetro, were all learned men, but their annotations are often complicated and difficult to follow. Trissino was also a learned man, and a good critic, and his 1562 Poetica was as faithful an interpretation of Aristotle as any of the great commentaries. Moreover, his Poetica was briefer, simpler, and clearer.

[2] Cicero, in De officiis, 1.5, quoting Plato, says that if one could see the face of honor (or virtue)—'faciem honesti'—it would excite a wonderful love of wisdom. Cf. Plato's Phaedrus, 250D.

THE SPANISH TRAGEDY,
OR BABYLON REVISITED

by S. F. JOHNSON

THOMAS KYD'S masterpiece, though extraordinarily successful in its day, has been more notorious than renowned since that time, and much of the interpretive criticism it has occasioned has tended to enhance its notoriety. My purpose in this essay is to argue a case for the careful contrivance and artistic unity of effect of *The Spanish Tragedy* as it has been preserved for us (without the later 'Additions') by proposing historically possible resolutions of some of the major difficulties that criticism has encountered.

One of the more obvious difficulties with the play as we have it is that Hieronimo's playlet in the catastrophic scene is printed in an English version rather than in the four different languages Hieronimo had specified in arranging for its performance. Before the 'actors' enter our text provides the following explanatory note:

> Gentlemen, this Play of Hieronimo, in sundrie languages, was thought good to be set downe in English, more largely, for the easier understanding to every publique Reader.

This unusual editoral interpolation implies that the playlet was performed in sundry languages and that it was somewhat shorter than the English version prepared for the reader. Some of Kyd's critics have doubted that the note should be taken at face value. M. C. Bradbrook, in her influential *Themes and Conventions of Elizabethan Tragedy* (1935), comments on the interest of the 'groundlings' in hearing "the sound of a strange language" and speculates that the playlet "may really

have been given in the 'sundry languages' "; but she adds that, "considering Kyd's reputation, it would be unlikely" (p. 84). More recently Philip
Edwards, in his invaluable edition for the Revels series (1959), has expressed his doubts more strongly, arguing that the playlet may have been
performed in English or, wordlessly, in mime (pp. xxxiv-xxxix).[1]

The main difficulty which these and other critics have felt in taking
the note at face value stems from their feelings that an Elizabethan
public-theater audience would not have understood what was going on or
would have been bored by dialogue they did not understand. Kyd has
anticipated the first objection by having Hieronimo tell the story of his
academic, humanistic tragedy at some length (17 lines of blank verse) and
by having him provide a 'book' of the play for the onstage 'audience,'
lest the real audience worry about *their* not understanding the action.
Moreover he has Balthazar, who has already objected to the presentation
of a tragedy at his wedding festivities (4.1.86, 155), protest that Hieronimo's plan to produce the tragedy "In unknown languages, That it may
breed the more variety" (173) will only breed "a mere confusion, And
hardly . . . be understood" (180). Hieronimo simply replies, "It must be
so," and asserts both that the invention will prove to be "good" and that
"tediousness" will be avoided (182-9). Kyd has prepared for the performance in strange languages as carefully as he could. He cannot have been
concerned with his audience's understanding the dialogue but rather
with some other effect, one which he seems to have had Balthazar unwittingly specify in objecting that Hieronimo's "variety" will be "a mere
confusion," for it is this last word that Hieronimo himself picks up in his
brief soliloquy that concludes the scene:

> Now shall I see the fall of Babylon,
> Wrought by the heavens in this confusion.
> (4.1.195-6)

"The fall of Babylon" is Hieronimo's description of the catastrophe
that Kyd has had him devise, and the device that he has wrought is
analogized both with the confusion of tongues wrought by the Lord at
Babel (*Genesis*, 11) and with the horrible destruction of both the historical and symbolic Babylons as prophesied in *Isaiah*, 13, *Jeremiah*, 51,
and *Revelation*, 18.[2] To Protestant interpreters, the symbolic Babylon

---

[1] Quotations from the play are from this edition, except for the note already quoted
which is from the old-spelling text in *The Works of Thomas Kyd*, ed. F. S. Boas (1901).

[2] Cf. Edwards's note (p. 108), where indebtedness is acknowledged to Mrs. E. E.
Duncan-Jones for the suggestion that Hieronimo may be thinking of "the tower of
Babylon, i.e., Babel."

was of course Rome, the whore of Babylon being equated with the Antichrist, in turn equated with the Pope, one of whose agents in Kyd's day was the King of Spain. It is possible that the reiterated phrase, "in one hour" (*Revelation*, 18.10, 17, 19), emphasizing as it does the suddenness of the destruction of Babylon, is to be recalled in connection with Hieronimo's promise that "all shall be concluded in one scene" (4.1.188). However that may be, Hieronimo's couplet equates Spain with Babylon and with Babel,[3] for Babel was thought to mean "confusion" (*Genesis*, 11.9, gloss), though as one of the cities of the kingdom of Nimrod it was to be distinguished from "another citie in Egypt, called also Babel" (*Genesis*, 10.10, gloss). The Egyptian Babel or Babylon, the modern Old Cairo, was nevertheless frequently confused with the Mesopotamian city, as apparently by Spenser who, according to W. L. Renwick, seems also to have accepted the Geneva Bible's "confusion of the Tower of Babel and the city of Babylon founded by Ninus."[4] The Egyptian Babylon suggests a possible association of the killing of the heirs to the thrones of Spain and Portugal with the slaying of the first-born of Egypt (*Exodus*, 12), an association which would analogize Kyd's Spain with Egypt as well as with Babylon, both traditional enemies of the chosen people—first the Israelites, later the early Christians, later yet, for Kyd's audience, the Protestant nations, particularly the English.

However fascinating the Apocalyptic, Mesopotamian, and Egyptian Babylon analogues may be, it is chiefly the Tower of Babel analogue that I wish to explore in this essay. The Biblical account of it was inevitably embellished both by the Jews and by the Christians, as Frazer's monumental *Folk-lore in the Old Testament* abundantly demonstrates. For my purposes, however, John Lydgate's typically expansive and compendious version of the story in his *Fall of Princes* is more than sufficient, and I shall touch only on its relevant features. It is the second 'tragedy' in the collection, the fall of Nimrod, who "bilt the toure of babilone to save him from noyous flodis which for his pride was put fro his magnificence

---

[3] The Geneva version uses "Babel" both for the site of the Tower and for the later city or empire throughout the Old Testament (some 275 times) and uses "Babylon" (12 times) only in the New Testament; these forms strictly and consistently transliterate the Hebrew and Greek originals. Biblical quotations that follow are from the copiously glossed Geneva version, with the New Testament in Tomson's revision, specifically a copy of STC 2206 (1609). I use the Geneva rather than the Bishops' or another version because the former was the common household Bible from about 1570 until some years after the publication of the King James version (1611), despite the fact that the Calvinistic bias of its marginal annotations was distasteful to many among the ecclesiastical authorities.

[4] As cited in *The Works of Edmund Spenser: A Variorum Edition, The Minor Poems* (1947), 2.305. See also note 15 below.

and his toure with sodeyne levene smyten doun" (ed. Henry Bergen, 1923, 1.28). Lydgate, following his "auctour Bochas" by way of Laurence, has the tower destroyed a first time "with thondir and with levene liht . . . The boistous wyndis and the rage skie" (1.32.1172-4), then rebuilt and destroyed a second time by a division "off tunges" which caused division "off ther hertis . . . Bothe off ther will, and off ther corages" (1.34.1216-22). The tower was therefore abandoned and Babel deserted; it may still be seen, but only from a safe distance:

> Off which werk thus it is befall,
> Off serpentis and many a gret dragoun
> It is now callid cheeff habitacioun,
>
> That no man dar, as ferr as thei it see,
> For wikkid heir and for corrupcioun,
> Bi a gret space and bi a gret contre
> Approche no neer that merveilous dongoun,
> So venymous is that mansioun
> And so horrible, no man dar approche. . . .
>   (1.32.1139-47)

This wasteland sounds rather like one of Lucretius's Avernian places, although it is certainly a typological back-assimilation from the biblical descriptions of the ruins of the historical and Apocalyptic Babylons: "And Babel shalbe as heaps, a dwelling place for dragons, an astonishment, and an hissing, without an inhabitant. . . . Her cities are desolate: the land is drie and a wildernes" (*Jeremiah*, 51.37-43; cf. *Isaiah*, 13.19-22 and *Revelation*, 18.19-24). When it is recalled that the Hanging Gardens of Babylon were one of the seven wonders of the ancient world, the biblical accounts of the sudden and violent devastation of the city and the venomous nature of its site thereafter afford striking parallels with the scene that Kyd inserts between Hieronimo's Babylon soliloquy and his preparation of a 'stage' for his playlet. It is the scene in which Isabella destroys the garden in which Horatio was murdered, curses it with perpetual barrenness, and kills herself. The "pleasant bower" (2.2.42) is made a poisonous wasteland:

> An eastern wind commix'd with noisome airs
> Shall blast the plants and the young saplings,
> The earth with serpents shall be pestered,
> And passengers, for fear to be infect,
> Shall stand aloof, and looking at it, tell,
> 'There, murder'd, died the son of Isabel.'
>   (4.2.17-22)

Isabella's action prefigures "the fall of Babylon" that Hieronimo is arranging, but his Babylon is Babel indeed, for three of the four players go to their deaths "in unknown languages," which Hieronimo had assigned with due care for decorum (4.1.175-8).

Hieronimo has promised that with him we shall witness "the fall of Babylon, *Wrought by the heavens* in this confusion" (my italics). In *Genesis*, 11.7, the Lord speaks: "Come on, let us goe downe, and there confound their language, that every one perceive not anothers speach." Like the Lord, Hieronimo has arranged to confound language and dull the perceptions of the villains to his and Bel-imperia's real purposes (the sharpness of her perception is communicated at 4.1.99 and 179). Before imitating that stunning heavenly action, however, he, like Hamlet, has had to bide his time (albeit, like Hamlet again, or Lear, more passionately than patiently) and to know how to recognize the appointed time when it arrived. As he has meditated in the *Vindicta mihi* soliloquy,

> Wise men will take their opportunity,
> Closely and safely fitting things to time:
> But in extremes advantage hath no time,
> And therefore all times fit not for revenge. . . .
> No, no, Hieronimo, thou must enjoin
> Thine eyes to observation, and thy tongue
> To milder speeches than thy spirit affords . . .
> Till to revenge thou know, when, where, and how.
> (3.13.25-44)

The Christian dispensation compensates for the confounding of language by the gift of tongues (*Acts*, 2), but the complementary Lesson to the story of the Tower of Babel, as ordained by Elizabeth's Bishops in 1559 for Whitmonday mattins, is not the account of the descent of the Holy Spirit on Pentecost but St. Paul's more generalized discourse on the spiritual gifts in *1 Corinthians*, 12. The official homilies comment on that chapter: "If any wisdome wee have, it is not of our selves, we cannot glory therein as begun of our selves, but we ought to glory in GOD from whom it came to us." In the same part of the same homily, we are told "how GOD giveth his elect understanding of the motions of the heavens, of the alterations and circumstances of time," and that those "that bee indued with this spirituall wisedome . . . can therefore attemper themselves to the occasion of the time." "There is no precept more seriously given and commanded," the homilist insists, "then to know the time."[5]

---

[5] "An Homilie for Rogation Weeke," in *Certain Sermons or Homilies* (ed. 1623, STC 13659 and 13675), 2.17.3, pp. 230-32. Cf. *Ephesians*, 5.15-17: "Take heede therefore that yee walke circumspectly, not as fooles, but as wise, Redeeming the season: for the dayes are evill. Wherefore, bee yee not unwise, but understand what the will of the Lord is."

Hieronimo is the wise man who watches and waits and recognizes the time. When Bel-imperia[6] upbraids him for his apparent reconciliation with Horatio's murderers, he knows that the time has come and that he is Heaven's 'scourge and minister':

> Why then, I see that heaven applies our drift,
> And all the saints do sit soliciting
> For vengeance on those cursed murderers.
>   (4.1.32-4)[7]

The "practices" that he devises so quickly, as if by inspiration, pat upon the entrance of the murderers, imitate those of the heavens themselves. He has become, in Edwards's words, "the agent of destiny" (p. lx; cf. p. lii on "the tools of destiny"), but to understand why things happen as they do, we must look once more at the Tower of Babel, this time through the eyes of John Calvin.

In his *Commentaries on Genesis*, as Englished by Thomas Tymme (1578, STC 4393), Calvin offers an explication of particular relevance for us:

> But firste Moses teacheth, that GOD for a while fared as thoughe he had not seene them, to the ende he breaking off the worke begun by the confusion of tongues, might the more evidently declare his judgment. For he doth oftentimes so beare with the wicked, that as one a sleepe

---

[6] Bel-imperia is the only 'living' character in the play who is linked with all the intrigues. Her "bloody writ" dropped from above as if in answer to Hieronimo's prayers (3.2.23 S.D.) and the function she serves here establish her as a link between the supernatural and human worlds of the play as well. Some critics have been severe with her, calling her "that ever new and dreaded portent, the 'new' woman, who flouts the mores with a lethal charm" (C. F. Tucker Brooke in *A Literary History of England*, ed. A. C. Baugh, 1948, p. 463), or "libidinous" and "a certain kind of woman" (Edwards, p. liv). These emphases seem misplaced. To an Elizabethan public-theater audience, Bel-imperia must have seemed a splendid creature of truly unparalleled loyalty. With one blow, she avenges the treacherous slayings of two lovers, both her social inferiors but the moral superiors of her brother and would-be husband—which only goes to show how perspicacious she (like the Duchess of Malfi) is in appreciating 'true nobility,' and how refreshingly free of false pride, as well as false modesty, a spirited aristocratic girl could be. With another blow, she (like Juliet or Cleopatra) succeeds in rejoining her lovers in death, though the plans of Don Andrea's ghost (4.5.17-22) do not include an Elysian *ménage à trois*. Nor is Bel-imperia's love for Horatio seen to conflict with her loyalty to Andrea; rather it grows out of it. For that very loyalty leads her to try to use his best friend, Horatio, to avenge him, and just because true friends were thought of as mirrors of one another, as alike as possible, she falls in love with Horatio and is equally loyal to him, even though this loyalty requires that she be confederate to the liquidation of her own brother.

[7] On the importance of this speech, see Moody E. Prior, *The Language of Tragedy* (1947), pp. 47 and 57.

he doth not only suffer them to take many wicked thinges in hand: but also he maketh them rejoyce at the successe of their wicked enterprises, that at the last he may make their fal the greater. . . . But he meaneth that GOD shewed himself a revenger by little and little, and as it were faire and softly. (p. 251) [8]

This image of God as the sleeping revenger goes far to account for the scene between Andrea's ghost and the sleeping figure of Revenge (3.15).[9] It also suggests that Hieronimo determines to imitate God's techniques as a revenger in the *Vindicta mihi* soliloquy:

> Thus therefore will I rest me in unrest,
> Dissembling quiet in unquietness,
> Not seeming that I know their villainies,
> That my simplicity may make them think
> That ignorantly I will let all slip. . . .
>   (3.13.29-33)

His pretended reconciliation with the murderers in the next scene seems so ingenuous that it deceives even its two most sympathetic onstage observers, Andrea's ghost and Bel-imperia, who conclude that Hieronimo has indeed abandoned his duty to avenge Horatio's death.

Hieronimo's duty is clearly spelled out in the Mosaic code, which Protestants believed to be quite as much the word of God as anything else in the two testaments. Where murder has been deliberate, the "avenger of the blood" must kill the murderer and not spare him, for "whosoever pardoneth murther, offendeth against the word of God" (*Deuteronomy,* 19.13, gloss; cf. *Hamlet,* 5.2.68-70). The avenger is defined

---

[8] Luther, in his commentary on *Genesis,* also emphasizes the image of God asleep as a human way of feeling about those times when "He neither punishes sin nor answers the prayers of the pious" (as translated, simplified, and abridged by J. Theodore Mueller, 1958, 1.193). Cf. the classical adage, "Dii irati laneos pedes habent," given in Tilley's *Proverbs* (1950) as G182, "God comes with leaden (woolen) feet but strikes with iron hands," where Lyly's *Euphues* is cited for the earliest English usage. Tilley does not include an instance from 1596 that occurs in a translation of a commentary on Du Bartas's account of the Tower of Babel (*Babilon,* tr. W. L'Isle, STC 21662a, p. 22, as cited in Roy W. Battenhouse, *Marlowe's Tamburlaine,* 1941, p. 112). Cf. also Hieronimo's perspective on Lorenzo in his 'security'; he "March'd in a net, and thought himself unseen" (4.4.118).

[9] Edwards (p. xxxiii) finds the text of this scene "extremely corrupt" and complains of the "inane repetition of 'Awake!' "; but the repetition has real point here. The figure of Revenge or Justice asleep and needing to be roused is an obvious way of presenting the idea of "God asleep"; cf. Spenser's allegory of the Temple of Isis (*The Faerie Queene,* 5.7.1-23) and the dumbshow (1.880) in *A Warning for Faire Women* (c. 1598-9).

as "the next of kinred [of the murdered man], who ought to pursue the cause" (*Numbers,* 35.12, gloss), and "the revenger of the blood himselfe shall slay the murtherer: when he meeteth him, he shal slay him" (*Numbers,* 35.19). However, the code continues: "Whosoever killeth any person, the *judge* shall slay the murtherer, through witnesses: but one witnesse shall not testifie against a person to cause him to die" (*Numbers,* 35.30).[10]

"Judge" is italicized in the Geneva version because it does not correspond to a word in the Hebrew (the King James version avoids the interpolation). The Geneva reading is doubly relevant to Kyd's play, for Hieronimo is not only the "revenger of the blood" but also the judge. He is the Knight Marshal of Spain (there being six explicit references to his office even before the murder of Horatio), and Kyd's audience would presumably have understood his function to be similar to that of the Knight Marshal of the English royal household, "who had judicial cognizance of transgressions 'within the king's house and verge,' i.e. within a radius of twelve miles from the king's palace" (OED, Marshal, sb. 6b; cf. Edwards, p. 5). More than half of the references to his official capacity occur after the murder of Horatio, the most poignant ones where Hieronimo is shown performing his judicial functions "in other men's extremes" while he cannot remedy his own (3.6.1-2). His Deputy reminds him (and us) that his "office asks A care to punish such as do transgress" (3.6.11-12). Even so, his first thought upon considering Pedringano's letter (the second 'deposition' of a witness in the case) is to "plain me to my lord the king . . . for justice" (3.7.69-70). When he is thwarted in that attempt by Lorenzo (3.12.28 and 67), who bears him down with his nobility (cf. 3.13.38), his melancholy induces a frenzy in which he offers to "surrender up my marshalship," capping this with a bitter pun: "For I'll go marshal up the fiends in hell, To be avenged on you all for this" (3.12.76-8). Lorenzo urges the King to accept Hieronimo's resignation (3.12.97), a proposal which Kyd, of course, has the King reject.

After the *Vindicta mihi* soliloquy which follows, four poor petitioners importune Hieronimo to plead their cases for them, providing a demonstration of "the common love And kindness that Hieronimo hath won

---

[10] This is, I think, a key to the relevance of the subplot, which presents us with an example of overhasty judgment based on the (false) testimony of only one 'witness'; it stands in anticipatory contrast to Hieronimo's judicial determination, based on the 'depositions' of two eyewitnesses. See William H. Wiatt's concise and perceptive essay on this relevance (*N&Q,* 5, 1958, 327-9). Wiatt sees much the same function without benefit of Scripture and points to Lorenzo's remark about Hieronimo's distraction (3.14.87-9) as a device to remind the audience of the contrast between the Viceroy's erroneous and Hieronimo's correct judgments.

By his deserts within the court of Spain" (3.14.61-3) and testifying directly to his rare integrity:

> for learning and for law
> There's not any advocate in Spain
> That can prevail, or will take half the pain
> That he will, in pursuit of equity.
> (3.13.51-4)[11]

It is unfortunate that most critics have tended to discount Kyd's emphasis on Hieronimo's official function and have seen him merely as a 'private' revenger, for in doing so they have missed the point of Kyd's brilliant invention: the tragic dilemma of the officially appointed minister of justice who is forced by circumstances to take justice into his own hands.[12] Hieronimo cannot be indicted under the general condemnation of 'private' revenge that Fredson Bowers outlines in the introductory chapter of *Elizabethan Revenge Tragedy* (1940).[13] Such a general condemnation is itself suspect, for the very fact that official and semiofficial spokesmen for state and church so earnestly condemned private revenge is an indication that Elizabethan attitudes toward it were mixed.

The treatment of this orthodox condemnation is rather like the more influential treatments we have of orthodox 'political theory.' They draw too exclusively on one item of oversimplified, official propaganda aimed at the commons, "An Homilie against Disobedience and Wilfull Rebellion," composed for and added to the official collection of homilies after the Northern Rebellion of 1569. This is the latest and longest of the homilies; but its inclusion among them did not lead to the suppression of the tenth homily in the First Book (1547), "An Exhortation concerning Good Order, and Obedience to Rulers and Magistrates." This homily, itself properly orthodox, is more complex although shorter than the later one. It points out loopholes in the doctrine of obedience and makes allowances for passive resistance that anticipate by a decade Calvin's

---

[11] On the distinction between justice and equity, and the considerable importance and popularity of the latter concept in Tudor England, see J. Wilson McCutchan, "Justice and Equity in the English Morality Play," *JHI*, 19 (1958), 405-10.

[12] See Prior, pp. 47-8; also Howard Baker, *Induction to Tragedy* (1939), p. 215: "it is clear that Hieronimo, in his magisterial capacity, has some prerogatives as a public avenger" (with reference to the last chapter of Calvin's *Institutes* as Englished by Thomas Norton).

[13] Bowers argues that Hieronimo adopts "Italianate Machiavellian tactics" (p. 80) and becomes "a villain to the English audience at the end" (p. 82), though he admits that the example of Hieronimo as villainous revenger "may seem the most debatable of the many available" (p. 40). John D. Ratliff's rebuttal, "Hieronimo Explains Himself" (*SP*, 54, 1957, 112-18), effectively demonstrates that he is presented as "an honorable, justified revenger" (p. 118).

liberalizing revision of the last chapter of the *Institutes*, "On Civil Government." Particularly relevant to Hieronimo's function are the 1547 homilist's comments on God's words, "Vindicta mihi":[14]

> Wee reade in the booke of Deuteronomie, that all punishment pertaineth to GOD, by this sentence, Vengeance is mine, and I will reward. But this sentence wee must understand to pertaine also unto the Magistrates which doe exercise GODS roome in judgement. . . . no man (of his owne private authority) may bee judge over other, may punish, or may kill. But we must referre all judgement to GOD, to Kings, and Rulers, Judges under them, which be GODS officers to execute justice. . . . And the same Saint *Paul* threateneth no lesse paine, then everlasting damnation to all disobedient persons . . . for as much as they resist not man, but GOD, not mans device and invention, but GODS wisedome, GODS order, power, and authority. (1.10.1, pp. 70-71)[15]

Many among Kyd's audiences must have been reminded of this or similar commentary while identifying with Hieronimo and being caught up in his dilemma.

We have already examined Hieronimo's 'inspired' scheme for performing his duty once he has perceived "that heaven applies our drift," and we have drawn considerable 'meaning' from his couplet in prospect: "Now shall I see the fall of Babylon, Wrought by the heavens in this confusion." It remains to be seen what can be said, against this background, of the aftermath of the Babelized playlet.

Of the survivors of the confusion at Babel, only Eber presumably retained the original language, but he was unable to instruct others, whose languages he did not understand (Luther, as cited in note 8, 1.194). Hieronimo is both Eber and somewhat more, for he breaks off "our sundry languages" and concludes "in our vulgar tongue" (4.4.74-5), apparently in order to reveal "the mystery, And serve for Chorus in this tragedy" (1.1.90-91). His lengthy 'explanation,' delivered over the corpse of Horatio and punctuated by a flourish of the "bloody handkercher," consists of (1) a conventionally rhetorical lament for his dead son, (2) a retelling of some of the events the audience has seen enacted, and (3) a

[14] *Deuteronomy*, 32.35; cf. *Psalms*, 94.1, *Romans*, 12.19, and *Hebrews*, 10.30. Bowers first pointed out (*MLN*, 53, 1938, 590-91) that Hieronimo's most important soliloquy begins with a biblical, not a Senecan, quotation.
[15] The homilist refers here to *Romans*, 13; and a Geneva gloss to 13.4 reads, "God hath armed the Magistrate even with a revenging sword." It seems pertinent to note that this section of the homily begins with a beautifully amplified statement of the concept of order and degree and proceeds to contrast it with a vision of the anarchic disorder that ensues when degree is taken away: "For where there is no right order, there reigneth all abuse, carnall liberty, enormitie, sinne, and Babylonicall confusion" (p. 69).

statement of his real purpose in staging his academic tragedy. Bel-imperia is spoken of only as an object of rival loves and, for love of Horatio, as a party to Hieronimo's revenge. Much of what Hieronimo knows, including all the details about how he came to know it, is not included in his 'explanation,' which is therefore hardly satisfactory to his stage 'audience.' He offers not the slightest proof of the guilt of his victims. Thus it is inaccurate, at the least, to say, as William Empson does, that "Hieronymo has just told the bereaved fathers everything he possibly could" (*"The Spanish Tragedy," Nimbus,* 3.3, 1956, 22), or, as Edwards does, that he "has told everything, yet the King, etc. are apparently still in ignorance and to their questions Hieronimo returns nothing but an inexplicable refusal to speak" (p. 117).

There may be some feeling that Hieronimo, like Eber, cannot instruct the others because they no longer 'speak the same language'; but that is at most an overtone, not a fundamental to this grand discord. Just before he bites out his tongue, however, he does give a fundamental explanation for his refusal to speak, though it is a mysterious one: "But never shalt thou force me to reveal The thing which I have vow'd inviolate" (4.4.187-8). We remember the vow made on the handkerchief over Horatio's corpse in the presence of Isabella (2.5.51-4), but that vow has been revealed (4.4.122-9). Strictly speaking, however, Hieronimo has made another vow involving a covenant with Bel-imperia:

> And here I vow (so you but give consent,
> And will conceal my resolution)
> I will ere long determine of their deaths. . . .
>   (4.1.42-4)

Bel-imperia has thus become Hieronimo's active "confederate" in revenge (4.4.176-9), but, contrary to his plans, she "miss'd her part in this" (4.4.140). The phrase may suggest, along with its primary sense, that her "part" was to have included helping 'explain' these events. However that may be, Hieronimo's second vow involved mutual concealment of purpose, and for Hieronimo to reveal what he knows of Bel-imperia's part in these events without her consent would, in a legalistic view, constitute a violation of that vow. His 'explanation' avoids any reference to the fact that she and her servant, Pedringano, were the two necessary witnesses whose letters established the identities and guilt of the murderers (3.7.53). If this reading is sufficiently Elizabethan in spirit, Hieronimo's motives for silence arise not from a sense of chivalry but from a proper horror of oath-breaking (cf. 4.4.152 and 182).

Rather than risk breaking his vow under the tortures that are threatened, Hieronimo bites out his tongue (perhaps a piece of uncooked liver,
as Charles Prouty suggests in the Crofts Classics edition, 1951). This
memorable and effective episode may be seen as a symbolic refusal to
participate in the confusion of the world after Babel. It more surely
serves to identify Hieronimo as admirably stoic, for he is imitating the
legendary action of Zeno of Elea, the traditional founder of the Stoic
school. In the biography in William Baldwin's *Treatise of Morall Phi-
losophie,* the death of "Zeno Eloates" is vividly recounted. He was being
tortured by a tyrant to force him to reveal details of a conspiracy. After
having endured the tortures for some time, he motioned for the tyrant to
come close so that he might whisper the details in his ear. When the
tyrant was in a position to hear them, Zeno firmly gripped his ear (or,
according to some, his nose) between his teeth and held fast until he tore
it off. This enraged the tyrant, who thereupon ordered more ingenious
tortures, finally having Zeno pounded by a gigantic pestle in a huge
mortar. While being pounded, Zeno delivered a stirring oration rebuking
his fellow citizens for enduring such tyranny, "and when he had so sayd,
because he would confesse nothing, he bit off his own tongue, and spat
it out in the tormenters face, who therefore killed him, as *Hermippus*
sayth" (STC 1269, c. 1640, p. 39v).[16]

The King of Spain is more amazed than enraged by Hieronimo's auto-
glossotomy, but he quickly recovers his determination to know all and
orders Hieronimo to write out a satisfactory explanation of his behavior.
Once more Hieronimo must dissemble to gain his ends. He motions for
"a knife to mend his pen," but he uses it to kill Castile and himself,
again amazing the onlookers. His reasons, if any, for killing Castile are
not even hinted at. He kills him because, in Edwards's words, he "is the
agent of destiny employed to avenge Andrea" (p. lx); that is, the reasons
for Castile's death are not Hieronimo's but Andrea's, and destiny, in the
figure of Revenge, is bound to gratify Andrea's ghost. It should also be
recalled that destiny, in this play, is arranged by Kyd to gratify his audience; and this brings us to another topic, the anti-Spanish bias of *The
Spanish Tragedy.*

Edwards rightly rejects as "ludicrous" Schick's attempts to read into
the play direct allusions to historical details of Spanish-Portuguese rela-

---

[16] I wish to thank my good friend and colleague, Professor William Nelson, for locat-
ing this version of the story for me in his copy of the *Treatise.* The life of Zeno occurs
in it at least as early as 1579, when the ninth edition was published. Boas (p. 413)
cites Schick's notice of Lyly's much briefer allusion in *Euphues* to the same event,
as derived from Plutarch.

tions (p. xxiv). It should be remembered, however, that Portugal was England's oldest ally, the alliance dating from the Treaty of Windsor (1386), in connection with which John I of Portugal married a daughter of John of Gaunt, thereby infusing his dynasty with English blood. In the play, John of Gaunt is the most glorified of the three English "Knights" who capture Iberian Kings in Hieronimo's first entertainment for the court (1.4.137-73).

After the death in 1580 of the last king among the legitimate heirs male in the dynastic line founded by John I, at least six claimants contended for the crown of Portugal, the most powerful of them being Philip II of Spain and the most popular Don Antonio, Prior of Crato, whose claim would have been unchallengeable had he not, like John I himself, been a bastard. Despite French support, he was unable to repel a Spanish invasion (1580) and was forced into exile. French attempts to establish him in the Azores were equally unsuccessful. He therefore came to England, where he found ardent supporters for his scheme to liberate Portugal from the tyranny of Spain. By early 1587, his cause was being advocated in Parliament. After the Armada, Elizabeth authorized an expedition which set out in the spring of 1589 to invade Portugal and seat Don Antonio on the throne. A landing was effected and the English marched on Lisbon but met with disastrous defeat. Don Antonio returned with the fleet, went back to France a few years later, and died there in 1595.[17] On many an occasion after 1580, he might well have echoed the last words of Kyd's Viceroy of Portugal, the last human speaker in the play: "Spain hath no refuge for a Portingale" (4.4.217).

These connections between Kyd's play and contemporary Anglo-Portuguese relations would have touched on the enthusiasms or disappointments of its audiences at any time from the mid-eighties to the early nineties. What must surely have gratified them hugely, however, are the last words of Kyd's King of Spain:

> What age hath ever heard such monstrous deeds?
> My brother, and the whole succeeding hope
> That Spain expected after my decease! . . .
> I am the next, the nearest, last of all.
>
> (4.4.202-8)

This is a lament for the end of a dynasty, and Hieronimo's avowed pur-

[17] J. B. Black, *The Reign of Elizabeth* (1936), pp. 304-8, 357-8; A. L. Rowse, *The Expansion of Elizabethan England* (1955), pp. 283-8; J. E. Neale, *Elizabeth I and her Parliaments: 1584-1601* (1957), p. 179; and Garrett Mattingly, *The Armada* (1959), pp. 395-7.

pose as an avenger was to kill, in his own phrase, "the hope of Spain" (3.14.140). By killing not only the King's nephew but also his brother, Hieronimo has created in Spain a situation like that of Elizabethan England: the nation has an aging sovereign, but that sovereign has no direct heir, and the question of the succession is cause for real anxiety. Whenever we may date the play, and at least until the accession of James I, English audiences would have rejoiced in this wishful discomfiture of the Spanish enemy. Not only has Hieronimo, as the working instrument of "the heavens," engineered "the fall of Babylon," but he has also performed an *acte gratuit* which confirms the feeling established at the end of Act 1, by means of the entertainment that Kyd so ingeniously devised for him to present to the Court, that he is a confirmed Anglophile who somehow has the best interests of Protestant England at heart.

One other point may be made. In the final scene of the play, Don Andrea's ghost assigns the nine characters who did not survive the action their eternal rewards and punishments. Obviously the audience is supposed to accept Andrea's dispensations as the judgments of God. Adequate justification for Kyd's fusion of classical and Christian otherworlds could be cited from many a more distinguished literary work than *A Mirror for Magistrates,* that worthy attempt by a group of middle-class Londoners to continue Lydgate's *Fall of Princes* to the beginning of the Tudor dynasty. But the second edition of the *Mirror* (1563) contains the most telling justification that I know of and one that must have been familiar to many in Kyd's audiences. It occurs in the prose comments on Sackville's contribution, which one of the company praises with this qualification: "where as he faineth to talke with the princes in hel, that I am sure will be mislyked, because it is most certayne that some of their soules be in heaven." William Baldwin, the chairman of the group, refutes the objection on theological grounds by adducing a special meaning of "Hell" as "the Grave" (often so used, he says, "in the scriptures, and in the writynges of learned christians"), adding that Sackville had himself told him that this is what he meant "and so would have it taken." A third speaker rejects Baldwin's defense as needlessly learned (and neatly bypasses the intentional fallacy into which Baldwin had fallen): "Tush . . . what stand we here upon? it is a Poesie and no divinitye, and it is lawfull for poetes to fayne what they lyst, so it be appertinent to the matter." It is pleasant to be able to report that Baldwin agreed with him, saying, "a poet may faine what he list . . . and [it] ought to be well taken of the hearers."

INTRIGUE IN
ELIZABETHAN TRAGEDY

by ALFRED HARBAGE

I T SEEMS SCARCELY mannerly at this late date to discuss the historical
importance of Kyd's *Spanish Tragedy*. The play has long been credited with introducing to the English popular stage the revenge motif,
with its Senecan panoply of ghosts, multiple murders, dire auguries,
moral sententiousness, and the like. With so many resemblances in fable,
dramatis personae, and theatrical devices to Shakespeare's *Hamlet,* it
must surely be considered portentous enough. Why encumber it further
with the dubious honor of anticipating the methods of better plays?

Nevertheless, perhaps something remains to be said. It may be argued
that our attention has been diverted by the conspicuous—that in observing the priority of Kyd's play within a specific genre we have somehow missed a point. I should like to propose that the historical importance of *The Spanish Tragedy* resides chiefly in certain details of its
action. These may not properly be considered Senecan at all, and their
influence is manifest not in the revenge plays alone but in nearly all
subsequent popular tragedies except the documentary histories. I refer
to the element of intrigue in Kyd's play, those considerable portions of
it where the entertaining complication of the action becomes an end in
itself. Perhaps Kyd's greatest innovation was to employ comic methods
with tragic materials, thus creating a species of comitragedy. Maneuvers
traditionally associated with the petty ends of petty tricksters are given a
sensationally lethal turn so as to win a new and oddly mixed response—
of amusement and horror, revulsion and admiration. To what extent

37

such a response is destructive of the dignity of tragedy and its presumed spiritual ends is an open critical question.

Classical and earlier Renaissance tragedy contains, to be sure, elements of intrigue. An instance is offered by Seneca's *Thyestes*. The victim is lured to his destruction by a ruse, and grim elements of humor appear: Atreus is clever and Thyestes is a gull. But in a sense the Agamemnon of Aeschylus is also a gull, as are many tragic heroes, and a distinction must be made at once. When the emphasis is upon the facts as they are and the facts as they appear to the victim, the effect is tragic irony. When the emphasis is upon the means by which that difference is achieved, the effect is something else. The appeal of intrigue is intellectual. Moral judgment stands partly in abeyance as we check the villain's calculations. Whereas we watch Macbeth commit a murder, we watch Iago play a game. Classical tragedy, mainly retrospective in its method and traditional in its matter, could not elaborate the action very far. Elaboration to the point of anything we may properly call intrigue is possible only when invention is permissible, and the heart of the fable is presented in a series of progressive episodes. The fables treated in classical and neoclassical tragedies sometimes contained intrigue, but in the process of dramatization it was canceled by the structure, surviving as a mere potential. The New Comedy, as represented by Plautus and Terence, despite the concentration of the action, was pre-eminently drama of intrigue.

The distinction is obvious enough in practice. When Kyd's Lorenzo maneuvers Pedringano into slaying Serberine, the authorities into arresting Pedringano, and the latter into remaining silent until the moment of his execution because of the hope of a pardon, he is behaving not like Atreus or Clytemnestra but like Matthew Merrygreek or Diccon of Bedlam. Not only is the effect of the action sometimes overtly comic, as when Pedringano stands with a rope about his neck while Lorenzo's Page comforts him with an empty box supposedly containing his pardon, but the very methods used are the traditional ones of comic intrigue. Diccon by means of a lost needle sets Dame Chat and Gammer Gurton at loggerheads. Matthew Merrygreek, by means of a mispunctuated letter, effects the same end with Ralph Roister Doister and Dame Custance. The resulting quarrels are trivial, hence in harmony with the trivial means used to foment them; but after Lorenzo's maneuvers with deceptive appointments and an empty box, Serberine and Pedringano are dead. So after the tampering with a letter by Hamlet, Rosencrantz and Guildenstern are dead. And after the manipulation by Iago of a piece of lost needlework (rather than a lost needle), Othello and Desdemona are dead. The ruse of Atreus in enticing Thyestes into his power is no more elaborate than need be. The difficulty of the end achieved justifies the complexity of the means employed. Such is not the case with the ruses of Lorenzo. He is sufficiently privileged in the state that he might slay Pedringano and Serberine out of hand, with few questions asked, and the intricacy of his methods must be recognized as entertainment for its own sake. Sometimes the later writers of tragedy found their intrigue in source fiction, itself progressive rather than retrospective in narrative method, but they usually complicated this intrigue further, as in the case of *Othello,* or supplemented it with pure invention. The tendency was for the intrigue to become increasingly elaborate from play to play, and from action to action within individual plays. In Marlowe's *Jew of Malta* Barabas disposes of the Christian suitors of his daughter by the relatively simple method of a forged challenge. Although "cunningly perform'd," this action is capped later in the piece when Iacomo is arrested for the murder of the propped-up body of a friar who has already been murdered by Barabas and Ithimore. Marlowe seems here to be letting his villains improve upon the methods of Kyd's Lorenzo.

That Elizabethan tragedy as it evolved is marked by an augmentation of intricacy, owing to a competitive response of playwrights to a taste for intrigue, scarcely needs to be argued. The whole of the plot of *The Revenger's Tragedy* is a multiplication of the devices of Lorenzo in disposing of Serberine and Pedringano, and of Barabas in disposing of Iacomo and the friar. Plays with a strong, simple, and reasonably plausible story line up to a certain point, like Middleton and Rowley's *Changeling* or Webster's *Duchess of Malfi,* will conclude in a welter of trickery, like the grand finale of a pyrotechnical display. Here all former 'notable cosenage' will be, so to speak, anthologized. As in the case of Webster's play the thickening of the plot, the density of the intrigue, is apt to begin where the dependence upon source materials ends. And even the tragedies which are least conspicuous for this trait, such as *King Lear,* are apt to contain at least one sequence in which a clever man manipulates several others to his own destructive ends, employing usually a concrete property, most often a letter, but also a dead body, a weapon, an article of attire, or (alas) a handkerchief.

Thomas Rymer called *Othello* a "bloody farce" and T. S. Eliot has called *The Jew of Malta* a serious "farce." Neither of these estimable critics has quite succeeded in bringing the critical issue into clear focus, and we can understand the reasons why. To the neoclassicist, Elizabethan

tragedy seemed so full of excesses and improprieties that his critical energies were fully deployed without the need for observing that tragedy of
intrigue is basically a mixed genre. He follows his authorities and objects
to the violation of 'the unities' in construction, or to the principle of
'decorum' in the presentation of character: Iago should not be presented
as both a soldier and a sneak! There is little need to meditate upon the
comic potential of the intrigue, when comic elements are so often overt,
as in the intrusion of the Clown. The modern belle-lettrist is apt to be
similarly diverted, but in a different direction and, of course, under
greater pressures to express approval. The horrific Barabas, with his self-
declared ferocity, seems to him seriocomic in the fashion of mordant
caricature quite apart from the nature of the devices he employs. But we
must recognize that *The Jew of Malta* and *Othello* are 'farces' only in the
same way in which most Elizabethan tragedies are, after a manner of
speaking, 'farces.' We are dealing with a pervasive feature of the tragedy
of the age with which we must come to terms.

We may as well concede at once that we rarely wish that there were
more intrigue in Elizabethan tragedy. It is this feature, rather than any
violation of 'unities' or any overtly comic elements, that makes us a little
uneasy under the quizzical glances of admirers of Corneille and Racine.
At least in the introductory stages, it is easier to win admiration for serious Elizabethan drama with English history plays like *Edward II* or
Roman tragedies like *Julius Caesar*. In these 'documentaries' or 'semi-
documentaries' the playwrights were working under restraints. No one
would wish that Shakespeare had elaborated the manner in which Cassius
duped Brutus with forged letters, and thus given the episode more substance than it possessed in Plutarch. It is partly the *absence* of intrigue,
in the mechanical sense, that gives plays like *Coriolanus* and *Antony and
Cleopatra* more innate dignity than plays like *Othello* and *Romeo and
Juliet*. They are 'classical' in more ways than one. Or in a quite different
category of tragedy, the highly original treatments of common domestic
transgression, we can often pinpoint the source of our critical discomfiture in the intrigue. The most embarrassing feature of Heywood's
Woman Killed with Kindness is not its alleged sentimentality, or the
intermingling of archaic and modern dramaturgical and didactic devices,
but the sequence of scenes in which Master Frankford grows clever with
duplicate keys. We wish he had exposed his wife and Wendoll in some
other way. He dwindles in tragic dignity not by exercising self-righteously
and loquaciously his moral code, but by becoming an intriguer.

Nevertheless, it would be risky to say that Elizabethan tragedy is admirable (on those frequent occasions when it *is* admirable) in spite of its intrigue. This would be a little like saying that certain Elizabethan poems are admirable in spite of their being sonnets. Intrigue in Elizabethan tragedy is so inextricably related to the kind of tragedy it is that to deplore it in general would be to deplore the tragedy in general—to wish it were some other thing. *Macbeth,* with its relative absence of intrigue, seems to me as to so many others a greater tragedy than *Othello,* with its relative abundance of intrigue, but I am by no means sure that intrigue itself, quantitatively considered, explains the difference in stature. *Macbeth* has incomparably the greater theme, with action and language appropriate to the theme. Although intrigue might well have spoiled *Macbeth,* intrigue does not spoil *Othello.* The *Revenger's Tragedy,* in spite of its widely acclaimed poetry, which proves upon examination to appear only in the first and a few later bravura speeches, strikes me as a bad play—but less because of its intrigue, thickened to the point of coagulation, but because it has so little else to offer. When an Elizabethan tragedy is bad, we seem to recognize the intrigue as a contributory factor, but in last analysis the play is bad not because of the intrigue but because the play is bad.

A generalization that holds here as everywhere is that an ingredient is good to the extent that it synthesizes with other ingredients to form a consistent whole. Intrigue is good to the extent that it is absorbed in the artistic process and serves the artist's end. An instance in which intrigue, featuring all the standard machinery, remains ludicrously *un*absorbed is provided by the episodes involving Bussy, Tamyra, and the interceding Friar in Chapman's *Bussy D'Ambois.* Dryden was inclined to consider *this* play a bloody farce, specifically a "mingle of false poetry and true nonsense." Although Chapman's star is at the moment ascending, it is harder to dispose of Dryden's view of *Bussy* than of Rymer's view of *Othello.*

The most obvious objection to intrigue in tragedy, apart from the fact that it can overtax the constructive skill of the playwright, is that it amuses us, makes us wish momentarily for its success, and creates in us a certain admiration for the intriguer and tolerance for his aims. However, in the case of *Othello* (and *Othello* is the most doubtful case among Shakespeare's major tragedies) our amusement at Iago, and covert admiration, may so involve us in his guilt as to contribute to our final feelings of revulsion against the thing he symbolizes. In the source story, Othello himself was an intriguer: Shakespeare altered that. In *King Lear,* Edmund's manipulation of Gloucester and Edgar by means of his faked letter is no detriment to the play. The intrigue is absorbed by the way it relates to Edmund's character and occasions his revelatory speeches. Great language is a great absorbent, and perhaps we do indeed owe some of the fine Elizabethan dramatic poetry to the gritty stuff it was forced to absorb. More dubious in *King Lear,* so far as artistic success is concerned, is Edgar's intrigue in achieving a trial by combat with Edmund, since deviousness is not a quality of Edgar's character and his ruses are not accompanied by speeches especially powerful. The contrast in effect of these two sequences of action is revealing in the extreme.

It appears that the Elizabethan playwright is most successful in exercising his spell upon us when he is being most true to his own traditions. Although intrigue itself might be new in tragedy, it was not new in its association with evil. The Vice, a traditional character, was often a comical fellow, but whatever the etymology of his name he symbolized the *vicious*; the awe-inspiring Machiavellian, with his masterful duplicity, merely filled in an ancient outline. One might be entertained by the methods of a Lorenzo, and even admire his cleverness, but such responses were tentative. Men might properly manipulate material things, but not their fellow men; cleverness in human relationships was evil, and should be associated only with characters who will ultimately be rejected. I think we may say that responses which are tentative, provisional, at war with ultimate moral judgment, are not inappropriate to spectators of tragedy, or destructive of ultimate tragic effects. Intrigue could be successfully employed in tragedy by a writer of constructive skill, so long as it was presented as evil in its effects and was associated with evil men.

But Elizabethan tragedy did not confine itself to intrigue in its mischievous aspects. In the comedy from which it borrowed the ingredient, no device was commoner than that of the tricker tricked, the underminer hoisted with his own petard. It was in imitating this feature of comic intrigue that Kyd and later writers muddied the tragic font. Lorenzo we can accept, but not Hieronimo—or Marston's Antonio, or others like him. Cleverness could be pitted against cleverness in comedy; poison could drive out poison, because it was not really poison after all, but only a useful purgative or emetic. In tragedy the poison was deadly, and so must retain its exclusive association with evil. It was possible to introduce a virtuous intriguer successfully, providing his maneuvers, like those of Friar Lawrence, were vain or catastrophic, or providing it was made clearly manifest that his intrigues, like his lust for vengeance itself, were eroding away his virtue. But such characters as Hieronimo and Antonio are supposed to retain our approval. They fail to do so, and the plays in which they appear fail to win our approval—at least as tragedy. Whether or not Chapman's Friar in *Bussy D'Ambois* is supposed to retain our approval is a moot point—his devices are certainly as catastrophic in their results as those of Friar Lawrence. Vendice in *The Revenger's Tragedy* ends thoroughly corrupted, but owing to his initial and single-minded devotion to trickery, he seems also to have begun corrupted. In neither case is the author's orthodoxy so much in question as his artistic sensibility.

Since all roads seem to lead to *Hamlet,* it would be strange if an essay on intrigue in Elizabethan tragedy failed to do so. If Hamlet was to remain a tragic hero, was to appear more virtuous than not in the eyes of Shakespeare's audience then and now, he could neither take premeditated vengeance nor be a successful intriguer, no matter how intellectually well-equipped. In the antecedent legend (and perhaps in an earlier play by Kyd) that is what Hamlet had been—a successful avenger, a successful intriguer. In Shakespeare's play, his one really successful ruse, disposing of Rosencrantz and Guildenstern, is only passingly reported and plays a negligible part in our total emotional response. His great stroke of intrigue, the mouse-trap play, by which he is so highly elated, resolves itself into an intellectual exercise. It catches the King's conscience but not the King's life. Hamlet meditates the killing of Claudius, but the killing of Claudius is not the fruit of those meditations. Hamlet tries to manipulate men and events, but a divinity shapes his ends. That his hand should slay Claudius is symbolically appropriate, but his hand upon the foil and the cup must be covered by the hand of Providence. Hamlet remains the tragic hero. Such characters as Hieronimo and Antonio are tragic heroes only in the hopeful eyes of their creators. It was an artistic necessity of the case that Hamlet should be so fertile in ideas, so sterile in actions, that upon his intrigues should be graciously conferred a soul-saving futility.

Although *Hamlet* is a success, its success is something of a miracle. The tragedy misses absurdity by a thin margin. Few Elizabethan tragedies are so adroit as Shakespeare's; we admire most of them for individual scenes, characters, and poetic passages, rather than for totality of effect. On the average, Elizabethan comedy, although less memorable in individual scenes, characters, and poetic passages, is more successful in synthesizing its ingredients. From the time of *The Spanish Tragedy* onwards[1] the ingredients of Elizabethan tragedy were hard to synthesize. We cannot say that intrigue spoiled Elizabethan tragedy, since particular plays survive to demonstrate the unique and powerful effects achievable with its use, but a tragedy of intrigue, a tragedy cross-bred from comedy, was too difficult for most talents. The playwrights were dealing with *almost* intransigent materials.

[1] My main point does not depend upon the priority of Kyd's play. If intrigue was introduced into popular tragedy by some other play, or by a more gradual process, or through the influence of some earlier mediator between comedy and tragedy such as Italian pastoral 'tragicomedy,' its significance remains the same. Nevertheless, I believe that Kyd was the innovator, and that the lasting notoriety of *The Spanish Tragedy* was, in some measure, the fruit of its initial novelty. R. B. McKerrow, with whom no one would rashly disagree, questioned the assumption that the slur in Nashe's Epistle to Greene's *Menaphon* (1589) was aimed specifically at Kyd, and Philip Edwards, in his recent excellent edition for the 'Revels' series, dates *The Spanish Tragedy* c. 1590. But to redirect the interpretation of the whole complex of allusions in Nashe's diatribe to some purely hypothetical playwright or shadowy 'group' of playwrights is to place an intolerable strain upon coincidence. After all, Nashe was referring, albeit in the plural, to *a non-university writer of popular 'Senecan' plays, successful enough to arouse his ire*. Even at this date it would be hard to name a candidate other than Kyd, and in view of the wrenched allusion to the "Kid in Aesop," along with two allusions to the profession of "Noverint" and the thrusting of "Elisium into hell" (to mention these items only), the case for Kyd becomes quite as strong as the case for Shakespeare as the object of the famous slur in Greene's *Groatsworth of Wit*. Concerning the latter, we can argue that "Shake-scene" is a common type of epithet, like "Tear-throat," and might indicate *any* allegedly bombastic playwright, but in view of the other particularities in the passage (each individually vulnerable), the case for Shakespeare becomes too strong to be denied, and few are inclined to deny it. I should say, further, that if Nashe was alluding to Kyd and *The Spanish Tragedy* (where the netherworld geography is—*pace* Edwards—open to cavil), then the play must have been written before the Armada. Absence of allusions to the Armada is not ordinarily a good dating criterion, but in a play with a Spanish scene, and with allusions to English victories over the Spanish, the absence of any allusion to the Armada (prophetic, let us say) would be something of a marvel if that play was written in 1588-9. I do not think that T. W. Baldwin's argument for a date at the beginning of the decade is convincing (*On the Literary Genetics of Shakspere's Plays*, 1959, Chapter 6), and I remain loyal to 1586-7. This, coincidentally, is about midpoint of the "five and twenty or thirty" years ago given by Ben Jonson in his induction to *Bartholomew Fair* (1614) as the era of *Andronicus* and "Ieronimo."

ROBERT GREENE AS DRAMATIST

by Kenneth Muir

R OBERT GREENE has had the misfortune to be regarded primarily as one
of Shakespeare's predecessors and as the author of the attack on him
in *A Groatsworth of Wit Bought with a Million of Repentance* (1592).
This is unjust to Greene in two ways: first because his best work was all
nondramatic, and secondly because critics have praised his plays for qualities which they do not possess. It may be worthwhile, therefore, to attempt a reassessment of his dramatic work.

It is probable that all his extant plays belong to the last years of his
life: *Alphonsus King of Aragon,* the most immature, must have been written after *Tamburlaine* (c. 1587). (J. Churton Collins, by means of dubious parallels, convinced himself it was written after Spenser's *Complaints,* printed 1591.) The "Address to the Gentlemen Readers" in
Perimides, published in 1588, would seem to show that Greene had by
that date written either an unsuccessful tragedy—which may have been
The Comicall Historie of Alphonsus—or else some other kind of play.
Greene mentions that two poets

> had it in derision for that I could not make my verses iet vpon the stage
> in tragicall buskins, euerie worde filling the mouth like the faburden
> of Bo-Bell, daring God out of heauen with that Atheist *Tamburlan* or
> blaspheming with the mad preest of the Sonne.

There are several plays which have been ascribed to Greene, including
Selimus[1] and *George a Greene*; but as the evidence is, to my mind, incon-

---

[1] The chief evidence for Greene's authorship of *Selimus* is the ascription to him of
two extracts from the play in *Englands Parnassus*; but the editor Robert Allott's
ascriptions are notoriously unreliable. When the play was reissued in 1638 it purported

clusive, it will be safer to confine this discussion of Greene as dramatist to the four plays of which he was the sole author and *A Looking Glasse for London and England,* written (as the title-page of the first edition claims) by Greene and Thomas Lodge.

No critic has found anything to praise in *Alphonsus* (c. 1587), Greene's absurd attempt to rival *Tamburlaine.* It was a failure on its first performance and Greene apparently never wrote the promised sequel. Characterization, construction, and versification are all feeble in the extreme. The induction is pointless. The main theme—the rise of Alphonsus by ruthless means—is interrupted in the third and fourth acts by a series of scenes concerning Amurack, scenes which contrive to be both boring and incredible. An enchantress called Medea—presumably not Jason's wife, though there is a later mention of the golden fleece—makes Amurack talk in his sleep; Mahomet, speaking out of a brazen head, deliberately prophesies falsely; and Fausta, Amurack's wife, banished for no very good reason, has a troop of Amazons at her command. At the end of the play, Alphonsus's father turns up in the guise of a pilgrim to arrange his son's marriage to Amurack's daughter Iphigina. Although he has not had the opportunity of talking with either Alphonsus or Iphigina he has mysteriously acquired knowledge not only of the state of their affections but also of their private conversation.

Two more examples may be given of Greene's carelessness. In the first act Belinus announces that he is going to relieve Naples; Albinius advises him to relieve Naples; and Belinus announces that he will follow this advice, as though he had not already decided on this course. Even more absurd is the speech in which Amurack decides to let his daughter marry Alphonsus. It is intended to display the conflict in his mind, but it is so crudely done that the effect is ludicrous:

> Now, *Amurack,* aduise thee what thou sayest:
> Bethinke thee well what answere thou wilt make:
> Thy life and death dependeth on thy words.
> If thou denie to be *Alphonsus* sire,
> Death is thy share: but if that thou consent,

---

to be the work of one T. G. These initials may have been intended to signify Thomas Goffe, who was however in his infancy when the play was first published in 1594. The evidence for Greene's authorship on grounds of style is even flimsier. It may be added that the play contains one undoubted echo of *Astrophel and Stella* (283-4); it was certainly influenced by *The Massacre at Paris* (which may have been written after Greene's death); and Selimus's long speech in seven-line stanzas (232-385) reads like a versification of Marlowe's table-talk, written by someone with little knowledge of the stage, and perhaps not originally intended for the public stage.

> Thy life is sau'd. Consent? nay, rather die:
> Should I consent to giue *Iphigina*
> Into the hands of such a beggers brat?
> What, *Amuracke,* thou dost deceiue thy selfe:
> *Aphonsus* is the sonne vnto a King:
> What then? then worthy of thy daughters loue.
> She is agreed, and *Fausta* is content;
> Then *Amuracke* will not be discontent.

A Looking Glasse (c. 1590) is a much more competent piece of work. The verse, though quite undistinguished and monotonously regular, is less clumsy than that of *Alphonsus*. The simple morality structure does not require subtle characterization or strong dramatic scenes. The main plot is concerned with the sins and timely repentance of Rasni, King of Nineveh, who commits incest and adultery and connives at murder. He is not dissuaded from his evil courses by the miraculous deaths of his incestuous bride and of his favorite counselor, nor even by the apparition of a burning sword; but Jonas succeeds in bringing about his repentance in the space of thirty lines. The episodes of the subplots concerning usury (for which Lodge was doubtless responsible), corruption, drunkenness, and adultery are a more relevant mirror of London vice than Rasni's flamboyant sins; and these scenes, mostly in prose, are written with much greater vigor and some humor.

There are, however, some serious dramatic weaknesses. The warning to London would have been obvious without the choric sermons of Oseas; it is uneconomical to have two prophets, Oseas and Jonas, performing a similar function; the episode of the whale is perfunctorily treated; and the class structure of society in Nineveh strains our credulity.

The divergences between the quarto of *Orlando Furioso* and the Alleyn manuscript of Orlando's part are considerable enough to show that it would be unfair to judge Greene's intentions by the extant text; but it is clear that, although some of the verse is not without eloquence, the characterization is still crude. The madness of the hero is quite unconvincing, and Greene bungles the climax of the play: Sacrepant's confession of his slander of Angelica falls flat because Melissa had already revealed this to Orlando.

It is on the remaining plays that Greene's reputation as a dramatist depends, and it may readily be admitted that *Friar Bacon* and *James IV* mark a great advance. It is possible after reading them to understand Nashe's praise of Greene as a plotter of plays, though some think that he was referring rather to the composition of scenarios than to the structure of the plays for which Greene wrote the dialogue.

If we accept the currently orthodox date of *Doctor Faustus* (1592-3), Greene would have had little time to exploit the interest in necromancy aroused by that play: he may therefore have been the pioneer in using magic as a dramatic theme.[2] So far as one can judge Marlowe's play from the textual ruins of the first two quartos, *Friar Bacon and Friar Bungay* (c. 1589), though inferior to it in poetical and dramatic power, is more competently constructed. Greene uses magic to link together the four plots—the making of the brazen head, the rivalry of the Prince and Lacy for the love of Margaret, the later rivalry of Lambert and Serlsby for her hand, and the competition between Bacon and Vandermast. The idea was a good one. It enabled Greene to preserve a rough unity while providing an attractive variety of incident; and on the whole it was carried out successfully. With a willing suspension of disbelief, we can accept Bacon's magic glass through which the Prince sees Lacy courting Margaret and through which the sons watch the fatal fight of Lambert and Serlsby. We can even accept the transport of Bungay, Vandermast, and Miles by diabolical means. Greene obtains some powerful dramatic effects, as when the Prince steps forward to stab Lacy whom he sees in the magic glass; but he is most successful, perhaps, with Miles's reactions to the brazen head and with his colloquy with the devil in the last act. The killing of the Lamberts and the Serlsbys is less easy to accept, since the death of one member of each family would have been enough to motivate Bacon's renunciation of necromancy.

But in spite of the variety of incident, which was the main factor in the success of the amateur production at Stratford-upon-Avon in 1959, the play will hardly stand up to serious critical examination. For the most part the verse is poor. Much of it reads like a weak imitation of Marlowe, relieved only by occasional effective lines. Greene is too fond of the more artificial figures of rhetoric, such as the ending of successive lines with the same word:

> But now the braues of *Bacon* hath an end,
> Europes conceit of *Bacon* hath an end,
> His seuen yeares practise sorteth to ill end:
> And, villaine, sith my glorie hath an end,
> I will appoint thee to some fatall end.

On the other hand, Miles's racy prose and skeltonic doggerel is often amusing.

---

[2] Apart from the difficulty of dating *Doctor Faustus* before the publication of its source (1592), the hero's proposal to wall all Germany with brass must have been imitated from Greene's play or from its source, since it is only a passing reference in *Doctor Faustus* and not an integral part of the play, as Bacon's project is in Greene's.

Greene has been enthusiastically praised for the characterization of his heroine. Certainly the pastoral descriptions of Margaret in the first scene are delightful and the first impressions we have of her bear out the descriptions. She is represented as a gay and unsophisticated country lass. But at moments Greene seems to forget her English simplicity and makes her acquainted with the classics.[3]

> *Phoebus* is blythe and frolicke lookes from heauen,
> As when he courted louely *Semele* . . . .
>
> Proportioned as was *Paris,* when, in gray,
> He courted *Oenon* in the vale of *Troy*.

In the fine scene (3.1), where Margaret takes the blame for Lacy's disloyalty, she is given some deservedly famous lines—

> Why, thinks King *Henries* sonne that *Margrets* loue
> Hangs in the vncertaine ballance of proud time?—

but we forget we are in Fressingfield when she rejects the Prince's offers in these words:

> if *Ioues* great roialtie
> Sent me such presents as to *Danae;*
> If *Phoebus* tired in *Latonas* webs,
> Came courting from the beautie of his lodge;
> The dulcet tunes of frolicke *Mercurie,*
> Nor all the wealth heauens treasurie affoords,
> Should make me leaue lord *Lacie* or his loue.

Later in the play, after Margaret is betrothed to Lacy, she foolishly gives Lambert and Serlsby to understand that she will choose one of them. Greene's purpose was twofold. He wished—unnecessarily—to demonstrate Margaret's constancy; and he wished to motivate the quarrel between her two suitors whose deaths were to cause Bacon to renounce necromancy. But Margaret, who is not intended to be stupid, has had her character sacrificed to situation. In the last act, as she is about to enter a nunnery, Lacy arrives in time to inform her that he is not married after all and that he had only pretended to be so in order to try her constancy. Margaret promptly forswears the veil; Lacy does not ask her forgiveness, nor does she utter a word of reproach: because of the Griselda convention neither they nor the author regard Lacy's stratagem as at all reprehensi-

---

[3] The classical allusions could be defended, as Richard Hosley reminds me, as part of the larger poetic structure of the play, providing a kind of 'heroic' tone which sorts well enough with Edward's duty as heir apparent to marry a princess; but it tends to spoil the contrast between court and country and to minimize the gulf between Lacy and Margaret.

ble. Here again character has been sacrificed to plot. Margaret is an uneasy compromise between two conventions; but the critics treat her as though she were as three-dimensional as a character in a novel and praise her for qualities she does not possess.

James IV (c. 1591), though purporting to be an historical drama, is based on a story by Giraldi Cinthio. Greene's dramatization is, on the whole, very skillful. The exposition is particularly fine: by the end of the first scene, James, just married to Dorothea, has employed Ateukin to win Ida's love. The conception of all the chief scenes is excellent, and some of them are well executed—notably Ateukin's two temptations of the King and Ida's refusal to listen to Ateukin's dishonorable proposals. The verse, too, is generally more successful than in Greene's previous plays: the influence of Marlowe is not so marked, there is less literary allusion, and the rhetoric is more controlled and more natural. Rhyme, moreover, when it is used (for example, Ida's moral sentiments in the first scene and her love-scene with Eustace in 2.1), is seen to have a dramatic function. But the play has corresponding weaknesses. Although rash critics have compared Bohan to Jaques and Aster Oberon to Shakespeare's Oberon and Prospero, the induction and the choric interludes between the acts are tedious and unnecessary. It is absurd for Bohan's sons to appear as characters in the play he is presenting before Oberon, especially as the events are supposed to have taken place in an earlier age; it is artistically confusing when Slipper is rescued from the gallows by the intervention of Oberon; and Greene does not explain how Nano, who takes service with Ateukin in the first act, should be in Dorothea's service in the second. It may be added that the scenes in which Lady Anderson falls in love with the disguised Dorothea are bungled, and nothing is made of Sir Cuthbert's jealousy. The debate between a Lawyer, a Merchant, and a Divine (5.4), which was presumably intended to illustrate the evil results of James IV's misgovernment, is never once brought into focus.

We could overlook these faults, as many critics have done, if the presentation of Dorothea and her husband were entirely successful. The main difficulty confronting Greene in dramatizing the story was that the hero's conduct was so atrocious that a happy ending was almost unthinkable. Greene tries to minimize James IV's guilt in various ways. Whereas in the source some years elapse between Astatio's marriage and his passion for Ida, Greene's hero is already in love with Ida when he marries Dorothea for reasons of state. Arrenopia's murder is planned by Astatio himself; in Greene's play the King is tempted by the villainous Ateukin. Astatio gives out that Arrenopia had committed adultery; James does nothing to blacken Dorothea's memory. But in spite of these mitigations, James is hardly a sympathetic character. Greene does not convince us, as he convinced Churton Collins (*Plays and Poems of Robert Greene,* 1905, 2.34), that James IV is "a man in whom the higher and lower nature is in conflict, and in whom the conscience of a naturally honourable and even chivalrous man is never asleep." James repents of his wickedness only when Scotland is invaded; he offers a reward for the finding of Dorothea not out of remorse but out of fear of her father, and his plea for forgiveness, eloquent as it is, comes rather late:

> Durst I presume to looke vpon those eies
> Which I haue tired with a world of woes,
> Or did I thinke submission were ynough,
> Or sighes might make an entrance to thy soule,
> You heauens, you know how willing I would weep;
> You heauens can tell how glad I would submit;
> You heauens can say how firmly I would sigh.

It is, no doubt, possible to forgive such wickedness, as Imogen forgives her husband and Hermione hers; but both Posthumus and Leontes believe that their wives have committed adultery and both undergo a long purgatorial period before they are forgiven. Dorothea speaks as though she had little to forgive:

> Shame me not, Prince, companion in thy bed:
> Youth hath misled,—tut, but a little fault.

James IV's fault was not little, and no woman could seriously believe that it was. Greene intends Dorothea's lines to express not her real opinion but her huge magnanimity in minimizing her husband's misdeeds; but the effect of the lines is to make her into an incredible paragon. This, indeed, is the impression left on us by the character as a whole. When, for example, she is informed of the King's faithlessness, she makes a speech which, in the opinion of many critics, exhibits the nobility of her character. But does it? Or does it not rather destroy the illusion of reality?

> He doth but tempt his wife, he tryes my loue:
> This iniurie pertaines to me, not you.
> The King is young; and if he step awrie,
> He may amend, and I will loue him still.
> Should we disdaine our vines because they sprout
> Before their time? or young men, if they straine
> Beyond their reach? no; vines that bloome and spread
> Do promise fruites, and young men that are wilde
> In age growe wise.

Even if we make due allowances for the belief in the theory of wild oats and for the medieval (and Elizabethan) admiration for patient Griseldas, such facile forgiveness, such inhuman lack of resentment, takes away from the reality of the character. She shrinks into pasteboard. Later in the play, when Dorothea learns that the King has issued a warrant for her death, she has an outburst of grief, but of grief unmixed with the indignation which even the most docile woman might be expected to feel:

> Ah poore vnhappy Queen,
> Borne to indure what fortune can containe!
> Ah lasse, the deed is too apparant now!
> But, oh mine eyes, were you as bent to hide
> As my poore heart is forward to forgiue,
> Ah cruell King, my loue would thee acquite!

When Ross urges her to write to her father to avenge her, she rejects his advice because her love for her husband is apparently undiminished:

> As if they kill not me, who with him fight!
> As if his brest be toucht, I am not wounded!
> As if he waild, my ioyes were not confounded!
> We are one heart tho rent by hate in twaine;
> One soule, one essence, doth our weale containe:
> What, then, can conquer him that kils not me?

Dorothea faints with grief when she hears that the King is deserted by his friends; and, when Lady Anderson advises her to return to her father, she replies in a speech which for complacent self-rightousness is unequaled in the whole body of Elizabethan drama:

> Ah Ladie, so wold worldly counsell work,
> But constancie, obedience, and my loue,
> In that my husband is my Lord and Chiefe,
> These call me to compassion of his estate:
> Disswade me not, for vertue will not change.

Lady Anderson may well be astonished:

> If English dames their husbands loue so deer,
> I feare me in the world they haue no peere.

It may plausibly be claimed that the impression such speeches give of self-conscious virtue is due to use of the convention by which characters, speaking out of character, inform the audience of their own virtue or villainy, so that the audience will know what their reactions ought to be. But Greene uses this convention so crudely that Dorothea becomes a mere puppet.

The other three women are only sketched. The Countess of Arran has been compared to the Countess of Roussillon in *All's Well That Ends Well*. Beyond the fact that both women are middle-aged countesses, there seems to be little resemblance. Lady Anderson, "an honourable woman struggling with a dishonourable passion," is not fully realized. Ida is perhaps the most successful of the three, and Greene contrives to suggest her virtue and charm.

The view I have taken of Greene's powers of characterization, especially of his women, is not the orthodox one. G. P. Baker tells us (*Cambridge History of English Literature*, 1910, 5.138) that by infusing into romanticism "sympathetic and imaginative characterisation," Greene "transmuted it into the realistic romance that reaches its full development in Shakespeare's *Twelfth Night, Cymbeline* and *The Winter's Tale.*" F. E. Schelling (*The English Drama*, 1914, p. 62) speaks of Greene's heroines as "three of the most genuine and charming women in the drama preceding Shakespeare"—which is not saying very much; Allardyce Nicoll (*British Drama*, 1927, p. 90) says that Dorothea is "the best-drawn woman figure in sixteenth century drama outside Shakespeare's comedies." Greene's heroines, he tells us, "are real; yet they have some elements in them which seem ideal." T. M. Parrott and R. H. Ball (*A Short View of Elizabethan Drama*, 1943, p. 73) write in the same strain. Greene's heroines (they say) "form a very charming trio. More fully realized, lifelike, and credible than the shadowy women of Lyly's plays, they strike a note of true romance and are in a sense the forerunners of such romantic heroines as Rosalind, Viola, and Imogen." J. M. Robertson (*Elizabethan Literature*, 1914, pp. 104-5) speaks of Greene's power of "presenting a recognizably real woman, tender and true, the moral superior of the men around her; and . . . Dorothea . . . forecasts the noblest types of womanhood in Shakespeare." Greene's editors are even more emphatic. Churton Collins assures us that Ida is "beautifully drawn, a Miranda nurtured in solitude," and that Dorothea "would do honour to Shakespeare; she is the soul of the drama, and as her presence pervades it, she redeems all the faults of the play." And T. H. Dickinson speaks of "the sweet and simple womanliness of Greene's gallery."

Paradoxically enough, these critics do Greene an injustice; for, in approaching the plays from a Bradleyan standpoint and in praising the fine powers of characterization displayed in them, they pass over the real qualities—the liveliness and variety—possessed by Greene. *James IV* has, of course, a superficial resemblance to some of Shakespeare's plays— Dorothea, like Imogen, escapes from the threat of murder by disguising herself as a boy; and, again like Imogen, she forgives her husband. But this does not justify an attempt to credit Dorothea with the qualities of a Shakespearian heroine. In reading the critics cited above, one gets the impression that they have confused virtue with verisimilitude. Margaret and Dorothea display an infinite capacity for forgiveness; therefore they are good; therefore they are well drawn.

It may be suggested that Greene's treatment of his own wife conditioned his portraits of wronged and forgiving womanhood. Dorothea may, as Robertson suggests, have been named after Greene's wife; and his deathbed letter expresses hope of the forgiveness which the heroes of his plays and novels invariably received. It is true that lifelike characters can be created on the basis of wish-fulfillments, but Greene was not writing in a convention which demanded realistic characters.

From the semifictional accounts of how he became a playwright in *Francescoes Fortunes* and *A Groatsworth of Wit,* it is apparent that Greene wrote merely "to mittigate the extremitie of his want." During the last few years of his life he made great strides as a dramatist, from the puerility of *Alphonsus* to the comparative maturity of *James IV*. But, although in some ways Shakespeare's plays are closer to Greene's than they are to Lyly's, Lyly was much the better artist. Artificial as his plays are, Lyly achieves perfectly what he sets out to do. Greene attempts to bring a wider range of incident and emotion into his plays and it is arguable that, though he is never fully successful, his plays were nearer than Lyly's to those of the greater dramatists who succeeded him. He was right to recognize that the "vpstart crow" was "well able to bombast out a blanke verse as the best of" the university wits. He did not realize that this same "absolute *Iohannes fac totum*" was shortly to leave them far behind.

MARLOWE'S *DIDO* AND THE TRADITION

by Don Cameron Allen

I.

EW OF THE GREAT women of antiquity exceeded "widow Dido" in historically established chastity or poetically invented tragedy. This
curious double existence over the space of fifteen centuries could be attributed to her unlucky yet fortunate choice of celebrating poets. The
historical Dido, who founded the city of Carthage and patriotically died
to defend it, is splendidly memorialized in Justin's *Epitome* of Trogus
(18.4-6); the Dido who inspired the poets and who is more alive to us
than her honest alter ego was invented by Virgil. We follow her amorous
career, as did our ancestors, through the second, third, and fourth books
of the *Aeneid,* and as Iris shears the lock from her forehead and releases
her passionate spirit, we feel, if we are romantics, that Aeneas paid too
great a price for Italy. In this conclusion we are made firm by her tear-
stained letter preserved by Ovid (*Heroides,* 7) or by her story retold
again by her sister Anna, now a shadowy Carthaginian goddess, in the
presence of Silius Italicus (*Punica,* 8.44-210). The annotations of the
grammarian Servius (4.459) or of the critic Macrobius (*Saturnalia,* 5.17)
inform us that none of it was so, that Virgil was a libeler, but we refuse
to have it that way—an Ariadne is always more fetching than a Judith.

Like us the Middle Ages knew Dido in both testaments. The poets
embraced the poetic lady. The moralists used both women because each
could be made to sing a moral tune. At the beginnings of this era, the
malice of Virgil was revealed by the almost Christian and almost medie-

55

val Ausonius, who converted a poem of the *Anthology* into popular Latin:

> Talis eram; sed non, Maro quam mihi finxit, eras, mens
> Vita nec incestis feta cupidinibus.
> Namque nec Aeneas vidit me Troius unquam,
> Nec Lybiam advenit classibus Iliacis.
>
> (23.2)

It is this woman of history, traduced by Virgil, who got the praise of Tertullian (*Anima*, 33) and who gave Jerome a text for a lecture on Christian widowhood (*Patrologia latina*, 33.286); it was the other woman, invented by the poet and abandoned by Aeneas, who made the tears (that should have been shed for Christ) spring in the eyes of the unregenerate Augustine (*ibid.*, 32.670). A thousand years later the poet of the *Roman de la Rose* moistens his pen with the same salt brine and complains about the founder of Rome. "Car li traitres s'en foi, Senz congie, par mer a navie, Don la bele perdi la vie" (ed. Langlois, 1922, 4.9-10).

Dante, as one might expect, struck the moral gong when he placed Dido in the second circle of Hell (5.61-2) and explained in the *Convito* (5.61) that Aeneas was a sort of unbridled stallion when he landed in North Africa, but that he put the bit in his mouth and pulled his load after the wild gallop was over.

> E quanto raffrenare fu quello, quando avendo ricevuto da Dido tanto di piacere, quanto di sotto nel settimo trattato si dirà, e usando con essa tanto di dilettazione, elli si partì, per seguire onesta e laudabile via e fruttosa, come nel quarto dell' Eneida è scritta.

Dante's editors, Benvenuto da Imola, Giovanni da Serravalle, Cristoforo Landino,[1] and Francesco da Buti, humanists of the fifteenth and sixteenth centuries, rebuked him for sending the good lady to the oven; in fact, da Buti puts it rather stoutly: "e però Virgilio fece molto male a dare tale infamia a sì onesta donna, per fare bella la sua poesia; e lo nostro autore Dante fece peggio a seguitarlo in questo" (*Commento*, ed. Giannini, 1858, 1.160-1).

Boccaccio, the first of Dante scholars, also knew the truth, but in spite of his knowledge he divided his allegiance between the two Didos. In his *Amorosa visione* (*Opere volgari*, 1833, 14.115-16) we hear Dido lamenting her faithless lover as his sails shorten on the road to Italy; but in the *De casibus illustrium virorum* (Paris, 1511, fols. 16v-17v) and the *De*

---

[1] See G. Biagi, *La divina commedia nella figurazione artistica e nel secolare commento* (1924), *ad loc.*

claris mulieribus (Berne, 1539, fols. 28-29v), he has described only the noble woman of the historians; in fact, in the latter work, he writes a homily in the manner of Jerome's on the duties of the Christian widow. It was the historical Dido who found her way from Justin via Boccaccio into popular encyclopedias like Jacobus Bergomensis' *De claris mulieribus* and who so perplexed Caxton that he gave her an opening round of applause before he brought her other half forward in the *Eneydos*. Francesco Petrarca also shared in Boccaccio's learning and was distressed that men who knew the two Didos were so seduced by the beauty, elegance, and sublimity of Virgil that they clung to his strange fiction. He found it difficult to understand why Virgil chose Dido out of a million other women—a woman praised by all for her chastity, fidelity to her dead husband, and patriotism—as an example of a lady tangled in the net of shameful love. He supposes therefore that Virgil perverted the legend for the sake of allegory, and so he expounds the fourth book of the *Aeneid* as a symbolic narrative of the pilgrimage of life in which the *vir fortis* resists all those temptations that would prevent his arrival at his destined goal (*Opera*, Basel, 1554, pp. 871-2).

Moral Gower in one of his *Balades* (43) can list Aeneas together with Jason, Hercules, and others as among the "tricherous," but when he uses Virgil's story in the *Confessio* (4.77-142), it is as an illustration of the sin of *acedia*. Aeneas, full of his mission, paused in Carthage and "hadde hise thoghtes feinte Towardes love and full of Slowthe, His tine lett." The Confessor warns all readers against "loves cause." Dido makes a similar Virgilian appearance in Chaucer's *Hous of Fame* and *Legend of Good Women* as a "martyr of love." There is no indication that Chaucer knew the historical Queen of Carthage nor does he condemn Dido and blame Virgil. The weight of Chaucer's accusation rests on Aeneas. In the *Hous of Fame* (267) the Trojan is given the epithet of "traitour," which is amply elaborated in the *Legend* (1326-9):

> For on a night, slepinge, he let her lye,
> And stal a-wey un-to his companye,
> And, as a traitour, forth he gan to saile
> Toward the large contree of Itaile.

There is little doubt, I think, that Chaucer understood Virgil's estimate of Dido and his emphasis on the destiny of Aeneas; it is probably equally certain that he knew the allegorical reading of the episode; nonetheless, he accepts the interpretation of the poet of the *Roman* that Aeneas is a traitor to *fin amour*. Fra Rocaberti, who lived a little later than Chaucer, abides by this decision and puts Aeneas in a lover's hell. The poet, who finds him in a pit in Love's garden, hears him say, like a citizen of the Inferno, "I am Aeneas and I suffer because of my ingratitude towards Dido. Love desires that love receive love, but following my will I did not know her worth."

> Eneas so, que per desconexenca
> De Dido so posat en tal turment.
> Amor qui es un conforme voler
> Vol que los fets sien tostemps conformes.
> Fent mos desigs no presi son valer.
> (*Gloria d'amor*, ed. Heaton, 1916, p. 92)

By the end of the Middle Ages the sympathies of men of letters are usually on the side of Queen Dido, who was either traduced by Virgil or shamelessly abandoned by Aeneas. To defend either the hero or the poet, men of the late fifteenth and of the sixteenth century[2] invoked the method of symbolic reading, which had also been attempted by Petrarch. In his *Allegoriae in P. Virgili Maronis opera*, Landino lays the whole blame on Dido's voluptuousness; it was she who proposed the affair. The fact that the union was consummated in a cave symbolizes those who seek for things in themselves. There is no question that Aeneas was snared by her love, and it turned him aside from his true course. If he had stayed with Dido, everyone not only would have blamed him but also would have felt sorry for him; and it is likewise plain that he would have forgotten his duties had Mercury not come to him (*Libri quattuor*, Strassburg, 1508, fols. 50-52v). A similar reading of the legend was made by Maphaeus Vegius, the author of the thirteenth book of the *Aeneid*, in his *De educatione liberorum*. For him the epic "conceals beneath the ornament of poetic imagery the highest mystery of philosophy." Aeneas is "the virtuous man" and Dido a fine woman.

> For what woman is not moved by Dido's example and set on fire with zeal for goodness, as she hears how earnestly the queen devoted herself to her task, established walls for her great city, regulated institutions and laws for the people in a spirit of justice, and, even though her husband was dead, won high renown and reverence for herself and inspired fear in her neighbors by keeping her faith and promise? And yet is the heart not shaken, terrified, and affrighted by the knowledge that she fell madly in love with her guest, a mere stranger, gave up the

---

[2] For examples of the charge against Virgil see Ariosto, *Orlando furioso*, 35.28; Betussi, *Il Raverta* (1544), in *Trattati d'amore*, ed. Zonta (1912), p. 73; Fracastorius, *Naugerius*, in *Opera* (Venice, 1555), p. 163; Tasso, *Discorsi*, 3.23; and Du Bellay, "Epistre a De Morel," in *Poésies françaises*, ed. Courbet (1919), 1.275. For samples of complaints about Aeneas see Bembo, *Gli Asolani* (ed. 1808), p. 65; and L. Dardano, *La bella e dotta difesa delle donne* (Venice, 1554), fols. 14-14v.

rule of her people, spent her time in such pursuits as merrymaking and feasting, and in the end forsaken by her lover, in grief and affliction, bereft of all hope, resolved to compass her own death? Will not a woman choose to devote herself to virtue, though it be austere, when its fruits are shown to be so sweet rather than to succumb to seductive passion, when its fruits are described as so bitter?[3]

Interpretations similar to these are provided for the Renaissance reader by Jodocus Badius Ascensius and Giovanni Fabbrino, editors of and commentators on the *Aeneid*. In his preface to Book 4, Badius Ascensius observes that each one of the six first books is to be equated with one of the six ages of man, and hence the book of Dido is devoted to young manhood. The moral of this book is the ill effect of love on a grave and pious man; in addition the story demonstrates how love-impatience drives a constant woman to suicide. The episode teaches us, Ascensius writes, that by keeping at a distance from luxury and ease we can avoid the lassos of Venus. Though Aeneas was caught in a moment of weakness, Ascensius does not feel that he can be charged with treachery; he is sure, in fact, that Virgil inserted lines 169-72 to clear his hero from blame (*Opera,* Lyons, 1529, *ad loc.*). While Ascensius puts the emphasis of his commentary on Aeneas, other critics—and especially Italians— were inclined to make Dido the center of their remarks.

Sperone Speroni in his *Sopra Virgilio* acknowledges the historical impossibility of the episode and thinks that Virgil brought it in so that he could warn men against Rumor, the Rumor that called Aeneas "treacherous" and Dido "unchaste." Could a woman of Dido's virtues, he inquires, fall in love with a man capable of treachery? The purpose of Book 4, Speroni observes, is to show how a noble woman is infatuated, a woman empty of affection because her husband is dead. The whole psychological course of love is described, and we are finally told how it turns to hate (*Opere,* 1740, 2.162-80). Fabbrino agrees with his countryman in pointing out that Dido was wounded by Cupid's golden arrow, whereas Aeneas was never touched by love. The Queen is first attracted by Aeneas's handsomeness, but slowly love, virtue protesting, fills her whole nature with an intemperate obsession. She pretends to admire Aeneas's character, but she really is taken by his physical charms (*Vergilio, Opere,* Venice, 1615, fols. 92-92v; 1st ed., 1588).

E però ci introdusse prima Didone per una donna castissima e prudentissima in governare la Republica, ma vinta poi da l' amore, e da la libidine, abbandona ogni buona operatìone, e si da a l' otio, e a la

---

[3] A. C. Brinton, *Maphaeus Vegius* (1930), p. 27. It is interesting that John of Salisbury takes the same objection to Dido's state dinner: *Policraticus,* ed. Webb (1909), 2.259.

lascivia. Da questo si conosce quanto facìlmente gl' huomini nelle cose prospere abbandonano la virtu, e si danno a le voglie sfrenate. (ed. 1615, fol. 96)

The departure of Aeneas teaches that the pious man should leave effeminate matters and strive towards the highest goods (fol. 118v), which, I suppose, though Fabbrino never says so, are masculine.

2.

According to the dissertation by Willem H. D. Suringar (*Dido tragoedia*, 1880), almost forty dramatists have written plays on the Dido legend, but to my knowledge no playwright of the Renaissance used the historical queen, tragic though her life was, as his subject. Although everyone probably knew of her existence, it was Virgil's Dido who took the fancy of poets. The three most important plays about her written before Marlowe's time were by Giraldi Cinthio, Dolce, and Jodelle. In 1888 Jakob Friedrich made a study of the Didos of Dolce, Jodelle, and Marlowe and found correctly that they had almost nothing in common to suggest that Marlowe had read his predecessors (*Die Didodramen des Dolce, Jodelle, und Marlowe,* 1888). In 1926 Robert Turner compared the plays on Dido by Pazzi de' Medici, Giraldi Cinthio, Dolce, Jodelle, and La Grange, and noted certain similarities between the *Didone* of Giraldi Cinthio and the *Didone* of Dolce (*Didon dans la tragédie de la Renaissance italienne et française,* 1926). Both of these investigators checked their texts against the great classical originals and found, as one might expect, interesting 'innovations.' The orthodox exercises of source and influence have been thus completed, but neither scholar has considered the literary tradition or explained the separate tones struck by the dramatists against the base of the tradition. I have attempted the first; I shall now move to the second.

In his preface to Alessandro d' Este, Giraldi Cinthio, whose play was written, performed, and printed in 1541, places his text in the allegorical tradition. "Ove Enea ci rappresenta uno prudentissime [*sic*] heroe, Giove la parte superiore dell' anima humana, Mercurio la discorsiva e ragionevole, e Didone la parte inferiore e sensuale" (*Didone,* Venice, 1583, pp. 4-5). The emphasis of the letter is retained in the prologue where we are informed that Aeneas, whose reason had been tricked by his senses, makes it conform to the fate ordained by God. "Ma sospinta Didon dal van disio, Da desperation fia interna vinta" (p. 8). In the course of the play, which follows the Virgilian framework closely, it is Achates who represents the reason's duty to God, and Anna who speaks for free will and so brings about her sister's doom. In the second act the sacrificial omens forbid the marriage, but Anna says that they are fraudulent means of cheating mortals. "Ma inganno le menti de i mortali Volendo lor mostrar quel, che non sanno" (p. 36). When Aeneas comments on the fine city and its beautiful queen, Achates reproves him for a weakness unbecoming to a hero with a heavenly destiny; Anna, however, urges Aeneas to suit himself and reminds him of the splendid humanistic doctrine of free will. Aeneas accepts her advice and succumbs to love, but not before Achates picks up the allegorical reading.

> Tutto in Didone trasformato i veggio,
> Sì, che nulla piu in lui riman d' Enea,
> Questi, il cui cor vincer non hà potuto
> Nè pericol di morte, nè la forza
> Di tutta Grecia, nè il furor del Mare,
> In tal maniera hor vinto è da Didone,
> Ch' egli come huomo effeminato, e molle,
> Tutto è sotto l'arbitrio di costei,
> Come tener fanciul sotto la madre.
> (p. 54)

Reason finally triumphs and Aeneas prepares to depart, mindful that he will be described through the ages as unjust, cruel, and unfaithful. Men may say this, but the "Signor" to whom he addresses his prayers and who knows the human heart also knows the truth (pp. 71-2). He almost gives in to love when he takes leave of Dido; but Achates, who has been lashed by a woman of Dido's entourage for encouraging his master to imitate Jason, Theseus, and Demophon, drags the wavering hero to the boats. Reason and the will of Heaven win against the desires of the flesh. The commentary on the whole action is supplied by a metaphysical chorus that sings at the end of Act 2 about the futility of ambition (one of Dido's faults), that urges a search for higher goals in Act 3, that comments on the supra-animal reason of man at the end of Act 4 and suggests that Dido follow its dictates. Finally, Aeneas gone and Queen Dido dead, the chorus sings a long piece on the instability of human fortunes and the fragility of human love (p. 128).

Giraldi Cinthio's play begins with the traditional encounter between Juno and Venus. Dolce's *Didone tragedia* (1547, in *Quattro tragedie*, 1776), which leans on its predecessor but is a far better play, opens with a soliloquy by Cupid, who describes himself as a cruel god. "Nell' una mano io porto Dubbia, speme, fallace, e breve gioja; Pene, sospir, e morti." Cupid, who is the only supernatural character in the cast, returns in the second act with the ghost of Sichaeus to whom he gives a snake torn from the head of a Fury and commands him to throw it in Dido's bosom. This play, which is concerned only with the departure of Aeneas and the suicide of Dido, is about the cruelty of love and the inescapability of destiny. Cupid's inaugural speech sets the first emphasis; Aeneas announces the second tone when he says early in Act 1: "O fallaci speranze, o vita incerta, Lieve, e mutabil piu, ch' al vento foglia!" (p. 18). Both doctrines are sustained by the choirs that sing at the end of each act; they tell us that Love is the cause of every ill and every shame that falls on "la meschinella gente" (p. 66); and they conclude the tragedy by chanting:

> Quel dì, che 'l miser uomo
> Veste qua guìso l'alma
> Di questo corporal caduco velo,
> Là su con lettre salde, e adamantine
> E' discritto il suo fine.
> Però a i fati cedete
> Voi, che felici, o sventurati sete:
> Ch' ogni cosa mortal governa il Cielo.
>
> (pp. 82-3)

Though Achates is present and acts as Aeneas's conscience, Dolce does not bow to the allegorical reading. He informs Aeneas, who is hesitant, that it is better for one woman to die than for the posterity of Ascanius to perish (pp. 21-2), and not only assures him that Dido has brought her evil on herself (p. 23) but also suggests means for a clandestine departure (pp. 24-5). Giraldi Cinthio had permitted Aeneas a self-exculpating speech; Dolce, sensitive to the charges against his hero, spends part of Act 2 and almost all of Act 3 in his defense. Aeneas admits that in leaving his wife of a year he is doing a disservice to lovers and to the most courteous lady the sun has ever seen (p. 22); he fears that she will kill herself and prays the gods to witness that he is innocent of evil.

> Ei mi sia testimon, che d' ogni caso,
> Ch' a lei possa avvenir, sono innocente;
> E che di tutti gli onorati pregi
> Che dar mi sento, e 'l meritar m' è caro;
> Alcun non è di che piu goda l' alma,
> Che del titolo illustre di pietoso.
>
> (p. 26)

The third act begins with the Messenger deriding Aeneas before the Chorus, which defends Dido by stating that she would never have married Aeneas "Per cagion lieve, o per lascivo amore" (p. 39). Achates has a long debate with the Chorus over the justice of Aeneas's actions, and the only sound argument he can find is that "il Ciel dispone" (p. 42). In this act, Aeneas uses the same argument with Dido; and when the Chorus assaults him as a typical betrayer of women and twits him with "che un gentil atto di pietad Onora l' um sovr' ogni umana sorte" (p. 51), he can think of nothing better to say than "Heaven wills it."

Jodelle's *Didon se sacrifiant* (1553-60, in *Les oeuvres,* ed. Marty-Laveau, 1868, vol. 1), by omitting supernatural characters, makes the story of Dido into a cold human tragedy. The gods are invisibly present, because Jodelle follows Virgil closely, but they are vague and distant, forces moving and directing the fates of men but speaking, like Christian angels, only in dreams. Curiously enough it is Achates in this play who makes sport of Aeneas's premonitory dreams; Ascanius and Palinurus advise obedience, for as the latter puts it, "Un mal passe le mal" (p. 158). The tragedy, though tedious, is gravely serious, almost sick with the hopelessness of man's fate. At the end of the first act, the Chorus describes the subjection of man to blind destiny (p. 167).

Jodelle writes about Dido and Aeneas, but these characters are only thin coverings for his dissertation on human despair and his tirade against the gods. Anna complains that the heavens are blind and punish the good for the crimes of the evil: "Qui traine incessamment l'innocence au supplice" (p. 172). Aeneas suffers in this tragedy as much almost as the Queen, but he too is in the harsh grip of the gods (pp. 196-7, 202). Jodelle also attempts to clear him of the charge of treachery, but the Chorus of Carthaginians, who are naturally prejudiced in their Queen's cause, see in the tragedy only the malice of the gods.

> Mais iniuste ie pense
> Chacune Deité,
> Qui iamais ne dispense
> Le bien à la bonté.
> Un seul hasard domine
> Dessus tout l'univers,
> Où la faveur divine
> Est deuë au plus pervers.
> (p. 217)

In this scheme of things, Love is as cruel as Dolce's Cupid had said, but Love is after all only a servant and minister of the blind evil of Heaven. Jean le Maire des Belges had, on one occasion, described how Love and Death exchanged bows, and Ronsard, Jodelle's contemporary, had said that Love and Death were the same thing. We cannot be shocked, then, when Jodelle comes to the same conclusion and writes for one of his final choruses a condemnation of love. "Il n'apporte que servitude, Et apporte, quand il est rude Tousiours la mor sur nous" (p. 224). This same neurotic reaction is put in the mouth of Barce, who brings the news of Dido's suicide: "Et bien souvent l'amour a la mort nous marie" (p. 227).

Though Giraldi Cinthio's play is the only one to follow the allegorical tradition, all three plays unite in defending Aeneas's desertion of Dido; however, the philosophical emphases of all differ. Giraldi Cinthio's play is the least complex in that it faithfully follows the *Aeneid* and presents the conflict as an heroic struggle between love and duty. With Dolce's *Didone* philosophical extensions are added, for though it makes plain that the divinely commissioned man must attend to his destiny and be absolved of blame for wrongs committed during his inspired career, it also states that human love is a cruel and bitter passion that men should avoid. The full melancholia of the hurt mind is brought into the legend by Jodelle. For him, love and duty are merely linguistic subterfuges that expound the malice of the gods; at best these passions are instruments that the heavenly forces use when, in their eternal blindness, they have their sport with mortals.

To turn from Jodelle to Marlowe is like going from a sanatorium to a masked ball. His *Dido Queen of Carthage* (in *Works,* ed. Tucker Brooke, 1910) was written for the Children of the Chapel Royal and presented to an audience that knew the classics and had some feeling for classical temperance. In a sense, he is in this play following the course set by John Lyly, but one must not think of his *Dido* in the same moment that one remembers *Campaspe* or *Sapho and Phao.* The subject is as grave as the poet is gifted. The play has been curiously unprized by critics partly because they do not know where in the Marlovian chronicle it belongs and partly because it seems not to move in the great swinging orbits of the universal tragedies. There is also the fact that Nashe had some share in it, though this share, if I may use the touchstone of my intuition, was certainly inconsequential. The important thing is that *Dido* was not written for the popular theater; hence Marlowe could be less blatant about his dramatic purpose.

Virgil is the stage director, and Marlowe follows, as Boleslaus Knutowski (*Das Dido-Drama von Marlowe und Nash,* 1905) makes painfully clear, the opening four books of the *Aeneid.* He keeps his eye so closely on the Latin text that he uses eight Virgilian lines that he either feared to spoil by translation or preserved for the sake of antique tone. He adds to the main text numerous small details that Knutowski and Tucker Brooke have tracked to classical or medieval origins and that probably come in some instances from the Renaissance editors of Marlowe's Virgil. What is of more importance are the grand alterations. Ascanius and Iulus are combined in one person; Iarbas, a small figure in the *Aeneid,* is given a fat part and is fancied by the virginal Anna; Dido dismantles the Trojan ships and they only get off for Italy through Iarbas's jealous aid; softer than his prototype, Aeneas has twice to be dragged to the wharf; finally, Iarbas, unlike himself, dies with Dido and Anna. Its continental predecessors were mainly concerned with the departure of Aeneas and the agony of Dido, but Marlowe's play sweeps through the whole Virgilian tale. The final distress of the Queen and her friends requires a hundred lines, an economy of poetic emotion that must be measured against Jodelle's eight hundred. The alteration of plot and the temperance of the English poet suggests that he was feeling his way towards the neoclassical technique of Corneille and Racine.

In the small cabinet of critical comments on this play, one comes most frequently on one ticketed 'inept portrayal of female characters.' This comment arises from what might be called 'folk psychiatry,' because the same remark applies equally well to Marlowe's male characters. Like the continental playwrights before him or, for that matter, like his own predecessors in the English drama, Marlowe is essentially a *rhétoriqueur.* If one goes by the speeches and never looks at the left-hand margin, one would have difficulty separating the men from the women or even the men from the men. It is true that Dido in this play is not so much a woman as a debutante. She makes love like an adolescent, and she curries her beloved's favor by loading him with gifts and honors. This is how one wins lovers in a schoolgirl's daydream. She also has a simple coyness that is proper in a young virgin but silly, though not unknown, in seasoned widows who are also empire builders. In spite of these defects, she cannot be shoved away with a customary statement; she must be observed within the formula, good or bad, that the poet has assumed.

When Dido first encounters Marlowe's Aeneas, he is a far more humble and self-depreciating hero than he had ever been before. Dido proceeds to cure this inferiority; she gives him the robes of Sichaeus; when he says that he is "too mean to be companion to a queen" (2.1.89), she makes him sit in her seat; then she becomes foster mother to his orphan child. She begs Aeneas, as is her literary custom, to tell the tale of Troy and the fate of its masters, but it is Helen about whom she is curious. This is purely *ewig weibliche*. In Act 3 she holds Cupid (Ascanius) in her lap and converses with her suitor Iarbas, and we observe her come under the power of the little god. First, like a modern widow, she worries about her reputation; then she says, "Dido may be thine" (3.1.19). As the amorous inoculation works, she first loves the little boy; then she begins to doubt her previous inclination to Iarbas. Finally, she sends the Gaetulian off abruptly and sighs, "Is not Aeneas fair and beautiful?" (3.1.62). Betussi (*Il Raverta*, p. 63), an expert in Italian love, complained that Virgil's Dido was too open, that she should at first have concealed her love; he reminds us of Marlowe's critics when he says that Virgil's queen is "inept." It is here that the coyness of Marlowe's woman helps. She does not fall in love the way one falls off a cliff. She boosts Aeneas's morale; then by showing him pictures of men who had sought her hand (Portia comes in here), she proves to him—though the action is naive—that she has some worth. At first all that she will say to Aeneas is that she does not hate him; afterwards, to herself, "O, if I speak, I shall betray myself" (3.2.171-2).

It is Marlowe's Aeneas who is the difficult character. Dido tells him of her love, and like Uriah Heep he remarks, "Aeneas' thoughts dare not ascend so high" (3.4.32). Shortly after, he is still acting humble, but handing her his heart and swearing by all that is sacred "Never to like or love any but her!" (3.4.50). Within a hundred lines or so, "Aeneas must away; Whose golden fortunes, clogg'd with courtly ease, Cannot ascend to Fame's immortal house, Or banquet in bright Honour's burnish'd hall" (4.3.7-10). He slips away to the docks; and when Dido finds him he says he is there only to say *bon voyage* to Achates. This dubious explanation is attended by a pompous speech (4.4.40-44) in which he describes himself as a man of iron; a moment later the iron man falls comfortably into Dido's arms. A second warning from the gods, whose commands he must obey, then separates Aeneas from his "dear love." Marlowe spares his audience the extended priggish orations that his continental forerunners had, at this point, written for the Trojan; he also avoids the lengthy rodomontade that they provided for the disconsolate and desperate Dido. She calls Aeneas a traitor, perjurer, and false lover, but this is part of the Latin tradition. There is no reason not to believe that Marlowe also looked down his nose at "pious Aeneas."

The gods have more to say and do in the English *Dido* than in any of the previous dramas. On this matter the late Una Ellis-Fermor, in her *Christopher Marlowe* (1927), wrote some interesting yet troubling lines.

But this concentration upon the relations of human beings to each other rather than upon the relationship of man to the universe is unlike Marlowe in any but the earliest stage of his career, before his strongest interests had grown clear, or in the latest stage, in which he had begun to set them aside.

She continues her remarks by stating that Marlowe "rejects the supernatural apparatus" and thus lowers the theme "from a half divine contest" to a "human story of the conflict between love and the instinct for action" (pp. 18-19). Almost a third of Marlowe's tragedy is given over to gods discoursing with other gods or with mortals, and in this sense the supernatural apparatus is emphasized rather than rejected. If, however, Miss Ellis-Fermor meant that the portrayal of the gods and of the divine forces is without high seriousness, she is exactly right.

The Jupiter who appears at the beginning of *Dido, "dandling Ganymede upon his knee,"* is hardly the dignified, antique gentleman of Virgil, but a Dives out of Petronius or Juvenal, a Roman Falstaff of the age of the Antonines. He swears "by Saturn's soul," and calls his catamite "Sweet wag," promising to entertain him with a jig by Vulcan and a chorus or two by the Muses. He amuses his "plump prostitute boy" by pulling a feather from sleeping Hermes' wing and presenting him with Juno's wedding jewels. The "female wanton boy," as Venus calls him, demands more presents and to this demand the *rector mundi et rex deorum* assents, "if thou wilt be my love." Twitted by disapproving Venus, Jupiter awakens that sound sleeper Hermes and sends him off to save the storm-wracked Aeneas. This is the first scene, and the irreverent tone does not lessen very much when Venus and Juno meet in Act 3 and talk like duchesses or charwomen. The Queen of Olympus is an "old witch" and a "hateful hag"; she is also a sly piece, as Venus observes when they have perfected their love plot. "You savour," says the implacable Aphrodite, "after my wiles." These episodes are not supernaturally divine but mortally comic, and they are in keeping with Marlowe's usual denigration of the divine. Marlowe is here a true son of Lucian, who wrote dialogues (4, 20) between these same gods that are filled with similar awe and wonder. Marlowe exhibits these high powers to us as commentaries on Aeneas's great decision: he would prefer to remain with Dido; he knows he is a transgressor against love; "Yet he must not gainsay the gods' behest" (5.1.127). What gods!

If the tone of the dialogues of the gods is Lucianic, those in which Cupid appears are Alexandrian. Ascanius and Cupid, little boys together, are as charming *putti* as the painters of the Renaissance ever drew. They sing songs, eat sugar almonds, and wear silver purses; they examine bows and quivers, play with doves, fan themselves with feathers, hunt, gather fruit, and sleep under quilts of flowers. One Pompeian episode follows another, and they all culminate in a scene that sits close to the Ganymede episode. In this scene (4.5) Cupid, disguised as Ascanius, is with the Nurse (Virgil's Barce), and suddenly the toothless old woman of eighty twitters with lascivious eagerness. "Four score is a girl's age," says she, "love is sweet; I'll have a husband or else a lover." Marlowe's purpose in this scene and in the others may be simply comic, but both are illustrations of what the Renaissance and the Middle Ages would call perverse love. The affair of Jupiter with Ganymede is an example of *amor illegitimus et praeternaturalis*; the awakened old woman is a fine sample of *amor illegitimus et naturalis*. (See Agostino Nifo, *De amore,* Leyden, 1641, pp. 288-98.) The impossible love of Dido and Aeneas, as the tradition proclaimed it, belongs in similar categories.

Though this play of Marlowe's does not move in the thundering realms of the universal absolutes which critics have found in *Tamburlaine, Faustus,* and *The Jew of Malta,* it does, I think, clearly reveal his characteristic attitude towards those who think that there is a divinity that shapes our ends. In his poetic philosophy men are surely better than their gods and have only one mortal weakness: they lend their ears and then their hearts to the advice and direction of the silly hulks they have themselves created. Marlowe is, of course, ironic, but in a sense he follows the traditions accepted by Dolce and Jodelle that Cupid is cruel and that the gods are blind blundering forces. By making Dido an attractive though immature woman and by showing us an Aeneas who is an obedient career pusher, but not overbright, he votes with his predecessors who held the Trojan guilty. There is also a possible allegorical reading of their love affair, but I am inclined to believe that if there is allegory, as there certainly is in Giraldi Cinthio, it is laughingly metaphysical rather than solemnly moral.

MARLOWE'S HUMOR

by CLIFFORD LEECH

"I HAUE (PURPOSELY) omitted and left out some fond and friuolous Iestures, digressing (and in my poore opinion) far vnmeet for the matter, which I thought, might seeme more tedious vnto the wise, than any ways els to be regarded, though (happly) they haue bene of some vaine conceited fondlings greatly gaped at, what times they were shewed vpon the stage in their graced deformities: neuertheles now, to be mixtured in print with such matter of worth, it wuld prooue a great disgrace to so honorable & stately a historie."[1] These statements appear in the address "To the Gentlemen Readers: and others that take pleasure in reading Histories" prefixed to *Tamburlaine* by Richard Jones the printer in 1590. The late Una Ellis-Fermor, in her edition of the play (1930), drew attention to the two possible meanings of the words—that Marlowe had originally included more comic matter than now appears in the text, and that actors' 'gags' had found their way into the copy in Jones's hands. But she evidently found greater probability in the latter interpretation (p. 67), and further considered that a number of passages in the extant text were gags that had escaped Jones's vigilance.[2] One of the recurrent features of Marlowe criticism has been the tendency first to deplore, and then to deny his authorship of, comic passages in the plays. And recently the disbelief in Marlowe's capacity for humor has made an especially vigorous appearance in C. S. Lewis's discussion of *Hero and Leander* in his *English Literature in the Sixteenth Century* (1954). Here

---

[1] Quotations from Marlowe are from *The Works of Christopher Marlowe*, ed. C. F. Tucker Brooke (1910).
[2] *Tamburlaine the Great*, ed. Una Ellis-Fermor (1930), notes on Part 1: 2.4.28-35, 3.3.215-27; on Part 2: 1.3.61-3, 3.1.74-5, 3.5.100-2, 3.5.136-7, 3.5.156-7.

we are told that, in such an undertaking as this poem, Marlowe had to be careful that his necessary realism of treatment did not awaken our disgust or incredulity; and Lewis adds: "Nor our sense of humour: laughter at the wrong moment is as fatal in this kind as in tragedy" (p. 487).

Against such views one may weigh T. S. Eliot's well-known assertion that Marlowe's "most powerful and mature tone" was that of a "savage comic humour," a humor akin to that of *Volpone* (*Selected Essays,* 1932, p. 123). Since Eliot's essay was published, it has become commonplace to echo this sentiment in relation to *The Jew of Malta,* but there has been less regard for its applicability to Marlowe's writing as a whole. In the present essay I wish to draw attention to the pervasively comic tone in *Dido Queen of Carthage,* in *The Massacre at Paris,* and in *Hero and Leander.* Ultimately there will come, perhaps, a recognition of the important part played by savage humor in *Tamburlaine* and in *Doctor Faustus:* they are tragic plays, but the tragedy is of the sort in which humor is at home, insisting on the bizarre and the puny coexistent with the splendid within the mind and behavior of each man, however single. That is not to say, of course, that the comic scenes in our extant *Faustus* come straight from Marlowe's pen: indeed, that is less than likely. But it is to suggest that Marlowe's vision of the world, as presented in these plays, included the comic. More easily than Shakespeare, he could laugh at his hero while sharing that hero's aspiration and anguish. In *Edward II* the situation is more complex, but Marlowe has not left humor out of account.

Nothing will be implied here concerning the dates of composition of the writings considered. *Dido* and *Hero and Leander* may have been worked at during Marlowe's Cambridge years, though the maturity of the style makes that difficult to credit; they may, on the other hand, date from the end of his short career. What I think may be suggested is that in Marlowe's writing as a whole, without any necessary relation to dates of composition, we can see varying ways in which humor may be woven into the fabric. In *Faustus* and *Tamburlaine,* as already asserted, it is part of a predominantly tragic response to the world, complicating but not destroying the tragic attitude. In *The Jew of Malta* and *The Massacre at Paris* the humor is more assertive, equally savage but no longer finding its place alongside a sense of a man's greatness: what is presented is a wry picture of a world of little men, dreaming of greatness and playing out their atrocities but—whether in Barabas or the Guise—exposing their puniness even in the moments of highest ambition. In *Edward II,* as notably appeared in the 1958 production by the Marlowe Society (acted in Cambridge, Stratford-upon-Avon, and London), we have a play of subdued tragedy, subdued comedy. The titular hero blunders and suffers, as do Mortimer and Isabella and Gaveston. We sympathize with them, we are shocked by the ends they meet, but Marlowe has kept all of them throughout at the mercy of circumstance, and lingers with pity over each error as it is made. And, as the dreams are modest here, so too is the occasion for laughter. Nevertheless, a fund of humor is available at need—in the baiting of a bishop by Edward and Gaveston, in Edward's infatuation, in the climbing antics of Young Spencer and Baldock, in Warwick's cruel jibe at the condemned Gaveston, in Lightborn's petty joy in his executioner's skill. But in *Dido* and in *Hero and Leander* the relationship between the comic and the serious is different from that in any of these. Although both stories end in death, the dominant tone is that of a gentle and delighting humor: the affairs of men and gods are seen as a spectacle engagingly absurd.

In the essay referred to, Eliot has drawn attention to the comic element in the style of *Dido,* a style "which secures its emphasis by always hesitating on the edge of caricature at the right moment" (p. 124). My concern is rather with the play's incidents and plan of composition. Throughout we are made aware of action on two planes, the human and the divine. In the beginning we see Jupiter dandling Ganymede, and Mercury and Venus also appear in the first scene. At the end of Act 1 Venus speaks to her son Aeneas, and their encounter and their relationship exemplify a recurrent interweaving of the two levels of being. Venus and Juno and Mercury all intervene in the human action. Cupid masquerades as Ascanius during a substantial portion of the play. Moreover, there are parallel relationships on the two levels: the divine boys Ganymede and Cupid are set against the human boy Ascanius; Venus and Dido are both mothers, Venus in actuality to Cupid and to Aeneas, Dido in fancy to Ascanius and to Cupid in Ascanius's shape; the rivals Venus and Juno (rivals for the apple and for Jupiter's love) are matched by the rivals Dido and Anna (for Iarbus's love). Because the mortals are ever at the gods' bidding, their stature cannot be great: it is Cupid in his disguise who causes Dido to love Aeneas; it is Mercury who gives to Aeneas the command to leave Carthage: in neither case is there the possibility of resistance or even much reluctance, for Aeneas, browbeaten as he is by Dido's reproaches, has only a fitful wish to stay with her. But not only are the mortals puny: the gods, interrelated with the mortals and echoing

their patterns of conduct, are trivial too. The opening of the play, showing Jupiter's infatuation with Ganymede, at once establishes the play's
attitude.

Virgil was Marlowe's primary source, and in places he followed the
Aeneid with, in Tucker Brooke's words, "schoolboy slavishness" (*Works,*
p. 390). Yet there are extraordinary differences between the ways in
which the two poets present the hero. The founder of the Roman fortunes is, in Marlowe's hands, not very much of a hero. In the tale to Dido
of Troy's destruction, he recounts how he failed to rescue three women
in his escape from Troy:

> O there I lost my wife: and had not we
> Fought manfully, I had not told this tale:
> Yet manhood would not serue, of force we fled,
> And as we went vnto our ships, thou knowest
> We sawe *Cassandra* sprauling in the streetes,
> Whom *Aiax* rauisht in *Dianas* Fane,
> Her cheekes swolne with sighes, her haire all rent,
> Whom I tooke vp to beare vnto our ships:
> But suddenly the Grecians followed vs,
> And I alas, was forst to let her lye.
> Then got we to our ships, and being abourd,
> *Polixena* cryed out, *Æneas* stay,
> The Greekes pursue me, stay and take me in.
> Moued with her voyce, I lept into the sea,
> Thinking to beare her on my backe abourd:
> For all our ships were launcht into the deepe,
> And as I swomme, she standing on the shoare,
> Was by the cruell Mirmidons surprizd,
> And after by that *Pirrhus* sacrifizde.
>
> (565-83)

It is Iarbus who asks, "How got *Æneas* to the fleete againe?" (586), and
Achates who replies, "As for *Æneas* he swomme quickly backe" (591).
The dramatic convenience of this is evident, for it establishes the hero as
a man ready to part company with a woman when necessity arises. But it
is important to note that here Marlowe has written independently of his
source. In the *Aeneid,* when Creusa is missing, Aeneas goes back for her
and searches in the heart of the burning city, abandoning the quest only
when so commanded by her ghost; Cassandra is referred to merely as
glimpsed during the fighting; and Polyxena does not appear in this
context.

In his relations with Dido, Aeneas is no more impressive than in his own account of his conduct in Troy. In 3.2, in the cave, he is a little absurd in his slowness to catch Dido's drift. When he accepts her love, he vows most solemnly to be faithful:

> With this my hand I giue to you my heart,
> And vow by all the Gods of Hospitalitie,
> By heauen and earth, and my faire brothers bowe,
> By *Paphos, Capys,* and the purple Sea,
> From whence my radiant mother did descend,
> And by this Sword that saued me from the Greekes,
> Neuer to leaue these newe vpreared walles,
> Whiles *Dido* liues and rules in *Iunos* towne,
> Neuer to like or loue any but her.
>
> (1038-46)

Yet just over a hundred lines later he is saying, "*Carthage,* my friendly host, adue" (1151), because Mercury has appeared to him in a dream. He considers whether or not to engage in a farewell encounter with Dido, but decides it will be safer to forgo it. When Anna insists on his seeing the queen, he lies:

> *Dido.* Is this thy loue to me?
> *Æneas.* O princely *Dido,* giue me leaue to speake,
> I went to take my farewell of *Achates.*
>
> (1222-4)

He is quickly made ridiculous when Dido replies that Achates may certainly go at once, and he has to invent the excuse that the weather is just now unfavorable, a subterfuge that Dido easily exposes. Then, to demonstrate his fidelity, he asks:

> Hath not the Carthage Queene mine onely sonne?
> Thinkes *Dido* I will goe and leaue him here?
>
> (1235-6)

Both Aeneas and Dido believe that Ascanius is with Dido (though actually it is Cupid in Ascanius's shape): unless there is an oversight here, Marlowe is implying that up to this point Aeneas has forgotten, or has been prepared to abandon, his son in his attempt to steal away.

Although Aeneas especially suffers from Marlowe's handling, Dido is not treated altogether gently. She has not much reticence or dignity as love comes on her, and she is as lavish with gifts as an insecure lover can be. When Aeneas asks if her citizens will not repine at her making him "their soueraigne Lord," she replies:

> Those that dislike what *Dido* giues in charge
> Commaund my guard to slay for their offence:
> Shall vulgar pesants storme at what I doe?
> The ground is mine that giues them sustenance,
> The ayre wherein they breathe, the water, fire,
> All that they haue, their lands, their goods, their liues,
> And I the Goddesse of all these, commaund
> *Æneas* ride as Carthaginian King.
>
> (1277-84)

The arrogance is a dim echo of Tamburlaine's, and the implicit criticism is stronger because this "Goddesse of all these" has already shown herself a mere woman indeed. Later she is ready to give up her throne if she may live privately with Aeneas, saying to Anna:

> Now bring him backe, and thou shalt be a Queene,
> And I will liue a priuate life with him.
>
> (1605-6)

So the King in *Edward II* was prepared to abandon England to his nobles if Gaveston could be his:

> Make seuerall kingdomes of this monarchie,
> And share it equally amongst you all,
> So I may haue some nooke or corner left,
> To frolike with my deerest *Gaueston*.
>
> (365-8)

Marlowe allows his Dido a stately ending, with Latin words to utter as she enters the fire. But there is a subdued casualness in the way the story is brought to its terminal point, the rapidly consecutive suicides of Dido and Iarbus and Anna—Dido for love of Aeneas, Iarbus for love of Dido, Anna for love of Iarbus—hinting at the comic.

In everything that has been noticed so far, the humor has shown itself indirectly, invoking the discreet smile, the detached shrug. There is direct comedy, however, in 4.5, where a Nurse has charge of Cupid in Ascanius's shape. She is taking him into the country, so that Dido may hold him as a pledge of Aeneas's fidelity. It is ironic that the pledge is Love himself, and that Love's mother has little heed for a mortal's love, being concerned only with her son Aeneas's fortunes. Moreover, the Nurse is infected by Cupid as Dido was: despite her eighty years, she begins to think of a husband. We have seen how the gods are made petty through their mirroring of human conduct, but now Dido's infection is mirrored in the Nurse's. For a moment there are three levels of action

—of the gods, of High People, and of Low People—and each is comically affected by the interrelation.

Marlowe may have been hurried in the composition of this play; he may have collaborated with Nashe, whose name appears with his on the title-page; in any event, it is not a fully achieved piece of writing. *The Massacre at Paris,* however, is much less than that in the 'bad' text that has survived. Here we have a play of only 1263 lines with a dramatic action covering a substantial stretch of time. The story of the massacre is over by line 540, and the whole sequence of events runs from Navarre's marriage to his accession as Henry IV. Superficially it is an anti-Guise play, but of all the characters only Ramus (for the brief moment of his appearance and murder) and Navarre are neutrally handled. Anjou, when he has become Henry III, gets favorable treatment in being presented as the ally of Navarre and the friend and admirer of Elizabeth, but his earlier conduct has been repellent. He is the murderer of Ramus. He exults in the Guise's death and in showing his dead body to the Guise's son:

> Ah this sweet sight is phisick to my soule,
> Goe fetch his sonne for to beholde his death.
>
> (1032-3)

Then he orders the deaths of Dumain and Cardinal Guise, and boasts to the Queen Mother of what he has done. This brutality is very different from the slaughter of the Damascus virgins or the many other barbarities of Tamburlaine. Anjou, like the Guise, can aspire, but his methods are those of common cunning and his musings on greatness are shoddy. Early in the play two Lords of Poland offer him their country's crown, and he accepts it on the understanding that it can be abandoned if the French crown becomes available. He is flattered by this Polish invitation, especially as it means he will have the Czar and the Turk as immediate foes:

> For Poland is as I haue been enformde,
> A martiall people, worthy such a King,
> As hath sufficient counsaile in himselfe,
> To lighten doubts and frustrate subtile foes:
> And such a King whom practise long hath taught,
> To please himselfe with mannage of the warres,
> The greatest warres within our Christian bounds,
> I meane our warres against the Muscouites:
> And on the other side against the Turke,
> Rich Princes both, and mighty Emperours.
>
> (459-68)

The reigning Czar was Ivan, and Süleyman the Magnificent had a few
years before been in command of the Turkish fortunes. Anjou in such
company is an unimpressive champion of Christendom, one incapable of
recognizing the grander manifestations of the aspiring mind.
The small brutalities of Anjou and the Guise have not the overt absurdity of Barabas's boast:

> As for my selfe, I walke abroad a nights
> And kill sicke people groaning under walls:
> Sometimes I goe about and poyson wells;
>   (939-41)

but the element of grim humor is evident enough. On occasion, however,
Marlowe's method is more direct, as it was with the introduction of the
Nurse in *Dido*. Fitting the more savage tone and pattern of event in *The
Massacre,* the humor is here of a more aggressive sort. After the death of
the Admiral, two unnamed figures debate in prose on how to effect the
disposal of his body: if they burn him, they think, the fire will be infected and then the air; if they throw him into the river, the water will
be tainted, then the fishes, then themselves; so hanging, they decide, is
best. Later the Soldier who has come, on the Guise's order, to shoot
Mugeroun, lover of the Guise's Duchess and minion of Anjou, has a
prose passage in which Mugeroun's relations with the Duchess are presented in a rapid sequence of gross images: the passage occurs in a slightly
extended form in Collier's version of the scene, allegedly dependent on
a manuscript leaf of the play. Moments such as these in *The Massacre*
and *Dido* show Marlowe underlining the comic element which is indeed
securely inherent in the writing as a whole. In *Tamburlaine* we can see
the sudden relaxations into comic prose, often in the midst of a blank
verse scene, as perhaps overemphatic pointers to the proper interpretation of the play. Although in all other respects *Dido* and *The Massacre*
are slighter and far less organized than *Tamburlaine,* the directly comic
moments are in them more shrewdly managed. Dido's Nurse, the Guise's
hangmen and hired assassin, are presented in isolation, and we are ready
to see the play's implications becoming explicit in their utterance. In
Tamburlaine the shifts from implicit to explicit are too sudden for us
to be at ease with them, except in the incident (in Part 2, 4.1) where
Calyphas loiters in his tent and provides a close analogue to the directly
humorous moments of these other plays.
    Hero and Leander has the quieter humor of *Dido,* but is far more ex-

pert in its control. As in the play, so here the worlds of gods and men are intertwined. Hero is *"Venus* Nun," Neptune would have Leander for his minion. There is an immediate irony in the notion that a priestess of the love-goddess should be vowed to chastity, and this is reinforced by the pictures of divine riot displayed on the crystal pavement of Venus's temple:

> There might you see the gods in sundrie shapes,
> Committing headdie ryots, incest, rapes:
> For know, that vnderneath this radiant floure
> Was *Danaes* statue in a brazen tower,
> *Ioue* slylie stealing from his sisters bed,
> To dallie with *Idalian Ganimed,*
> And for his loue *Europa* bellowing loud,
> And tumbling with the Rainbow in a cloud:
> Blood-quaffing *Mars* heauing the yron net,
> Which limping *Vulcan* and his *Cyclops* set.
>
> (1.143-52)

There is comic reticence in the withholding of Venus's name in the last couplet here, but indeed the comedy comes through in every line. Rarely have the gods been treated with such concentrated fun: "headdie" with the casual catalogue of line 144, "slylie stealing" and "sisters" in line 147, the swift change from "dallie" in line 148 to "bellowing" in line 149 and "tumbling" in line 150, the ludicrous "Blood-quaffing" for Mars and the richly associative "heauing" in line 151, together might almost justify a charge that Marlowe was overdoing the comedy, were it not that the poem (as Marlowe left it) is so consistent in tone that we are made at ease in a world of extravagance. The slyness with which the poet refrains from inserting Venus's name here is anticipated fifty lines earlier, when we are told:

> The men of wealthie *Sestos,* euerie yeare,
> (For his sake whom their goddesse held so deare,
> Rose-cheekt *Adonis*) kept a solemne feast.
>
> (1.91-3)

The formality of "held so deare" and "solemne feast" is mocked by "Rose-cheekt," and the poem's intertwining of gods and mortals at once appears in that the first encounter of Hero and Leander takes place at a time when the memory of Adonis is being honored. In the long passage at the end of the first sestiad, where it is explained why Cupid could not win the favor of the Destinies for Hero and Leander, this intertwining is presented more elaborately. The enmity of the Fates, we are told, arose from the love of Mercury for "a countrie mayd": she resisted his vigorous wooing until, thirsting after immortality ("All women are ambitious naturallie"), she demanded a cup of nectar as the price of her favors. Mercury stole the nectar from Hebe ("*Hebe Ioues* cup fill'd") and gave it to the girl. Jove came to know of the theft ("as what is hid from *Ioue?*") and "waxt more furious Than for the fire filcht by *Prometheus.*" So Mercury was banished from heaven, and Cupid, in pity for him, persuaded "the Adamantine Destinies" to dote on Mercury. From them, to effect his revenge, Mercury secured the restoration of Saturn and the banishing of Jove to hell. So for a time the golden age returned:

> Murder, rape, warre, lust and trecherie,
> Were with *Ioue* clos'd in *Stigian* Emprie.
> (1.457-8)

But Mercury soon neglected the love of the Destinies, and they in revenge restored Jove to power. Mercury's punishment was

> That he and *Pouertie* should alwaies kis.
> And to this day is euerie scholler poore,
> Grosse gold from them runs headlong to the boore.
> Likewise the angrie sisters thus deluded,
> To venge themselues on *Hermes,* haue concluded
> That *Midas* brood shall sit in Honors chaire,
> To which the *Muses* sonnes are only heire:
> And fruitfull wits that in aspiring are,
> Shall discontent run into regions farre;
> And few great lords in vertuous deeds shall ioy,
> But be surpris'd with euerie garish toy;
> And still inrich the loftie seruile clowne,
> Who with incroching guile keepes learning downe.
> Then muse not *Cupids* sute no better sped,
> Seeing in their loues the Fates were iniured.
> (1.470-84)

This ending, appropriate enough for a University Wit, might seem oversententious without the familiar tone of the final couplet and its cunning juxtaposition of "loues" and "Fates." The unexpected extension of the satire to the condition of human society brings the parallel between gods and men before us in a new way. Previously the small loves and angers of the gods had been exposed: even Prometheus does not escape when the word "filcht" is used of his gift of fire to men, and the mock-reverence of "as what is hid from *Joue?*" follows quickly on the casual mention of the filling of Jove's cup.

In this ending of the first sestiad, it is "a countrie mayd" whose resistance to Mercury causes revolution and counter-revolution on Olympus, disorders human society, and sets the Fates against all lovers, including Hero and Leander. Moreover, the account of Mercury's rough wooing and the girl's resistance is an anticipation of Leander's approaches to Hero in the second sestiad. Fleetingly we may be reminded of the association of Dido and the Nurse in their common subjection to Cupid. In this poem, however, the lovers are handled with a frank delight. Sensual and comely, with a tripping or a swimming or a panting motion, they move delicately through the verse. They are taken no more seriously than Dido and Aeneas, but their existence gives us far more pleasure. At their first meeting love is immediate, Leander feeling "Loues arrow" and Hero's gentle heart being struck by the fire that blazed from Leander's countenance. It is a speed the poet approves: "Who euer lov'd, that lov'd not at first sight?" But if love is immediate, mutual comprehension is not. Leander kneels, but Hero does not guess that she is the object of his devotion:

> He kneel'd, but vnto her deuoutly praid;
> Chast *Hero* to her selfe thus softly said:
> Were I the saint hee worships, I would heare him,
> And as shee spake those words, came somewhat nere him.
> (1.177-80)

One of Marlowe's recurrent devices in this poem is the use of dissyllabic rhyme, which he manages in such a way as to achieve a familiar tone and a sense of human hesitation. Here the effect is reinforced by the pause after "words" and the modest suggestiveness of "somewhat." In the ensuing eighteen lines there are three more examples of dissyllabic rhyme, and the last of them, at the end of the verse-paragraph, has a broad, oddly Byronic effect:

> At last, like to a bold sharpe Sophister,
> With chearefull hope thus he accosted her.
> (1.197-8)

Here "bold sharpe" unexpectedly presents Leander in a fresh light, as he waxes in a young man's sudden confidence, 'Sophister' being a Cambridge term for a second- or third-year undergraduate. This broadness can be found at times in the poem's descriptive imagery, as in:

> Who builds a pallace and rams vp the gate,
> Shall see it ruinous and desolate.
> Ah simple *Hero,* learne thy selfe to cherish,
> Lone women like to emptie houses perish. . . .
> (1.239-42)

—an image echoed perhaps at the beginning of the second sestiad:

> And therefore to her tower he got by stealth.
> Wide open stood the doore, hee need not clime.
> (2.18-19)

The comedy does indeed grow more vigorous as the love affair develops. The near-approach to consummation at the second meeting, Leander's second crossing of the strait and Neptune's wooing of him, the shivering of the cold and wet Leander as he begs for the warmth of Hero's bed, the ensuing contest that fully engages the poet's wit, the coming of daylight to the lovers—all these things help to achieve a comedy that is never out of control, never ill-tempered, never mean or ungenerous. There is, indeed, an almost moving touch—almost, because we must never feel that our sympathies are completely engaged—in the account of Hero's embarrassment in the morning. And Marlowe, fittingly enough, does not resist a comparison between Leander and Dis:

> Whence his admiring eyes more pleasure tooke
> Than *Dis,* on heapes of gold fixing his looke.
> (2.325-6)

The poet has some affection for his small human figures, but rather less for the gods.

"*Desunt nonnulla*" we read at the end of Marlowe's share in the poem, and perhaps the task of finishing defeated him. A scourge of God could be shown at the moment of death, but the story of Leander's drowning might have been difficult to treat in the manner of the poem. Dido could enter the fire, but she is not alive as the lovers in the poem are, and she has not been treated with the same affection as they. The thing could have been done, but perhaps the tone of voice would have been awkwardly changed. Indeed the last lines of the second sestiad have a harshness that is new and not easy to accommodate to what we have previously known:

> By this *Apollos* golden harpe began
> To sound foorth musicke to the *Ocean,*
> Which watchfull *Hesperus* no sooner heard,

> But he the day bright-bearing Car prepar'd,
> And ran before, as Harbenger of light,
> And with his flaring beames mockt ougly night,
> Till she o'recome with anguish, shame, and rage,
> Dang'd downe to hell her loathsome carriage.
> (2.327-34)

The inert catalogue of the penultimate line, with the heavy alliteration that follows, seems to lack the full assurance of the rest of the poem, and perhaps Marlowe felt it.

The humor in *The Jew of Malta* and in *Faustus* presents, of course, larger problems than are touched on here. The object of the present exercise has been to urge fuller recognition of the variety of Marlowe's humor, and its high degree of integration with the fabric of his writing. Above all, I have tried to present *Hero and Leander* as a major comic poem.

MARLOWE'S *DOCTOR FAUSTUS* AND THE ELDRITCH TRADITION

by MURIEL C. BRADBROOK

DOCTOR FAUSTUS, most concentrated of Elizabethan tragedies before *Macbeth,* also ranges widely and is composed from the union of several older traditions. Hardin Craig has called it a perfectly generalized morality *(English Religious Drama of the Middle Ages,* 1955, p. 386). The bond by which Faustus gives himself to Lucifer is valid because it is made in the presence and against the miraculous intervention of God, the Judge in whose court the agreement is registered. *Doctor Faustus* is a tragedy of responsibility and choice, though not till the final scene does the full realization of his action come to the doomed magician when, like Everyman, but with such a different anticipation, he is called to his reckoning. Set against these tragic issues, much of the conjuring which fills the middle of the play may seem now irrelevant and tasteless. Perhaps it would become more explicable, if not more acceptable, were it seen as a development of what I shall call the eldritch tradition. Eldritch diabolism, while both comic and horrific, is amoral and does not involve personal choice or the notion of personal responsibility. The cackle of ghoulish laughter is essential to winter's tales of sprites and goblins, phantoms and illusions. Country mumming was and still is designed in the comic-horrific mood, whether this is displayed in the blackened faces of Plough Monday men, or the huge wicker monster of the Padstow Hobby; but in the early sixteenth century William Dunbar, a court poet, could exploit the same area of feeling. Of Dunbar, C. S. Lewis has written:

In him more than in any other, the comic overlaps with the demoniac and the terrifying. He also is of the 'eldritch' school; the wild whoop of his noisiest laughter has, and is meant to have, something sinister in it. . . . in "The Dance of the Seven Deadly Sins" . . . these "sweir bumbard belly huddrouns" and these highlanders whose clatter deaves the devil himself are intended to make us laugh. But notice, on the other hand, that we are laughing at torture. The grotesque figures skip through fire, jag each other with knives, and are constantly spewing out molten gold with which they are constantly refilled "up to the thrott." (*English Literature in the Sixteenth Century*, 1954, pp. 94-5)

Compared with an earlier grave treatment of the Seven Deadly Sins, such as that in "A Disputation between a Good Man and the Devil" (*Minor Poems of the Vernon MS*, EETS, 1892, pp. 329-54), the eldritch quality which Dunbar shares with *Doctor Faustus* involves the reader or spectator much more intimately, and is therefore by nature more dramatic in its appeal.

In his "Visitation of St. Francis" ("How Dumbar wes desyrd to be ane Freir"), the Scottish poet provided another illustration to *Doctor Faustus*. Seeing Mephistophilis for the first time in his own form, Faustus commands him to

> Go, and return an old Franciscan Friar,
> That holy shape becomes a devil best.
>   (1.3.25-6)[1]

In Dunbar's poem, the poet, being visited in a dream by St. Francis and offered a friar's habit, declares that sanctity is more often found among bishops; that he has already worn the friar's habit and did not find it led to holiness.

> Als lang as I did beir the freiris style,
> In me, God wait, wes mony wrink and wyle;
> In me wes falset with every wight to flatter,
> Quilk micht be flemit with na haly watter:
> I wes ay reddy all men to begyle.

> This freir that did Sanct Francis thair appeir,
> Ane fiend he wes in likenes of ane freir:
> He vaneist away with stynk and fyrie smowk:
> With him me thocht all the hous end he towk,
> And I awoik as wy that wes in weir.

---

[1] I have used the parallel-text edition of *Doctor Faustus* by W. W. Greg (1950); quotations are from his accompanying *Tragical History of the Life and Death of Doctor Faustus: A Conjectural Reconstruction* (1950).

Dunbar expressed the eldritch in savage energetic movement; and in *Doctor Faustus* the clowns' patter supplies a verbal equivalent to the galvanic frenzy of the Seven Deadly Sins of Dunbar. They "bounce at the gate" and rush into the Duke's presence with merely comic bustle, but in the scene between Wagner and the Clown, images of hell-fire and the torn flesh of the victims are evoked by the backchat:

> *Wagner*. . . . The villain's out of service, and so hungry that I know he would give his soul to the devil, for a shoulder of mutton, though it were blood-raw.
> *Clown*. Not so, neither; I had need to have it well roasted, and good sauce to it, if I pay so dear, I can tell you. (1.4.8-12)

Faustus's own tricks vary from those of the common conjurer to those of the eldritch 'shape-changer'; his transformations, though devoid of the moral significance which burns in the scenes of choice, combine the comic and the horrific, being designed to raise at once a shudder and a guffaw.

Benvolio and the knights who cut off Faustus's head, only to find that, "Zounds, the devil's alive again," are deceived by an old trick, popular at Christmas feasts. Perhaps this very trick is behind the most eldritch of all monsters, the Green Knight of the fourteenth-century romance, who after a beheading picks up his head and rides away. For at the end of the poem the Green Knight confesses he was sent to Arthur's hall by the enchantress Morgan le Fay to terrify Guinevere. This final revelation that his magic shape was due to conjuring at once reduces its fearsomeness, placing it on a different supernatural footing. The beginning of the poem is altered by this disclosure at the end.[2] When such figures appeared at real medieval feasts, they would be as gigantic as the Green Knight, because the player's whole body would be encased in a false trunk, its shoulders appearing at the level of his eyebrows, with the false head fixed on top.

Conversely, the early jests about false heads and false legs which Faustus sheds so lightly gain a terrible retrospective irony when in the last scene the Scholars find his mangled remains—and it may be that the stage properties were identical.

> *Second Scholar*. O help us heaven! see here are Faustus' limbs
> All torn asunder by the hand of death.
> *Third Scholar*. The devils whom Faustus served have torn him thus.
> (5.3.7-9)

[2] I would see the end of *Sir Gawain and the Green Knight* as a comical transformation, dissolving some of the horror of the beginning; it becomes more of a traditional Christmas game, or at least that possibility is raised. For the traditional views, see Albert B. Friedman, "Morgan le Fay in *Sir Gawain and the Green Knight*," *Speculum*, 35 (1960), 260-74.

A voluntary act of this sort was reputed to have saved a Pope who had sold himself to the Devil but who, unlike Faustus, contrived to evade the bargain:

> Silvinus, þe pope, dede homage to þe devyl to come to hyȝ astate. ffirst he was a munke, whan he spak wyth þe feend, & dede hym homage. Þanne, þe feend dede helpe hym up, to be an erchebyssechop, & afterwards to be pope. Þanne he askyd þe feend, how longe he schulde lyve? Þe feend seyde, tyl he dyde synge a messe in ierusalem. (*Jacob's Well*, Chapter 4, EETS, 1900, pp. 31-2)

Singing mass one day, Silvinus heard a great din of fiends and found that the name of the church was Jerusalem. But after shriving himself, he hacked off the limbs with which he had worshipped the Devil and had his body laid in a cart drawn by wild beasts, to be buried wherever they should take him. They bore the corpse to the church of St. John Lateran, where he was buried.

> And in signe þat he hath mercy of god for his penaunce, ȝit, fro þat tyme hyderward aȝen þe tyme þat ony pope schal dye, his bonys in þe grave make dyn, and swetyn out oyle in signe of mercy.

For those who faithfully believed in hell-fire and the physical torture of the damned, this story would carry an eldritch mirth it no longer possesses. The Devil had cheated with the same pun that was later to cozen King Henry IV, but he had been cheated in his turn.

Other medieval poems bring horrific jesting very close to pure terror. Such is *The Aunters of Arthur,* with its yelling ghost rising from the Cumberland tarn, or the Auchinleck version of *St. Patrick's Purgatory,* where the devils jest with unnerving irony, extending their menace in playful threats; similar grotesquerie is found in St. Brendan's voyage. Gargoyles and the grotesques carved on capitals and misericords exemplify the same tradition. Grand, dignified, and melancholy devils belong to the sixteenth century rather than to earlier times; Mephistophilis is of this new order. Perhaps the conception of a deliberate rejection of God could be seriously entertained within a religious context only when a degree of general scepticism was well established.

In Marlowe's day, eldritch mirth is most frequently found combined with antipapal stories, with scurrilities and fabliaux in the popular jest-books of the common press. These play boisterously with notions of hell-fire, combining obscene tales with parody of holy water, sacred relics, and other rejected objects of veneration from the old faith. As though some lingering fear of summary vengeance forbade such mockery except under the protecting form of jests, there is a defensive refusal to risk a straight penalty by straight challenge.

One of these works, *Beware the Cat* (1570), attributed to no less a personage than William Baldwin, author of *The Mirror for Magistrates,* tells how witches in Ireland send to market fine red swine who, when led to the water, turn, like Faustus's horse, into wisps of hay. This book is full of magic shape-changes effected by the witches' familiars, the cats.

Tarlton's Newes out of Purgatorie (1590), presented by Robin Good-fellow, comes a degree nearer to the stage; it shows the famous clown—a baiter of papists and of precisians in his time—returning to witness for the existence of Purgatory, "pale and wan." The writer attempts to conjure him: "Depart from me, Satan, the resemblance of whomsoever thou dost carry."

> At this, pitching his staff down on the end, and crossing one leg over the other, he answered thus: Why, you whorson dunce, think you to set Dick Tarlton *non plus* with your aphorisms? . . . Oh, there is a Calvinist; what, do you make Heaven and Hell *contraria immediata*? . . . yes, yes, my good brother, there is *quoddam tertium*. (ed. J. O. Halliwell, 1844, pp. 55-6)

He urges that men of old would never have paid so much for dirges and trentals for no gain; and writes further:

> if any upstart Protestant deny, if thou hast no place of scripture ready to confirm it, say as Pythagoras' scholars did, *ipse dixit,* and to all bon companions it shall stand for a principle. (*ibid.,* p. 57)

In *Tarlton's Newes* this championing of a papal doctrine is combined with extreme scurrility, as in the tale of Friar Onion, who pretended to be the Angel Gabriel in order to have his will of a woman. (The story is from Boccaccio, *Il Decamerone,* 4.2, though the name of Friar Onion is from 6.10.) The reckless jesting which was associated with Marlowe had its counterpart in the recklessness of Tarlton and other early clowns, and so contributed to the force of the comic scenes in *Doctor Faustus;* Wagner's assumption of the voice of a precisian is very like that of Tarlton in the jestbook.

Another work of similar kind, though like *Beware the Cat* directed especially aginst the Irish, was Barnaby Rich's *Greene's Newes from Heaven and Hell* (1593).[3] The ghost of Robert Greene, excluded from

---

[3] Pamphlets about wandering spirits, whether by Robin Goodfellow or depicting him, carry on the same tradition as Dunbar's *Ballad of Kind Kittok,* where the goodwife rides to Heaven on a snail in company with a newt, slips in when Peter is not looking, and slips out again for "the aill of hevin wes sour."

Heaven for writing about coneycatchers and from Hell for disclosing their tricks, comes to recite his adventures and ends up as "the maddest goblin that ever walked in the moonshine." There is a tragic undertone to this ribald work, for Rich was vainly seeking redress against a powerful enemy, Adam Loftus Archbishop of Dublin, and his complaints are slipped in between churl's tales of a henpecked bricklayer who goes to Hell to avoid his wife, and of the ghost of a miller whose lecherous plans had recoiled upon himself and made him agent to his own cuckolding; he was now transformed into

> a most deformed creature, with a monstrous pair of horns, growing from the upper part of his forehead, the tips whereof turned round into his eyes, and growing there again into his head, had made him stark blind, that he had no manner of sight. (ed. R. B. McKerrow, 1911, p. 44)

This eldritch monster, as terrifying as the fiend which Edgar describes at Dover Cliff in *King Lear,* is not perhaps more horrible than some of the cardboard monsters used on the stage for shows of detraction and scorn. These were often of a 'religious' intention. One such was given at Court on Twelfth Night in the first year of Elizabeth's reign, where cardinals, abbots, and bishops were presented in monstrous animal forms; later, according to Lyly, Martin Marprelate was brought on the public stage with "a cock's comb, an ape's face, a wolf's belly, cat's claws &c" (*Pappe with an Hatchet,* 1589; see E. K. Chambers, *The Elizabethan Stage,* 1923, 4.232).

So Mephistophilis transforms the Clowns into an ape and a dog, and this scene (3.3) follows immediately upon the scene of Pope-baiting. The grotesque hobgoblin pranks played by Faustus upon the Horse-courser and the Ostler are of the kind recounted in jestbooks, where they are connected with antipapal stories, and it seems very likely that, in the popular theaters, the Clowns' afterpieces were largely composed of such matter.[4] By bringing these jests and the Devil's fireworks within the compass of the play, something was achieved for Marlowe's contemporaries, if not for audiences of a later day; this was possible because the strength of the comic-horrific mood gave to these jests a macabre quality they no longer possess. There was something dangerous in the Clown's role; he was apt to be treated with sudden unexpected violence as when in *Titus Andronicus* he is condemned to death and goes off with a wry jest: "I have brought up my neck to a fair end."

[4] As late as 1681, such monstrous animals were used in antipapal processions, carried out on the anniversary of Queen Elizabeth's accession, 17 November, and culminating in the burning of the Pope opposite the statue of Queen Elizabeth at Temple Bar; see Sheila Williams, *Journal of the Courtauld and Warburg Institutes,* 21 (1958), 104-18.

By repute Marlowe died unrepentant and shared the fate of his own hero, as all the orthodox were convinced; but Robert Greene, another jester with holy things, lived to write his repentance in the very accents of *Doctor Faustus*. He began his reckless career with:

> Hell (quoth I) what talk you of hell to me? I know, if I once come there I shall have the company of better men than myself, I shall also meet with some mad knaves there, and so long as I shall not sit alone, my care is the less. (*Repentance of Robert Greene*, 1592; Bodley Head Quarto, 1923, p. 11. Cf. *Doctor Faustus*, 1.3.58-60, 2.1.125-33)

And he ended with:

> Oh, I feel a hell already in my conscience, the number of my sins do muster before my eyes, the poor men's plaints that I have wronged cries out in mine ears and saith, Robin Greene, thou art damned; nay, the justice of heaven tells me I cannot be saved. . . . I am taught by the scriptures to pray; but to whom shall I pray? To him that I have blasphemed? . . . Oh that my last gasp were come, that I might be with Judas and Cain, for their place is better than mine. . . . (*ibid.*, p. 14)

Greene's Vision gives an even clearer echo of Faustus's opening speech at its own opening:

> I know Stipendium peccati mors, O then shall I fly from thy presence? (*Works*, ed. A. B. Grosart, 1881-3, 12.205)

These works may have been contributed to the Greene legend by other writers; he remained a popular figure, often coupled with Tarlton (who was given also some edifying ballads of repentance). Greene was alternately presented as a mad merry rogue, chronicler of coneycatchers, or as a tragic repentant blasphemer—the two sides of Greene's legend match the two sides of Faustus's story.

In the tragedy, however, implicit reconciliation of these two opposite states is attempted through different levels for the conjuring, which leads continuously from horseplay up to tragedy. This is not an argument for unity of composition, for it seems clear that Marlowe had a collaborator and also that the text was modified in transmission. It is a plea for unity of conception. The naive attitude which produced the jestbooks was incorporated in *Doctor Faustus* because the boldness of his intellectual challenge demanded this protective or compensatory relief. In real life, any situation of unusual danger will often call out the impulse to ridicule or laughter. The "savage comic humour" which T. S. Eliot felt in Marlowe has a historic basis in the eldritch tradition, here and in parts of *The Jew of Malta*. Today these are relatively inaccessible; they can be recovered best, perhaps, from the fooling in the tragedies of Shakespeare, especially of course in *King Lear*; but Shakespeare is so much subtler than Marlowe that the comparison does not greatly help. It is rather by comparison with literature of an earlier time, such as the works of Dunbar, that it may be possible to estimate the weight of the eldritch tradition in *Doctor Faustus*.

It is the comprehensiveness of the play that prevents it from being fitted into any of the earlier 'kinds.' What remains in it of the morality has been generalized, not only by the daring of Faustus's challenge and the pity and fear of his last hour, but also by the balance supplied in the figures of Mephistophilis, the Scholars, the Old Man, and even the Clowns.

Faustus's daring is embedded in familiar protective jest; the ingredients of this play were popular, however the transformation of the whole made them into something new.

Not only the scope, but ultimately, as I believe, the dignity of the play is increased by combining the intellectual aspiration and heroic dreams of the great scholar with the comic ghoulishness of the folk; by combining the fine and sensitive mind lured to self-destruction with the gross simplicity that has not yet reached the level of making a moral choice, whose terror is fitly represented by roaring property dragons and devils with fireworks. Faustus himself appeared in full canonicals; and perhaps, in view of the many tales about the visible appearance of the devil in this play (see Chambers, *The Elizabethan Stage*, 3.423-4), the cross was felt a necessary protection for the chief actor.

> The gull gets on a surplis
>   With a crosse upon his breast,
> Like Allen playing Faustus,
>   In that manner he was drest.
>   (S. Rowland, *Knave of Clubs*, 1609, p. 29)

MARLOWE'S 'TRAGICKE GLASSE'

by IRVING RIBNER

CHRISTOPHER MARLOWE'S career as a dramatist was very brief, but it was also very varied, and even on the basis of the seven plays we can attribute to him with certainty it is possible to trace a development not only in dramatic technique but also in philosophical scope. It is with the second of these that I wish to deal, for Marlowe's great achievement lay in the development of English tragedy, and tragedy depends upon ethical and metaphysical assumptions which the dramatist must invite his audience to share with him. Marlowe, perhaps more surely than any of his contemporaries, mirrored in his plays his own changing vision of man's place in the universe; thus at some point in his intellectual progression tragedy became possible. Certainly it could never have sprung from the view of the world reflected in his earliest plays. *Dido Queen of Carthage* falls far short of tragedy in spite of the death of its heroine, and if we are to view *Tamburlaine* in a "tragicke glasse," as the prologue invites us to do, this glass reveals only pathos in the deaths of those lesser figures who must be destroyed to prepare the path of the conquering superman with whom Marlowe is primarily concerned. Marlowe came slowly to tragedy; only when he came to recognize the frailty and limitation of humanity did this mode of drama become possible for him.

It would be far easier to trace Marlowe's changing perspective and the corresponding growth of his tragic vision were it not for the vexing problems of text and chronology which plague every student of his plays. It is difficult to assess the achievement of *The Jew of Malta* since we have only the corrupt quarto of 1633, with its obvious signs of Heywood's distortion in the final acts of Marlowe's original conception. *The Massacre at Paris*

91

remains a perpetual puzzle, for the unmistakable hand of Marlowe which is evident throughout this botched and wretched text gives intimations of a grander vision of human failure than what has survived the process of corruption. That we have no real evidence of when this play was written only adds to our confusion.

It is possible, however, to find two polar positions in Marlowe's view of the world. There is at one end an emphasis upon the limitless potentialities of mankind which we find in *Dido* and the first part of *Tamburlaine,* and not so much diminished in the second part as some writers have supposed. At the other end of the spectrum there is that sense of human limitation and defeat, what Una Ellis-Fermor called the "mood of spiritual despair," which we find in *Edward II* and *Doctor Faustus (The Jacobean Drama,* 1936, pp. 1-5). That these were Marlowe's final plays seems very likely; most commentators today would place *Doctor Faustus* as the later of the two, and if we may make any guesses about *The Massacre at Paris,* we must suppose that it belongs with these final works, perhaps, as I shall suggest, between *The Jew of Malta* and *Edward II.* The second part of *Tamburlaine* shows the first faint signs of change from the confident optimism of the first part, and it seems to have been followed by *The Jew of Malta,* a play which stands midway between the two extremes of Marlowe's vision. If we could know it fully, it might emerge as the play in which the values of *Tamburlaine* are first held up to scrutiny and found wanting. Certainly the Machiavellian view of the world so proudly asserted in *Tamburlaine,* is in *The Jew of Malta* subjected to some ridicule.[1]

If the first part of *Tamburlaine* was sketched while Marlowe was still at Cambridge, as most commentators believe, Marlowe's turning to the drama must have coincided with a turning away from the theological studies to which his Parker Foundation scholarship committed him, for *Tamburlaine* stands in opposition to every religious principle which Anglicans like Matthew Parker revered. Marlowe's turning away from theology must bear some relation to an absorption with classical poetry which he seems to have developed at Cambridge, since we must also date from his student days his translations of Ovid's *Amores* and Lucan's *Pharsalia,* indicating a concern for the two themes to which he was constantly to return throughout his career, love and war. The first stage of Marlowe's development seems to have been one of change from Christian contemplation of the divine to a pagan concern with the sensual aspects of man and his political involvement in great affairs. It is easy to see

---

[1] See my "Marlowe and Machiavelli," *Comparative Literature,* 6 (1954), 348-56.

Dido and *Tamburlaine* as the product of these two concerns; in *Dido* especially we see their relation to one another. Although *Dido* was not printed until 1594, critics have long discerned that this text represents a later recension of the play, for the blank verse seems to illustrate two separate stages of artistic maturity. If the name of Thomas Nashe, which appears on the title-page along with Marlowe's, means anything, it may be that the work in its earliest form was the product of their initial association as fellow students at Cambridge. Indeed, in the play as we have it there is little which we have any reason to attribute to Nashe, though it is possible that in some earlier version he may have had a larger share. We shall never know the answer, but we do know that the play bears every sign of Marlowe's hand and that it needs to be considered with *Tamburlaine* as springing from the same period of classical study and reflecting the same stage in Marlowe's development.

When Marlowe wrote the first part of *Tamburlaine* in 1586 or 1587, he did something which never before had been done in English drama. He took a historical figure—praised in a long series of humanistic historical accounts as a successful ruler and as one who had stemmed the Turkish advance over Christian Europe at Ankara in 1402, an instrument of Divine Providence whose cruelty was the visitation of punishment upon evildoers—and he framed a play which would exalt such a figure by revealing his steady movement towards the conquest of the world. His play became an episodic sequence of scenes each of which was designed to make more clear the greatness of his hero. Marlowe, in fact, applied the episodic technique of the miracle drama to a secular figure, and he used him as the symbol of a way of life which denied every Christian premise dear to the Elizabethan establishment. The first part of *Tamburlaine* makes no pretense at being anything other than a heroic celebration of the ruthless conquering hero's triumph, "the man of humble birth," as F. P. Wilson has written, "who rises from victory to victory to the noon or meridian of his fortunes, where the dramatist leaves him a happy warrior and a happy lover" (*Marlowe and the Early Shakespeare*, 1953, p. 19). This conception is Marlowe's initial view of Tamburlaine, and if in the second part some elements intrude to diminish the hero's brightness, we must remember that the sequel is a later addition which represents a further stage in Marlowe's growth, and that the first part was conceived entirely independently of it.

Marlowe approached his historical subject not with the Christian view of history as the working out of God's purposes on earth, but rather with the premises of the classical historians he had read at Cambridge. He seems to have been influenced in particular by Polybius, who in his history of Rome had exalted individual prowess, seeing historical event as the product of human ability and will in a world ruled only by a blind fortune. The greatness of the true hero of history lay in his ability to assert his individual will in opposition to fortune and to master it for as long as possible. Finally he must be cut off by death, and this being so, he must accept his end with stoical resignation and fortitude. Of this human ability to master fortune the first part of *Tamburlaine* provides a supreme example, while the second part depicts the inevitable triumph of death in spite of human prowess. In Marlowe's hero there is also the Machiavellian ideal of the lawgiver, the superman who by his own *virtù*, his power of mind and will, can arrest the processes of decay to which all civilizations are subject and create new nations. While doing so he stands outside of all morality.

In Tamburlaine we have also the static quality of the movers of Roman history. He is at the play's beginning a fully drawn man of destiny, and he passes from one static scene to the next as he goes about his conquest of the world, the dramatist never displaying change or development in his hero's character. His end of world conquest is implicit in his initial characterization—an end from which nothing can deter him, not even the tears of the Zenocrate he loves. He must destroy her native city because it is in his nature to do so. The Virgins of Damascus must be slaughtered because his unalterable principles of warfare decree it. The play is concerned not with development of character, but with its revelation. In this, as I have suggested, Marlowe was following the historical method of Polybius, whose subject was the conquest of the world by an initially complete but ever expanding Rome.[2]

The addition of a second part to *Tamburlaine* could not change the conception of the first; it certainly could not make of it, as Roy W. Battenhouse has suggested (*Marlowe's Tamburlaine*, 1941), the first movement of a ten-act morality play illustrating God's punishment visited upon a blasphemous infidel. The subject of the sequel play is the death of the hero, and in George Whetstone's *English Mirror*, which may well have been Marlowe's principal source,[3] Marlowe would have read that "this great personage, without disgrace of fortune, after sundry great victories, by the course of nature died." This view of Tamburlaine's death

---

[2] I have developed these points at greater length in "The Idea of History in Marlowe's *Tamburlaine*," *ELH*, 20 (1953), 251-66.

[3] See Thomas Izard, "The Principal Source of Marlowe's *Tamburlaine*," *MLN*, 58 (1943), 411-17.

is in accord with a general treatment of the subject by humanist historians, going back at least to Poggio Bracciolini who had told the story of Tamburlaine in his *De varietate fortunae,* written between 1431 and 1448, close to the events themselves of Tamburlaine's career. They had seen him as the superman who had mastered fortune for as long as it was possible for any man to do so, that is until death finally had triumphed. His death could not be viewed as a punishment for his life, but rather as the necessary culmination of his greatness, for he was cut off, as classical historians held that the great man should be, at the very peak of his glory. Marlowe's Tamburlaine until the moment of his death is a reflection of that same humanist ideal of the superman by the light of which Machiavelli shaped his *Life of Castruccio Castracani* (1520, printed 1532), and whom he envisaged as the savior and unifier of Italy.[4]

Marlowe's hero dies only because all who live must die. His conquests are undiminished; the one son incapable of following in his footsteps has been destroyed, and his two remaining sons are ready to complete their father's domination of the world. That historically they did not do so, but instead brought about the dissolution of their father's empire, is a consideration outside the scope of the play. Marlowe's final estimate is in the last words of the play, spoken by Amyras:

> Let earth and heauen his timelesse death deplore,
> For both their woorths wil equall him no more.
> (*Works,* ed. Tucker Brooke, 1910, 4645-6)

Since the death of Tamburlaine alone was not sufficient matter for a play, Marlowe had to fill in his historical scene with diverse matter from various sources, some of it entirely extraneous to his story. The treachery of the Christian King Sigismund of Hungary has been taken as Marlowe's indictment of the moral pretensions of Christianity, but it could just as easily be taken as a defense of true Christianity against the doctrine of equivocation being preached in some papal quarters. It is probably an instance of Marlowe's filling in his plot by the use of a moral exemplum which he could exploit for its dramatic possibilities, and it may have no more relation to the death of Tamburlaine, which is his basic theme, than does the story of the suicide of Olympia which he borrowed from Ariosto.

[4] These points have been developed by Eric Voegelin, "Machiavelli's Prince: Background and Formation," *Review of Politics,* 12 (1951), 142-68, where the humanist Tamburlaine legend is seen as one of the most important shaping elements in Machiavelli's conception. Marlowe, I believe, influenced by the same writings that had influenced Machiavelli, saw Tamburlaine in the same light in which Machiavelli viewed him.

These elements do, however, contribute to a change of tone in the second part of *Tamburlaine* which detracts from the theme of the triumphant conqueror which runs through Part 1. They convey a sense of futility and death which supports the sombre return to reality in the very fact that Tamburlaine must die. In the second part there is a reminder of human mortality and human loss, a note first sounded in the death of Zenocrate, the decay of beauty and strength. The basic conception of Tamburlaine's death is still that of the humanist historians, but there is also, in the futile preservation of Zenocrate's embalmed body, the burning of the Koran, and the mockery which answers Tamburlaine's ineffectual challenge of the gods, a sense of futility, frustration, and waste which in another context might be tragic.

It is an overstatement, however, to say (as Harry Levin does) that Marlowe "was forced, by the very impact of his creation, to face the genuinely tragic conflict that was bound to destroy the monster he created" (*The Overreacher*, 1952, p. 35). That Tamburlaine's sickness follows immediately upon his burning of the Koran does not mean that we are to take his death as divine punishment for blasphemy. We are not to regard the scene as Marlowe's defense of religion, with Christianity and Islam strangely identified. Coming at the moment when it does, the sickness of the hero is Marlowe's ironic manner of showing the futility of Tamburlaine's attempt to master those powers of the universe which no man can master, to win the ultimate victory over fortune by the conquest of death itself. Death strikes at the very moment when he is loudest in his defiance; the "daring God" who torments his body is neither Christ nor Allah, but that inscrutable force in the universe which decrees death even to the greatest and most powerful of men. There is no 'genuinely tragic conflict' in this situation. The madness of Tamburlaine's defiance of the inevitable is succeeded by the calm of the deathbed scene in which the hero accepts the inevitable, dying the superman he has always been. In the final triumph of fortune we have only an awareness of human limitation of which there is no hint in the first part of *Tamburlaine,* but which when considered more deeply and developed in other contexts may at last give rise to genuine tragedy.

In its classical aspects *Tamburlaine* is related to *Dido Queen of Carthage,* which presumably was conceived during the same period of Marlowe's development. We sometimes tend to dismiss this play as evidence only of a young scholar's fascination with classical myth, giving full range to his most sensuous verse in exploitation of one of the world's great love stories. Miss Ellis-Fermor called it a play which stands apart both from

Tamburlaine and the plays which Marlowe wrote at the close of his career. "The theme of *Dido*," she says, "is one which Marlowe never chose again as the main subject of a play and only very rarely introduced in a subsidiary one; that theme of love which, with the single exception of *Hero and Leander,* he treated always unusually and often, it must be confessed, ineptly" (*Christopher Marlowe,* 1927, p. 18). But there are elements in *Dido* other than its love story, and not only do these relate to *Tamburlaine,* but the love story itself looks forward to things which are to come in later plays.

We must remember that although Marlowe had just translated Ovid, it was not to Ovid that he turned in what probably was his first play, but to Virgil, and that Virgil's theme always is the destiny of Rome. Although Marlowe allows his imagination to dwell on the personal emotional aspects of Dido's plight, and though he captures the poignancy of frustrated love with an effectiveness such as the stage never before had witnessed, the general conception of the play still owes much to Virgil's epic, which, in fact, Marlowe translates directly in passage after passage. Although there is the suffering of Dido, paralleled by that of Anna and Iarbus, and though there is even the temptation of Aeneas to linger in Carthage, which Marlowe introduces at the end of the fourth act, and his remorse as he departs in the fifth, all of this matter constitutes but an episode in the career of a superman who, like Tamburlaine, is destined to create an empire. The difference is that whereas Tamburlaine relies only upon himself, Aeneas is the chosen instrument of the gods. This allows Marlowe to dwell for a moment on the possible opposition between divine will and human desire, and it is this which creates in the play all that is intensely personal and human. Aeneas shows a brief susceptibility to human passion, which for a moment deters him from his purpose, but this is quickly pushed aside and destiny is allowed to resume its course. I would suggest that Marlowe, even when most absorbed in the sensuous details of his love story, is still concerned with the superman, the man of destiny. In *Dido* he dealt with such a man in a mythological framework, as an instrument in a conflict among pagan deities which was to give rise to the greatest empire the world had ever known. From this subject he turned to history and chose a secular figure with a similar destiny, but one whom he could treat without reference to the affairs of a mythical Olympus, in terms not of classical poetry but of classical history.

As drama *Dido* is as static as *Tamburlaine.* It opens with a still pageant, the curtains parting to reveal Jupiter with his Ganymede; Venus interrupts to plead for his assistance to her son; Jupiter explains the heroic destiny which awaits him, and then we pass to a succession of scenes which reveal Aeneas obeying the impulses of destiny. What impresses the reader is the one-sidedness of the love affair, the passivity of the lover for the greater part of the play. It is not until the beginning of the third act that Dido falls in love with Aeneas, and when he declares his love for her in the cave scene at the end of that act, his speech is merely an acceptance of Dido's offer of marriage agreed on beforehand by Juno and Venus (1036-46). But immediately afterwards he is ready to obey the call of destiny and to leave Carthage without any acknowledgement of the solemnity of the vow he has made to Dido. He wishes that Dido will release him, but he knows that he must go whether she will or not. There is never any real conflict in his mind at this point. He pays only a token respect to the lover's obligations:

> I faine would goe, yet beautie calles me backe:
> To leaue her so and not once say farewell
> Were to transgresse against all lawes of loue: . . .
> (1196-8)

Only briefly, at the end of the fourth act, does he succumb to Dido's blandishments, renew his vow, and agree to remain as King of Carthage:

> This is the harbour that *Aeneas* seekes,
> Lets see what tempests can anoy me now.
> (1265-6)

This is the momentary weakness which stays the hero from his duty. We find him preparing to remain in Carthage at the beginning of the fifth act, but immediately Hermes appears to remind him of his duty and there is never again any question of staying. For the rest of the play he is concerned only with the manner of his departure. Marlowe's momentary concentration upon the human aspect of his story does not impede the forward march of the superman toward his destined goal.

It is Iarbus rather than Aeneas who represents male passion in the play, and it may have been in part to contrast him with Aeneas that Marlowe developed his role, for which there is only the slightest warrant in Virgil. Aeneas is as changeless as Tamburlaine, as impervious at last to the tears of Dido as Tamburlaine is to those of Zenocrate. Aeneas permits Dido to give him her aid, her treasure, and herself, for which he promises himself in return—but when fate calls he leaves her. Although Dido kills herself for love, this love, all-consuming on the human level though it may be, is still the human result of a stratagem by which the goddess Venus seeks to forward the destiny of her son; it is all part of the larger plan. The play is about a heroine who dies for love, but this event must be seen within the larger context of the story of a hero who will not permit love to deter him from the role which everything in his creation decrees that he must play. There are tragic implications in the human cost which such obedience to destiny involves, and this element is something foreign to the first part of *Tamburlaine*. It is not so foreign to the second part, where the death of Zenocrate and the cowardice of Calyphas draw from the superman powerful human emotions, and if the suicide of Olympia has any function it is to repeat the theme of the human cost of power, a motif to which Marlowe constantly is to return and which is to give birth at last to real tragedy.

As a play about human achievement rather than human failure, *Dido* is therefore no more a tragedy than *Tamburlaine*. The sufferings of Dido are no more significant in the universal scheme of things than are those of the Virgins of Damascus whom Tamburlaine is impelled to slay. Love is the human weakness above which the founder of nations must rise, and if Aeneas must make two attempts before he is at last able to leave Carthage, this is to stress the difficulty of the role he must fulfill, that the hero must rise above the human feelings of ordinary man. Marlowe began his dramatic career as a writer of conqueror plays on classical models, his concern being always with the fortunes of the man of destiny. *Dido* and *Tamburlaine* illustrate varied aspects of this theme, and it is therefore important, I believe, that we preserve the traditional view, recently challenged,[5] that these plays were written close together in time and that at least in their initial conceptions they are the product of Marlowe's Cambridge years. Taken together they represent the first stage of his development, a stage still far removed from tragedy yet showing faint signs of the matrix from which tragedy is to emerge.

No matter how we may take the charges of atheism which were leveled against Marlowe both before and after his death—and the external evidence is extremely strong, even while we recognize that Robert Greene's accusations may be the product of malice and envy—his earliest plays would indicate an intellectual position which allies him with the currents of Renaissance skepticism which were challenging the medieval notion of a harmonious creation, observing degree and order and ruled over by

[5] By T. M. Pearce, "Evidence for Dating Marlowe's *Tragedy of Dido*," in *Studies in the English Renaissance Drama in Memory of Karl Julius Holzknecht*, ed. Josephine W. Bennett, Oscar Cargill, and Vernon Hall, Jr. (1959), pp. 231-47.

the providence of a loving God. Marlowe stands at the beginning of his dramatic career in opposition to the Christian humanism of Richard Hooker; he is in the company of Bruno, Montaigne, and the Machiavelli by whose writings he seems so strongly to have been influenced.[6] In its simplest terms the conflict between these two opposing attitudes may be narrowed to an opposition between rival views of nature and the power of human reason in relation to it. Nature for the Christian humanist is the creation of God controlled only by God, and human reason is an attuning of human will to divine will in recognition of the divine law which operates in all of nature, and thus a willingness to live by those moral laws—the altruistic feelings, love, kindness, loyalty, and others— which all men intuitively recognize and which are enshrined in Christian belief as reflections in normal human intercourse of the love of God by which the whole creation moves. The skeptics, on the other hand, exalt the power of man to control the universe by his own strength and reason, without regard to divine influence. They see nature not so much as the reflection of divine will, but as something governed by immutable laws which may be studied; nature can be controlled once these laws are understood. They envision man as the potential master of his environment. The movement from the control of physical nature to that of human social and political relations is a natural and easy one, and Machiavelli made it in his attempt to glean from the classical historians, and from his own observation of contemporary affairs, laws which could apply, to the problems of government.

   Tamburlaine and *Dido* stand opposed, each in its own way, to the Christian humanist position, *Tamburlaine* in its exaltation of *virtù*, and *Dido* in its implicit denial of love as a legitimate concern in the execution of the purpose of the gods, and in its very view of the universe as governed by the capricious, quarrelsome deities of classical myth. Human *virtù* could manifest itself in two forms, as Machiavelli had explained, the strength of the lion and the cunning of the fox, and Machiavelli held that each was necessary to the successful ruler. The strength of the lion is obvious in *Tamburlaine*. That cunning is the weapon by which the ends of the gods are assured in *Dido* is not always so obvious, but the entire Ascanius-Cupid subplot is, after all, little more than a cunning device by which Dido is outwitted so that the destiny of Aeneas may be forwarded. Venus uses Ascanius first to trick Dido into loving Aeneas so that his fleet may be repaired, and then she uses Ascanius as the false

[6] For the strongest statement of Marlowe's challenge to Elizabethan orthodoxy, see Paul H. Kocher, *Christopher Marlowe* (1946).

hostage that creates the sense of security on Dido's part which permits Aeneas to escape.

This kind of cunning, the manipulation of worldly affairs and of other men by one's own powers of fraud and deception came to be known as 'policy,' this being merely one of the means by which the skeptic could assert his control over events by the power of his reason. In Shakespeare and Chapman, policy is the object of scorn and derision. Marlowe, in *The Jew of Malta, The Massacre at Paris,* and *Edward II,* went on to explore the implications of policy in human affairs, and it is important that we note that in doing so he was exploring the implications of the system of values he had postulated in *Dido* and the two parts of *Tamburlaine.*

The first two acts of *The Jew of Malta* are so different from the final three that no conscientious reader of the play can fail to share Wilson's judgment (p. 65) that "to suppose that the same man who wrote the first two acts was wholly responsible for the last three is revolting to sense and sensibility." The aspiring superman of the play's beginning has been converted by its end into the caricature of a villain upon whom retribution is visited in conventional terms of poetic justice. That the end of the play does not give us what we have been led to expect at the beginning, however, should not obscure the fact that the focus of the play in its original conception must still have been upon the failure of its central character, whereas that of Marlowe's earlier plays had always been upon his triumph. Barabas at the beginning of the play is like Tamburlaine a man of boundless power and imagination; he rules the world by his wealth as Tamburlaine rules it by his strength. Like Marlowe's earlier heroes, Barabas stands deliberately in opposition to Christianity; Tamburlaine is a Scythian and Aeneas a pagan Trojan; all three stand for essentially non-Christian ideals, and Barabas by his name is specifically marked as the antithesis of Christ.

The play as we have it is blatantly anti-Semitic, castigating the Jew as a remorseless villain, holding him up to ridicule, and showing him finally as the victim of a punishment as ludicrous as it is merited. But if we limit our consideration to those parts of the play which are manifestly Marlowe's, it is at least as anti-Christian as it is anti-Semitic, and on moral grounds Barabas certainly gets the better of his quarrel with Ferneze in the first act. Kocher (p. 130) has argued that Marlowe uses Barabas as an instrument for attack upon Christianity, not out of affection for Jews but out of scorn for Christians. Barabas is not a comic or a craven figure at the beginning of the play. He is not "a shrunken figure withered in body and mind."[7] He is the aspiring pagan, drawing his wealth from all corners of the world, wielding global power, and delighting in all of the felicity which wealth can convey. We get in his speeches the intoxication of expanding empire which Elizabethans could experience in the exploits of Hawkins or Drake and which no poet has conveyed more perfectly than Marlowe:

> What more may Heaven doe for earthly man
> Then thus to powre out plenty in their laps,
> Ripping the bowels of the earth for them,
> Making the Sea their seruant, and the winds
> To driue their substance with successefull blasts?
>
> (145-9)

He delights in the things of the world, and in his love of wealth he stands in opposition to Christianity:

> Who hateth me but for my happinesse?
> Or who is honour'd now but for his wealth?
> Rather had I a Iew be hated thus,
> Then pittied in a Christian pouerty:
> For I can see no fruits in all their faith,
> But malice, falshood, and excessiue pride,
> Which me thinkes fits not their profession.
>
> (150-56)

The behavior of the Christians in the play merits the contempt with which Barabas views them. When they steal his gold, Marlowe tells us in unequivocal terms that Barabas has been deeply wronged:

> What? bring you Scripture to confirm your wrongs?
> Preach me not out of my possessions.
> Some Iewes are wicked, as all Christians are:
> But say the Tribe that I descended of
> Were all in generall cast away for sinne,
> Shall I be tryed by their transgression?
> The man that dealeth righteously shall liue:
> And which of you can charge me otherwise?
>
> (343-50)

The lines are amazingly modern in their indictment, and through them rings Marlowe's scorn for Christian pretensions to virtue. There seems little doubt of Marlowe's sympathies in the initial act.

Marlowe's conception in *The Jew of Malta* seems to involve the pagan superman who is wronged by Christian policy and who then seeks by

---

[7] M. M. Mahood, "Marlowe's Heroes," in *Poetry and Humanism* (1950), p. 75.

policy in turn to repay his wrongs, but the very exercise of policy viti-ates the superman and destroys his heroic image, lowering him beneath even those who have sinned against him. Barabas becomes the avenger who, like Seneca's Atreus, must repay his injuries with greater evils than those to which he himself has been subjected. He comes finally to be the incarnation of evil, a vehicle for the morality of Satan himself, though Miss Ellis-Fermor is certainly correct in holding (*Christopher Marlowe,* p. 100) that he becomes "a Satanist who rebels against a world-order of unclean and unjust things." Barabas moves from the amoral to the utterly immoral, but we must remember that this represents a progres-sion from what he is at the beginning of the play. *The Jew of Malta* is not the "farce" which T. S. Eliot has called it (*Selected Essays,* 1932, p. 123); it is Marlowe's first tragedy because it portrays the degeneration of a man through the manner in which he reacts to evil in the world. We no longer have the simple movement of an initially complete and static figure as in *Dido* and *Tamburlaine.*

This tragic conception comes through even the crude buffoonery of the final acts, and in the murder of Abigail, whose father at the beginning of the play holds her "as deare As *Agamemnon* did his *Iphigen*" (175-6), we are reminded, as we are to be more effectively reminded again in *Edward II,* of the human loss which is the price of policy. We have in *The Jew of Malta,* I believe, a play in which the limitations of Chris-tianity are exposed even more surely than in *Tamburlaine,* but where the failure of policy receives the greater dramatic emphasis. It is certainly a play in which Marlowe has already begun to question the faith in the power of human mind and will which he had so proudly asserted in *Tamburlaine.*

If we search for the source of Barabas's failure, the collapse of his policy, where are we to find it? Levin has suggested (pp. 78-9) that it is in his need for love, his awareness of the simple fact that man cannot depend upon himself alone, as one who places his hope either in strength like Tamburlaine or in policy like Barabas must always do. The begin-ning of his downfall is in his choice of a companion, Ithamore, and the final collapse of his power comes from his human desire for reconcilia-tion with his enemies, his need to trust those whom the true man of pol-icy would have known could never be trusted. Caricature of the 'Machi-avel' as Barabas is, he violates the most essential elements of Machiavelli's creed, and his defeat is the failure of the Machiavellian ethic. In this fact we may find perhaps Marlowe's final recognition of the value of those altruistic feelings which might have spared the Virgins of Damascus or which might have made Aeneas the victim of a truly tragic conflict. In this dimension of *The Jew of Malta* is one measure of the distance which Marlowe has traveled.

The departure from *Tamburlaine* is further made clear by the prologue to *The Jew of Malta,* where "Macheuil" himself appears to set the scene. However, this figure is not the Machiavelli to whose view of the world Marlowe had given his assent in *Tamburlaine.* This is the Machiavel of burlesque tradition, and the precepts he speaks are those of Innocent Gentillet's *Contre-Machiavel* (printed 1576), bearing little relation to anything Machiavelli himself had written.[8] The entire prologue was actually translated from Gabriel Harvey's *Epigramma in effigiem Machiavelli,* itself based upon Gentillet, and as Levin points out (p. 61), "both scholar-poets were in a position to know how greatly they distorted Machiavelli's doctrine and personality." The conduct of Barabas himself, though supposedly Machiavellian, is almost always in direct contradiction to Machiavelli's actual principles. What is significant is that in this play Marlowe, in order to make clear the deficiency of policy, was able to use a stereotyped caricature of what in an earlier play he had seriously espoused.

In *The Jew of Malta* we have the defeat of policy, but we do not have the triumph of its antithesis, for Ferneze the Christian and Calymath the Turk are each as guilty as Barabas, and if there is any victory at the end of the play, it certainly is not one of moral principle. Jew, Christian, and Turk in this play all live by the same code, the success of the one following upon the downfall of the other, as each is able to seize the advantage and practice his policy the more efficiently. For the triumph of virtue we must move a step further to *The Massacre at Paris,* and it is because this play seems to supply an element which is missing from *The Jew of Malta* that I would suggest—very tentatively—that it is the play which came next to be written. We have the self-defeating policy of the Guise, drawn on an even more lavish scale than that of Barabas, without the comic element and with more corpses littering the stage than in any other of Marlowe's plays, to say nothing of the hundreds of whose drowning in the Seine we are told. But we have also in opposition to the Guise the quiet virtue of King Henry of Navarre, and it is this virtue which at the end of the play is triumphant. That Navarre never really comes alive in the play, that his speeches are flat and insipid, consisting of little more than platitudinous moralizing, does not obscure the fact that his role in the play is to stand for anticlericalism (he specifically allies himself with

---

[8] See my "Significance of Gentillet's *Contre-Machiavel*," *MLQ,* 10 (1949), 153-7; and Kocher, *Christopher Marlowe,* pp. 196-200.

Queen Elizabeth of England) as the Guise represents the power of the Papacy, and thus to provide the final victory of a force antithetical to that represented by the Guise. He stands for the triumph of a political as well as a religious position, and we must consider that the political in this play may have been Marlowe's primary concern. It is difficult to believe that the Navarre of our received text retains much of what must have been the author's original conception. There is, in fact, little other than some speeches of the Guise which sound at all like Marlowe.

The soliloquies of the Guise reveal to us the self-reliant man of policy like Barabas, but one who, unlike Barabas, vaunts his deliberate villainy from his very first appearance. He seeks a crown by the deliberate exercise of immorality, and it is the very danger of the quest which he enjoys:

> Oft haue I leueld, and at last haue learnd,
> That perill is the cheefest way to happines,
> And resolution honors fairest aime.
>
> (94-6)

He relies upon his own power exclusively, using religion only as an instrument of policy:

> For this, from Spaine the stately Catholickes
> Sends Indian golde to coyne me French ecues:
> For this haue I a largesse from the Pope,
> A pension and a dispensation too:
> And by that priuiledge to worke vpon,
> My policye hath framde religion.
> Religion: *O Diabole.*
>
> (117-23)

These lines have the unmistakable ring of Marlowe, linking the aspirations of this character to those of Tamburlaine and Barabas. The goal for which the Guise strives by villainy is that "sweet fruition of an earthly crown" which Tamburlaine had sought by strength. It is only Navarre who stands in his way, whom he must overcome as Tamburlaine had destroyed Mycetes and Bajazeth, and in the failure of the Guise to overcome Navarre is a measure of the difference between these plays. The action of *The Massacre at Paris* is episodic like that of *Tamburlaine,* the simple detailing of the Guise's villainies until he reaches the height of his power, only to be murdered at last as he outreaches himself. There is also a kind of thematic elaboration in the role of Henry III, a weak, lascivious practitioner of policy as the Guise is a cruel and forthright one, who comes however to a similar end, murdered as his own policy recoils upon him.

We must note that the cause of the Guise's downfall is similar to what destroys Barabas: his inability to cope with the ordinary human emotions, the affections of his wife and his own concern for honor and esteem. We have the ludicrous spectacle in this play of the all-powerful manipulator of kings revealed as a cuckold. He incurs the enmity of the King which must at last destroy him when to defend his honor he kills the King's favorite who has been his wife's lover. The Guise, master of policy, is destroyed when he allows the passions which the man of policy must control to defeat his own policy. In doing so he gives rise to the counter-policy of Henry III, who lives by a code no different from that of the Guise and whose murder at the end parallels that of the Guise, emphasizing for a second time the futility of all policy. Henry of Navarre stands in contrast to these two, the champion of true religion, placing his faith not in policy but in the protection of God. And it is Navarre who comes at last to the French throne.

From this one might suppose that by the time of his writing *The Massacre at Paris* Marlowe had returned to the faith of his youth and had been reconciled to the church he had opposed in his earlier work. Of this we cannot be sure. The religious sentiments which Navarre expresses may bear little relation to what Marlowe originally wrote, and it is, in any case, to the political rather than doctrinal issues of anti-Catholicism that Marlowe gives his support. But we can be sure that this play does embody a renunciation, even more pronounced than that in *The Jew of Malta,* of the individualist amoral faith of *Tamburlaine.*

As tragedy the play is much like Shakespeare's *Richard III,* almost medieval in its display of the sudden fall from power of the aspiring villain, though there is none of the terror or remorse of conscience which comes at the last to Shakespeare's Machiavel. *The Massacre at Paris,* as we have it, is by far the least successful of Marlowe's plays, and there is little in it to arouse the tragic emotions. In his brief career Marlowe was to write only two plays of real tragic scope and intensity, but those plays, *Edward II* and *Doctor Faustus,* represent a development from all which had gone before. I would suggest that it would have been difficult for Marlowe to have come to them without the experience of his earlier plays. *Edward II,* which I take to be the earlier of the final two, recapitulates the career of the Guise in the rise and fall of Mortimer, but there is an important difference in that Mortimer is not evil when the play begins; he is not even amoral like Barabas. Marlowe no longer needs a ready-made villain. He can now present a loyal, patriotic gentleman, devoted entirely to the good of his country, and in the process of his decline demonstrate the corrupting force of aspiration to power such as he had never been able to do before. He could do so within a truly tragic context, detailing the decline of one man through his own destruction of his human instincts, while in the parallel tragedy of King Edward II he could display the destruction of a man forced by necessity to wield a power which he is incapable of wielding because of his own human instincts. Marlowe holds these two situations in relation to one another, with Edward as he declines in power acquiring to at least some extent a new humility and self-understanding through suffering which win for him the sympathy of the audience, while Mortimer, rising as Edward falls, is alienated from the audience as they behold the slow erosion of his humanity. This pattern of rise and fall is a unique structural achievement in *Edward II*, from which Shakespeare was to learn much in his own *Richard II*.

Marlowe has abandoned his faith in the amoral superman like Tamburlaine. He had shown in *The Jew of Malta* and *The Massacre at Paris* that an egocentric self-reliance may degenerate into a demonic force destructive of itself as well as of the social order, and he demonstrates this again in Mortimer. In *Edward II*, however, there is no evidence that Marlowe has come to accept the Christian humanist view of order and degree in a divinely controlled and harmonious cosmos, with what Tudor theorists considered to be the proper role of the king in that system. *Edward II* and *Doctor Faustus* are plays of a terrible pessimism, for while they detail the futility of individual aspiration and the corrupting effects of power they offer no alternative which mankind can fully embrace. They are plays without affirmation. If there is any reconciliation at the end of *Edward II*, it may be in the audience's knowledge that the new king, Edward III, did in fact go on to become one of England's greatest kings, that it was possible for at least one king to escape the corrupting effects of power which the play has made clear.

The political setting of *Edward II* involves the same amoral world of *Tamburlaine,* where the events of history represent not the workings of a divine plan for humanity, but the results of human action and human error. There is no mention in *Edward II* of the divine right of kings or of their responsibility to God. A king's power rests only upon his own ability to maintain it in spite of opposition, and when he cannot assert this power he loses all of the attributes of royalty:

> But what are kings, when regiment is gone,
> But perfect shadowes in a sun-shine day?
> (2012-13)

Edward II is born into a position in which to survive he must be a Machiavellian superman like Tamburlaine or Mortimer; and since he is not, he is destroyed. That is his tragedy. But the tragedy of Mortimer is that he is destroyed by being precisely what Edward is not. There is nothing in the play of the Christian attitude which might have emphasized the fall of Mortimer as punishment for sin. His is the inevitable fate of all who aspire beyond the limits of mortality. To be incapable of exercising power like Edward is to be destroyed; to exercise it fully is to destroy one's self like Mortimer. This is the human condition, and man can only meet it by the assertion of the stoic fortitude with which Mortimer accepts his death:

> Base fortune, now I see, that in thy wheele
> There is a point, to which when men aspire,
> They tumble hedlong downe: that point I touchte,
> And seeing there was no place to mount vp higher,
> Why should I greeue at my declining fall?
>
> (2627-31)

If the tragedy is moral, this is because it embraces a comprehensive view of human experience, while it displays the relation of good to evil and the plight of a humanity which is prey to necessity and its own human nature. It is a consistent vision and a tragic one, but the only resolution it can offer is in terms of a classical stoicism.

The only one of Marlowe's plays which is cast in a deliberately Christian context is *Doctor Faustus,* perhaps also the most difficult of his plays to come to terms with, for of the two inadequate texts which have come down to us only a small part can be from the pen of Marlowe. What follows here is based upon the reconstruction by Sir Walter Greg, which must remain our most reliable guide.[9] It is obvious that *Doctor Faustus* is a play about human damnation and that the contrary alternative of salvation in specifically Christian terms is always present in the dramatic context, but this need not mean that Marlowe had returned to Christian belief when he wrote this play any more than his authorship of *Dido* need indicate that he was ever a pagan Greek. Christian doctrine was one of Marlowe's most vital concerns throughout his career. Only in *Dido,* of all his plays, is it not an important issue. Kocher has argued that much of his dramatic activity may be explained as a struggle against the theo-

---

[9] *The Tragical History of the Life and Death of Doctor Faustus: A Conjectural Reconstruction* (1950). Greg's date of 1592-3 (argued in his parallel-text edition, 1950, of the quartos of 1604 and 1616) seems to be generally accepted. That *Faustus* is Marlowe's latest play had been argued on bibliographical grounds by F. S. Boas, *Christopher Marlowe* (1940), pp. 203-4.

logical training of his youth: "However desperate his desire to be free, he was bound to Christianity by the surest of chains—hatred mingled with reluctant longing, and fascination much akin to fear" (p. 119). The damnation of Faustus could be taken by the Elizabethan audience, as it no doubt was, as a perfectly orthodox warning to sinners, an exemplum in the medieval manner delineating what the church held to be the mental state of the damned and dwelling at last upon all of the physical horrors of the soul's being carried off through the traditional Hell-mouth.

Marlowe may well have known Nathaniel Woodes's morality play, *The Conflict of Conscience,* and he may even have known the story on which that play was based, the despair and death of Francesco Spiera, an Italian Protestant who had renounced his faith.[10] But Marlowe's *Doctor Faustus* is not a Christian morality play, for it contains no affirmation of the goodness or justice of the religious system it depicts with such accuracy of detail. It is, rather, a protest against this system, which it reveals as imposing a limitation upon the aspirations of man, holding him in subjection and bondage, denying him at last even the comfort of Christ's blood, and dooming him to the most terrible destruction. The religion of the play is a Christianity from which, as Michel Poirier has pointed out (*Christopher Marlowe,* 1951, p. 141), Christ is strangely missing.

There is a terrible warning for humanity in the final chorus:

> *Faustus* is gone, regard his hellish fall
> Whose fiendful fortune may exhort the wise,
> Onely to wonder at vnlawful things,
> Whose deepenesse doth intise such forward wits,
> To practise more than heauenly power permits.
> (1481-5)

The price of aspiration, of seeking to probe beyond the ordinary limits of man, is death in its most horrible form. If the progress of Doctor Faustus is, as Miss Gardner has written (p. 47), "from a proud philosopher, master of all human knowledge, to a trickster, to a slave of phantoms, to a cowering wretch," this is not to say that the order of things which decrees such human deterioration as the price of aspiration beyond arbitrary limits is affirmed by Marlowe as a good or just one. The

---

[10] This has been suggested by Lily B. Campbell, "*Doctor Faustus:* A Case of Conscience," *PMLA,* 67 (1952), 219-39. Miss Campbell sees the play as a tragedy of despair in the medieval theological sense of refusal to accept the mercy of God. For similar Christian interpretations of the play, see M. M. Mahood, *Poetry and Humanism* (1950), pp. 67-74; Helen Gardner, "Milton's 'Satan' and the Theme of Damnation in Elizabethan Tragedy," *English Studies,* 1 (London, 1948), 46-66; and Leo Kirschbaum, "Marlowe's *Faustus:* A Reconsideration," *RES,* 19 (1943), 225-41.

play does not preach a pious submission to divine law. It is a terribly pessimistic statement of the futility of human aspiration. In this play Marlowe is using a Christian view of Heaven and Hell in a vehicle of protest which is essentially anti-Christian.

Greg has shown that the framework of the Good and Bad Angels who plead for Faustus's soul and even the Old Man who offers him salvation at the end are probably the work of Marlowe's collaborator, but he has argued that these elements must nevertheless have been a part of Marlowe's original conception. This machinery of medieval exemplum does not make such an exemplum of the play. Rather than the play of Christian affirmation which some critics have taken it to be, *Doctor Faustus* is the tragedy of the human being who will not surrender, in return for the promise of salvation, those heroic attributes—the cravings for knowledge, wealth, power, and delight—for which Marlowe still sees it as in the nature of mankind to yearn. Marlowe has come a long way from *Tamburlaine,* for while he once may have seen these goals as attainable, he now sees them as only an illusion whose very pursuit must be man's destruction.

He has come also to see that the Christian faith of his youth may provide one escape for mankind, but it is a faith he still cannot bring himself to accept, and I believe that Miss Ellis-Fermor is correct (*Christopher Marlowe,* p. 62) in seeing *Doctor Faustus* as a play about Marlowe's own sense of loss and frustration. It is the most terribly personal of Marlowe's plays, perhaps of all Elizabethan drama, but we must not confuse the poignant longing for belief, for salvation, perhaps for rescue in orthodox Christianity from the doubts and perplexities which were Marlowe's humanistic heritage, with the signs of acceptance and resignation. *Faustus* does not preach a creed. The play is a mirror not of Christian certainty but of agnostic intellectual confusion. The contrary systems of value in *Doctor Faustus* are as clear-cut as in Shakespeare's *Lear* or *Macbeth*—submission to divine will versus defiant belief in one's own power to control nature—but the author's response to them is entirely different. *Doctor Faustus* is a play in which man by his own deterioration and final torture pays the price of his independence of mind, and it is a play which, unlike Shakespeare's, can offer little hope for humanity. Unlike the damnation of Macbeth, that of Faustus leads to no affirmation of order or harmony in the universe, and there is no compensating rebirth of the good.

Faustus, like Tamburlaine or Barabas, seeks to enlarge the ordinary scope of human life so that man on earth may equal the state of the God he envisages in Heaven. Faustus is the knowing and deliberate apostate:

> Had I as many soules as there be starres,
> Ide giue them al for *Mephastophilis:* . . .
> (338-9)

And he proceeds to enumerate the things he seeks: kingship like Tamburlaine, limitless power, and ability to control the physical universe. There is never any doubt in his mind before he makes his bargain that what he seeks is worth the price of damnation. The tragedy does not involve an unknowing choice of evil, or even a defect of judgment. Faustus is not tempted by Mephistophilis as Othello is by Iago. Mephistophilis, in fact, is almost sorrowful as he warns Faustus of his fate. The tragedy lies in that what Faustus receives in exchange for his soul is finally worthless, that wealth, power, and sensual pleasure are revealed to him as having only a delusory value which disappears as soon as they are possessed. The restricting force of Christian submission is made clear in Faustus's opening soliloquy; that the alternative is equally without value is the burden of the rest of the play. Faustus can receive no answers to the questions he asks. The broad comic matter which takes up most of the central portion of the play is not from the pen of Marlowe, but it is clear that these scenes, which follow the source closely, are an essential part of the story, and that even if they were written by a collaborator, they must have been a part of Marlowe's conception of the total play.[11] These central scenes are designed in part to illustrate the futility of what Faustus gains, and they are still effective in doing so.

There are three movements in *Doctor Faustus,* following closely the divisions of the source-book. First there is the hero's choice of damnation, which springs not only from his awareness of the limitations which Christianity places upon him, but also from his syllogistic conclusion that in Christian doctrine his death through sin is already implicit:

> If we say that we haue no sinne,
> We deceiue our selues, and theres no truth in vs.
> Why then belike
> We must sinne, and so consequently die.
> I, we must die an euerlasting death: . . .
> (70-74)

The syllogism is a false one because it ignores the atonement of Christ for man's sins and the possibility of salvation through grace, but this is

---

[11] See Greg, "The Damnation of Faustus," *MLR*, 41 (1946), 97-107; and Wilson, *Marlowe and the Early Shakespeare*, pp. 70-77.

not made clear by Marlowe, and Faustus's view of Christianity is the only one made explicit in the play. The God of *Doctor Faustus* is one singularly without love, a God of terrible justice without mercy; no more than Lucifer himself will Marlowe's God show Faustus any mercy once his bargain has been made. If Christianity offers Faustus nothing but sin and death, he will turn elsewhere. The second movement of the play shows the shallowness of what Faustus receives for his soul, his growing awareness of this shallowness, his own deterioration as he exchanges his heroic aspirations for petty trickery, and the constant pressure he feels to renounce his bargain and accept salvation on Christian terms. In the final movement of the play is the delineation of the last stage of Faustus's deterioration as he pleads for mercy, the horror of his destruction, and the realization that it has all been for naught.

There is nothing in *Doctor Faustus* of the Calvinistic bias which shapes Woodes's *Conflict of Conscience*; the way of repentance is always open to Faustus, as these central scenes constantly make clear. But for Faustus to repent is for him to reject those human aspirations which had led him to make his bargain in the first place, and although again and again he is driven to repentance by fear, the thought of worldly power and delight keeps him steadfast to his bargain. Whether Helen of Troy be a succuba or not, the lines with which Faustus greets her (1328-47) are still among the most lyrical Marlowe ever wrote, and their poetry alone evokes a sympathetic response to that for which Faustus gives his soul. I do not believe the audience ever see Faustus as a fool; if they did there could be no tragedy. Although we may pity him and certainly are horrified by his fate, we may still emotionally identify ourselves with him and feel the magnificence of what he seeks. Faustus accepts damnation rather than acknowledge a limit to man's capacity to seek the unknowable and the unattainable. If Marlowe's final view of Christianity is implicit in this play, it is that the Christian promise of salvation may be one way out of the human dilemma, but one which he cannot yet bring himself to take. If he had lived longer, perhaps Marlowe might have written a play of true Christian affirmation, but he did not do so in *Doctor Faustus*. The tragedy of this play, and of humanity as Marlowe sees it at this point in his career, is that neither Christianity nor its alternative presents a choice which mankind wholeheartedly can embrace.

The death speech of Faustus reveals none of the stoic resignation with which Mortimer accepts his fate. Marlowe wishes in this play to show the final degeneration of what had been heroic, to reveal a futile longing for faith such as Marlowe himself may have suffered, and to illustrate

the final bleak terror of the human situation. We have a poignant pleading by Faustus for escape from what the play has revealed cannot be
escaped. The abject terror of Faustus serves to emphasize both the un-
heroic stature to which he has shrunk and the struggle which continues
to the last within his own soul:

> O Ile leape vp to my God: who pulles me downe?
> See see where Christs blood streames in the firmament.
> One drop would saue my soule, half a drop, ah my Christ.
> Ah rend not my heart for naming of my Christ,
> Yet wil I call on him: oh spare me *Lucifer*!
>
> (1431-5)

The final stage is a frantic pleading for the mercy which Marlowe's stern
God of justice will not show; the power of Lucifer finally prevails. In the
death of Faustus the terror and futility of the human condition are revealed as they never had been before in English drama, with no compensating hope of any kind.

This survey has been brief and the proposed chronology of the plays
necessarily conjectural. Nevertheless it may still be possible, while we
keep in mind the many areas of Marlowe's life and thought about which
we can have no certainty, to conclude that he came to the writing of
tragedy as he abandoned the optimistic individualism of his Cambridge
days, but that he did not live long enough to find a faith which could
take its place, though in *Doctor Faustus* he seemed to be moving closer
than ever before to traditional Christianity. If we assess his final achievement in tragedy, we find that in his last two plays he was able to present
a comprehensive view of mankind and to make some statement about the
relation of good and evil in the world, as every tragic vision must. He
could however, find no real principle of order in the universe, no hope
for human triumph over evil, and the only consolation he could afford to
mankind was in the heroic stature of a stoic acceptance and submission
to what must be.

This is something quite other than the tragic vision of Shakespeare,
who when Marlowe died had approached tragedy only in *Titus Andronicus* and *Richard III*, but who was to go on to achieve in the plays of his
maturity the kind of tragic reconciliation of which Marlowe was incapable, relating good and evil in terms of a Christian humanist view of the
world, and finding in creation a moral order which made suffering meaningful and which provided a basis for renewed acceptance of life.[12] Al-

---

[12] I have developed this theme in *Patterns in Shakespearian Tragedy* (1960).

though Marlowe taught Shakespeare much of his dramatic technique, he did not bequeath to him his own pessimistic "tragicke glasse." Marlowe's true successors in this respect were the Jacobean dramatists like Webster, Middleton, and Ford, who rejected the Shakespearian synthesis and, beginning with Marlowe's skeptical view, sought in their independent ways for a comprehensive vision of reality.

MORE SHAKESPEARE
SONNET GROUPS

by Brents Stirling

I N "A SHAKESPEARE SONNET GROUP" (*PMLA*, 75, 1960) I proposed a new effort to answer some old questions raised by Thorpe's quarto of 1609. The quarto sonnet order is often unsatisfactory, but so have been most attempts to improve it. I tried to meet the difficulty with a standard of multiple evidence. First considered were sonnets 63-8, all of which are addressed to Shakespeare's friend in the third person and distinguished further by a uniform epithet, "my love." Surprisingly, five remaining sonnets of third-person address (a very limited category) also contain the epithet: 19, 21, 100, 101, 105. When the eleven sonnets with this double hallmark are read together they show added signs of linkage: a close unity of theme, a constant echo of image and phrase, and a conventional structure—beginning, middle, and end. Three additional factors complete the picture. Sonnets 63-8, already joined in Q, show that Shakespeare 'intended' a poem of the kind proposed; the five remaining sonnets, separated in Q, are all in questionable position; and removal of 100-101 from the Q order leaves 97-9>[1]102-4 with a new sequential unity.

Right or wrong, my point was simple: of the connective elements just described, one or two could be fortuitous but there is not much chance of accident in the total combination. Thus I believe that the eleven sonnets belong together, presumably in the order 100, 101, 63-8, 19, 21, 105. Further, since this new group and its 'by-product' 97-9>102-4 both

---

[1] In this essay the symbol > means 'followed immediately by.' In the present instance 97-9>102-4 means sonnets 97-9 followed immediately by sonnets 102-4, the whole forming a unified group.

show a consistency found in authentic sequences such as 1-17 and 76-86, it becomes likely that Shakespeare's text was more coherent than much of Q implies; that although he plainly linked sonnets by 'associational' motif, his habit was to avoid non sequitur whether of logic or tone. There is still much to be learned from close reading so long as we adopt standards which minimize accidental or merely general connection between sonnets.

No one will be surprised at this continuation of an earlier study. Few revisers of the 1609 sonnet order ever retreat to prepared lines of defense. Remembering this, I expect a skeptical reception and will welcome it if based on a fresh reading of the text and an understanding that Q has no authority governing sequence except where groups of sonnets speak for their own continuity. I ask only that an old question be reopened experimentally, and above all that the experiment be addressed to Shakespeare's own lines. No argument for amending the 1609 text can be self-sufficient; it can only point to what may be found if certain sonnets are carefully reread and recompared. For those who may wish to do this there is a suggestion which should be helpful. Use two copies of the Sonnets; few distractions defeat close comparison so much as backward and forward page-thumbing.

With the questionable position and the relocation of five sonnets discussed in a previous essay (hereafter referred to as SSG), we can turn here to some additional sonnets among the first 126 which may be displaced. These are of two kinds: (1) sonnets which 'agree' in some way with adjacent sonnets but which interrupt and cancel the design of a larger series; (2) sonnets either at odds with adjacent sonnets or 'out of touch' with them (except, of course, for those which clearly introduce new groups). In 'Class 1' are sonnets 36-9, 46-9, 113-16. In 'Class 2' are sonnets 24, 32, 69-70, 81, 95-6. The lists are not complete; they merely set the limits of present discussion.

To decide at the outset that these sonnets are out of position because they induce non sequitur would beg the question. Hence, in the discussion of any suspected sonnet the beginning point will be simply that its placement can be questioned, and that the questioning can rest on tangible grounds. Further, unless the position of a sonnet is open to specific doubt, there will be no attempt to relocate it by a 'multiple-factor' test, and only if its position is exceptionally doubtful will displacement be counted as one of the factors supporting relocation.

In considering faulty sequence we need not face all of its implications. For example, if sonnets 113-16 break the continuity of 109-12>117-21, we might ask which of the elements is 'actually' displaced—the disruptive sonnets, the first segment of the broken series, or the second segment. It is not likely at present that such a query can be answered, but it can be separated from the problem of restoring a Q group. If restoration of sonnets 1-126 as a continuous poem were in issue, the question would have to be met. We may be sure, however, that no such issue exists. In agreement with most modern editors and critics, my premise is that the Sonnets are a publisher's collection of distinct groups written at different times, some short (pairs, threes) and some longer; some independent and some related. The location of a group in relation to other groups is an ultimate editorial problem, but our first concern with a fragmentary or disturbed group should center upon its internal restoration.

In discussion to follow, extensive acknowledgment of previous opinion is impossible and unnecessary. Reference to Rollins's Variorum edition (1944) will often show a dozen arrangements affecting sonnets dealt with here. In some cases my disposition is new, in others only partly so; but in general the basis of multiple evidence upon which rearrangement is grounded differs either in nature or extent from that of earlier analysis.

In this essay all italics in lines quoted from the Sonnets have been added for the sake of clarity or emphasis. Quotation is rendered with modern spelling and punctuation; in the current problem an archaic text is not useful as evidence unless its form determines meaning or style. Variations from the original text, including accepted emendations, are indicated wherever they might affect interpretation.

Doubtfully placed sonnets will be discussed not in their Q order but in one that favors clear exposition. From this standpoint we can begin with sonnets of Class 1, those which may fit loosely with adjacent sonnets but nevertheless destroy the continuity of a group. The advantage of starting here is that a showing of doubtful placement will require proof of a design which is disrupted, one quite like that of recognized Q groups and of the eleven-sonnet group proposed in SSG. Thus, if the evidence of design is clear it will expand the number of groups which reflect a Shakespearian standard of continuity. It will also help to make later discussion clearer, shorter, and perhaps more convincing.

In considering sonnets of Class 1 the first step in each case will be an attempt to restore an interrupted Q group; the second step, if opportunity permits, will be an effort to relocate the interrupting sonnets. Not all possibilities of relocation can be set forth, but those discussed will be numerous enough to illustrate the nature of multiple evidence and its application.

THE GROUP 43-5>50-51 AND SONNETS 46-9

Ultimately we can infer the misplacement in Q of sonnets 46-9 only from their breaking of the impressive connection between 43-5 and 50-51. Rearrangers listed in the Variorum do not exploit this connection but Pooler, one of the best editors, noted it (1918). My contribution will be an attempt to describe Shakespeare's characteristic way of achieving it. No matter what the result, we shall know where we stand. Traditional comment has often accepted sonnets 46-9 in their Q position on grounds of loose thematic relationship with neighboring sonnets, and I shall question this associational or tangential linkage in supporting the far more pointed one between 43-5 and 50-51. Thus differences will become clear: either a strongly coherent design prevails over the lax framework of 'thematic' interpetation, or it does not.

Sonnet 42 humorously resolves the 'crisis' of poet, friend, and mistress on a note of mutual identity, and 43 begins a new series. Here the young man's "shadow" comes by night to enhance the poet's dreams; yet how much more blessed would it be if he should appear "in the living day." "All days are nights to see till I see thee, And nights bright days when dreams do show thee me." This anxious wish and its accompaniment of disembodied visitation now finds expression in 44: "If the dull substance of . . . [the poet's] flesh were thought," no "injurious distance" could thwart him; but he is not made of thought, whose nimbleness "can jump both sea and land"—he is "so much of earth and water wrought," that he "must attend time's leisure. . . , Receiving naught by elements so slow But heavy tears. . . ." Linked syntactically with 44, sonnet 45 proceeds from the "slow" elements of earth and water to "the other two, slight air and purging fire." The first, air, is the poet's thought, "the other [his] desire." When these two "quicker" elements are gone in "embassy of love" to the friend, the poet's "life," "being made of four" and left "with two alone," sinks to melancholy until air and fire return to recount the youth's "fair health" (compare the impalpable visitation in 43). The poet is then joyful but "straight grow[s] sad" as he sends air and fire back in a new embassy. There is no reason to dispute the Q order 43-4, and there is no question that 45 follows. But what of 50-51? If, tentatively at this point, we remove sonnets 46 through 49, the theme of 43 and the theme, imagery, and phrasing of 44-5 are assumed by 50-51 with a directness that compels recognition. "How *heavy* do I journey on the way" (50.1); the tired beast plods "to bear that *weight* in me" (50.5-6). Compare these lines with 44.13-14: *"heavy* tears," and with 45.7-8: "my life . . . *sinks down."* Note "on the *way*" (50.1) and "stop my *way* (44.2);

"Thus far the *miles are measured*" (50.4) and "to leap large *lengths of miles*" (44.10). The *"dull* substance" of the poet's flesh (44.1), heavy and spiritless, now becomes imaged in the poet's *"dull* bearer" (51.2), the "beast" that "plods *dully* on" (50.5-6; Q "duly"), that answers *"heavily"* the poet's "spur" on the reluctant course away from his friend. On this outward journey love can excuse the poor beast's plodding, but what excuse will love find for slowness in the return? "Then should I spur, though *mounted on the wind"* (51.7). Compare the air-borne motion here with the thought-air equation of 45.1-3 which stems from the "nimble thought" that can "jump both sea and land" (44.7). "Then can no horse with my *desire* keep pace, Therefore *desire* . . . Shall neigh—*no dull flesh*—in his *fiery* race" (51.9-11). Recall again the *"dull* substance of my *flesh"* (44.1) and the equation of "desire" and "fire" (45.1-3). Finally, note the *slow–woe, slow–go* rhymes in the couplets of 44 and 51.

Some of these echo-links may be incidental but most of them are inseparable from the identity of theme and progress of thought in 43-5>50-51. They effect a continuity which no attentive reader, I should say, could regard as accidental. They reproduce, moreover, just the sort of straight-line development, enhanced by incremental repetition and variation, which we find in sonnets 1-17, in other existing Q groups, and in the eleven-sonnet series which I have sought to restore in SSG.

What can be the editorial reason for retaining sonnets 46-9 in the midst of such an apparently authentic and consecutive group? This is the Q order, but again, Q has no authority respecting arrangement except where the sequence is self-justifying. Sonnets 46-7 do speak of absence and bodiless visitation in absence, but in an elaborately new context which smothers that of 44-5>50-51. Besides (for what it is worth), in 46-7 the friend, not Shakespeare, seems to be traveling (47.11). At first glance sonnet 48 has a fair claim for retention; in it the poet travels, and the opening line closely resembles the opening line of 50. Yet, as in 49, the dominant note of 48 is alienation, a subject not even present by implication in the concentrated group we are considering.

The case against keeping sonnets 46-9 in their Q order is simply that their presence cancels the extensive interconnection between 43-5 and 50-51. Four sonnets intervening between 45 and 50 negate completely the thematic unity, thought development, and echo-linkage which we have observed, and any poet would know this to be their effect. For that matter, even one intervening sonnet (48, if allowed to stand) which introduces a new theme would go far toward such a disruption. Finally, anticipating the objection that 43-5 and 50-51 could be 'companion-pieces' separated by 46-9, one must say that the separation under these circumstances would be equally destructive of the poet's art.

Relocation of Sonnets 46-7 with 24. If they belong together these three sonnets spin out an elusive conceit. We have the friend's picture (24) with the poet's eye as painter, his heart as the canvas or "table," and his body as a perspective-frame. There is a legal dispute, with a jury ("tenants to the heart"), over rights of the eye and heart to the picture (46), and an accord or settlement between plaintiff and defendant (47). The general idea is clear enough, but the perspective (pun intended) shifts in such a way that it is hard to settle specific meanings. Of the eye and heart in 46.3-4, for example, which is subject and which object? If the picture is "stelled" on the heart and hangs in the bosom (24) why should eye presume (47.6) to invite heart to a feast of gazing on the heart's own possession? Such questions have ready but conflicting answers, and the game is scarcely worth the trouble. The sequence can be read 24, 46-7; or 46-7, 24. Brooke (1936) kept 24 apart, declaring that 46-7 refer to a real picture, 24 to a metaphorical one. On the same grounds I suggest that the three may belong together with 24 concluding the series: thus the friend's *"true"* picture would finally be the one in the poet's "bosom" (24.6-7), which would supplant the physical portrait of 46-7. This reading implies a beginning *in medias res* (with 46), hardly an unusual procedure. It has the advantage of minimizing much of the contradiction and confusion.

We can be sure, in any event, that 46-7 belong together, and I agree with Pooler and others that 24 may be integral with them. Yet, if it is not, this much can be said: examination of Shakespeare's 154 sonnets will show that the three in question have no clear relation to any other sonnet or sonnet group, and no violence is done by placing them together but apart from the rest. If 24 is not integral with 46-7, it is at least a likely companion-piece or sequel.

The ultimate placing of sonnet 48 must be discussed in a later essay. For the present I shall merely suggest its graphic likeness to 52. Although the two sonnets when left by themselves express antithetical ideas, their close similarity of motif and imagery makes it likely that they belong to the same group. Should this prove true, the argument against interrupting and spoiling 43-5>50-51 by leaving 48 in its Q position will be strongly reinforced.

Relocation of Sonnet 49 with 87-90. Rearrangers have linked 49 with 88 but have not included 87 in the scheme. Here, the relationship between 49 and 87 will be a key to the relocation of 49, by multiple evidence, with the group 87-90.

1. In 87-90 the poet releases his friend from all allegiance and, declaring himself unworthy, resolves to justify an end to the relationship. Sonnet 49 plainly fits this situation but, since similar notions appear elsewhere, more specific parallels are needed. At the outset of 87-90 the crisis is presented in terms of a legal issue, argued in legal terms, with the poet as his friend's advocate. Sonnet 87: "The *charter* of thy worth gives thee *releasing*"; "My *bonds* in thee are all *determinate*"; "how do I *hold* thee but by thy *granting?*"; "my *patent* back again is swerving"; "thy great gift, upon *misprision* growing, Comes home again." In 88 there are terms of lay discourse which are also legal terms: "wherein I am *attainted,*" "for thy *right.*" Now, sonnet 49: "Whenas thy love hath cast his utmost sum, *Called to that audit* . . ."; "When love, *converted* . . ." (compare the common-law term 'conversion'); and the concluding couplet, "To leave poor me thou hast the strength of *laws,* Since why to love I can *allege no cause*"—a lawyer's summation of the whole matter.

2. Additional terminology of this kind is combined with phrasal echo. Compare "*Upon thy part,* I can set down . . ." (88.6), supplemented by "Against thy *reasons* making no defense" (89.4), with "To guard the *lawful reasons on thy part*" (49.12); also note "*reasons*" in 49.8. In the sense found here, these two terms do not occur elsewhere in the Sonnets. Likewise echoed is some nonlegal phrasing; "I will *acquaintance strangle and look strange,* Be absent from thy *walks*" (89.8-9) closely resembles "When thou shalt *strangely pass,* And *scarcely greet me*" (49.5-6).

3. Expressing exactly parallel ideas, sonnets 88 and 49 have rhetorically parallel opening lines: "*When* thou shalt be disposed to set me light, And place my merit in the *eye of scorn*" (88); "*Against that time,* if ever that time come, When I shall see thee *frown on my defects*" (49). This may be the reason for Pooler's brief observation relating the two sonnets.

4. No evidence of the kind we have considered supports an alternative relocation of sonnet 49. The friend's alienation justified by the poet is a theme present in several groups other than 87-90, but in all of them there are elements fundamentally distinct from the subject or tone found here. On first impression 49 seems to follow nicely after 35 in the Q series 33-6; there is alienation, and the poet (35.10-11) vindicates his friend in the kind of legal language present in 87 and 49. The great difference, however, is that 34-6 are sonnets which depict the young man as affectionately contrite over an injury to the poet, and the poet as tenderly concerned only lest the friend dishonor himself. With its clear note of a

time when the more fortunate of the two shall despise the other, and of a despair tinged with recrimination, sonnet 49 is very far from 33-6. For similar reasons it deviates from 95-6 (which I shall later link with 36). Sonnets 40-42, also concerned with alienation, are likewise quite out of tone with 49 and 87-90. Nor does 49 agree with the subject and attitude (sweet resignation) of the rival-poet sequence, 76-86. Sonnets 109-21 refer to alienation, but there the poet has sinned against the friend and is repentantly returning to his good graces. Except for 87-90, the only sonnets with which 49 fits are the linked 57-8; they share its hurt despair, and 58 speaks of the friend's "charter," a legalism that parallels the "charter of thy worth" in 87, thus echoing a primary note of 49. Sonnets 57-8, however, are distinct from neighboring sonnets and plainly belong together. It is quite possible that they connect in some way with 87-90 and 49, but if so the likely relationship is one of a pair in proximity with a longer series.

THE GROUP 33-5>40-42 AND SONNETS 36-9

Here again a number of sonnets so break the continuity of a group that their Q placement must be questioned. Brooke and a number of other editors recognize this, but few sonnet problems call for the detailed reconsideration that will be attempted here. Beginning the interrupted group, sonnets 33-4 introduce as a sun-obscuring cloud the "stain" of the young man's sin against the poet. He has repented; but of what relief, the poet asks, is the "offender's sorrow" to one who must bear "the strong offense's cross?" In a quick resolution by couplet (34.13-14) the question is settled: "Ah, but those tears are pearl which thy love sheds, And they are rich, and ransom all ill-deeds." Sonnet 35 resumes the note of forgiveness, echoing 33 and 34 with "clouds" which "stain both moon and sun." "All men make faults," including the poet who corrupts himself by "salving" his friend's misdeed (a further echo—compare "salve," 34.7). Then in another resolving couplet (35.13-14) appears the first descriptive hint of the youth as transgressor: "that sweet thief which sourly robs from me." What the robbery actually is will become clear in sonnet 40, but preparation for the disclosure begins in 35. There the poet undertakes to justify the wrong he has suffered; assuming a legal role, he declares himself both "thy adverse party" and "thy advocate," who "'gainst myself a lawful [i.e. legal] plea *commence*." Readers of the Sonnets will recall the elaborate tongue-in-cheek casuistry of 40-42 which concludes in a dramatic turn of couplet similar to those of 34 and 35, that since "my friend and I are one," "she loves but me alone." But it is not well understood that sonnets 40-42 complete the "plea" which the poet avowedly begins in sonnet 35. At the same time they reveal progressively the nature of the "robbery" announced but not explained in 35.14. And the reference back is unmistakable: "I do forgive thy robb'ry, gentle thief" (40.9) echoes "that sweet thief which sourly robs from me" (35.14). In addition, the "loss"–"cross" note of 34.10-12 recurs with identical rhyme in the corresponding lines of sonnet 42. (In 34 Q misprints "crosse" as "losse" in line 12.)

Only from the complete text can we properly estimate the coherence of this group. A poet who was also a playwright would have understood that the presence of sonnets 36-9 in the midst of it spoils the whole design. For Pooler it was "not easy to believe" that 35 and 36 are connected, and Brooke (p. 27 of his edition) removed 36-9 from the Q sequence, finding their sincere regard for Shakespeare's friend incompatible with 33-5 and 40-42, which "deal so poignantly with his offense." I prefer to support rearrangement on other grounds: an elaborate change of subject in 36-9[2] destroys obvious dramatic and poetic development, development of the kind found in recognized Q sequences. Again, if we dismiss this conclusion as subjective, we assume the alternative of a poet who could put into full play the extraordinary logic of his art and at the same time wreck it, not by inadvertence but by composing several extraneous sonnets. Whatever an editorial policy based on this assumption may be, it is hardly conservative. Yet, there is a conservative alternative here, a recognition that Shakespeare after all may have composed and transmitted these sonnets in their Q order: first 33-5, then 36-9, and finally, as a continuation of 33-5, sonnets 40-42. But if we could know that this happened what should govern a modern edition? Should order of composition or transmission prevail over internal evidence of the author's unifying intent?

If sonnets 36-9 are in doubtful order their possible relocation becomes a problem. A simple solution would be to place them, as Brooke does, after rather than before 40-42. In effect, this may be the solution but it will be complicated by the disposition of additional sonnets.

Relocation of Sonnet 36 with 95-6. Relocation of 37-9. The Q order, 95 after 94, upsets good sense in a manner hardly convertible into paradox, and thus it is apparent that the pair 95-6 is questionably placed. Presumably addressed to the young man, the last two lines of 94 warn

---

[2] These sonnets do contain the note of identity between poet and friend which is carried to a resolution in 40-42. But 38-9 depart entirely from the theme of sin and injury committed by the youth, and 37 joins them in breaking continuity between the beginning of the poet's "plea" in 35 and its continuation in 40-42.

him that "sweetest things turn sourest by their deeds; Lilies that fester smell far worse than weeds." The first lines of 95 then impulsively tell him, "How sweet and lovely dost thou make the shame Which like a canker in the fragrant rose, Doth spot the beauty of thy budding name." The friend as festering lily is something less than kin to the friend as festering rose. Sonnet 94 concludes that evil linked with beauty is doubly noxious; without transition, sonnet 95 declares that the youth's evil linked with his beauty becomes sweet and lovely. It will not do to call this a dramatic shift in point of view, for fatuity is never dramatic. Nevertheless, 95-6 can be read as an independent pair, and for this reason even the absurdity of the 94-5 transition does not itself establish a displacement—although we can be reasonably sure that the Q editing, which invites continuous reading, is at odds with authorial intention. Fortunately, there is good evidence for a relocation of 95-6 in combination with 36, a possibility which editors and rearrangers have neglected. Thus joined, the three sonnets become related as a series to the larger group 33-5>40-42.

1. First, we need to consider the relationship, just mentioned, between these sonnets and the larger group. Sonnets 95-6 point to the friend's "shame" or sin, which is the general subject of 33-5. Other sonnets, of course, deal with this, including 93-4 from which I propose to separate 95-6, but the latter agree with 33-5>40-42 in combining two much more specific notes: both sequences strike a nice balance between censure and justification, and both resolve alienation between friend and poet by an appeal to identity or oneness (42 and 96.13-14).

2. Sonnets 95-6 also appear related to 33-5>40-42 through verbal echo, much of it admittedly conventional: "rose," "bud," "canker" (35.1-4 and 95.1-3); "sweet," "sweets" (35.14 and 95.1-4); "faults," "fault" (35.5, 9 and 96.1,3,4); "shame" (34.9 and 95.1). And in 40.13 there is "lascivious grace in whom all ill well shows," which is paralleled not only in idea but in the combined phrasing—"lascivious," "grace"—of 95.5-8 and 96.1-4.

3. Although it interrupts the continuity of 33-5>40-42 and is therefore in questionable order, sonnet 36 should retain at least its proximity to that series. Some interpreters of 36 read it as declaring the poet's guilt and the young man's innocence, an outright reversal of the idea in 33-5. But the "blots that do with me [the poet] remain" (line 3) imply a guilt shared by the poet and his friend, which is what 40-42 describe. It is interesting, too, that sonnet 36 can be understood in two ways; it can be read 'straight,' reflecting the mutual attachment of two men, and as playful *double entente* in which "undivided loves," "two loves," and "separa-

ble spite" all refer to the love of poet and friend for the same woman—again their mutual sin which leaves "blots" with both, and requires that they remain apart in order to avoid public spectacle and public surmise. This reading of the sonnet is in tune with Shakespeare's light touch when dealing with identity-in-division (40-42 and 37-9). Still, the reading does not justify retention of 36 in the midst of 33-5>40-42, for its very complication would add to the disruption, previously discussed, which the Q sequence inflicts upon that group.[3]

Sonnet 36 has a further claim to proximity with 40-42. Its interesting phrase "separable spite" (line 6) describing the divisive force between poet and friend has a parallel in the equally arresting "Kill me with spites, yet we must not be foes" (40.14).

4. There is finally the evidence of pointed linkage between 36 and 95-6. A minor but by no means negligible echo is "blots"–"blot," denoting sin or disgrace (36.3 and 95.11; but note 92.13). Outweighing all else, however, is the word-for-word duplication of couplet in 36 and 96: "But do not so. I love thee in such sort, As thou being mine, mine is thy good report [i.e. reputation]." If 95-6 are followed by 36, this couplet echo will complete a pattern already begun by the reference to "ill report" in 95.8, and the scheme will thus bridge all three sonnets.

Here we meet difficulties, some of them bibliographical. The exact repetition of last lines could be a scribe's error of eye. If so, the two sonnets must once have been close together, which is my conclusion but not the reasoning behind it. With sixty sonnets intervening in the Q copy, the duplication is not a likely 1609 printing error.[4] The theory that

---

[3] Although there is a possible echo of "undivided loves" (36.2) in "Take all my loves" (40.1), which would carry the *double entente* of 36 into 40, the linkage would provide does not match the pointed run-on between the last line of 35 and the first line of 40. With its excursion into the wisdom of parting and of outward estrangement, 36 introduces a new subject in a convoluted fashion, and thus separates the beginning of the poet's plea on the friend's behalf in 35 from its pointed continuation in 40-42.

[4] No matter what order of typesetting is assumed, whether seriatim by pages or by formes (see G. W. Williams, "Setting by Formes in Quarto Printing," *Studies in Bibliography*, 11, 1958), it is most unlikely that in setting sig. G1 the compositor set the first seven lines of that page (sonnet 96.6-12); then erroneously turned to a much earlier point in the copy (corresponding to sig. C4v in Q) to set the couplet of sonnet 36 as 96.13-14; and finally returned to the correct point in the copy to resume setting the next following sonnet (97)—all this without being aware of his error, or (if aware) without correcting it. But even if there were evidence that a printer's error might readily have occurred, we should still have to explain how a mistakenly repeated couplet could make not ordinary but perfect sense in both sonnets which contain it. In checking these matters, a reader is sure to be interested when he sees that the last nine lines of 36 stand at the top of C4v and the last nine lines of 96 correspondingly at the top of G1. Further examination will show, however, that this line-division, or a close approximation of it, occurs in Q at the top of every fifth page. Uniform length of sonnets with close uniformity in number of lines per page is, of course, the explanation.

Thorpe's editor supplied a missing couplet by copying one from another sonnet is gratuitous. Brooke accepted the couplet repetition as it stands, regarding it as a repeated epigram which in sonnet 96 would have stirred the friend's memory of past events and of the earlier sonnet's reference to them.

Historically, a linkage of 36 and 96 has been resisted manfully, probably on the ground that proximity of two sonnets with identical couplets amounts to poetic crudity. This depends altogether on the poet's handling of the repetition, and in any event the device is not antecedently improbable. Actually, the most telling point here is the aptness and grace which couplet repetition achieves when 36 follows 96. Both sonnets continue the substance of 33-5>40-42—the divisive "blot" or stain, with mutual identity resolving the division. In each of the two sonnets the repeated couplet underscores the common theme and a distinct variation of it. Sonnet 96: do not dishonor yourself by intimacy with others (the "gazers"), for "mine is thy good report"; sonnet 36: do not dishonor yourself by intimacy with me ("public kindness"), for "mine is thy good report."

Disposition of sonnet 36 has thus involved a disposition of 95-6. I suggest a linkage of the three in the order 95, 96, 36 and their placement as a series immediately after 33-5>40-42. Sonnets 37-9 can readily follow. The result will be three successive poems on a common theme, identity-in-division between friend and poet. The first of these speaks of the youth's sin against the poet and involves the two in a triangular 'arrangement'; the second dwells upon the youth's loss of reputation and the poet's share of mutual guilt. Both poems settle the divisive wrongdoing by appealing to spiritual or psychic oneness. The second, however, introduces the need for physical separation (36). The third series, 37-9, turns to the poet's continued praise of his friend, complicates this by resumption of the common theme, psychic identity, and meets the predicament exactly after the fashion of the second poem by calling, again in the final sonnet (39), for physical separation.

THE GROUP 109-12>117-21

The problem here is again that of the two interrupted groups previously discussed. Since a number of rearrangers, including Brooke, have noted the breaking of this series by sonnets 113-16, I shall simply mention it in the belief that an attentive reader can determine for himself whether the two pairs, 113-14 and 115-16, nullify an ordered development and a harmony of detail. If they do, another group should be restored and another instance of Shakespearian coherence noted. I shall not attempt at this time to relocate what I take to be the two intrusive pairs.

So far, we have considered the restoration of three groups disrupted in Q by doubtfully placed sonnets of Class 1. We have also considered relocation of sonnets which break two of the three groups. The pair 46-7 has been joined with 24 in an independent series; and 49 has been placed with 87-90. Sonnet 36 has been connected with 95-6, and 37-9 moved intact, thus forming two series related to and following 33-5>40-42. Next in order are some questionably placed sonnets of Class 2, those which simply contradict adjacent sonnets, or depart from them, without disrupting a group.

SONNETS 32, 81 AND THE Q GROUP 76-86

There are good reasons for relocating sonnet 32 with the 'rival-poet' series, sonnets 76-86. Perhaps the most interesting of these is that the linkage 'rehabilitates' sonnet 81. Commonly considered at odds with the group, 81 no longer appears so when it is joined with 32. This relationship with its unifying result has not been recognized.

1. It is possible to 'justify' 32 in its Q order by observing that it refers to the poet's approaching death after 31 has recalled the death of friends. One can also surmise with Pooler that 32 is "a dedication of the previous five sonnets, and perhaps others now out of place." Such explanations of the 1609 text are made doubtful, however, by the entirely new theme which 32 introduces: other poets with "style" have "outstripp'd" Shakespeare's "poor rude lines." This departure from the theme of preceding sonnets is matched by a lack of tangible connection between 32 and sonnets which follow it.

Sonnet 81 seems anomalous in the midst of 76-86, a group which, aside from the clearly misplaced 77, discourses on a rival poet and other versifiers with "compounds strange." The theme is invidious, stressing the poet's flagging muse and his anxiety lest others usurp his place. Sonnet 81 intrudes here with a serene promise of immortality in verse: "You still shall live—such virtue hath my pen. . . ." In the middle of the series as it stands, point of view is vacantly changed and development interrupted.

2. Sonnet 32, which lacks relevance in its Q position, expresses the rivalry among poets depicted in 76-86. This agreement in subject is unusually pointed: the rivalry is part of a new "age" or fashion, and our poet's simplicity contrasts with the ingenuity of his competitors. Sonnet

32 also voices a second theme of the group, which is set forth in 76: "Why . . . do I not glance aside To new-found methods . . . ?" "O know, sweet *love,* I always write of *you* And *you and love are still my argument."* (See SSG, p. 340). With this compare 32.7, 14.

3. In tangible theme 32 fits no group other than 76-86. Certain other sonnets express ideas which border on those of 32, but a comparison of these approximate parallels with the thematic likeness between 76-86 and 32 will show the difference between peripheral and close relationship. To check this, note the less pointedly related sonnets: 38, 59, 67, 71-2, 102-3, 105-6, 125.

4. In addition to voicing the themes of 76-86, sonnet 32 echoes language of the series: "My sick Muse" (79.4), "My tongue-tied Muse" (85.1), and " 'Had my friend's [the poet's] Muse grown with this growing age . . .' " (32.10); "my rude ignorance" (78.14) and "these poor rude lines" (32.4). If these similarities are thought conventional, compare further: "Making his [the rival's] *style* admired everywhere" (84.12), "In others' works thou dost but mend the *style"* (78.11), and " 'Theirs [the rival poet's lines] for their *style* I'll read . . ." (32.14). There is also "reserve" (85.3 and 32.7); in both cases the reference is to poems and the word means 'to preserve.' "Style" and "reserve" occur nowhere else in the Sonnets. Although this evidence is appreciable, none of the parallels cited matches a final one: "Why with *the time* [the new age of poetic fashion] do I not glance aside . . . ?" (76.3), "Some fresher stamp of *the time-bettering days"* (82.8), and "Compare them [the poet's lines] with *the bettering of the time"* (32.5). Again the similarity of usage in 81 and 32 is unique.

5. Thus far we have viewed 81 as a displaced sonnet, and it appears to be one until 32 is added to the group. When 32 is placed after 81, a surprising change takes place. The two sonnets form a unified pair, and in the new context 81 now fits very well in its Q position. Sonnet 81 commences, "[Either] I shall live your epitaph to make, Or you survive when I in earth am rotten." The sonnet then elaborates upon the first alternative, the poet's survival and his "gentle verse" as a "monument" to the dead friend. But what of the second alternative? In its new position 32 completes the either-or contingency with rhetorical balance. Sonnet 81 begins: either I "shall live" or *"you survive . . ."*; sonnet 32 opens, *"If thou survive. . . ."* After this linkage with 81 by syntax and echo, 32 then brings the survivorship note of 81 into a direct relationship, hitherto lacking, with the rival-poet theme expressed by other sonnets of the group. And we may recall that it does so with graphic parallels of sub-

theme, imagery, and phrasing. It is important to understand that the primary reasons for placing 32 with 76-86 (paragraphs 2-4) are quite independent of those for joining 81 and 32 as a pair. Thus one set of reasons corroborates the other.

SONNETS 69-70 AND THE Q GROUP 91-4

The pair 69-70 contradicts sonnets which precede it in Q and has no connection with those that follow. Unless intended as a separate two-stanza poem, it is out of place. Sonnets 66-8 depict Shakespeare's friend as the only pattern of truth and beauty surviving in a now degenerate world of "infection" (corruption). Sonnets 69-70, however, present him as so prone to corruption that his "fair flower" exudes "the rank smell of weeds." Further, in 66-8 the young man stands apart from all others, but in 69-70 he has become "common" (69.14). No two sonnet series could be more antithetical.[5] Between 69-70 and ensuing sonnets there is no contradiction; there is simply a complete change of subject, which means that 69-70 can be separated from 71-4 with no disturbance of the text. Connective elements between this pair and 91-4 are extensive and pointed. Although rearrangers have occasionally linked 69 with 94, they apparently have not observed the plan of connection which we shall consider.

1. The theme of 91-4 is the friend's beauty which can deceptively hide an inner corruption. In the Q order, sonnets 95-6 'continue' this theme but do so with an unsettling breach of logic (pp. 123-4). Sonnets 69-70 will continue it without contradiction. And in the process, 69 will remove still another awkwardness from the Q sequence. In 93 it is said that the friend's outward mien can reveal nothing but innocence, no matter what evil may lie beneath. Sonnets 95-6, however, assume that the "vices" which underlie innocent appearance have been revealed widely, that they are common knowledge. Sonnet 69 replacing 95 provides transition here instead of inconsistency: it notes first that the friend's outward qualities convey nothing but goodness, thus expanding 93, and then explains in due course that a look beyond outward traits ("By *seeing farther* than the eye hath shown") will disclose evil in the youth's "mind" and "deeds."

2. In completing the theme of 91-4, sonnets 69-70 supplement its imagery. There is the 'heart' note—"Want nothing that the thought of hearts can mend" (69.2), and "thou alone kingdoms of hearts shouldst owe" (the vivid conclusion of 70)—an emphasis which follows well from 93.4, 7, 11: "thy heart in other place," "the false heart's history," "thy

---

[5] Besides, 66-8 show strong signs of belonging to a distinct group. See SSG. For a discussion of Brooke's questionable linkage of 69-70 with 66-8, see SSG, p. 347.

heart's workings." This is a repetition not so much of apposite idea as of motif. Thought and phrase combine, however, in another connective scheme. Lines 9-14 of sonnet 94 introduce the "summer's *flower*" which, should it meet with infection, will fall in dignity below the "basest *weed*." "For sweetest things turn sourest by their *deeds*; *Lilies* that fester *smell far worse than weeds.*" Sonnet 69 carries both the idea and its image to a direct application: others will measure the friend not by his beauty but by his *"deeds,"* and to his "fair *flower*" will add *"the rank smell of weeds."*

Pertinent and detailed as these parallels may be, they invite the objection that infected flowers or cankered roses grow everywhere in the Elizabethan sonnet garden. I am convinced, however, that it is good practice not only to question the use of commonplaces, but also, on the second convolution of skepticism, to question the questioning. In this instance it pays. Examination will show that the infected-flower note with a "weeds-deeds" accompaniment occurs nowhere in the Sonnets save in 94 and 69.

3. Between 93-4 and 69-70 there are further and stronger links of the kind just described. After stressing the friend's comeliness as a concealment of any inner evil or unfaithfulness, sonnet 93 ends, "How like *Eve's apple* doth thy beauty grow If thy sweet virtue answer not thy *show.*" Pointedly in its opening lines, sonnet 94 continues the thought and echoes the word: "They that have power to hurt and will do none, That do not do the thing they most do *show,* Who *moving others* are themselves as stone, Unmoved, cold, and to *temptation* slow." Thus the "show," which in 93.13 is like Eve's apple, is outward temptation again in 94 which speaks of that which privileged and good men "most do show" (invite) but "do not do." Lines 3-4 which amplify lines 1-2 leave no doubt of this meaning.[6] Now, if 69-70 are allowed to follow 94, the verbal link just described will be extended by continuation of 93's couplet rhyme in the couplets of both 69 and 70; the rhyme is *grow–show* and *show–grow* in 93 and 69, *show–owe* in 70. Nor will this complete the linking process, for there is an accompaniment: "If thy sweet virtue *answer not* thy show" (93), "why thy odor *matcheth not* thy show" (69), and "If some suspect of ill *masked not* thy show" (70). Finally, these interlocking couplets express a progressive logic: if your character and

---

[6] In order to rescue Shakespeare from allegiance to the "cold" and "unmoved" who move others, this sonnet has occasionally been found ironical. By his own phrasing, however, Shakespeare appears to admire men who are "to temptation slow"—hardly a priggish sentiment. In any event, when tempted to find irony in sober Elizabethan moralizing, we too should be "slow," no matter how stuffy we may find it.

appearance should not agree . . . (93); what it is that prevents their agreement (69); if only they did agree . . . (70).

4. In composite detail the connective elements described in paragraph 3 are shared only by 93-4 and 69-70. In one of its lines, however, sonnet 40 duplicates the "show" note: "Lascivious grace, in whom all ill well shows" (40.13). This is not surprising, since the group containing 40 (33-5>40-42) likewise deals with a friend whose good looks are at once his peril and a cause for the poet's alarm. In fact, there are a number of parallels, all arising from this situation, which tend to relate 33-5>40-42, 95-6>36, and 91-4>69-70. We have already considered a relation between the first two of these groups (pp. 122-6). It is quite possible that the third belongs in some way with them.

If the conclusions of earlier discussion can be trusted, eighteen sonnets are doubtfully placed in Q. Five of these are 'singles' separated from companion sonnets and now found in isolation: 24, 32, 36, 48, 49. Ten are in pairs that in spite of apparent displacement remain intact as pairs: 46-7, 69-70, 95-6, 113-14, 115-16. The remainder form a series of three: 37, 38, 39. Evidence in SSG raises the number of doubtfully placed sonnets to twenty-three by adding three singles: 19, 21, 105, and one intact pair: 100-101. The total thus includes eight singles, six pairs, and one unit of three.

Since questionable sonnet arrangement has been inferred from close reading and literary judgment, it is encouraging that a pattern appears which may tell something about the manner in which disarrangement occurred in the manuscripts. These manuscripts may have been the separate sonnet groups given to the addressee on different occasions, copies of them, or copies of copies. In the copying process, moreover, separate groups may have been brought together in single collections. Varied, successive dislocation must have occurred, and in the course of it six pairs of sonnets apparently could become scattered but still survive as pairs. The number of sonnets dispersed in this way, plus the number dislocated in one series of three, is greater than the number of sonnets disarranged as singles. The proportion is 15 to 8. A plausible way of explaining this is to assume loose-leaf manuscripts with sonnets often appearing two, and sometimes three, to a leaf. If a pair is on one leaf it will remain as a pair no matter how extensive the disturbance of leaves (for example, 69-70 or 95-6). On the other hand, if a pair occupies successive leaves it may easily lose its identity in the shuffle (for example, 81, 32).

Sonnets appearing three to a leaf may be the explanation not only of 37-9 being displaced as an intact series of three, but of 33-5>40-42 being split in the middle with both fragments (threes) undisturbed.

The manuscript conditions thus implied by sonnet displacement appear to square so far with those implied by sonnet relocation. Relocation has also rested upon literary evidence; yet none of the restored pairs suggests an original sonnet group with abnormal manuscript leafing— such as erratic alternation of two-to-a-leaf and one-to-a-leaf arrangements. Sonnets 69-70 (hypothetically two-to-a-leaf) fit at the end of 91-2/93-4 (also explainable as two-to-a-leaf). With a similar consistency, sonnets 100-101 (SSG) fit before 63-8 in an even-numbered sequence divisible two-to-a-leaf. Sonnets 95-6 appear to belong before 36, a single, which suggests an original series of three, with the first two on one leaf and the third or concluding sonnet on a leaf by itself. The same arrangement can account for 46-7>24.

Sonnets 32 and 49 are not so readily explained. Both appear displaced as singles, and both have seemed to fit *in the midst* of existing Q groups— 32 after 81 within 76-86, and 49 after 88 within 87-90. The original sonnet arrangement in these two groups may have been one-to-a-leaf and, if so, the separation of a single sonnet like 32 or 49 is easy to understand. Existing manuscripts, however, indicate that a two-to-a-leaf order was more likely, at least in a sizable group like 76-86. In that event the loss of a single sonnet from the middle of a series, with its reappearance elsewhere, becomes far less plausible. This implies a possible fault in our relocation of 32 and 49, and brings to mind a principle already noted in the discussion of pairs. No matter what the sonnet content by leaves in a manuscript group, the concluding sonnet, if 'left over,' may be on a leaf by itself. Thus if 32 and 49 are terminal sonnets the trouble will disappear, a possibility that calls for re-examination of the 76-86 and 87-90 groups.

We may recall that strong evidence points to 32 as a continuation of 81 (pp. 128-9). Hence, if 32 is to be the end-sonnet left over in a two-to-a-leaf arrangement,[7] 80-81 (on a single leaf) should precede it, possibly following 85-6, the terminal sonnets in Q. This is just what a second look at these sonnets tends to confirm. Note that 86 introduces "the *proud* full *sail* of his great verse" which is echoed by "the *proudest sail*" of 80.6, the beginning of an eight-line metaphor of the two poets as ships.

---

[7] If the clearly intrusive 77 is removed, the 76-86 series with 32 will come to eleven sonnets, a number consistent with an original two-to-a-leaf arrangement, plus an end-leaf with the concluding sonnet.

Surprising additional echoes are "spirit" as an epithet for the rival poet (86.5 and 80.2), and "tongue-tied" (85.1 and 80.4). Finally, no sonnet could serve better than 32 in concluding the group. Sonnet 32, therefore, is in far more likely position at the end of the 76-86 series than it is in the middle. The order of leaves would be: . . . 85-6/80-81/32 (end-leaf).

It is hard to believe that reappraisal of sonnet 49 would yield similar results; yet it does. Although there is unusually good evidence for placing 49 with the group 87-90, its position after 88 (see pp. 120-21) again invites an assumption of sonnets arranged one-to-a-leaf; otherwise, how would 49 alone have vanished from the 'interior' of the group to reappear elsewhere? Here, as before, we encounter difficulty. In the manuscripts I have seen, both sides of the leaves were generally used; a one-sonnet-to-a-leaf arrangement must have been rare. But if 49, like 32, is an end-sonnet, a two-to-a-leaf order—87-8/89-90/49 (end-leaf)—becomes possible. Is it likely? At first it would appear that 49 cannot come at the end of 87-90, for 90 seems to voice a terminal climax. Rereading, however, will suggest that 49 could aptly end the series as a reflective quieting of the 'outburst' in 90, and as a fine summation of the 'legal' metaphor which dominates the group. Note also the parallel first lines which 90, 49 would have as concluding sonnets: "Then hate me when thou wilt. *If ever* now" (90); "Against that time, *if ever* that time come" (49). Here again literary evidence agrees with the tentative assumptions of manuscript form.

Nevertheless, in view of the likely copying and recopying of manuscripts prior to the 1609 printing, we can hardly expect to account for all anomalies. The three separated singles relocated in SSG appear to disrupt the manuscript leafing order implied by other sonnets in the group. We have seen that the first eight sonnets of the restored series suggest an original two-to-a-leaf arrangement: 100-101 (one leaf), 63-8 (three leaves). This scheme hardly accounts for the last three sonnets— 19, 21, 105—which appear scattered in Q as singles, thus suggesting an original one-to-a-leaf order. Sonnet 105 offers no problem, however, since as the eleventh sonnet it would have been 'left over' on an end-leaf; the trouble lies with 19 and 21. If these two were only consecutive, the two-to-a-leaf hypothesis consistent with the first eight sonnets would hold up nicely in an arrangement of 19, 21 on the next-to-last leaf and 105 by itself on an end-leaf. But 19 and 21 are not consecutive; so we are left with an hypothesis that 'almost' holds. As a tactical measure, perhaps one should claim this as the one flaw which saves a theory from overconfirmation. It may well be. Yet, perversely, I must call attention to the nature of sonnet 20 which separates the two in question. It is wittily obscene and, of all the Sonnets, the one most likely to circulate by itself. A copyist who found it in his possession, and who wished (understandably) to include it in his collection, would have faced two choices. He could have begun or ended his manuscript with the sonnet, or he could have copied it between two other sonnets. Assuming that our copyist and his problem existed, he apparently took the latter course; in any event sonnet 20 came to rest between 19 and 21, two sonnets which belong together (see SSG), and which now have but one sonnet between them. Thus, prior to a copying process which introduced sonnet 20, they could readily have appeared on a single leaf which had been displaced from a two-to-a-leaf manuscript containing the SSG group.

In this essay and in SSG the relocation of sonnets has been controlled by a standard of multiple evidence. It now appears that the results may in turn be controlled by checking them against the manuscript conditions which a given sonnet arrangement implies. What are the prospects? I am sure that my hypothesis of manuscript history can be improved, whether by limitation or expansion, but its ultimate usefulness may be restricted. Had the Sonnets been printed from a single consistent manuscript in which only the leaf-order was disturbed, the text might be restored with comforting objectivity. It is likely, however, that Thorpe's was not a single manuscript, and that his materials represented various histories of disarrangement, copying, and recopying. In addition, Thorpe here and there may have contributed some irresponsible editing. Witness Benson in 1640.

Under these conditions the success of nonliterary evidence may vary widely with different sonnet groups. It is possible that sonnets 127-54, a small, separate, and largely homogeneous collection, will offer good chances of manuscript reconstruction from the evidence of disarrangement.[8] At any rate, in working with it I have sensed two possibilities which should be passed on to anyone willing to take part in this necessary but possibly thankless effort. A two-to-a-leaf arrangement, with one sonnet on each side of a leaf, may explain the transposition of certain sonnets which editors have noted as a flaw in Thorpe's text. A loose leaf simply turned over would account for the reversed order. A two-to-a-leaf hypothesis may also furnish an occasional clue to the order of sonnet

---

[8] Since finishing this essay, I have found additional evidence that sonnets 127-54 suffered disarrangement by two's, which indicates disarrangement of manuscript leaves containing two sonnets each.

groups. Assume two sonnets which are consecutive in Q, and displaced. Assume also that they are unrelated (that is, not paired like 69-70). Despite their lack of apparent connection, they may belong together. From the likelihood that they were inscribed on a single disarranged leaf, it may be inferred, with the help of internal evidence, that the first of them ended one series and the second began another.

These tentative ideas and others like them may be useful in a hoped-for improvement of Shakespeare's text, though ultimately, of course, the evidence of content and style will be controlling. Whether or not the restorations attempted here are accepted, I hope one matter has become clear: that where continuity exists in Q, or where it can be restored by valid means, sonnets will be found linked not by general ideas or single parallels but by distinctive combinations of idea, subordinate idea, parallel phrasing, image recurrence, and cumulative development. If this principle is recognized, a better text should be inevitable, whatever its resemblance to the one I have suggested.

THREE HOMILIES IN
THE COMEDY OF ERRORS

by T. W. Baldwin

1. LUCIANA'S HOMILY ON THE 'SUBJECTION' OF THE
WIFE'S 'STUBBORN WILL,' 2.1.7-25

I N *The Comedy of Errors,* Luciana is trying to impress upon her impatient sister the Christian duty of a wife, as stated typically in "An Homelie of the state of Matrimonie": wives "relinquish the lybertie of their owne rule" (*Certayn Sermons or Homilies,* ed. 1587, sig. 2G7). Luciana had said, "A man is Master of his libertie" (2.1.7). This Adriana resents: "Why should their libertie then ours be more?" (10).

> *Luciana.* Oh, know he is the bridle of your will.
> *Adriana.* There's none but asses will be bridled so.
> *Luciana.* Why, headstrong liberty is lasht with woe.
> (13-15)

This dialogue is partly in terms of *Proverbs,* 26.3 (Bishops' Bible, 1573): "Vnto the horse belongeth a whip, to the asse a bridle: and a rod to the fooles backe." The "headstrong liberty" of the ass gets not only the proverbial bridle for its "will" but is also "lasht with woe," as the horse is with a whip and the fool's back with a rod.[1] But the dialogue is also partly in terms of "An Homelie of the state of Matrimonie," which warns the wife against 'stubborn will': "That wicked vice of stubburne wyll

---

[1] Richmond Noble, in *Shakespeare's Biblical Knowledge* (1935), p. 237, sees a probable application of this passage in *Timon of Athens:* "Page. [*to the Fool*] Why, how now, captain? What do you in this wise company? How dost thou, Apemantus? *Apemantus.* Would I had a rod in my mouth, that I might answer thee profitably!" (2.2.77-80).

and selfe-loue, is more meet to breake & to disseuer the loue of the heart, than to preserue concord" (*Homilies*, sig. 2G4v). Thus Shakespeare reproduces the 'official' position of the *Homilies* on the wife's will, combining it with the figure of the stubborn ass from *Proverbs*.

This prologue on the "headstrong liberty" of "will" introduces a homily on 'subjection' in an ordered Christian world. Noble (p. 107) quotes the Bishops' Bible (the Geneva Bible does not have "subjection"): "*Psalms*, 8.6-8: 'Thou makest him to have dominion of the works of thy hands: and thou hast put all things in subjection under his feet; All sheep and oxen: yea and the beasts of the field; The fowls of the air, and the fishes of the sea: and whatsoever walketh through the paths of the seas.' See also *Genesis*, 1.26 [Bishops' Bible: 'God sayde, Let vs make man in our image, after our lykenesse, & let them haue rule of the fishe of the sea, and of the foule of the ayre, and of cattel, & of al the earth, and of euery creepyng thyng that creepeth vpon the earth']. Cf. *Ecclesiastes*, 3.19B, 'a man hath no preeminence aboue a beast.' "

This biblical triplicity, "the beasts of the field; The fowls of the air, and the fishes of the sea," becomes the rhetorical framework for Luciana's homily on 'subjection':

> There's nothing situate vnder heauens eye,
> But hath his bound in earth, in sea, in skie.
> (16-17)

The corresponding animate creatures in these three divisions are "The beasts, the fishes, and the winged fowles" (18). All these "Are their males subiects, and at their controules" (19). Similarly for man:

> Man more diuine, the Master of all these,
> Lord of the wide world, and wilde watry seas.
> (20-21)

Here, to care for the triplicity, the "wide world" has to serve for the "winged fowles" (which are land-based) as well as for the "beasts." Then the reason for man's mastery is given: he is

> Indued with intellectuall sence and soules,
> Of more preheminence then fish and fowles, . . .
> (22-3)

According to the basic passage that is being echoed, "thou hast put all things in subjection under his feet." Here is the "subjection" (not in Geneva) of all things to man, under his "rule." But the word "preheminence," as Noble points out, is from the Bishops' Bible, *Ecclesiastes,* 3.19: "For it happeneth vnto menne as it doth vnto beastes, euen one condition vnto them both: as the one dyeth, so dyeth the other: yea, they haue both one manner of breath: so that in this, a man hath no preeminence aboue a beast, but are al subdued vnto vanitie." The gloss is also reflected: "There is no difference betwixt a man and a beast, as touchyng the body, which of them both dyeth: but the soule of man lyueth immortally, and the body of man riseth vp agayne by the mighty power of the spirite of God." In his body, man has no "preeminence" over the beasts; the "preeminence" is in "the soule of man," because men are "Indued with intellectuall sence and soules." While the beast is not specifically mentioned here, nevertheless he is the basic member of the triplicity. The Geneva gloss plays down man's distinctive "reason, & iudgement" as ineffectual, as opposed to faith. While Shakespeare also refers to this difference of "intellectuall sence," he does so with a much different emphasis.

Shakespeare's phrase belongs to the psychological jargon of his time, being in terms of the three souls or parts of the soul, "vegetative, sensible or sensitive, rational or reasonable" (OED): "1398 Trevisa Barth., *De P. R.,* 3.7 (1495), 53. In dyuers bodyes ben thre manere soules: vegetabilis, that yeuyth lyfe and noo felinge, as in plantes and rootes; Sensibilis, that yeuyth lyfe and felynge and not reason in vnskylfull beestes; Racionalis, that yeuyth lyf, felyng and reason in men. . . . 1531 Elyot, *Gov.,* 3.24. The thirde parte of the soule is named the parte intellectuall or of understandynge." By virtue of the "intellectuall sence," the third of his souls, man is above all other creatures. So God has given him "preeminence" over them. The natural conclusion to this syllogism of analogy is that men also "Are masters to their females, and their Lords" (24). Shakespeare is here 'varying' the current phrase of lord and master— "called their husbandes Lordes," says the homily. And so the necessary conclusion of the whole is: "Then let your will attend on their accords" (25). The Christian code does not tolerate for a wife "headstrong liberty" of "will." The statement of the Bishops' Bible is typical: "But as the Churche is subiecte vnto Christe, likewise the wiues to their owne husbandes in al thinges" (*Ephesians,* 5.24; cf. *1 Peter,* 3.1, *Colossians,* 3.18, etc.). While the theme of the 'subjection' of all to Christ is actually from the Bible, yet Luciana deduces it from the order of nature "vnder heauens eye," as given in the Bible, with all things under Heaven in subjection to man as the pre-eminent being in the lower hierarchy.

2. ADRIANA'S FIRST HOMILY ON ADULTERY, 2.1.104-15

Twin homilies on adultery by Adriana have caused trouble in posing the major textual cruces of the play. In the first (2.1.104-15), she looks at the case of the adulterer and his 'name' from the point of view of the effect upon the adulterer himself; in the second (2.2.132-48), from the point of view of the effect upon the innocent wife and, through her, of the reflected effect upon the husband also.

The 'matter' and the technical phraseology of Adriana's speeches come from the official homilies of the day, where "The second part of the Sermon against adultery" laments "what corruption commeth to mans soule thorough the sinne of adultery" (*Homilies,* sig. K6), and asks "Is not that treasure, which before all other is most regarded of honest persons, the good fame & name of man and woman, lost through whoredome? . . . Come not the french-pocks, with diuers other diseases, of whoredome?" (sigs. K8-8v). Adriana expresses her fear to Luciana that her husband, because of his association with "minions" (2.1.87), will not "keepe faire quarter with his bed" (108); and she states her commonplace in aphoristic style worthy of grammar-school Cato himself: ". . . no man that hath a name, By falshood and corruption doth it shame" (112-13). The passage immediately in question runs as follows:

> I see the Iewell best enamaled
> Will loose his beautie: yet the gold bides still
> That others touch, and often touching will,
> Where gold and no man that hath a name,
> By falshood and corruption doth it shame: . . .
> (109-13)

Here we have the "good fame & name" of the homily, which will suffer "corruption," as indeed will even the soul itself, by whoredom, as is there stated repeatedly. In the homily, this "treasure" of "good fame & name" cannot be lost without defrauding Christ, who "hath bought vs from the seruitude of the diuell, not with corruptible golde and siluer, but with his most pretious & deare heart bloud" (*Homilies,* sig. K7). This phrase "golde and siluer" appeared prominently also in the original marriage ceremony (1549), along with "Iewels of golde." The wide use of "golde and siluer," "treasure," "Iewels," and so on, in Biblical and liturgical language aided in turn the promised chain in bringing on the figure of the corruptible jewel of enamel and gold, in which Adriana obscures her first homily. This gnomic commonplace, clinched with rhyme in a conventional form, is thus correctly stated, and its meaning is clear: No man of name (fame, reputation, honor)[2] should shame it with the falsehood of "company," as the husband is doing, which will occasion the corruption of whoredom, as the wife fears. The various suggested emendations of this aphorism, beginning with Theobald's (1733) of "By" to "But" (accepted by Malone, 1790), are certainly wrong.

It must be remembered that Adriana's complete simile grows out of a stated situation. She says of her husband that

> His company must do his minions grace,
> Whil'st I at home starue for a merrie looke. . . .
> I know his eye doth homage other-where, . . .
> (87-8, 104)

He has promised her a chain:

> Would that alone, a loue he would detaine,
> So he would keepe faire quarter with his bed: . . .
> (107-8)

This promised chain then introduces the figure of "the Iewell best enamaled" (109), to rhyme with "bed." The falsehood to his marriage vow of company with, and eye-homage to, minions may be tolerated, if only the husband does not proceed to the actual corruption of whoredom. To achieve the comparison between the external of "company," involving the "homage" of the eye to "minions," contrasted with the fundamental of the marriage "bed," the subject of the simile is complicated from the usual gold of good name into a jewel of enamel and gold (109-10), a characteristic figure (see note 2). Stated directly instead of obliquely, the resultant simile becomes: touching will tarnish the beautifying enamel of a jewel, even if it does not affect its gold, "and" falsehood and corruption will shame a name (without reservation). The two parts of the simile are joined, not by "as . . . so," but by the conjunctive "and" (111), which is thus in rendition rhythmically emphatic (as is "man," which is the 'word' of the commonplace, and the contrast with "jewel"). Theobald emended line 112 by suggesting "so" to follow this conjunctive "and" ("and so no man"), in order to amend the meter. However, so far as the technical structure of the simile is concerned, such a "so" is wholly re-

---

[2] For echoing statements on good name, reputation, honor, see *Richard II*, 1.1.177-8; *All's Well That Ends Well*, 4.2.45-51; *Othello*, 2.3.262-5, 3.3.155-61. With the last passage ("Who steals my purse steals trash") may be compared a passage in the *Homilies:* "many times cometh lesse hurt of a theefe, then of a rayling tongue: for the one taketh away a mans good name, the other taketh but his riches, which is of much lesse value and estimation, then is his good name" (sig. L8v). Compare also my *William Shakspere's Small Latine and Lesse Greeke* (1944), 2.275.

dundant. Logically, it could be used in the sense of 'consequently'; but it is not in the text, and there is nothing about the text itself to suggest that it should be there. The suggestion is a redundant addition by way of wrongly inferred improvement.

As to the alleged metrical irregularity of line 112, Malone objected to inserting either Theobald's "so" or Steevens's "though," since "Wear" or "Where" is "used as a dissyllable," a judgment that elicited from Chedworth (1805, p. 47) the pontifically damnatory pronouncement, "some commentators seem to have no ear." But even if a syllable should be missing, the technical structure clears the sense. A modern reader needs only suitable punctuation between "gold" and "and" (111) to set off the two halves of the simile. Failure to recognize this technical structure has been the cause of all our woe.

The "touching" here is stated as by "company" and by "homage" of the eye paid to "minions" (who occupy the place of the professional loose women of the *Menaechmi,* and get localized as the suspected Courtesan). This touching will spoil the beauty of the enamel, even if it does not affect the gold. Similarly, "falshood and corruption" tarnish a name (113). The husband is guilty of "falshood" in company and eye already, and the wife hopes only that he will not proceed to the "corruption" of whoredom against his "bed." For, as the homily warns, whoredom will not merely shame the name, the beautifying enamel; it will corrupt even the soul itself, the very gold of one's being. So in the conclusion no reservation is made for gold, such as had been made in the premise. The corruption of whoredom will be absolute.

The conjunctive "and" of line 112 is certainly correct, joining the two parts of the simile. This, as we have seen, in turn clears the conclusion of the simile. Most of the premise also falls naturally into place:

> I see the Iewell best enamaled
> Will loose his beautie: yet the gold bides still
> That others touch, . . .
>
> (109-11)

The difficulty is in the immediately following lines:

> . . . and often touching will,
> Where gold and no man that hath a name,
> By falshood and corruption doth it shame: . . .
>
> (111-13)

As the text stands, "will" must be completed grammatically by the next precedent verb, "bides." In that case, "often touching" becomes the object, and the statement becomes, 'gold will bide often touching.' Then "Where gold" becomes the condition—'if it really is gold.' The comma following "will" is in keeping with this interpretation, whereas if "often touching" is taken as the subject, and "Where" is replaced by "Wear," then the line should run on, without a comma, as does the preceding line, with which it rhymes. Theobald's suggested "Wear" (after Warburton) reverses the grammatical structure, which is bolstered by the punctuation.

Spence (1894) retained the folio reading "Where" but did not elucidate it or fit it into his freehand interpretation. Cuningham (1907) followed Theobald in reading "Wear gold; and so no man," and devoted an appendix to explanation of "this somewhat vexed and difficult passage." Apparently independently of Spence, J. Dover Wilson (1922) objected vigorously to Theobald's "Wear." "Theobald reads 'wear' for 'where,' and all mod. edd. follow, ignoring the fact that 'touching will wear gold' flatly contradicts 'the gold bides still that others touch.' " Dover Wilson prints "Where," though he obelizes the line and, postulating a cut of two or more rhyming lines, suggests that "the line is hopelessly corrupt." Analyzing the figure a few years later (1927), I argued that "Where" is the correct word, a judgment which our fuller knowledge of the genetics of the figure now justifies. Kittredge (1936) read "Wear" for "Where" (112) and "But" for "By" (113). Hardin Craig (1951) accepts Theobald's "Wear" but obelizes the reading. Peter Alexander (1951) retains the folio text intact, adding only punctuation (most notably, a semicolon after "Where gold"). G. B. Harrison (1952) retains Theobald's "Wear" and interprets the basic figure as one of testing gold by means of a touchstone. C. J. Sisson (1953, and *New Readings in Shakespeare,* 1956, 1.91) breaks the basic structure of the simile to emend "the whole passage," reading "that" for "yet" (110), "yet" for "and" (111), and "Wear" for "Where" (112). It now appears, however, that the passage is not "hopelessly corrupt," even though we might well wish that Shakespeare had paid somewhat less attention to sentential profundity and a little more to sense.[3] But the common background of this bit of wisdom gave him and his contemporaries the sense. I hope they enjoyed and profited.

Adriana charges that her husband has already been false to the enamel of his name by "company" and the "homage" of his "eye," and hopes only that he will not proceed to corrupt the gold of his name and of his

[3] In *Albions England* (ed. 1589) William Warner had admonished the English against the error of mixing similes and sententiousness: "Onely this error may be thought hatching in our English, that to runne on the Letter, we often runne from the Matter: and being ouer prodigall in Similes, wee become lesse profitable in Sentences, and more prolixious to Sense" (sig. ¶4).

soul itself by unfaithfulness to his marriage bed. She laments that she cannot please even his eye, as his "minions" do:

> Since that my beautie cannot please his eie,
> Ile weepe (what's left away) and weeping die.
> (114-15)

Proper sentimental self-pity from time immemorial!

3. ADRIANA'S SECOND HOMILY ON ADULTERY, 2.2.132-48

When Adriana thinks she has cornered her husband but has cornered Antipholus of Syracuse instead, she bestows on him a companion homily on the innocent wife adulterated by her husband, and the reflected effect upon him. The passage is built up as a thrice-stated figure in syllogistic sequence. In the first statement she poses the hypothetical case of her own infidelity:

> How deerely would it touch thee to the quicke,
> Shouldst thou but heare I were licencious?
> And that this body consecrate to thee,
> By Ruffian Lust should be contaminate?
> (2.2.132-5)

In the second statement she claims that, though innocent, she had been contaminated as though she were indeed guilty of adultery:

> I am possest with an adulterate blot,
> My bloud is mingled with the crime of lust: . . .
> (142-3)

And in the third statement she accuses her husband of having effected this contamination:

> For if we two be one, and thou play false,
> I doe digest the poison of thy flesh,
> Being strumpeted by thy contagion: . . .
> (144-6)

His "crime of lust" introduces a "poison" to his "flesh" (there is no "grime," as Dover Wilson and other editors would emend); and this in turn causes a 'contamination,' a 'mingling,' a "contagion" in her "bloud." Thus she is made into a 'strumpet'; his "crime of lust" results in her suffering the "stain" of an "adulterate blot."

It will be remembered that the homily on adultery had been quite specific as to the results of whoredom. "What gift of nature . . . is not corrupted with whoredome? Come not the french-pocks, with diuers other diseases, of whoredome?" (*Homilies*, sig. K8v); and are not wives also "corrupted . . . through whoredome?" The homily on matrimony gives as the first reasons for matrimony "to bring foorth fruit, and to auoide fornication. By which meane a good conscience might be preserued on both parties, in brideling the corrupt inclinations of the flesh, wythin the limits of honestie. For God hath straitly forbidden al whoredome and vncleannesse, and hath from time to time taken greeuous punishment of this inordinate lust, as all stories and ages have declared" (sig. 2G3v). (On the prohibition against "whoredome," see *Hebrews*, 13.4, *1 Corinthians*, 6.9, *Revelation*, 22.15, etc.) So, on the purely physical side, her husband will pass on to Adriana any "poison" of his "flesh," such as the "french-pocks" threatened by the homily; and he will do so because of his "crime of lust"—"inordinate lust," to use the language of the homily, for which God may mete out "greeuous punishment."

"The second part of the Sermon against adultery" says that the first part had shown "finally what corruption commeth to mans soule thorough the sinne of adultery." The second part then quotes various passages of Scripture (the principal being *1 Corinthians*, 6), and continues as follows: "he saith, do ye not know that your bodies are the members of Christ? shall I then take the members of Christe, and make them the members of an whore? God forbid. Do yee not knowe, that hee which cleaueth to an whore, is made one body with her? There shalbe two in one fleshe (saith he) but he that cleaueth to the Lord, is one spirite" (*Homilies*, sig. K6v-7). Adriana therefore claims that, though she is innocent of adultery, her husband has, because man and wife are one flesh, made her into just such a strumpet as the Courtesan with whom she suspects him of having played her false. She concludes logically:

> Keepe then faire league and truce with thy true bed,
> I liue distain'd, thou vndishonoured.
>
> (147-8)

That is, if her husband does his duty by his "true bed," he will punish her as a strumpet, so that "I liue distain'd, thou vndishonoured." She will remain "distain'd" indeed, as he has unjustly made her, but he will have vindicated his honor and so will himself be "vndishonoured."

Both lines of this clinching gnomic distich are clear in their genetics. The underlying figure of the second line is of stained honor. This is the figure regularly used in Italian discussions of such cases of honor, and in these the ruling is the same as Adriana's. Annibale Romei in his

Courtiers Academie (1596) twice rules that when a wife is unfaithful, "with her owne, shee also staineth the honour of her husband" (p. 97); "with her owne, she staineth also the honour of her husband" (p. 126). Benvenuto Italiano, in *The Passenger* (1612), has the same approximate phraseology: "she being marryed and accompanying with others, together with her owne, she staines her husbands honour also" (p. 609). Romei also rules typically that the husband "looseth not his honour, but when hee conuerseth with a married woman" (p. 97), though if he "falsifieth the oth of matrimony, frequenting with a loose woman," he is "worthy of some blame" (p. 96). But both writers agree that the wife stains both her own and her husband's honor by any deviation at all.

So the second line of the distich has been balanced on the "stain" and "honor" of this Italian ruling, which was a paradox. By any deviation the wife stained her honor, but the husband did not, unless with a married woman. But Adriana had been contending at length that husband and wife are one, and that consequently, if the husband goes a whoring, he makes a strumpet of his wife. So, in that case, "I liue distain'd, thou vndishonoured." Adriana has shaped the Italian phraseology correctly into her paradoxical line. Long before I knew the genetics of the line, I wrote: "Adriana points out to Antipholus that they two are undividably one, and that he would punish any erring on her part. But if so, he ought now to punish her, because he has sinned, and thus in their undividable oneness has made her guilty, without any act of her own. She again advises him therefore to keep fair league and truce with his bed by punishing or distaining her. So will he clear his own honor" (ed. 1927, p. 81). And Shakespeare himself did not change—or need to change—this original phraseology.

The first line of the distich, "Keepe then faire league and truce with thy true bed," is a restatement from Adriana's first homily, "would keepe faire quarter with his bed" (2.1.108). Thus "bed" has kept its place to become the rhyme to "vndishonoured," botched up with the inevitable epithet "true"; "with his" has been adapted as "with thy," and "would keepe" has been adapted to the sentence structure as "Keepe then"; "faire quarter" has become "faire league and truce," the word "truce" doubtless being suggested as balanced alliteration with "true." The two homilies have been tied together; the condition of the first has naturally become the exhortation of the second.

Each line of the distich is as Shakespeare wrote it, and each separately is quite correct. And each line separately states a correct conclusion for the preceding speech, as do the two together. It seems clear also that

Shakespeare wrote the second line first, as a correct conclusion of his idea, and then adapted the first line of it from a line in the earlier homily to tie the two homilies together, and to make of the two lines a distich. So far as this text is concerned, then, any scholarly edition can only retain and explain the folio reading.

It seems clear that in Adriana's two homilies the printer accurately reproduced the copy that had been set before him; and thus we owe him a debt of gratitude. In these passages, and in Luciana's earlier homily, we are very close to Shakespeare's pen in the white heat of unblotted composition. The technical rhetorical forms, such as syllogistic reasoning, triplicity, sentential distich, and so on, are all readily at hand, well prepared for the heated flow. Considerable skill is already evident, awaiting that practice which sometimes makes perfect; but without evidence of that meticulous self-correction which is sometimes alleged to be necessary to attain complete perfection. "Would he had blotted a thousand," said the meticulous Ben, whose efforts were already too late; ours may well be more profitably expended upon our own miracles of composition.

Here we have watched the young Shakespeare applying his rhetorical skill to ideas from the official homilies of his day to produce three homilies for two of his characters, all centering on Adriana's problem husband. These homilies in turn throw light on what Shakespeare intended the positions and resultant emotions of those characters to be. Adriana has heard her Job's adviser Luciana, but like the stubborn ass she continues, with the most 'righteous' motives and on the basis of impeccable authority, to betray herself to her own eventual reproof. In doing so, she, like her sister, has been made by Shakespeare to think and speak in the official and conventional language of his day.

PYRAMUS AND THISBE ONCE MORE

by MADELEINE DORAN

WHEN SHAKESPEARE wrote his burlesque of "Pyramus and Thisbe" for *A Midsummer Night's Dream* in the 1590's, the story was already worn from countless retellings and appeared ready, doubtless, for parody. Yet it was to survive for nearly three centuries more as serious drama or as opera.[1] The fortunes of such a perdurable story, retaining its identity under all the accidental elaborations and shifts of emphasis brought about by the changing sensibilities of different eras, may be an interesting thread in the history of taste. I propose to look at two versions of the story, a twelfth-century one and a mid-sixteenth-century one, and to note what survived and what varied between the two points.[2] It may be possible, even, by viewing the story in such a wide context, to throw some new light on Shakespeare's handling of it.

It is necessary, first, to take a reminding look at the tale in the *Metamorphoses,* for Ovid laid down its permanent features. Moreover, his telling was never discarded, but from time to time was returned to as a point of fresh departure. In Ovid's story of the beautiful young Babylonians whose love was thwarted first by parents and then by a cruel and accidental fate, action is simple and swift. Circumstances of the falling in love and of the parental opposition are left vague; motivation is not explored. But the scenes at the wall and at the spring are developed, and rhetorical heightening is given the speeches of pathos—the address

---

[1] See especially Émile Picot, introduction to *Moralité nouvelle de Pyramus et Tisbee* (1901). The latest production Picot gives is of an opera at Frankfort in 1872.
[2] This is a case of fools rushing in. Douglas Bush discreetly forbore to plunge into the long and complicated history of the story; but see his *Mythology and the Renaissance Tradition* (1932), especially pp. 17-18, p. 50, n. 7, and bibliography.

of the lovers to the wall, Pyramus's self-condemnation, Thisbe's calling on her dying lover, and her apostrophe to the tree and to her parents before she kills herself. The irony of their union in death is tersely stated: "quodque rogis superest, una requiescit in urna." The effect of the whole narrative is pictorial and pathetic. Yet the rhetoric is also hyperbolic. The art is economical, but the mood is hardly restrained.

Except for occasional omissions, of the burial in a common urn and of the change of the mulberry fruit from white to purple as a memorial of the lovers' death, all the main features of the Ovidian tale remain in later tellings: the youth and beauty of the lovers, the opposition of the parents to the marriage, the conversation through a crack in the party wall between the houses, the tryst by moonlight beside a spring near the tomb of Ninus, the frightening away of Thisbe by the thirsty lioness (or lion), the beast's mouthing of Thisbe's dropped cloak or veil, Pyramus's late arrival and misinterpretation of the signs, his suicide, Thisbe's return, and her suicide with the sword of Pyramus.

It is easy to see why such a story was of perennial interest. Under all the subsequent moralizing and rhetoricizing the tale was to undergo, the essentially pathetic irony of young and innocent lovers brought to death by unfriendly fortune was to remain and to reassert itself. But it is also perhaps easy to see why no telling ever quite achieved tragic greatness. The wall as the obstacle to love-making and the lioness as an agent of destiny always hovered on the edge of ludicrous possibilities. These are only too clearly revealed in the many illustrations of the story in the early printed editions and translations of the *Metamorphoses*.[3] At any rate, it was not Pyramus and Thisbe but a cognate and perhaps derivative story—the story of Romeo and Juliet, from which these features were omitted and to which new human agents and motives were added as complication—that was to find truly tragic expression.

Nevertheless, Pyramus and Thisbe must often have satisfied local and temporary standards of tragedy. Perhaps the telling, after the Ovidian one, that best endures later scrutiny is the Norman *lai* by an unknown author of the twelfth century.[4] Ovid's 112 lines are expanded into 932.

[3] A long and complicated subject in itself. Some reproductions may be found in M. D. Henkel, "Illustrierte Ausgaben von Ovids *Metamorphosen* in 15., 16., und 17. Jahrhundert," *Vorträge des Bibliothek Warburg*, 1926-7 (1930), and in the standard histories of early book illustration: Brun, Essling, Hind, Kristeller, Sander, etc. For some representations of the fable in the Middle Ages, see Paul Lehmann, *Pseudo-Antike Literatur des Mittelalters* (1927), introduction and reproductions.

[4] Critical edition by C. de Boer, *Piramus et Tisbé, poème du 12e siècle* (1921); also by F. Branciforti in *Biblioteca dell' Archivum Romanicum*, 57 (1959). My quotations are from the latter edition. I am grateful to my colleague, Professor Julian Harris, for help with interpretation.

It is the earlier part, on the circumstances of the love affair and the torments the lovers suffer, that is most changed and enlarged. "Piramus" and "Tisbé" are introduced as children more beautiful than any ever were and as paragons of nature:

> Tant com gemme sormonte voirre,
> Or argent, rose primevoirre,
> Tant sormonterent de biauté
> Cil dui toz ceulz de la cité.

The children are stricken by the dart of Love at seven; at ten they spend their days together, fasting more than they ought at their age and reluctant to return to their "ostaus" at night. As they grow, their precocious affection is observed by an attentive servant and they are separated by their parents, between whom there has long been "un grans maltalans," "une tençon," and "une envie," and who therefore do not wish their children to marry. The young people suffer increasing torments of love until they are fifteen, when longer endurance seems impossible. They weep, they faint, they cannot eat or sleep; their suffering destroys their strength and beauty. In desperation, Pyramus goes to the Temple of Venus to pray for aid. Thisbe, finding a crevice in the wall of her room, the very wall of the boy's room on the other side, puts the pendant of her girdle through it to attract attention, and Pyramus, seeing it, knows a way has been found for them to speak together. In a lyric change of metre (in which dissyllabic lines are irregularly interspersed among the regular octosyllabic couplets), they describe their love and their torments to one another. At a second meeting, Thisbe tells Pyramus how he appeared to her in a dream, unable to reach her; how he appeared again, sad and thoughtful; and then how she heard a voice calling her many times:

> "Tisbé, cognois tu ton ami?
> Esveille toi, alons de ci,
> Tisbé."

Arguing that the gods have commanded them to go, she tells Pyramus to meet her at the fountain, under the mulberry tree, where Ninus is buried; they make no plans beyond the meeting. When Thisbe steals out of the "palais" that night, she does not heed the omens: in descending the stairs, she puts her left foot forward, she hears thunder above her to the right and feels the whole palace shake, she sees the hoot owl and the screech owl ("le huant" and "la fresaie"). She is observed by a watchman as she goes along the city wall, yet is so beautiful that he takes her for a goddess and does not try to stop her.

From this point the story moves much as in Ovid, except that the lioness becomes a lion, the *velamina* becomes a "guimple" (wimple), Thisbe hides in the shadow of an "alemandier" rather than in a cave, Pyramus revives enough to speak before he dies ("Tisbé, amie, Pour Dieu, qui vost remist en vie?"), and there is no meeting of the parents or common burial. The speeches of lamentation or "duel" are enlarged by various rhetorical devices of amplification: with repetition and elaboration; with apostrophes, not only to lions, parents, and tree, as in Ovid, but also to the night, the fields, the fountain, the sword, the moon, fortune, love, and death; and with witty figures like *adnominatio* and *traductio* or *conduplicatio:*

> Mors, que demores? Car me prens!
> He, mors,
> Pour quoi demores? C'est grans tors
> Que ie ne sui orendroit mors.

The rhetoric of amplification, however, remains the instrument of a genuinely poetic purpose.[5] Here, as in the first part, the interspersed short lines, rhythmic variation, and repetition give the speeches of passion a lyric effect:

> Nuiz de dolour, nuiz de torment,
> Moriers, arbres de plorement,
> Prez, qui du sanc estes sanglent,
>   Fontaine,
> Que ne m'avez rendue saine
> Cele cui sanc gist en l'araine!
> Com soudement est fete vaine
>   M'entente,
> M'esperance, m'amour, m'atente!

With the death of Thisbe, the narrative is brought to a swift close. As she falls on the body of Pyramus, she embraces him, kissing his eyes, his mouth, his face,

> Tant com sens et vie li dure,
> Tant com li dure sens et vie
> Se demoustre veraie amie.
> Ici fenist des deus amanz,
> Con lor leal amor fu granz.

Their passion has been headlong and reckless, but the author's final word is only praise of their true love. There is no moral. At one point

---

[5] Branciforti, in the introduction to his edition, makes an important study of the rhetoric in its relation to the rhetoric of the schools. See also Helen C. R. Laurie, "Piramus et Tisbé" (*MLR*, 55, 1960, 24-32), on both the rhetoric and the psychology of love in the poem.

in the poem, when they are in doubt whether to go or not, the author reflects on their fatal choice, the choice of will rather than reason, not in the vein of condemnation but of tragic insight. In them at that moment, longing and fearful imaginings are counterpoised:

> Delitent soi au porpenser
> De ce qu'il doivent assemblez
> Et divisent en lor corage
> Lor duel, lor mort et lor domage.

But they cannot draw back: "Mes toutes ores vaint Amour." Throughout the poem, Love is an incurable sickness, an unquenchable fire, a faithless tyrant who keeps his followers in subjection, and against whose dart everyone, young and old, is helpless. Hence the poem has tragic pathos. The dominant note is the remorselessness of love, and the response asked for is pity: pity for the beautiful adolescents—"li jovenciaux" and "la pucele"—who seem made for each other, pity for their helpless suffering at the hands of irresistible love, pity for them in the unlucky chance which leads them to death.

This *lai* was widely known, as shown by contemporary references to it, and it had a profound influence on other *romans courtois*.[6] Courtly poets, both French and Provençal, made Pyramus and Thisbe walk beside the great lovers of legend and romance: Ytis and Biblis, Paris and Helen, Flor and Blancheflor, Tristram and Iseult, Lancelot and Guinevere. Arnaut de Mareuil, for instance, writes of his love for his lady in a common formula:

> Qu'anc, Domna, ço sapchaz,
> Non fo neguns amans
> Que tant be ses engans
> Ames com eu am vos,
> Neih Leander Eros,
> Ni Paris Elenan,
> Ni Pirramus Tisban.

"Believe me, Lady, never was there any lover who loved so well, without deceit, as I love you—not Leander, Hero; nor Paris, Helen; nor Pyramus, Thisbe" (from "Tan m'abellis," quoted in Faral, *Sources latines*, p. 11). This is the kind of universality the twelfth century gave the story: Pyramus and Thisbe became types of constant love. And since their love was also fatal, they became, like Tristram and Iseult, symbols of the common destiny of lovers. Drawing up lists of particular instances under

---

[6] Edmond Faral, *Recherches sur les sources latines des contes et romans courtois du Moyen Âge* (1913), pp. 14 ff. He quotes many passages (pp. 9-13) referring to the story from French and Provençal poets of the twelfth century.

categories was a way the Middle Ages had of generalizing; hence by its inclusion in these categories of experience, the story of Pyramus and Thisbe takes on a tragic significance beyond what may be found in any single version.

Although the story was not always told in the Middle Ages in so purely literary and sympathetic a form as in the *lai,* being mostly labored as a theme for rhetorical exercise or as a text for theological or moral allegory, it was to survive this treatment to reassert itself in the Renaissance simply as a story. Nor was the romance version of it to disappear; it continued to be known throughout the Middle Ages as well as the Ovidian original, and perhaps better. The *lai* was incorporated whole in the monumental *Ovide moralisé,* an early fourteenth-century translation and expansion of the *Metamorphoses,* accompanied by allegorical expositions and running to 70,000 lines of French verse.[7] The *Ovide moralisé* had various redactions into prose, one of which, abridged somewhat and contaminated with another set of allegorical interpretations from the *Reductorium morale* (c. 1337-42) of Petrus Berchorius, was published by Colard Mansion at Bruges in 1484; as *Le Bible des poètes* it was reissued in a handsome illustrated folio by Antoine Vérard in Paris in 1493, and several times later by himself and others. This same prose version of the *Ovide moralisé,* but now shorn of all allegories, was printed at Lyons in 1532 as *Le grande Olympe des histoires poétiques du prince de poésie Ovide Naso en sa Metamorphose.* The *Grande Olympe* continued to be printed at Lyons and Paris during the century in small inexpensive formats (octavo, duodecimo, and decimosexto), usually with woodcut illustrations.[8] Thus a lively and readable, though shortened, text of the medieval story was readily available—that is, a version which especially emphasized the extreme youth of the lovers, their sufferings in the throes of a helpless love, their blameless constancy, and their pitiable deaths. It must be noted, however, that with the omission of the dream, the omens, and large parts of the lovers' speeches, and with the loss of the poetry, the special emotional intensity and beauty of the *lai* were gone.

---

[7] Edited by C. de Boer, *Ovide moralisé: poème du commencement du 14ᵉ siècle,* 5 vols. (1915-38). On relations and influences of the poem see further his edition of *Ovide moralisé en prose* (1954); also Faral, *Sources latines,* pp. 57-61; F. Ghisalberti, "L'Ovidius Moralizatus de Pierre Bersuire," *Studi romanzi,* 23 (1933), 5-132; and Joseph Engel, *Études sur l'Ovide moralisé* (1945).

[8] Sometimes under the title *Les 15. livres de la Metamorphose . . . contenans l'Olympe des histoires poétiques.* Graesse gives nine editions by 1597; George Duplessis, *Essai bibliographique sur . . . Ovide . . . aux 15ᵉ et 16ᵉ siècles* (1889), gives eleven; see also Robert Brun, *Le livre illustré en France au 16ᵉ siècle* (1930).

But in the sixteenth century, of course, fresh translations and adaptations of the *Metamorphoses* burgeoned, particularly in Italy. Among these was Giovanni Andrea dell' Anguillara's free and greatly lengthened *Metamorfosi* in *ottava rima* (Venice, Griffio, 1561). The most popular of all the Italian translations, it went into at least twenty editions by 1601.[9] Anguillara's handling of the Pyramus and Thisbe fable is therefore an excellent one to compare with the *roman courtois;* it is, moreover, extended to about the same length (920 lines, in 115 stanzas), and is highly wrought though in a different manner, a high Renaissance manner— realistic yet artfully rhetorical, dramatic in action yet copious in detail. If Anguillara knew the romance version, as a number of details suggest he may have done, he did not imitate it. Like the medieval poet's, his inventions are greater in the first half, but for quite different purposes. Instead of dwelling on the prolonged anguish of unsatisfied love, Anguillara augments motivation, circumstances of the action, descriptive details, and new sensations—in short, he seeks to give fresh verisimilitude and credibility, psychological naturalness, and a different kind of suspense to the old story.

The intention of increasing verisimilitude is obvious in the handling of the characters. The traditional hyperbole of the lovers' unsurpassed beauty ("iuvenum pulcherrimus alter,/altera, quas Oriens habuit, praelata puellis") is varied with differences according to their sex, and appropriate differences of temperament are noted as the story progresses, such as that the lady is quicker of thought and more tender of heart, and that the man is stronger and more severe. Again, up to the night of the escape, Pyramus (the man and hence able to move about freely) is made to be preoccupied with the responsible business of the elopement; Thisbe (the girl, shut in and necessarily obliged to follow orders and to wait) is shown as undergoing more emotional stress. He worries about the execution of his plans; she worries about the honesty of his intentions towards her. In most tellings of the story, the lovers simply fill their undifferentiated roles as intense and unhappy adolescents in love, though Thisbe may sometimes appear more eager because her part in the story requires that she arrive first at the tryst. Even in Anguillara individuality of character may be less in question than decorum, a sense of what is fitting to either

[9] See Brunet, Graesse; also British Museum *STC Catalogue of Books printed in Italy* (1958). My quotations are from the better of the two editions dated 1584 (Venice, Giunti; Folger 1584a; Huntington 241777). I have consulted my colleague Professor Gian N. G. Orsini on troublesome readings.

sex. Although Thisbe is said to be "ne l' amore più calda, e viva," she is yet put decently back in her place, as it were, from her bold role in the romance. The verisimilitude is social as well as psychological. Still, any difference at all heightens the impression of realism, and Anguillara handles these domestic situations with great naturalness.

Verisimilitude is also achieved with circumstantial detail. The family quarrel (merely stated in the romance and not even necessarily implied in Ovid's bare "sed vetuere patres") is given body with new details about the fathers' behavior, such as keeping the house keys under their pillows at night. Most important, the preparations for the elopement are much extended. It is only after Pyramus has thought out fully all the practical steps to be taken (for he means to marry Thisbe in another city, and in the meantime to have her chaperoned by parents of friends) that they plan the tryst at Ninus's tomb. And by nightfall, Pyramus has completed extensive preparations: he has got counterfeit keys made for the doors of their houses, has managed to get some money together, and has arranged to have horses and necessaries for the journey ready in a nearby village. Eleven stanzas are expended on Thisbe's escape: her drugging her attendant aunt with a sleeping draught; her watching the stars from the balconies to be sure of the time; her taking her aunt's keys to unlock the door of her chamber; her feeling her way around the walls of the "sala" or great hall to find the door the "adultera chiave" will open; her counting her way down the staircase; her opening the main gate.

Not only do these touches give the setting freshness by creating the atmosphere of a big Renaissance town house ("hostello" or "casa"), but also they put the suspense in a different place. In the romance it is in the increasing frustration of the lovers, until suddenly (when by escape the chance of fulfillment is at hand) the mood changes to anticipation. The doubts are brief. The climax of decision is only a minor climax in the emotional movement of the poem, a step towards the major double climax of the suicides, and this sense of it is kept by Thisbe's reckless disregard of the unfavorable omens as she leaves the palace. In Anguillara, however, the suspense is in the action and its consequences—in the preparations for the elopement and in the natural emotional turmoil they give rise to on the long day of waiting. The conflict between longing and anxiety, generalized in the romance for both the lovers and without a setting, is given by Anguillara to Thisbe alone, waiting in her room; besides, the anxiety which foresees possible death in the future is transformed into an immediate anxiety about the success of Pyramus's business that day. There is great naturalness in all this, of course. Watching for the setting of "il pigro Arturo" and the rising of Capricorn,[10] Anguillara's Thisbe thinks it better to be too early than too late, and so her impatience takes her to her doom. But there are no omens. Hence, in spite of her imprudent haste, her successful escape from the house is intensely climactic and brings a temporary relief.

Anguillara must then build to the second and tragic climax. This time he leaves the original swift action pretty much alone, and adds only a few circumstantial details. Suspense is mainly built by a set of interpolated apostrophes which sharpen (as did Thisbe's haste in leaving her house) the awareness of time. The poet apostrophizes the moon to darken her light lest Pyramus see the bloody garment and the lion's tracks in the sand; prays the stars to send some passerby to struggle for the sword with Pyramus; and prays the plants, if neither men nor gods will hear, to trip him with their roots, hold him with their leaves—anything for a moment's delay; for Thisbe is already on her way back from the cave to tell him of her adventure. In emphasizing the terrible fatality which lies in the timing, these speeches are meant to arouse pity as well as to increase suspense.

The genius of the story is pathos; and from Ovid on, in all tellings, the lovers' passionings are the chief points of heightening. Anguillara does not fail expectation. He amplifies the suicide speeches in a perfectly traditional way. He keeps the Ovidian themes: self-blame; the irony of the deaths; apostrophes to lions, the surrounding caves, the sword, the parents, the mulberry tree. But he 'varies' these themes, in Renaissance fashion, with new horrors (How many beasts must have torn Thisbe with teeth and nails, and divided her flesh to feed "lor voraci figli leoni"?); new ironies (Why do not the heavens show Pyramus her bones? "Who will show me the road I must walk to find what I do not want to find?"); new conceits (The naked and pointed sword, the good sword which would have killed anyone else more willingly than its master, Pyramus, could not fly from killing him—

> Il miser disperato s' abbandona,
> Quando nol prende alcun, nè gliè conteso;
> E lascia ruinar la sua persona
> Sopra il pungente acciar con tutto il peso.
> L' ignuda spada sua, pungente, e buona,
> Ch' ogni altro hauria più uolentieri offeso,

[10] This interpretation of Anguillara's rather ambiguous indication as to which "segno" was rising, which setting, is the only one that will give his statement astronomical application; such a condition is met in the latitude of Rome at midnight in early July, or at 1 a.m. about Midsummer Night!

> Non può fuggir di far quel crudo effetto,
> E passo al suo Signor la ueste, e 'l petto) .

To Thisbe the sword was both "omicida, e innocente." Anguillara elaborates, moreover, the complaints against fortune, not explicit in Ovid, but by now thoroughly traditional:

> Ahi, quanto, ahi quanto à noi voi fate torto,
> Siate stelle, destin, fortuna, ò fato,
> A far in questo amor rimaner morto,
> Chi non ha punto in questo amore 'errato.

The story ends with the parents building a common tomb for the dead lovers. This has an ironic fitness, because they disjoined those whom love had joined and by their rigor brought about the children's deaths. In this account, it is the cruel parents who are primarily to blame, rather than cruel Love. As in the romance, there is no moral spoken against the lovers. Morality is guaranteed, nevertheless, by the assurance that the lovers intended to enjoy each other according to law, human and divine. The affair is altogether more respectable and prudential, and to that degree less moving.

Although the rhetoric of amplification may be no greater quantitatively in Anguillara than in the romance, it seems so. The figures of thought—such as description, comparison, similitude, interrogation, apostrophe—are more extended in Anguillara; every conceit is pushed to a tasteless extreme. The differences are also qualitative. One gets the impression of fewer aural schemes of repetition and of more dramatic schemes of contrariety; that is, of less anaphora and anadiplosis (figures which chime), less polyptoton and paranomasia (figures of wordplay), and of more antithesis, paradox, and synoeciosis (varieties of *contentio*). There is much more sense of strain in Anguillara; catachresis, or the wresting of words from their normal sense, is pervasive. And the lyrical note of the passionate speeches in the romance is altogether absent. In short, the rhetorical effect is greater than the poetic.

To modern ears, Anguillara's 'copiousness in exclaims' grows wearisome. But it is Renaissance taste we are concerned about, not ours, and we have a very clearly defined statement of that in the "Annotationi" of Giuseppe Orologgi appended, in editions from 1563 on, to each book of Anguillara's *Metamorfosi*. The notes are partly explanatory (in the medieval eheumeristic tradition), partly moral, partly critical. Those on Pyramus and Thisbe ("Annotationi del quarto libro") are confined to an analysis of the style of Anguillara's version of the fable. The very thing

Orologgi likes best about it is its enrichment with "spiriti" (probably passages of feeling), "affetti" or speeches of passion, "conversioni" or apostrophes, comparisons, descriptions, indeed with every poetic ornament; and he singles out for praise particular passages of action, description, and feeling, especially the "bellissime e vaghe conversioni" or apostrophes I have described. He also commends Anguillara for his service to decorum in various places. Everything, he says, is transformed in the spirit of Ovid who, if he had had to write the story of these two unhappy lovers in our Italian language, would not have been able to dress it in more beautiful and artificial ornaments.[11] The digressions Anguillara introduces throughout the poem would be out of place in a literal prose translation, but in verse they are permitted, so long as they are appropriate, for adornment and delight; Ariosto's ornamentation of Boiardo's older romance is sufficient precedent ("Annotationi del secondo libro"). What Orologgi admires, then, besides the new touches of decorum and the story-telling skill, is the whole overlay of the brief fable with rhetorical amplification and poetical ornament.

A product of the high Renaissance and pleasing to its taste, Anguillara's "Piramo e Tisbe" is dramatic in emphasis, realistic in setting and psychology, weighted with passion yet safely moral, copious and highly wrought in detail. It is thoroughly sophisticated and overripe. After Anguillara, the story was to be treated to many excesses, rarely with so much assurance and mastery as his. Only literary genius could bring it back to a moving simplicity, and no literary genius was to touch it but Shakespeare, whose 'simple' treatment of it was to be of the murderous kind.

The versions Shakespeare shows certain evidence of knowing have been described most recently by Kenneth Muir in *Shakespeare's Sources* (1957) and by Geoffrey Bullough in *Narrative and Dramatic Sources of Shakespeare,* 1 (1957). Except for Ovid's original Latin and Chaucer's forthright English rendering of Ovid in his *Legend of Good Women,* they are all bad. Golding's translation (1565, 1567, etc.), with its cantering fourteeners and bouncing diction, hardly induces a tragic mood:

> This said, she tooke the sword yet warme with slaughter of her loue
> And setting it beneath hir brest, did to hir hart it shoue.

The "new Sonet" or ballad in *A Handful of Pleasant Delights* (1584, but perhaps a new edition of the "pleasaunte Sonettes" of 1566) and the versi-

---

[11] The better known poet and critic, Varchi, had a similar opinion; on this and on Anguillara's contemporary reputation, see M. Pelaez, "La vita e le opere di . . . Anguillara," in *Il Propugnatore,* 4.1 (1891), 40-124.

fied tale in *A Gorgeous Gallery of Gallant Inventions* (1578) are appalling in their ineptitude, as we all know.[12] The story in the *Gorgeous Gallery* follows the *Grande Olympe* closely and hence, in outline and much detail, if not in spirit, is like the medieval romance. Whether Shakespeare had acquaintance with any other versions in English, such as Gower's or Christine de Pisan's, or with any continental versions directly, we have no means of knowing. But he cannot have helped knowing that the story was traditional and hoary, that Pyramus and Thisbe as types of tragic lovers were everybody's property, a theme for schoolboy exercises and for pretentious poetasters. Besides, there had been coming out sporadically since the beginning of Elizabeth's reign, and now in a rash, tales in verse about other pairs of Ovidian lovers, including Marlowe's *Hero and Leander* and his own *Venus and Adonis*. These tales may have given impetus to Shakespeare's "Pyramus and Thisbe" in *A Midsummer Night's Dream*. It was a subject appropriate to the play and must have seemed especially ripe for parody.

In any case, what is interesting from the point of view of the present essay is that Shakespeare's parody catches not only the features of the story unchanged from Ovid's time (the wall with its crannied hole or chink, the moonshine by which the lovers meet, the lion vile which stains Thisbe's mantle, the bloody blameful blade which broaches each lover's breast); but also the features that were most amplified or that were altogether new in post-Ovidian tradition. Shakespeare describes the beauty of the lovers in the trite formulae of romance and ballad: Thisbe's breath, like flowers, has "odious savors sweet"; "most radiant Pyramus," "sweet youth and tall," is "lily-white of hue, Of color like the red rose on triumphant briar," and his eyes are "green as leeks." The lovers apostrophize Night—

> O grim-looked night, O night with hue so black,
> O night, which ever art when day is not!

the Moon—

> Sweet moon, I thank thee for thy sunny beams;

the Sword—

> Come, trusty sword,
> Come, blade, my breast imbrue!

and Nature—

> O, wherefore, Nature, didst thou lions frame,
> Since lion vile hath here deflow'red my dear.

---

[12] On date and relationship of these poems see editions by Hyder E. Rollins of the two miscellanies (1924, 1926).

They call on cruel destiny to end their miserable lives:

> Approach, ye Furies fell!
> O Fates, come, come,
> Cut thread and thrum,
> Quail, crush, conclude, and quell!

They are paired with other lovers famous for constancy:

> *Pyramus.* . . .   I am thy lover's grace;
> And, like Limander, am I trusty still.
> *Thisbe.* And I, like Helen, till the Fates me kill.
> *Pyramus.* Not Shafalus to Procrus was so true.
> *Thisbe.* As Shafalus to Procrus, I to you.

Thisbe 'means' at great length and as in the romance her passion ends the play. The style parodies the worst excesses of 'varying' and of 'hunting the letter,' exemplified not only in the Pyramus and Thisbe poems Shakespeare knew from the anthologies, but also to some extent in Turbervile's translation of Ovid's *Heroical Epistles* (1567), another set of tragedies of love.

It is interesting to note that if the commonly accepted chronology of the plays is correct, Shakespeare handled Pyramus and Thisbe and its cousin-story of Romeo and Juliet within a year or two of each other (1594-6). Muir thinks that in the Pyramus and Thisbe interlude he was parodying himself, because he knew that *Romeo and Juliet* was no tragedy. One could as well argue the reverse—that having handled the story offhand and comically in *A Midsummer Night's Dream* he got interested in the theme and decided to give it the serious treatment it seemed capable of in a variant form; and one might suggest that Mercutio's digressive Queen Mab speech sounds like left-over stuff from the comedy. I am not arguing for such a sequence, only presenting the supposition to show that it is quite as plausible as the contrary one; for I believe that such speculations, if they go beyond merely playful guessing, are futile. We cannot know why Shakespeare chose either story or in what order. What can be observed, and what is interesting artistically, is that he took the same fundamental story in opposite directions, one to its zenith, the other to its nadir. The Romeo and Juliet story he brought to the fruition of its artistic possibilities, to its most poignant and poetic expression as a tragedy of adolescent love crossed by unfriendly circumstances. And perhaps one can say that in the outrage he perpetrated on the Pyramus and Thisbe tale he only brought it to the absurd extreme its accidental features—its Wall, its Lion, and its Moonshine—had always been asking for.

HENRY V AS HEROIC COMEDY

by ROY W. BATTENHOUSE

SHAKESPEARE'S *Henry V* offers us opportunity for reviewing an action of piety and patriotism which to many readers has seemed ideal. The king and the clergy, in this play, are seen working together in friendly collaboration. United around a common interest, they forge a common purpose. In the name of God and country they undertake a war with France whereby the English people are rallied to high heroism and achieve, almost miraculously, a famous victory and a new international status. What dream of man could wish more? Yet the meaning of this illustrious accomplishment is open to diverse interpretation. What shape of significance has Shakespeare given to this ideal? Has he formed it as an epic of praise and celebration or, conversely, as a drama of surface splendor hollow at the core? Does he understand it as a comedy, or as a tragedy, or as epic history? Over these questions the critics have differed.

Nearly all have agreed, however, on two points: that the play's hero typifies in some sense 'the successful Englishman,' and that his success represents an Elizabethan ideal. The Tudor historian Hall had written in his *Chronicle* (1548):

> This Henry was a king whose life was immaculate and his living without spot. . . . He was the blazing comet and apparent lantern in his days; he was the mirror of Christendom and the glory of his country; he was the flower of kings past, and a glass to them that should succeed. No Emperor in magnanimity ever him excelled.[1]

And this estimate is reflected in Shakespeare's play when the Chorus hails Henry as "mirror of all Christian kings" and "star of England." The

[1] Edition of 1809, pp. 112-13, as quoted by J. Dover Wilson in the new Cambridge *King Henry V* (1947), p. xviii.

163

Chorus suggests also (Act 5) a parallel between Henry's French expedition and the Elizabethan campaign into Ireland by the Earl of Essex, whose return in great triumph was expected at the time of the play's first staging. Parallels at other points, especially as between the tactics described in Act 1 and those of state and church under Elizabeth, have been noted by Lily B. Campbell (*Shakespeare's Histories,* 1945, pp. 257-71). An audience in the summer of 1599 could see mirrored in this play the national consciousness of their own day.

But 'historical' explanation, if taken no further, cannot answer our original question: What judgment does Shakespeare imply regarding the cultural pattern he is mirroring? Toward what meaning does he shape it? Let us begin by inquiring of the critics.

1.

Some of them, such as E. M. W. Tillyard and Mark Van Doren, find a total lack of consistent shaping and regard the play as a dramatic failure. In their view the fault lies in Shakespeare's submitting to popular tradition, letting puerile patriotism do the work of dramatic construction. According to Tillyard, Hal's brilliance has been jettisoned to make him into a simple copybook hero; and the play's comic scenes contribute nothing but aimless variety (*Shakespeare's History Plays,* 1946, pp. 304-14). Van Doren charges that the ideal English king collapses into "a mere good fellow, a hearty undergraduate"; and he finds the rhetoric hollow. Shakespeare's genius was here "at loose ends" (*Shakespeare,* 1939, pp. 170-79).

Not so, however, in the view of J. Dover Wilson and J. H. Walter, editors of the New Cambridge (1947) and the new Arden (1954) texts. They defend both the play and its hero as altogether admirable—in the *epic* mode. They see Shakespeare as fulfilling the epic requirement of moral instruction by exhibiting for his audience a hero "perfect above the common run of men"—in fact, a Christian model. With eloquence Wilson compares the Chorus to "a priest leading his congregation in prayer and celebration," in "tones of eager entreaty from the playwright's own lips." Neither editor discusses the comic scenes or credits the dramatist with any irony. Nor does G. Wilson Knight, who lately has praised the play as "a new epic and heroic drama blending Christian virtue with martial prowess" (*The Sovereign Flower,* 1958, p. 37).

But a third group of critics denies that Henry is Shakespeare's ideal king. A. C. Bradley long ago took this stand, remarking simply that Henry's religion has too much "policy" and some "superstition" in it;

and that he shows an inability to "spare love for anyone outside the family" (*Oxford Lectures on Poetry,* 1909, pp. 256-8). John Palmer, more recently, has called the play "an exposure of the wicked futility" of Henry's quest for glory, a supreme instance of Shakespeare's "moral detachment" (*Political Characters in Shakespeare,* 1948, p. 228). And H. C. Goddard, in a long and penetrating chapter in *The Meaning of Shakespeare* (1951), has developed the thesis that

> through the Choruses, the playwright gives us the popular idea of his hero. In the play, the poet tells the truth about him. (p. 218)

That truth, as Goddard sums it up, is that

> not maliciously and in cold blood but against the grace of his own nature and by insensible degrees, the man who began as Hal and ended as Henry V made himself into something that comes too close for comfort to Machiavelli's ideal prince. (p. 267)

Goddard sees not epic but irony. He sees "ransom" involved in Henry's paying off Williams; parody of Henry in Pistol's braggings; and a "confusion of Mars with the Christian God" in Henry's piety. He believes Shakespeare is quite aware of the analogy between highway robbery in *Henry IV* and imperialism in *Henry V,* and aware that the 'unity' it forged was counterfeit, doomed soon to collapse under Henry VI. To these points Allan Gilbert has added a few, in a recent article suggesting that "satire" is interwoven with patriotism in the mixed fabric of the play.[2]

My own view involves a basic extension of this third position, mostly through new examples in support of it, together with some suggestions for a larger perspective by which to see the drama coherently. It seems to me there is satire, but not of the 'cankered-muse' type practiced by Shakespeare's rivals. Rather, Shakespeare's satire is Chaucerian, both gently sympathetic and covertly hilarious. It is grounded in irony; and in this case in an irony which is already present, although probably unwittingly, in the chronicles themselves. As expanded in drama, this irony gives rise to what I prefer to call 'heroic comedy,' or else 'comic history.' I see this mood and mode as controlling the entire action of *Henry V,* pervading all its strands and levels. Schlegel spoke of heroic comedy, long ago, in noting the 'marriage of convenience' with which this play ends. What he did not notice, however, was that such a marriage has its analogy in Act 1 when state and church join hands. Does not their politic court-

[2] "Patriotism and Satire in *Henry V,*" in *Studies in Shakespeare,* ed. A. D. Matthews (1953), pp. 40-64.

ship anticipate that of Henry and Katherine? If so, the theme of court-ship of worldly advantage may be germinal to the whole drama. But before we pursue further this suggestion, let us pause to consider yet another kind of approach to the play, offered by Derek Traversi in some recent essays[3] which would stress the 'tragic' implications of *Henry V.*

To the portrait of Henry in the chronicles, Traversi believes Shakespeare added his own reading of the 'tragedy' implicit in the kingly office. Inheriting a conception of Henry as a ruler "perfectly aware of his responsibilities and religiously devoted to the idea of duty," Shakespeare chose to emphasize "the obstacles, both personal and political," that lie between this conception and its fulfillment. He saw the very conditions of kingship in a light akin to the tragic. For kingship demands a perfection of self-control in the ruler, yet how precarious is the human will's ability to maintain that control! To show how the exercise of power brings out defects of human frailty, Shakespeare lets us see flaws in Henry—in his shifting the responsibility upon the archbishop in Act 1, and in his later outbursts of temper. On the other hand, Henry's merciless reprisals are necessary to "the public function he has accepted." The administration of justice demands "a detachment which is almost inhuman and borders on the tragic." Shakespeare has focused on certain "contradictions, moral and human, inherent in the notion of a successful king."

That Traversi finds contradictions in Henry's kingship is a point worth noting. But why ascribe these to pressures of office simply, and not to Henry's interpretation of his office? Suppose we ask what kind of justice demands an almost inhuman detachment. And what kind of success involves contradictions inherent in it? Must we suppose that every kind of justice and every kind of political success involves these? That would be to overlook certain other kings in Shakespeare, such as pious Edward in *Macbeth,* or Duncan and his appointed successor Malcolm, or Richmond whose kingship has ghostly appointment from both royal lines in *Richard III,* or the King of France in *All's Well.* These were Christian kings who, either in office or prior to their being crowned therein, succeeded in fulfilling a kingly duty without engaging in any shuffling of responsibility or merciless reprisals. Is not Goddard correct, then, in associating Henry's politics with a "close to Machiavellian" practice, and in questioning whether its 'success' was really success at all? Perhaps, actually, Henry was the victim, not of his office, but of his misdirecting his efforts in that

---

[3] *Shakespeare from Richard II to Henry V* (1957), pp. 166-98, an expansion of his earlier essays in *Scrutiny* (1941) and *Approach to Shakespeare* (1956).

office, serving convenience rather than true welfare. And if so, was he "perfectly aware of his responsibilities"? Traversi's phrase, in fact, goes a bit beyond the chronicles.

The chronicles do give the impression that Henry was perfect in meeting the responsibilities that earn for a prince worldly fame; but they do not pause to ask whether such fame constitutes a 'perfect awareness' of a prince's true responsibility. My distinction here is a subtle one but important. For we have only to remember that the Pharisees in biblical times, and some pious pagans in Roman times, seemed perfect in responsibilities they were aware of. Nevertheless, between them they put to death Jesus, Paul, and others, and brought on the eventual ruin of Jerusalem and of Rome. With irony Jesus called the first group "whited sepulchres," while the second earned Augustine's praise for their "splendid vices." Their popular reputation, however, was as paragons of virtue. People who thought otherwise went silent or else unheard. Shakespeare may be adverting to such a situation when Henry boasts (5.2.296) that "the liberty that follows our places stops the mouth of all find-faults"; or, earlier, when Canterbury boasts that England's "chronicle [is] as rich with praise As is the ooze and bottom of the sea With sunken wrack" (1.2.163). Such is the irony of the pursuit of fame, and of the virtues perfected in its service. We might call this tragic; yet if the pursuer in his lifetime remains wholly content with his goal, do we not more commonly praise his folly as 'comic'? Such seems to me Shakespeare's view of Henry.

Now the chroniclers and Shakespeare agree in describing the popular view of Henry. Shakespeare, however, enlivens and punctuates it with the deeper insight I have just described. It might perhaps be argued that Hall or Holinshed had some inklings of this deeper insight, but in their eulogies deliberately avoided it for safety's sake. That is possible, yet seems hardly likely. In any case, what their eulogies state is the popular portrait; and what I am suggesting is that Shakespeare could accept their statements as true within this framework. Thus when they say that Henry's "life" was "without spot," their words can be read as describing, not Henry's heart or soul, but his public behavior as seen by contemporaries. And when Hall says that Henry was the "apparent lantern in his days," this phrase can be read in the sense in which it would apply equally to Alexander the Great in his days. Further, to call Henry "the mirror of all Christendom" does not prohibit viewing all Christendom as, say, Dante did in *Purgatorio* 32, as a presently tattered realm to be sighed over. If Henry is "the flower of kings past," as Hall asserts, may he not then be the flower of Richard II's deceptive piety and of Henry

IV's cold ambition? And, finally, when Hall says that no emperor ever excelled Henry in "magnanimity," this credits him merely with one of the sub-Christian virtues, the one particularly exalted by the Renaissance. Thus a strictly literal reading of Hall does not require anyone to impute to Henry an authentically Christian *spirit,* or the distinctively Christian virtues. I doubt that Hall or Holinshed saw this fact, yet the details which they recount of Henry's actions, as we shall presently see, imply this limitation quite plainly.

May not Shakespeare, therefore, have undertaken to portray a Henry —and indeed the whole society which he heads—as admittedly illustrious but bounded within the limits of sub-Christian virtue? Within such limits, Shakespeare can add appropriate detail to his sources without risk of contradicting them, so long as whatever behavior he adds does not imply the inner operation of any genuinely Christian motive in the persons portrayed. There can be "glistering semblances of piety," yes. But the heart of the action will suggest no substantial Christianity. Thus reconstructed the history will be double-edged. It will allow some spectators, blinded by a surface patriotism, to admire as their own ideal its particular heroism. But it will permit others to discern, as various modern critics have, an ultimate emptiness in the pageantry, a suspicious fulsomeness in the rhetoric, and a kind of heroism in Henry more suggestive of "a very amiable monster" (Hazlitt's phrase), or of "some handsome spirited horse" (Yeats's phrase), than of a truly human being.

If we will recall that Dante placed Alexander below the minotaur in Hell's circle of the violent, we may have a key to Shakespeare's moral estimate of Henry. For does not Fluellen patriotically compare Henry to "Alexander the Pig" (adding that this is all one with "magnanimous") in a comic scene invented by Shakespeare? The pronunciation "Pig," of course, results from Fluellen's Welsh accent, but Shakespeare is making his own serious jest. Dante, in commenting on Alexander, had cried out:

> O blind cupidity both wicked and foolish, which so incites us in the short life, and then, in the eternal, steeps us so bitterly. (*Inferno,* 12, Temple Classics translation)

Shakespeare, I think, saw this cupidity in Henry's career, as an underside to the portrait drawn by the Tudor chronicles. Without directly stating this judgment, he implies it repeatedly. For example, he shows Henry invoking Alexander's name at Harfleur, in a speech urging the English to fight like tigers and pursue their game like greyhounds. And at the play's very beginning, the Prologue speaks of crouching hounds and of proud horses' hoofs, of a "cockpit" and of "upreared and abutting fronts." War as animal sport, clearly, is a theme in the play's action. But will not a heroism thus blind to its own cupidity inevitably have "contradictions moral and human" inherent in it?

To achieve his purpose, Shakespeare has invoked a complex dramatic structure. In his main characters he has delineated a worldly professionalism, which continually confesses itself in ironic evasions. Then, at a secondary level, he has invented characters such as Fluellen and Macmorris, who by speaking wiser than they know serve to reveal flaws in their leaders. And finally, at the level of Pistol and company, he has provided antic clowning which parodies the main action of the play. Although epic and farce are technically polar opposites, Shakespeare by intertwining them has been able to write a history which is also heroic comedy.

2.

It is important to recognize that the chronicles themselves, despite their high tone of eulogy, provide a basis for irony in the very facts they report. There are ominous undertones, for example, in Holinshed's details describing Henry IV's passing. We are told how the son overhastily claimed the crown as his "right," grasping for it on superficial evidence, careless of the deeper truth of the situation. May not this action be symptomatic—of the way he will later grasp for the French crown? Equally symptomatic is his attitude when the father awakes and reproves Hal for his "misuse [of] himself." Not shame or repentance, but what Holinshed calls "good audacitie" characterizes his reply. And the scene continues:

> "Well, faire sonne" (said the king with a great sigh), "what right I had to it, God knoweth." "Well" (said the prince), "if you die king, I will have the garland and trust to keep it with the sword against all mine enemies as you have done."[4]

Why the king's great sigh? He is remembering (is he not?) his own misuse of himself in grasping another man's crown. The kind of right he himself has taught—based on a will to have and to keep by the sword—now

---

[4] *Holinshed's Chronicle* (Everyman's Library), ed. Allardyce and Josephine Nicoll (1927), p. 68. My further references to Holinshed will be to this text. However, an additional passage in Boswell-Stone's edition (1896), pp. 159-60, deserves notice; for in it Holinshed, after referring to the journey which Henry "pretended to take" to the Holy Land, goes on to describe Henry's subsequent sickness as "not a leprosie, stricken by the hand of God (saith maister Hall) as foolish friars imagined, but a very apoplexie. . . ." Does Holinshed's verb "pretended" mean merely 'intended'? Or is there a suggestion of 'professing falsely'? And is Holinshed quoting Hall to agree with him, or to hide behind him?

stands before him in the person of his son. How can he gainsay the son's apology, seeing that his own right to the crown God alone knows? Let higher standards of rectitude not be insisted on.

And a second irony comes immediately next in Holinshed. He juxtaposes mention of Henry IV's belated plans to go to Jerusalem with the fact of his dying instead (as if by divine judgment?) in an English room named Jerusalem. Thus not the reality of a true crusader's death, but instead its English counterfeit, must serve as the measure of Henry IV's career. Yet the old king takes comfort from the counterfeit as if it were the real:

> Lauds be given to the father of heaven, for now I know that I shall die here in this chamber, according to the profesie of me declared, that I should depart this life in Jerusalem.

Is this not irony compounded? A king who cannot distinguish empty fulfillment from the real (may we not say?) is about as superstitious as Macbeth. (And Holinshed's statement that Henry was stricken at Saint Edward's shrine reminds us of that other usurper, the Scottish one, to whose overthrow pious Edward likewise contributed.) Usurpation, superstition, an ironic death—these are Henry IV's legacy to his son, if we pay close attention to the unspoken implications of Holinshed's facts, as Shakespeare no doubt did.

Can Henry V's reign be different from his father's? The details with which Holinshed ushers it in do not hint so:

> He was crowned the ninth of April being Passion sundaie, which was a sore, ruggie, and tempestuous day, with wind, snow, and sleet; that men greatlie marvelled thereat, making diverse interpretations what the same might signifie. But this king even at first appointing with himselfe, to shew that in his person princelie honors should change public manners, he determined to put upon him the shape of a new man. For whereas aforetime he had made himselfe a companion unto misrulie mates of dissolute order and life, he now banished them all from his presence. . . .

Here what most critics have noted and applauded is Henry's change in public manners. But does that differentiate him in any way from his father? Rather, it marks a move toward duplicating the father's kind of excellence. He will henceforth put on the manners of respectability—the "shape" of a new man. Not necessarily, however, the "new man" which Scripture recommends. There lies the significant irony, overlooked by many readers of Holinshed and perhaps by Holinshed himself. But Shakespeare could have, and I think did, recognize it. Surely he knew that the "new man" of which St. Paul speaks is achieved not by putting on "princelie honors" but by counting them as nothing; not by reshaping one's public image but by being renewed in "the spirit of the mind"; not by banishing misruly companions but by suffering for them and among them. Hence, the "new man" which Holinshed has described is nothing new at all but simply old Henry *redivivus*. And like his father, young Henry is dedicating himself to a counterfeit morality rather than a true morality, ignoring duty's substance for duty's shadow. Everything that Passion Sunday stands for in the Christian calendar is quite opposite in kind to the new kingliness Holinshed is ascribing to Henry. No wonder, then, that Passion Sunday turned stormy on Henry's consecration day. The omen's implications are pretty certainly negative as far as Heaven's blessing is concerned. Holinshed does not pause to decipher them. Nor can Shakespeare introduce the omen literally into the closing scene of *2 Henry IV*; yet that scene figures the omen's import analogously enough in the sleety and windy passion which the new Henry bestows on his friend Falstaff.

Elsewhere too in *Henry IV* it is well hinted that the direction of the new Harry's reign will be no more Christian than old Harry's projected crusade. And the exact measure of that project's Christianity may be gathered from the father's words of advice to the son:

> [I] had a purpose now
> To lead out many to the Holy Land,
> Lest rest and lying still might make them look
> Too near unto my state. Therefore, my Harry,
> Be it thy course to busy giddy minds
> With foreign quarrels; that action, hence borne out,
> May waste the memory of the former days.
>
> (Part 2, 4.5.210)

Whereas Holinshed had been silent regarding the motive of Henry's "pretended" crusade, Shakespeare here supplies a plainly selfish and politic motive—not out of line with the import of Holinshed's surface facts (which we have already noted), but yet constructing for their underside an appropriate order of psychological fact. Shakespeare's lines make clear to us (though not to their secular-minded speaker) that the crusade, if it had been carried out, would have been a travesty of kingly responsibility—an action aimed not at "redeeming the time" but at wasting "the memory of the former days" and thus redeeming the monarch's own status. Suited as this advice may be to mastering "giddy minds," it inevitably commits the *head* of state to outgiddying the giddy. Huge comic implications thus inhere in the role which the father has set for his son.

But the new Henry has a remarkable aptitude for his role. His launching of a quarrel with France, as Shakespeare presents it, is managed with such an adroit show of "right" and of "conscience" that no one within the world of the play seems to recognize the counterfeit of justice that is being fabricated. By the end of Act 1, Henry's "well-hallowed cause" has taken on the color of a crusade, led by a "Christian" who goes forth "by God's grace" and in His name—to play a set of tennis for the rule or ruin of France! Surely old Henry IV could have dreamt nothing finer. The magic of it all is the product not merely of the "muse of fire" and "heaven of invention" invoked by the play's Prologue, but also of subtle fires of cupidity and inventions of piety which Shakespeare allows for in the characters of his story.

Does his portrait distort Holinshed's facts? Rather, it incorporates them within a fuller context. The archbishop's two-part argument for the war, so carefully reported in Holinshed, is given conspicuous prominence. In fact, it is put the more in the limelight by Shakespeare's shifting its setting from Parliament to Court. By this same shift, moreover, Henry's role at the helm of things is enhanced, lest the king seem, as in Holinshed, the mere dupe of a "sharp invention" set going by the clergy. For if sharp invention be ascribed solely to the clergy, this would hardly square with Holinshed's praise of Henry, elsewhere, as pre-eminent in "policy" and noted in particular for the secrecy with which he developed his purposes. Henry, says Holinshed in a final summing up, "never enterprised anything before he had fully debated and forecast all the main chances." If so, should there not be, from the very beginning, circumstances to indicate this fact? Shakespeare supplies them. He constructs a scene at Court which contains covert hints of sharp invention by both parties, reciprocally catalytic. And, to give Henry priority in all matters, he ascribes to him (rather than to the bishops, as in Holinshed), the earliest stirring-up of the war question. But this fact is allowed to emerge indirectly, when we hear that Henry is awaiting the French reply to claims he has transmitted through diplomatic channels. This tucked-in detail also implies balance at the moral level: if the clergy are venally concerned about titles to lands, so is Henry.

Henry doubly so, for it is he who is permitting the Commons to raise a claim to the lands of the church. Why? Perhaps to let the church know that its title to old rights may disappear, unless rights to the King's old

titles can be made to appear (like the magician's rabbit) to draw attention elsewhere. Certainly at the level of titles and rights, which may
easily be substituted for truth and justice by a little evasion, these gentlemen ought to be able to cooperate. With one of them figuratively up a
tree, and the other stumped, they have common ground, or at least re-
ciprocal grounds, for closer brotherhood. Or to change our metaphor,
now that the King's one hand is on the church's throat, and the other on
France's tail, the church can help the King's predicament by raising a
cry for a fox hunt. Canterbury can ransom himself (that is, his status)
with golden words and coin—just as, later in the play (4.4), the French
Gentleman does when Pistol has him by the throat. Shakespeare is already outlining a type-situation for later parody. In fact, he is epitomizing
the basic action of the play, for which there will be several analogous
expressions later. In thus proceeding he is not wrenching Holinshed's
chronicle. Merely, he is bringing into better focus the basic story in
Holinshed, by touching it up with latent circumstances that will better
shape up the full historical comedy.

One wonders how Holinshed, in detailing so carefully the archbishop's
oration, could have failed to see its irony. The initial argument against
the Salic law boils down to a single point: French *usurpers* have never
accepted this law as a bar to *their* kingship, therefore neither can it bar
the "princes of this realm of England of their right and lawfull inheritance" (Holinshed). In strict logic, this must mean: either that the "lawfull inheritance" of English princes has no dependence whatever on
French law (which is true, but ruinous to any legal claim to France), or
else that English princes have as their "lawfull inheritance" the task of
emulating French usurpers (which turns out ironically as a fact). The
usurper Hugh Capet, argues the archbishop, established his claim
through the female line. True; but only a juggling which reminds us of
Chaucer's art can twist this fact into evidence for Henry's claim. (And
was Shakespeare perhaps aware of Dante's comment on Hugh Capet in
Purgatorio 20? Dante calls Capet "the root of the evil tree which over-
shadows *all* Christian lands.") Shakespeare plays up the irony by letting
the archbishop play rhetorically on the word "bar," while otherwise the
syntax is getting so tangled that no one can quite follow the logic by
which the speaker pirouettes to his triumphant conclusion.

Then comes the second argument, as overbrief as the first was overlong.
"The archbishop," says Holinshed, "further alleged out of the booke of
Numbers this saying: 'When a man dieth without a sonne, let the in-

heritance descend to his daughter.'" That is all. But Shakespeare makes explicit the implied sequitur, when he lets the archbishop leapfrog his logic and conclude:

> Gracious lord
> Stand for your own, unwind your bloody flag,
> Look back into your mighty ancestors . . .

and invoke the "warlike spirit" of the Black Prince! The Black Prince, in such a context, becomes a veritable Prince of Darkness; and the archbishop's serpentine unreason goes beautifully with his golden rhetoric.

Meanwhile we should not overlook Shakespeare's setting. He has seen to it that Henry's question, from which the skyrocket response is launched, is a very limited question: "May I with right and conscience make this claim?" Exactly *what* claim is shrewdly left vague, while the word "right" neatly avoids thinking of "justice," and "conscience" shelves a considering of "truth." Similarly, Henry's first question had been narrowed to "Why . . . *bar* us in our claim?" Only so much has the archbishop been asked to "religiously unfold." In the "name of God," however, he has been charged to take heed "*How* you awake our sleeping sword of war," and told to speak under this "conjuration" (a term ironically apt for the show-of-divinity both speakers make). In advance, Henry assures Canterbury of his readiness to believe "That what you speak is in *your* conscience washed As pure as sin with baptism." Exactly: a baptizing of sin is what is here desired. Such is Shakespeare's implication—though auditors who understand only 'poetic' theology may miss the point. They may fail to see also that what they have been watching is a masterpiece of evasive shuffling by two magicians (dramatized by a third, Shakespeare). Confederates know how to prime one another. They speak each other's language.

And there is a deeper irony. In strict logic, if the "let descend" of *Numbers* is read as *must* descend in civil law, would it not justify first of all (as Goddard notes on p. 222), not Henry's antiquated claim to France, but rather Edmund Mortimer's claim to the English crown Henry now wears? To insist on inheritance through the female is to undermine Henry's own present position. Blindly, Henry does not see this. Nor apparently does Holinshed. Yet Holinshed mentions a parallel case in his reference, a page later, to the living wife of the Earl of Cambridge, a female in the royal line, through whom this Earl hoped to claim the English throne as his wife's "inheritance." This Earl is the very man we see in Act 2 of the play, there executed by Henry on the charge of selling out his country to the French, a charge which hides the Earl's real intention. Hence the huge irony of Act 2: with great show of piety Henry executes his rival—essentially for the treasonably English and all-too-Frenchified dream of inheriting through the female! Thus does the pot call the kettle black. And Henry's accompanying sermon on the "fall of man" is double-edged irony: for it unwittingly describes not only his own moral fall from grace, but also his fall from manliness in yielding to a female ambition.

This episode prepares us for the crowning irony of Act 5. What Henry there achieves, as the reward of all his labors, is merely the title "heir." Henry never becomes "king" of France; and Shakespeare highlights the point by silence as to the lesser honor mentioned by Holinshed, "regent" of France. Henry gets, instead, the title of "son" to the French king (which rather diminishes Henry's former title); and he gets this (as both Shakespeare and Holinshed carefully state) by marrying the *living* female Kate, not by reason of any dead great-great-grandmother's claim. In other words, he inherits through the female by marrying her—an appropriate answer, surely, to his demand in 2.4.103 (and in Holinshed) that France deliver up the crown "in the bowels of the Lord," thus taking "mercy on poor souls" for whom war opens the jaws. With ironic mercy, Henry's own jaws are fed a bride, while the crown is delivered from his threat and into France's safe keeping. In fact, in a bawdy sense, Kate becomes his "lord," whose bowels may deliver up to him a "French crown." (Her non-virginal status is hinted at in her kissing Henry after saying that "maids" do not, 5.2.280.) Hence Kate's importance to Act 5. The marriage negotiations have overtones of a shotgun-marriage, with Henry holding the shotgun; but he ends up with no status other than as consort to the delicately bawdy Kate.

Earlier, according to the prologue to Act 3, Henry "likes not" the French offer of Kate together with some "petty and unprofitable dukedoms." Yet what else but this is he accepting at the play's ending? Is there not dramatic appropriateness, therefore, in opening Act 5 with a scene in which Pistol is made to eat the leek which he likes not? Surely this is a prophecy, through parody, of Henry's fate. (And though the leek's more specific symbolism is not explained,[5] its association with St. David suggests the biblical hero's winning of nonvirginal Bathsheba, a

[5] An audience might remember, however, that the leek is associated with love of the fleshpots of Egypt, in *Numbers,* 11.6. The OED cites Cowley as using "leek" in this sense in his *Plagues of Egypt* (1656), where it connotes "the Flesh-pots love . . . and sordid roots below." See also OED, Paynel (1528), to the effect that leek is "nat holesome for temperate bodyes," and OED, Herbal (1597), that it is "hot and dry and doth attenuate." Aphrodisiac connotations as well as religious backsliding seem well established.

triumph which he liked not when its badge was forced on him to accept with shame.) Likewise, Pistol's references to "base Trojan" permit us to recall the empty and sordid outcome of the Greek war for Helen.

3.

And has not Shakespeare elsewhere, through parody, foreshadowed an overall reading of Henry's expedition to France? At the beginning of Act 2 he shows us Ancient Pistol preparing to carry away Nell Quickly from an intimidated Nym. Let us see if we cannot read Nym as an antici-patory symbol of the French, and in particular of Burgundy. Nym is being robbed of his "troth-plight," but "when time shall serve there shall be smiles." Why? Because "I dare not fight; but I will wink and hold out mine iron." Recall Monsieur Le Fer in 4.4. Recall, also, Burgundy's yielding of Kate to Henry (5.2.333): "I will wink on her to consent, my lord, if you will teach her to know my meaning." Like Nym, the French are ready to play at bragging and at dueling but know also how to yield when the opponent gets the upper hand—for "though patience be a tired mare, yet she will plod" (2.1.25), just as Burgundy plods in the peace negotiations.

"Couple a gorge," shouts Pistol, a cry we shall often hear, at times ac-companied by a "permafoy" (4.4.39). Does it not epitomize Henry's tactics? We have noted his figurative resort to it in Act 1 and in Act 5. At Agincourt he uses it conspicuously, when having killed one batch of prisoners he threatens to slit the throats of another batch unless the French surrender. "Fearing the sentence of so terrible a decree," says Holinshed, the French yielded "without further delaie." Wisely they might.

For what shall we say of Pistol's second theme, "Base is the slave that pays"? It parallels Henry's scorn of demands for ransom. Yet when it comes to making peace Pistol goes beyond Nym's request for "eight shillings," freely offering him a "noble" with "present pay," together with "liquor" and "brotherhood." For "I'll live by Nym, and Nym shall live by me. Is not this just?" Let us say it is as just as what Henry offers France in Act 5. For note what is involved in Henry's insisting that France address him as "Notre très cher Henry, Roy d'Angleterre, Hériteur de France." Together with "present pay" of homage, France gets a "noble" Henry as *our* Henry. And as for the "brotherhood," let us listen to Henry's words to Kate:

> take me by the hand, and say "Harry of England, I am thine": which word thou shalt no sooner bless mine ear withal, but I will tell thee aloud "England is thine, Ireland is thine, France is thine, and Henry

Plantagenet is thine"; who, though I speak it before his face, if he be
not fellow with the best king, thou shalt find the best king of good
fellows. (5.2.254)

Precisely: he remains king of "good fellows," but Kate is being made
Queen of all his lands. "Dat is as it shall please de roi mon père," says
Kate.

Thus the patient fox has outwitted the valorous mastiff. Just so the
French had predicted (3.7.142) that the "fat brained" English "curs"
would "run winking into the mouth of the Russian bear and have their
heads crushed." Or, let us recall Nym's warning to Pistol: "I will cut thy
throat, one time or another, and *in fair terms*; that is the humour of it."
Or recall Fluellen's words (3.2.64): "Th'athversary, look you, is digt himself four yard under the countermines." And to cap the humor, there is
Henry's own jovial phrase to Kate: "St. Denis be my speed" (5.2.193). Do
readers remember St. Denis—the man who was reduced to carrying his
severed head in his own hand?

The early scene between Pistol and Nym at Hostess Quickly's is, in
fact, a mirror scene with reflections in other directions too. It reflects a
light of analogy, for example, on Henry's dealings with Williams. Figuratively, Henry has Williams by the throat when, glove in hand, he claims:
" 'Twas I indeed thou promised'st to strike. . . . How can thou give me
satisfaction?" (4.8.43). Williams must bow and beseech pardon, whereupon Henry offers "fellow"-ship by extending, not his hand, but a glove
full of crowns. In this case, of course, the analogy focuses on a contrast:
Williams will have none of Henry's dishonorable "glove" or ransoming
gold. Unlike Nym, Williams is no pander to Mistress Quickly, but instead true-plighted to Lady Honor. He is content to seem to lose, knowing himself to be the actual victor morally. Henry's triumph is merely
verbal. Symbolically, the king now plainly has a "leek" in his cap, "For
I am Welsh, you know . . ." (4.7.110). As a St. Davy he is no less ironic
here than as a St. Denis later.

But the "mirror scene" of 2.1 looks in still another direction—backward, on the events of Act 1. Perhaps we should have carried through
this analogy first, since it is the most immediate. Nym resembles Canterbury who, when Henry's gloved hand had threatened his throat, yielded
gracefully. Also like Nym, Canterbury in due time outwits Pistol-Harry.
For he maneuvers him into handing over to the prelates the office of
magistrates in England during his absence. In a sense, then, there is truth
in Henry's later boast at Agincourt: "It yearns me not if men my garments wear; such outward things dwell not in my desires." Not Henry
but the bishops have secured the garments of his authority within Eng-

land, while Henry has carried off merely the "honor" he so sinfully covets (4.3.28)—in this case, the honor of Mistress Sanctity, the church's hostess, whom the bishops have prostituted to their temporal gain.

The way in which Henry continues to prostitute sanctity can easily be seen at Agincourt. What "fellowship," for example, can Saints Crispin and Crispianus have with the work Henry is about? These brothers were humble shoemakers. They were martyred by Diocletian—perhaps because Diocletian did not like their efforts to shoe public actions with a "good" justice (obeying St. Paul's "feet shod with the preparation of the gospel of peace"). In William Shakespeare's play, the efforts of Williams are similarly unwelcome to Henry. For Henry has his own sense of what is fit and right: War is God's beadle. Or let the Irish Macmorris speak for Henry: "The trumpet call us to the breach; and we talk, and, by Chrish, do nothing: . . . It is a shame, by my hand; and there is throats to be cut and works to be done" (3.2.115). Probably Diocletian felt similarly. So he shooed the Crispins out of his sight—just as Henry shoos his opponents time and again in the play (for example, at 4.7.62). But holy smoke, what a name Crispin provides any king to conjure with! (It "most excellently suggests the word Christian," says Wilson Knight, p. 169.) So let us imagine, when the troops return home, how they can roll up their sleeves and say: "These wounds I had on St. Crispin's day"! (4.3.48.) Thus, with only a hint from Holinshed, Shakespeare supplies the mockery and the pathos of Elizabethan England's 'vigil' of St. Crispin.

Shakespeare sees also, as Holinshed apparently does not, the ironic connection between Henry's murdering of the prisoners and his pious eagerness, immediately afterwards, to give God's "arm" the whole credit for the victory. "To thine arm alone, ascribe we all," says Shakespeare's Henry—and, in the next breath, proclaims a penalty of "death" on any soldier who boasts of a share in the victory. Having gone that far in irony, Shakespeare could hardly risk mentioning the psalm which Holinshed says Henry ordered sung, *In exitu Israel de Aegypto*. Historical comparisons might explode the whole joke. So Shakespeare risks only the words *Non nobis* and *Te Deum*. Try imagining, however, what would happen if a Hollywood producer were to introduce a choir distinctly singing the full text of these songs.

We have critics, nevertheless, who wax enthusiastic over Henry's piety at Agincourt. Commenting on Henry's line, "How thou pleasest, God, dispose the day," Dover Wilson writes (p. xli): "It is a statement of the ultimate heroic faith, a faith which, like that of the martyrs, puts him who holds it beyond reach of mortal man." Perhaps so. But just how like is it, really? As like as shadow to substance, is what Shakespeare's irony tells us. His drama makes plain whose arm disposed of the prisoners and also who disposed the French to yield.

By now my reader will scarcely need the help of a commentator on Henry's famous prayer before Agincourt. Its opening line, "O God of battles steel my soldiers' hearts," distorts both God's nature (which is not *of* battles but *above* them) and His work (which is to soften by grace, not to steel). Henry's petition is Turkish piety, in the spirit of an Amurath (despite *2 Henry IV*, 5.2.48). Moreover, what should be mentioned first in any Christian prayer—namely, penitence—comes at the tag-end of Henry's, and in the weasel form of "imploring pardon," not mercy. In this context his confession that "all that I can do is nothing worth" is ironically correct. For all that he has been able to do is to boast of his philanthrophies—exactly like the Pharisee in the biblical parable. And instead of "God be merciful to *me,* a sinner," there is the almost farcical plea that God *not think* on "my *father's* fault"—"Not to-day, O Lord, oh, not today." Only the pre-established rhythm of the blank verse hides the inner rhythm of blank panic.

Henry's language gives him away at other times too. Only once, and then as an insinuation from under disguise, does he term the war just— in the phrase "his cause being just." Williams at once moves toward the heart of this matter, only to be shuffled off by the king's evasive sermon in another direction. Holinshed had put the words "our just cause" and "our just quarrel" squarely into Henry's mouth at Agincourt. Shakespeare is a better psychologist; he understands the evasions of a guilty conscience. Also he knows its proneness to inadvertent self-revelation. Note, for example, Henry's reply to the French ambassadors:

> We never valued this poor seat of England;
> And therefore, loving hence, did give ourself
> To barbarous licence.
>
> (1.2.269)

Or notice, at Harfleur, his threatening of "infants" in the name of *"Herod's* bloody-hunting slaughtermen" (3.3.41). Or at Agincourt, his threatening of the French with stones "from the old *Assyrian* slings" (4.7.65). Such allusions speak loud, louder than the direct "We are no tyrant but a Christian king" of Act 1. The same Henry who orders Bardolph hanged for stealing a "pax of little price" (3.6.47) will later swear, "by the mass," that his soldiers' hearts are in trim to steal French

"new coats" (4.3.115). Ah, yes, the new "coat." By the mass, that's what
will make the New Man of St. Paul's teaching!

4.

The comic language lesson in 3.4, located at a central point in the
play's structure, is also pivotal for interpretation. Shakespeare does not
waste scenes of farce; he makes them carry theme as well as immediate
entertainment. Here the scene is placed between, on the one hand,
Henry's "impious war" over Harfleur, replete with imagery of rape, and,
on the other hand, a scene in which the French speak with bawdy innuendo of the "barbarous" English. What kind of 'language,' then, do
the English speak? Katherine is about to find out. She discovers a body-
language which amazes her, yet arouses her desire to repeat the lesson
"une autre fois."

The words Katherine asks about have an order suggestive of a progress
in love-making,[6] though devoid of any words for heart or soul. Beginning
with attention to the hand, the focus of interest moves up the arm to the
neck and chin (as if for a stolen kiss) and then downward to what we
may call fundamental matters, adequately deciphered by Katherine's
broad wit. Quite well enough she understands that the English tongue
is bent on "sin" and, in the end, on things too naughty to mention in
polite society. The wordplay of the dialogue, as if in epitome of the
play itself, hovers between suggestions of robbery and rape. The connotations on this level prepare us for the later love-scene in Act 5, where
Katherine professes to "understand well" when Henry talks of desiring
to "possess" her by winning at "Leap-frogge" and getting her by "scam-
bling." In that scene his request that she "mock me mercifully . . . because I love thee cruelly" (5.2.215) is as truly fulfilled as is the cruelty
of his love. Indeed his proper match is Kate, who as Burgundy suggests
is "well summered and warm" to "endure *hand*ling."

But besides overtones of bawdy in the language lesson, the fact that it
starts out with vocabulary for the "hand" and its parts is itself significant.
At Harfleur, let us recall, Henry has pictured his English army as a
"blind and bloody soldier with foul hand" (3.3.34); and one of his cap-
tains, Macmorris, goes around swearing characteristically "by my hand."
Moreover, an undertone of legerdemain has been noticeable in the play
from its beginning, and at the end we will overhear Henry's comic surrogate, Pistol, resolving to turn bawd and "something lean to cutpurse

---

[6] I am indebted for this observation to my colleague Robert Davis.

of quick hand." Thus 'hand' has a primary importance in understanding the English order of values. In the outreach of the hand's parts and powers may we not see delineated the ethos of Henry and his fellows? Katherine's lesson, through its farce, implies and plays on this truth.[7] She is shown learning about (the) English, so to speak, from head to toe —which ironically in this case means from the nailed hand to the indecent foot, with nothing worth mentioning above the chin. The vignette is its own commentary. But of the various verbal puns which accompany it, Katherine's associating of the hand's "nails" with English "males" is particularly apt, since it amusingly links English men with claws or a bestial kind of manhood. Moreover, "nails" will be mentioned in a later scene (4.4.75) as characteristic of "the roaring devil in the old play."

Much of what the language lesson has hinted as to the English character we can find openly ascribed to Henry, later, in Pistol's eulogy. Valiant fist, beau-cock habits, and even dirty foot are here praised. In fact, the whole of Pistol's admiring tribute might well be engraved as Henry's epitaph:

> The king's a bawcock, and a heart of gold,
> A lad of life, an imp of Fame,
> Of parents good, of fist most valiant:
> I kiss his dirty shoe, and from heart-string
> I love the lovely bully. . .
>
> (4.1.44)

As an imp of fame with a dirty shoe, our Harry-hero's version of John Bull does indeed deserve aesthetic admiration—the more so when *we* understand its marvelous incongruity with Christian heroism. Recognition of the obscene belongs to art's morality. Hence we may say likewise,

---

[7] A textual problem, related here only incidentally to our argument, may be worth mentioning. The Folio's text of the French in this scene is notorious for its botched spellings and genders. Editors have regarded these as printer's or compositor's faults and accordingly have tidied up the French. But can we be sure that all the Folio's oddities of French are contrary to Shakespeare's intention? May not some of them be a deliberately fractured French for purposes of farce? At the beginning, for example, when Katherine asks, "Comient appelle vous le main en Anglois?", Alice replies: "Le main il & [*et* = phonetic *est*] appelle de Hand." Here "Le main il" involves faulty gender in both article and pronoun. But just possibly there is a dramatic reason: an auditor alert to puns might *hear* "Le main" as a question about "Man," or even about "the man" Henry. Such an auditor would then have the fun of understanding this opening gambit as follows:

> *Katherine.* What is (the) *Man* called in English?
> *Alice.* (The) *Man, he* is called the Hand.

In the light of what the play elsewhere lets us see as to the hand's importance in the English ethos, the reading here suggested is attractive as lending an even more forcible emphasis to a thematic point.

with Nym: "The king is a good king; but it must be as it may; he passes some humors and careers" (2.2.125).

And of course Henry's opponents in the play come off no better, or no worse. The French are repeatedly characterized as magnificently frivolous, shrewdly pusillanimous, and sinuously bawdy. They call themselves "bastard warriors," and Pistol calls one of them a "damned and luxurious mountain goat" (4.4.20). Thus the goatish and horsey French balance against the piggish and bullishly barking English. The whole play, in its undertones, is a splendid contest between London gunstones and Paris balls; between Greeks with an Achilles heel and Trojan Paris-lovers (the pun in 2.4.132) with their Nell; between Ares and Aphrodite, between Jove and Europa—all the various aspects of Renaissance paganized Christendom. Nor is such a spectacle really new within Christendom. The Epistle of St. Peter describes at length certain Christians who, after having known the way of righteousness, slide back into the defilements of the world, uttering "great and swelling words of vanity," and whose "last state is become worse than the first." In fact, St. Peter has an indelicate proverb for this: "The dog is returned to his own vomit again, and the sow that was washed to her own wallowing in the mire" (2 Peter, 2.22). Shakespeare tucks this proverb (in French) in the middle of his play (3.7.68), with the added comment, "thou makest use of any thing." Could it be the play's motto?

Shakespeare's prologue to Act 4, provided we know how to read it, states well enough his dramatic purpose. The drama's pitiful and ridiculous "foils," says the Chorus, are "mockeries" by means of which we are invited to discern truth:

> And so our scene must to the battle fly;
> Where, O for pity! we shall much disgrace
> With four or five most ragged foils,
> Right ill-disposed to brawl ridiculous,
> The name of Agincourt. Yet sit and see
> Minding true things by what their mock'ries be.

Pity for the human imagination's mockeries of heroism and of grace: such is the Christian playwright's request of us as we read with him the history of Agincourt. A pitiful history of 'foiled' cupidity is the comic theme. Or, ironically stated, the theme is: How to put off the old man and put on the New. The recipe for this is an heroic comedy.

TUDOR INTELLIGENCE TESTS:
MALVOLIO AND REAL LIFE

by C. J. SISSON

1. THE PROBLEM

EVEN AFTER SOME centuries of continuous and industrious exploration on a scale unprecedented in literary history, there remain some small islands in the Sea of Shakespearia still practically unvisited and uncharted. The immense mass of commentary upon *The Merchant of Venice* almost neglects Launcelot's contribution to palmistry in 2.2, or dismisses it as mere nonsense. It is, in fact, clear evidence that Shakespeare was well acquainted with the science, for he keeps Launcelot close to the principles laid down by early authority, even in respect of dangers of drowning and of widows and maids in the number of prospective wives.[1] A second unexplored islet, with which we are here concerned, is the ordeal to which Malvolio was subjected to test his sanity, put in question by Olivia in 3.4 of *Twelfth Night*. She charges Maria and Toby to take care of him, and they enter with zest upon their psychiatric duties. Toby diagnoses at once diabolical possession as the cause of his madness, and Maria and Fabian concur with relish. They confine him in a dark room and very properly arrange for a visit by a clergyman in the hope of exorcizing the devil in him. Feste puts on a gown and beard, and adopts the name of Sir Topas the curate, an obvious choice of name for those who know how to treat madness, having perhaps learned from Reginald Scot's *Discovery of Witchcraft* (1584) that "a topaz healeth the lunatic person of his passion of lunacy," a belief supported by the au-

---

[1] See John Methan, *Works*, ed. Hardin Craig, EETS (Orig. Ser.), 132 (1906), 111-12. It is odd that Professor Craig, when he later came to edit Shakespeare, cited (*Complete Works*, 1951, pp. 512-13) only an almost irrelevant reference from Furness. But almost fifty years separate the two books.

183

thority of Cardan. (See Robert Burton, *The Anatomy of Melancholy*, 2.3.1.4.) The inquiry is conducted in 4.2, with an interrogatory by Sir Topas, to which Malvolio manfully replies in defense of his challenged five wits.

Curiosity is naturally aroused as to whether this scene bears any relation to the normal processes of inquiry in the real life of Shakespeare's time into actual or supposed cases of lunacy, whether it is a caricature, however gross, of such inquiries, or whether it is pure fantastic nonsense, as Launcelot's palmistry is not. A full account of one such inquiry would satisfy this curiosity, and would also be of exceptional interest in the history of psychology, as the earliest available evidence of the nature of intelligence tests in their true sense, as distinct from the recently fashionable sense of ascertaining mental agility. The case now to be reported is fully recorded in early Chancery depositions and ran its course through the last years of Edward VI and the reign of Philip and Mary (P.R.O., C24/43/Ford v. Rythe). Among the dramatis personae is, incidentally, the steward of a great house, Robert Pickes, of a dignity comparable to Malvolio's.

2. BACKGROUND TO AN INQUIRY INTO LUNACY

The political background to this story of Henry Windsor, son and heir of Sir Anthony Windsor, Lord of the Manor of Harting in West Sussex, near Petersfield, and brother of Lord Windsor, is one of unrelieved hideousness. The death in 1547 of that man of power who had held the crown of England in firm hands, the dread King Henry VIII, left his throne to be occupied by a sickly boy, as a pawn in a game in which the stake was high indeed, no less than the crown of England. It was fought between two great families, the Seymours and the Dudleys, whose unscrupulous maneuvers in pursuit of their unbridled ambitions for power, and whose exercise of power, achieve the difficult feat of making one think more kindly of Henry VIII. Their rival plots to supplant the Tudors by the Seymours or the Dudleys ended upon scaffold after scaffold. Some months after Sir Anthony Windsor's death, Edward Seymour, Duke of Somerset, was arrested, and after an uneasy truce rearrested and beheaded upon a charge of conspiracy against John Dudley, Earl of Warwick and presently Duke of Northumberland. During Northumberland's time of full power, Henry Windsor's affairs, and his own person, fell under the oppression of the Duke's son Sir Andrew Dudley and of the Privy Council, from Dudley's stronghold at Petworth. In due course, Northumberland came to the axe under Mary, after his attempt to place on her throne Lady Jane Grey, whom he had married to his son Guildford Dudley. As the shadow of the Dudleys receded from Sussex, it became possible to appeal to justice from tyranny.

With this change in political power, a change of religious sympathies favored the Windsors, and we see in these litigations the spectacle of changing fortunes from Edward to Mary, from Mary to Elizabeth, so often to be observed under the Tudors. There was little doubt where the Windsors stood in these matters. Their ally Sir Anthony Browne, friend of Henry VIII, Knight of the Garter, guardian to Prince Edward and Princess Mary, and executor under Henry's will, lord of wide lands around Midhurst and Petworth, builder of a great house at Cowdray, was placed by John Fox among the 'Papists' on the Privy Council, a "principal pillar" of Stephen Gardiner's power (*Acts and Monuments,* 1631, 2.529, 647). Browne had died a year later than Henry, and his support was lost under Edward. His son Anthony, no less faithful, rose to be Viscount Montague under Mary. The Windsors may have conformed, but under Elizabeth a later Lady Windsor gave refuge in her London house to two fugitive priests, Cuthbert Mayne and William Wigges (P.R.O., C24/303/6). Edmond Ford was Sir Anthony Browne's man of business and managed his manors in West Sussex, including the Honour of Petworth, and could hardly be of the opposing party in religious matters. He was the son of Erasmus Ford, a Merchant of the Staple, of considerable wealth and possessed of lands round Thames Ditton and Kingston. Edmond clearly had incurred the enmity of Sir Andrew Dudley in his projects for setting up as Lord of the Manors of Harting. Henry Windsor calls Ford "brother Ford," probably as husband by a first marriage to a sister of Ford. Ford himself married Eleanor Cheesman.

Henry, son and heir of Sir Anthony Windsor, aged thirty-six in 1550, had now married Eleanor Burbage, of a Hertfordshire family, aged thirty in 1558, whose sister Mary was wife to John Brock, a London physician and a principal witness, along with Eleanor, in the events now to be described. After Henry's death, Eleanor married Hugh Partridge, of Hertfordshire. Henry's sister Constance had married Thomas Rythe, whose cousin George Rythe was Sir Anthony's man of business and an executor of his will.[2] Thomas was man of business to the Earl of Southampton.

The Harting Manors had long been in the possession of the Hussey

---

[2] *The History of Harting,* by the Rev. H. S. Gordon (1877), a vicar of Harting, among other errors, gives this name as "Riche." It also mentions Windsor's idiocy as established. Nevertheless it is a valuable compilation.

family, and their male line of entail ended with Sir Henry Hussey. Constance, his only surviving child and heiress, married Henry Lovell, and their daughter Elizabeth, the next heir, married Sir Anthony Windsor. They had two children, Henry and Constance, and the Manors were naturally entailed solely upon these grandchildren of Constance Hussey, though Sir Anthony by a second marriage had six other children, as we learn from Henry Windsor himself.

It is clear that Henry and Ford had agreed to effect a conveyance of the Manors to Ford. Even before Sir Anthony's death in September 1549, they had agreed upon a lease, in reversion for twenty-one years from the date of his death, of Harting and part of West Harting. The conveyance of the fee simple, upon his death, offered difficulties, for it involved a breach of the entail upon Constance and required her consent. Inducements were offered by Ford to her and to the Rythes, which they accepted. (The birth of a child to Henry and Eleanor would, of course, have extinguished the rights of Constance.) Constance and Thomas were to have 400 marks in cash or an annuity of 20 marks. George was to have 200 loads of firewood a year forever out of Harting Combe. The conveyance, now unopposed, was completed by process of Fine and Recovery in the Court of Common Pleas before Sir James Hales in Michaelmas 1549. At this stage Sir Andrew Dudley and his friends in Sussex intervened, to invoke one last desperate expedient. The Rythes, submissive to so powerful an ally, who could be so dangerous an enemy, joined in his attack. There was no question that the price paid for Harting was adequate and that the sum of £1,930 had been paid and was fully acquitted.

The conveyance was challenged on the grounds of undue influence and of Henry's incompetence by reason of idiocy to conduct affairs. The King's Escheator in Sussex was charged with an inquiry *De idiota inquirendo,* with a view to placing Henry's estate under the Court of Wards and Liveries and so, obviously, entrusting it to Dudley. Henry Windsor was removed from Harting and held incommunicado at Burton in the house of Sir William Goring, near Petworth, where the inquiry was held at Whitsuntide 1550 by the Deputy Escheator Mr. Birche, with a jury of local worthies, at least one of whom, "an ancient yeoman" Nashe, proved to be recalcitrant to such an inquiry and was replaced. Henry elected to answer for himself, and the questions put, with his answers, were quoted verbatim in subsequent litigation. They were unsatisfactory for the proposed purpose, and an attempt was made to involve Henry's wife, and with her help Henry himself, in a fresh inquiry at Horsham, in which he would play the part of an idiot in answering questions. The record of his answers would then be used in a trial for disseizin of Harting at the assize to be held at East Grinstead. It was urged that their safety lay in submitting to this course, and Mrs. Windsor was brought before Sir Andrew Dudley in his London house of Petty Callice in St. James, where also Henry was then held prisoner in the charge of Dudley's steward Robert Pickes. Subjected there to intense pressure, with the threat of the anger of the Duke of Northumberland and the determination of the Privy Council to have Henry declared an idiot and to ruin Ford, she at last submitted, and her consent won Henry's agreement. Windsor was taken to Horsham, to Henry Hussey's house, and there was tutored in his part. The jury, carefully 'framed' for the purpose (the word is in common Tudor use in this sense), found as required. The Privy Council, subservient to the Dudleys, expelled Ford from Harting and imprisoned him in the Fleet, as soon as 'the office was found,' that is, as soon as the finding of the inquiry was declared. Nevertheless the trial at the Assize ended in the dismissal of Rythe's case. It rested almost solely on the question of idiocy, and the evidence for Windsor's real sanity was overwhelming.

A new situation arose with the death of Henry Windsor, and with the fall of the Dudleys upon the accession of Mary in 1553. In the meantime Edmond Ford had gained a valuable ally in John Brock, Windsor's brother-in-law, who had been deeply involved in the plot against him. Brock, smitten by conscience, had sworn in 1551, before Ford and three gentlemen of standing in Sussex, to a long and detailed account of the plot, which Ford could produce in evidence and which Brock would stand to as a witness in any subsequent suit. The evidence of Henry's wife Eleanor was no less damning. She also had made a statement in November 1553, a few months after the trial for treason of Northumberland and Sir Andrew Dudley. Both were produced in due course when the case reached the Court of Chancery and came to final settlement in 1558 in favor of Ford's ownership and of Windsor's sanity. Ford and his descendants reigned at Harting Manor for two centuries. He himself was buried in Harting Church on 5 December 1568, and the Parish Registers record his family history. A bronze plaque in the Chancel reports their later alliance by marriage with Baron Grey, whose son Forde Grey became Earl of Tankerville. Of the Rythes there is no trace in Harting.

3. IDIOT OR WISE MAN: THE INQUIRY

The alternative to being an 'idiot' was to be a 'wise man,' in the terms normally used in records of inquiry. It is evident that no especial expert qualification was required for competence to judge in this matter. The inquiry at Petworth was presided over by the Deputy Escheator, assisted by the Feodary (an official of the Court of Wards) and a jury of ordinary men of the neighborhood acquainted with Windsor, such a jury as might serve on the manorial Court of Harting. Questions were put to Windsor in turn by the Escheator, the Feodary, and the Jury. A verbatim record of the inquiry was produced at the Assize trial by Thomas Boundy, a London lawyer who was one of Ford's clerks and appeared there for him. He gave it again in evidence before the Court of Chancery, and it is transcribed in the depositions, "fol. xix Examinacō Henr Wyndesore Capta apud Petworth in Cōm Sussex die Jovis in Septimana Pentecost Anno rs E vjᵗⁱ quarto [i.e. 1550]."

The Eschetors
demaunds

Examynyd of what age he aunseryd xxxvjᵗ Requyryd to tell it he told perfectly what was his fathers name he aunseryd Sir Antony Wyndesore knyght Also what his mothers name was he aunseryd Elizabeth

What his graundfathers name was on the parte of his father he aunseryd he knew not his name.

What was his graundmothers name on the parte of his mother he aunseryd Constance Lewknor and she had two husbands the first husbands name was Lovell and her second husbands name was Sir Roger Lewknor.

Also how meny wyffs his father had he aunseryd three the ferst was his mother the second namyd Annise and the third namyd Jane.

fol. xx. Ferther was demaunded how meny brethren and Susters he had by one father and one mother he aunseryd one Sister and by the second wyff his father had six childern Andrewe Elizabeth Peter Antony Edith and Honor whereof thre were on lyve and thre were decessed and by his last wyff he had no chyld

There was also demaundyd of hym what a pece of gold of half a soūaign of ten shillyngs was he aunseryd xˢ a Reyall

Demaundyd of hym what a pece of gold was of xˢ of the last coyne wᵗ a crowne on the hed he aunseryd xˢ

Also what a pece of gold of the newe coyne was wᵗ a pollyd³ hedde of xˢ he aunseryd xˢ of the newe coyne

---

³ That is, with the head ending at the neck, as if beheaded.

Also what a crowne of v^s was he aunseryd v^s

Also what a pece of gold callyd an old Aungell was he aunseryd an old Aungell worth x^s

And what a pece of gold callyd an old Royall was he aunseryd an old Royall of the old coyne

And what it was worth he aunseryd xij^s

The Feodaryes
Demaunds

Demaunded whether he would prove hymself a wyse man by his councell then being there or by his owne aunswer he aunseryd by his owne Aunser

Demaundyd howe meny dayes ys in a moneth besyds the Sondayes he aunseryd foure Sondayes and xxiiij dayes

Demaundyd howe meny fyngers he had besyds his two thombes he aunseryd eight fyngers

Demaundyd howe meny was v and vij he aunseryd xij

Demaundyd howe meny was vij and v. he aunseryd xij

Demaunded what a pece of coyne callyd an old testern was he aunseryd an old testern

And what a pece of coyne callyd a Shyllyng was he aunseryd xij^d

Demaunded what the lands was worth by the yere he sold to Mayster Foord he aunseryd one hundred marks by the yere

And what money he receyuyd therfore he aunseryd xix^C pounds

Demaunded howe meny yeres purchase that was after the rate he aunseryd twenty yeres purchase and uppeward

Demaunded howe meny shillyngs was xiiij grotes he aunseryd iiij^s viij^d

Item he was requyred to rede Englysshe he redde it perfectly

Demaunded howe meny pence were in fyve grotes shewyd vnto hym he aunseryd xx^d

The Juryes
Demaunds

Item requyred to tell xx^s in grotes dyd tell it perfectly and after to tell howe meny grotes were therof he told it out by lx grotes perfectly

Demaunded why he dyd sell his land being so feyre a possession he aunseryd because he myght gayn moore yerely by lettyng out his money after x^{li} in the hundred

Demaunded to whome he had so lett it he Aunseryd he woold not declare that

Demaunded to wrytt his owne name his fathers name and his moothers name he dyd wrytt there names perfectly Henry Wyndesore Sir Antony Wyndesore and Elizabeth Wyndesore

per me Joñem Byrche

and in the presence of vs Thomas Carpender Thomas Stoughton Thomas Shelley Phi. Browne

Some significance may perhaps be read into the regions of inquiry entered upon in each group. The Escheator, concerned with the succession of land by due inheritance, inquires into Windsor's knowledge of his family history. But he also tests his knowledge of the coinage. The Feodary's catechism contained some exercises in mental arithmetic concerning money and elementary finance, as befitted the treasurer of the Court of Wards, along with some miscellaneous oddments. He also tested Windsor's ability to read English, whereupon "he redde it perfectly." The intrusion of catch questions brings us nearer to a modern 'intelligence test.' When asked how many days there are in a month besides Sundays, Windsor answered four Sundays and twenty-four days. He could hardly have been thinking of February, with its twenty-eight days, for the inquiry was held at Whitsuntide, and in 1550 Whit Sunday fell on 25 May. He seems to have presumed that the question referred to a lunar month rather than to the varying calendar months, and so escaped its complexity. There was perhaps even an element of unfairness in two successive questions upon adding first seven to five, then five to seven, with the implied suggestion that these were different problems. Doubtless the Feodary sought appreciation of the shrewdness of his searching inquiry. But Windsor was not bemused. The Jury tested his ability to 'tell' money, and his understanding of capital value in relation to rental value of land. Here his answers were of perfect cogency, as were his answers to similar questions from the Feodary. Certainly £1,900 let out on interest at 10%, the usual rate of the time, would produce an income of £190, as compared with an income from rents of 100 marks or £66. The purchase price represented more than twenty years' purchase, a Windsor said, indeed almost twenty-nine years of an income of £66. The Jury's insistence upon the apparent strangeness of parting with "so fair a possession" as Harting sprang from the deeply ingrained attachment of these country folk to the ownership of land as the supreme good. For the rest, they tested also Windsor's skill in writing his own name and those of his father and mother, which he did perfectly. They themselves for the most part could but make their mark. There was no question of Windsor's confidence in himself in this ordeal. The Feodary offered him the alternative of representation by a lawyer, and Windsor chose to answer for himself.

He certainly knew what was important in his family history. He did not know the name of his paternal grandfather, but that of his maternal grandmother was of greater significance, and he knew that it was Constance Lewknor, she being wife in turn to Mr. Lovell and to Sir Roger Lewknor. It was, of course, through Constance that Harting came to the Windsors, and Henry's sister was named after her. He knew of his father's three marriages, of his second wife Annis and their six children, named in order, and of his third wife Jane, though the entail of Harting rested upon himself and his full sister Constance alone. He knew his way about the jungle of early Tudor coinage apparently. These were days when the gross debasement of the coinage in Henry's last years, continued under Edward and Mary, was a very live and disturbing issue, and a man had to have his wits about him in dealing with a most complex coinage of varying gold and silver content according to its age. There might for example be a considerable divergence in the value in shillings of a 'new' or an 'old' sovereign or ryal.

The most ample evidence is given by a variety of other witnesses to Windsor's competence in the managing of his affairs and of his Harting lands. A number of documents produced as exhibits, in his own handwriting, record his dealings with his farmer and others, and are quoted verbatim. One document contains an interesting analysis of his sources of income before his father's death:

The land I bought of my brother Foord by yere xiij^{li} vj^{s} viij^{d}

The Anuyte I haue of my father by yere xiij^{li} x^{s}

The Anuyte I haue of my brother Foord by yere x^{li}

The allowance I haue of my father for my bord vj^{li} xiij^{s} iiij^{d}

The yerely proffetts of my woods x^{li}

The yerely pencyon I haue of my father for the land Mayster Gage bought of me iij^{li}

Sma totlys of all my hole yerely lyvyng ouer and aboue all charges is lvj^{li} and x^{s}

An autograph letter from Windsor to Ford is cited and is a model of form and style. It also evidences Windsor's independence in his dealings with Ford. His reference to his own wife as "my bedfellow your sister" is made before 1549, and is explicit. For the most part the extensive further evidence covers the same ground of civilized and controlled social behavior and competence in daily affairs. It is recorded that he and his father said mattins and evensong together in Harting Church. But we have a glimpse of Windsor's wider interests in his friendship with the Rev. Anthony Clerk, Prebendary of Chichester Cathedral and formerly schoolmaster there, a frequent visitor to him at the Manor House. Clerk played 'Irish' at the tables with him, and 'Post' at cards, and also interested him in dramatic performances at the school. Windsor lent Clerk costumes, of which he made a list himself, for the purposes of playing "a comedy callyd filius prodigus," some one of the many Prodigal Son plays of the time in the Terentian manner.

No transcript has survived of Windsor's examination by the Escheator at Horsham, but in an extraordinary confession by his brother-in-law John Brock, then twenty-eight years of age, in which he records his part in the whole affair, he reports some of the questions for which Windsor was tutored to answer in counterfeit folly. The confession was made before Ford and three Justices of the Peace, William Hustwayte, Robert Sennyng, and Robert Pecock, in Hustwayte's house on 27 February 1551, and the verbatim transcript is a notable literary document of Tudor prose, of considerable length. It opens thus:

> Mr. Forde I am nowe comen vnto you to open a matter wherewith I haue not byn a little troubled syne the devill first putt in my head to attempt the same, God I take to record by no mans procurement but onely of myne owne deuelishe mynde procured therunto.

He then explains the reasons for his great fears for himself, his certainty that the Privy Council was bent on declaring Windsor an idiot, and his belief that Ford was his enemy.

> Thus being by the devill enflamed agaynst you I saught meanes to serue their turne in all that I colde. But er I declare vnto you how and the cyrcomstance thereof I here before theis three honest men ask you hartelye forgyuenes desyring you for the passyon of Chryst to pardon me, or els I am sure I can not be saued, for nothing forceth me this to do, but only that I am so troubled in my conscience that I can neyther eate drynck nor slepe in quiett but euer this mater is in my head. God I knowe is mercifull, and farre he runnys that neuer turnys therfore for Gods sake forgyue me. And I wyll (withoute feare or dread of any man) shew vnto you the truth euyn as I haue don and therby shame the devill and procure grace and fauor at Gods hande.

Upon Ford's assurance of Christian forgiveness, Brock proceeds to report conversations with Sir Andrew Dudley, to whom he suggested that extraordinary measures would be necessary with Windsor, "for I knowe although he be not wise, yet he is far from suche an ydeote as the lawe calleth an ydeot," and offered his services, with proposals to enlist the influence of his sister-in-law, Windsor's wife, who alone could persuade him. "She is half at her wytts end allredy," and will be amenable if Dudley "handles her gently and promyses her fayer." She was taken to Dudley's London house, and Windsor was brought there to meet her. When they parted, she showed him two bent silver pennies, to serve as tokens to validate any future message from her. She was then taken to Windsor Castle, to Dudley's room there, when she signed a statement of her husband's idiocy drawn up by Sir Henry Hussey, without reading it. At Horsham, Brock and Mrs. Windsor's brother Robert Burbage produced the tokens to Windsor, and overcame his resistance. Hussey therefore instructed Windsor in their presence:

> Cosyn Wyndesor I am not a litle glad you haue shewed yourself so conformable to your friends for hereby you shall fynde moche friendship. But one thing I must lesson you in and that is this when you be brought into the Courte before the people as you were at Petworth you must answer in all things contrary and ouerthwartlye as this, yf my cosyn Goryng or I ask you any nomber that you can tel, answer cleane contrary as if you be asked what is twoo and twoo say seven, what is three and three say five. And so likewise vnto like questions for allthough I know that you can tel thies and suche other small nombers well ynough, yet must [you] mysse for the nones for that will best content the people, for we will axe you no harde questyon, because you shall remember the better to mysse of purpose or willingly, but one other thing of all other you must chiefly remembre. When I bid you tel twenty tel it as I know you can but mysse in some place and then I and my cosyn Goryng will prayse and comend you and will say that it is a shame that any such as you ar should be brought in question to be an ydeot that can tell twenty so well. And then by and by I will require you to tell twenty backwarde, and furthwith before all the people turne your back toward vs and tell twenty as you dyd before, and in your gesture and countenance and yn all things els shewe your self as folishly as you can deuise for it for it is all for your proffitt and advantage.

Brock concludes his confession in melodramatic passion:

> By gods blood if there be any suche mater in hand I will open such a gap as will make them all ashamed to here of it, for now I perceive this is the only marke they shote at to haue his lordship to come to

the king by Atteynder [of Ford] for I will neuer whiles I live for no
mans plesur consent to shed ynnocent blood I had rather be toren in
peces with wild horses for if this shold com to passe Mr. Hussey you
haue made a fayer shoote.

He has a considerable repertory of rhetorical colloquialisms. "A foole
he shold be founde spyte of his teethe." So indeed has Mrs. Eleanor
Windsor. "Mr. Dudley would neuer leave him vntill he had sett him ouer
the cooles." She confirms Brock's story at all points in her confession. We
may think the better of Brock's sincerity when we realize that his statement was made in February 1551 when the power of the Dudleys was in
full tide and had overwhelmed even the Duke of Somerset whom they
were soon to bring to the scaffold. Eleanor's statement was made in safer
waters, some months after their fall and the execution of Northumberland, under Mary.

4. THE STEWARD OF A GREAT HOUSE: A TUDOR MALVOLIO

Of all the corroborative evidence recorded at both the Assize Court
and in the Court of Chancery, in confirmation of the normality of Windsor's intelligence, that of Robert Pickes has exceptional interest as coming from the steward of a great house, in a situation similar to that of
Malvolio, and his evidence throws some light upon Shakespeare's probable conception of Malvolio's status in Illyria. Pickes was 'Steward in
Household,' as he informed the Court, to Sir Andrew Dudley from 1551
to Dudley's arrest in July 1553, and thereafter to Francis Earl of Hunt-
ingdon. (It is obviously important to distinguish the office of 'Steward
in Household' from that of a Steward of a Manor or of other estates.)
Pickes served Dudley in this office both at his castle of Guisnes, during
Dudley's Captaincy of Guisnes, and at his London house, 'Petty Callice,'
in St. James's Park. He gives his age as being thirty-seven on 17 February
1558, describing himself as "Gentleman." His signature "per me,
R. Pickes," followed by an elaborate paraph, is of exceptional size and
ceremony. His evidence is given with a similar weight and dignity, with
some apparent sense of his own importance, and conveying a certain independence of judgment and moral integrity.

What we learn of Pickes's functions in Dudley's household may well
lead us to reconsider the nature of Malvolio's control, by delegated authority from Olivia, over Sir Toby and Sir Andrew as well as over Maria
and Feste. When Dudley's household moved with him from one to
another of his seats, it moved as a whole with Pickes in command, and it
is evident that in Dudley's absence Pickes had sole authority. With the

household moved also the family and guests, voluntary or involuntary, of Dudley. Among them was Dudley's prisoner or enforced guest Henry Windsor, who was moved from Guisnes to Petty Callice, whence upon Dudley's fall Windsor was taken away by Mr. Sturton ("Keeper of Whitehall") into the Queen's protection. Pickes explains that he

> had the Orderinge and gouernment as well of Henrie Wyndesore late decessyd then being in the Custody of Sir Androwe as other his howsholde seruantts and familye in the Castell of Guiynes duringe the tyme Sir Andrewe was capitayne there, and also on this syde the Seas, at his howse in saynte James parke, called petie Callice.

The government of the family as well as of the servants is explicitly stated, as also of the guest Henry Windsor. Pickes explains further his opportunities for judging Windsor's intelligence by the fact that "Henrie Wynsore sate at meate and meale contynuallie with this deponent," and describes "his behavore at the borde." It is apparent that Pickes presided over a Steward's Table as representative of his Lord,[4] at which the son and heir of a Knight might properly sit, with members of the Lord's family, and probably with household servants of a certain status. The pleasing picture is evoked off-stage in Shakespeare's Illyria of Sir Toby, Sir Andrew, Maria, and Feste all sitting at Malvolio's table for dinner, under his judicious and observant eye, and under his presidency, while Olivia sits remote in her dining-parlor. Pickes, like Malvolio, can claim to speak "as I am a gentleman," and indeed is of a degree far superior to any "yeoman of the wardrobe." Viola and Olivia alike speak of Malvolio as "a gentleman." At table Pickes had observed Windsor closely:

> I neuer sawe but that he wolde sitt and eate his meate discreatlie and soberlie, nor neuer sawe hym vse any vayne or wylde communycačon as Idieyotts dothe accostomhable vse nor lightlie wolde answeare to any communycačon, vnlesse the talke had byn mynesteird vnto hym, or that one had axed hym a question then he wolde have answeared the matter so reasonablie as most men wolde haue done, and not like no Ideyott.

Windsor was meticulous about his own dress, and saw to it that his man gave his clothes proper attention. If his man had been slothful, spending too much time in the town in search of his own pleasure (a touch of Malvolio here) Windsor warned and admonished him. As for such money as was placed at his disposal, Windsor kept it "warily in his purse." Dudley, he told Pickes, was making a very good thing out of him and

---

[4] The parallel throughout with the office at Court of the Lord Steward of the Household is very close here.

could well pay for all he needed. Windsor played cards. The only game Pickes saw him play was 'saunt' (a form of piquet played with piquet cards),

> at the whiche playe he wolde number his Cardes as well and as redilie as any man sholde and make his game as warelie, wich game is not for any Ideyott to playe at.

It is fair to add here that other witnesses testify to Windsor's equal prowess at 'Irish' and 'Lurch,' forms of 'Tables' or backgammon, and at the card-game of 'Post' or 'Post and Pair.' There was nothing 'fantastical' about Windsor's letter-writing, as may appear from available letters. Dudley indeed, concerned about the impact of such evidence, ordered Pickes to deprive him of pen and ink, and forbade Windsor to see kins-folk or friends, or to leave the house. This led to Windsor's feeling ag-grieved against Pickes, to his concern.

Pickes's conscience, indeed, operated with something of a puritanical severity. His evidence, written in his own hand, is given

> Not for feare of any Creature lyvinge, nor for the proffyght or lucre of worldlie goods, nor for affection of Brother or kyndred, But with a good Conscience to declare the truthe.

It is not only in his function that Pickes helps us to an understanding of Malvolio, but also in the essential dignity and conscious worthiness of his personality, which is plainly impressive even at a remove of four centuries. There was that in him, as in Malvolio, that might put him at the mercy of Maria's plot in *Twelfth Night*.

5. LEGAL ASPECTS OF THE INQUIRY

A full account of all the legal proceedings in sequence before the Chancery trial is given in evidence there by Thomas Romney, a lawyer of the Inner Temple, who was Ford's clerk and administered under Ford Sir Anthony Browne's manors, and who presented Ford's case at the Assize trial at East Grinstead. He had discussed the question of idiocy with various legal experts and Justices of the Peace, and had studied it in all available books. His case that Windsor "was of sane and artificiall memory and not an Ideott" rested upon the following principles:

> An Ideot was he that could not gouerne hym self nor order his lands goods nor chattellys, and he must be suche a person that cold not accompt in nomber xxd nor cold tell who was his father or mother nor what age he was of, so that it might appere that he had not any intendement

of reason what shuld be for his proffet and what to his hurt, and he
must be suche a one as hath not suche vnderstanding as he can atteyn
to the knowledge of letters nor to rede by instruccyon of others.

In support of this argument, he produced to the Judges and jury

> Mayster Justyce Fitzherbert's booke of natura brevium and redde the
> tytle of the wrytt de Ideota inquirendo . . . to proue that he was not a
> foole and a naturall Ideott and suche a one as the lawe entendeth an
> Ideott to be.

Romney's authority is Sir Anthony Fitzherbert's famous *La nouelle
Natura breuium,* which cites the form of the writ and explains the circumstances in which a writ is issued and the nature of the inquiry. It is
issued by the Crown upon information laid. In this case Hussey and
Goring were the informers. The Escheator for the relevant county is
charged with the inquiry. The Crown's interest lies in the proper main-
tenance of lands held by Knights' Service, in the alienating of such lands,
and in the dissipation of substance. The inquiry must consider these
matters, and decide also whether the subject of inquiry is a 'natural fool'
from birth, or has developed idiocy later in life, and if so is rather a
lunatic with lucid intervals. The Escheator is to report the results of his
inquiry to Chancery, and an appeal lies only with the Privy Council.
Romney's arguments, supported as they were by a transcript of the Petworth inquiry, keep very close to Fitzherbert's language, in Romney's
translation of his grisly law-French (ed. 1567, pp. 232-3). It is apparent
indeed that the interrogation of Windsor followed Fitzherbert's instructions, except in the precise question of numbering up to twenty, which
however figured in the further Horsham inquiry. There were evidently
set lines prescribed for the conduct of such inquiries, with such variations
in detail as might illuminate further their main principles. The issues
are thus reported from "Beverly's Case" in Cowell's *Law Dictionary* of
1607 (ed. 1727, sig. 2G4v):

> If one have understanding to measure a yard of cloth, number twenty,
> rightly name the days of the week, or to beget a child, he shall not be
> counted an Ideot, or naturall fool, by the laws of the realm.

The only conceivable basis for the attempt upon Windsor seems to be
that he was undersized, of poor physique, that having married twice he
apparently had no children, and that Brock defines him as 'not wise,'
though no idiot.

6. MALVOLIO'S ORDEAL

It is apparent that in the highly informal inquiry in *Twelfth Night* into Malvolio's sanity we are moving in a different world from that of any established legal procedure. The conspirators might plausibly argue some authority to conduct their inquiry from the Lady of Illyria, implicit in her instructions: "Let this fellow be looked to. Where's my cousin Toby? Let some of my people have a special care of him" (3.4). And presently Maria charges Toby, "Sir Toby, my lady prays you to have a care of him." Sir Toby presumes diabolical possession, and orders Malvolio to be bound and confined in a dark room, there to be visited by Feste in the guise of the parish priest Sir Topas, whose concern is to exorcize the devil who has entered into Malvolio and bereft him of his wits.

Maria's diagnosis of his condition is that "the man is tainted in his wits," a parallel to Viola's observation (3.1) that "wise men folly-fallen quite taint their wits," and that "he is sure possessed." Malvolio struggles in his examination by Sir Topas with the suggestion that he is "mad," and demands inquiry into his intellect and understanding. A searching question upon transmigration, a theory attached to the name of Pythagoras,[5] evokes a most reasonable and well-informed answer, which Sir Topas rejects as unorthodox. The inquiry indeed is not into a case of alleged idiocy, but into madness or lunacy. Here the function of priestly exorcism might well be valid in Elizabethan eyes, as many a case certifies, resting upon the authority of the Gospels. The practice of exorcism of places and persons was well established in the old Church. It has indeed been undertaken at the present day in respect of haunted houses, though rarely. I do not find, however, that the law in Tudor England takes diabolical possession into account in its treatment of disordered minds, though the instigation of the Devil is assumed in charges of felony, as is stated in the formula of indictment. In the tragedy of *Macbeth,* indeed, we have a dramatization of such diabolical influence exerted through the Weird Sisters, the instruments of the Devil. The infection has involved Lady Macbeth too: "More needs she the divine than the physician."

There is, however, something more than a hint of the processes of Tudor thought as reflected in law, in Coke's commentary upon Littleton (*Institutes of the Laws of England,* ed. 1639, pp. 246-8). Section 405 deals with the definition of *non compos mentis,* "of none sane memory," which is not necessarily to be identified with *amens, demens, furiosus, lunaticus,*

---

[5] It is generally held that the 'Pythagorean' philosophy was of Buddhist origin.

fatuus, or *stultus.* The true 'idiot' is so from birth, a 'natural idiot,' the only case in which the land in question falls under the Crown. But loss of understanding and memory may supervene as a result of exceptional events, such as grave sickness or overwhelming grief. Or it may be brought about by a man's own vicious acts and will, by a *voluntarius daemon,* by drunkenness for example. (It is important to realize here that diabolical influence can be exerted only with the consent and collusion of its subject.) Finally, there is the special case of the lunatic, who enjoys intervals of understanding, a condition related generally with the phases of the moon.

It is plain that there was legal authority to encourage the belief that Hamlet might have lost his balance of mind through the extreme grief which he expresses in his very first appearance in the play. The insistence in the law upon 'memory' is significant, moreover, in the light of Hamlet's words (1.5):

> Remember thee?
> Ay thou poor ghost, whiles memory holds a seat
> In this distracted globe, . . .

—a phrase that gives pause in considering the meaning here of "globe," which may well mean 'my head.' Claudius sees him as feigning "turbulent and dangerous lunacy" in intervals of quiet days (3.1), and Gertrude's suggestion evokes from Hamlet a denial of "madness." Like Malvolio, he answers, "Bring me to the test" (3.4). By 4.1, after the slaying of Polonius, it might seem that both Gertrude and Claudius accept "his very madness." Polonius early in the play suggests genuine madness due to his treatment by Ophelia (2.1), and Ophelia's description of Hamlet's neglected dress recalls the insistence of all witnesses upon Windsor's care to be well-appareled, as evidence of his sanity.

The law clearly recognized that some are born idiot, and that some achieve idiocy or lunacy, but certainly not that some have idiocy thrust upon them, as with Windsor and Malvolio. It does, however, in the procedure of *De idiota inquirendo,* give reasonable assurance against fraudulent information laid against a subject's sanity. The inquiry takes place in his own district. The Escheator is a notability of his county. The Feodary is a professional expert in affairs. And the jury is composed of men drawn from his own surroundings who know him and his family. He may be legally represented at the inquiry. The interrogation was eminently fair and was directed towards practical ends, seeking to examine the fitness of the subject to play a normal part as a member of society. No attempt was made at the inquiry to bring into consultation a physician or a clergyman or an expert in the law, to give professional evidence or to examine the subject. At all points, Malvolio's examination was at complete variance with legal procedure under such a writ. The treatment of his supposed madness may have been in accordance with the practice of the time in some respects, notably in his confinement in a dark cell and in calling upon a clergyman to deal with a supposed diabolical possession. But nothing in this famous scene can be interpreted as a reflection even in caricature of any public process of the law or of any probable experience in real life. It is farce, indeed, a pure theatrical fantasy, with a certain element of cruelty which can be felt to be offensive. Whatever Malvolio's faults, in this scene he bears himself with dignity against an outrageous attack upon the citadel of his being. On the modern stage, certainly, the scene is consequently very difficult to play and fails of its intended comic effect, whatever Feste's antics as Sir Topas. The story of Henry Windsor makes it even more difficult to attune oneself to the comic spirit as thus exemplified in *Twelfth Night*.[6]

[6] This article has been prepared with assistance from the Central Research Fund of the University of London for photostat reproductions, and from the Sharpe Fund of University College. The Rev. F. Hunter, Rector of Harting, kindly placed his Registers at my disposal and was most helpful. Material from Chancery records is reproduced by permission of H. M. Stationery Office.

HAMLET'S DEFENSE OF THE PLAYERS

by WILLIAM A. RINGLER, JR.

HAMLET'S TWO SCENES with the players (2.2 and 3.2) have been often commented upon from varying points of view. The dumbshow before the play-within-the-play of 3.2 has received most attention; but other parts of the scenes have been discussed as examples of Hamlet's ideals of playwriting or of Shakespeare's own ideals of acting, or as containing topicalities of concern to players and playgoers in Shakespeare's time though perhaps no longer of concern in ours. The topicalities that have received most attention are the references to the competition of the children's companies with the adult companies (the "ayrie of Children"), and the indications of personal animosities among rival groups of playwrights and actors (the so-called War of the Theaters).[1] A third set of topical references, which though noticed have been less adequately commented upon, have to do with the attacks upon the stage that were continuous through most of the last quarter of the sixteenth century. The concern of this essay is to show that references to these attacks are more numerous in *Hamlet* than has generally been supposed, and that the two scenes, though they incidentally present a defense of playing, do so for reasons essential to the structure of the play rather than for the sake of introducing material of merely topical interest to members of Shakespeare's immediate audience.

The Elizabethan attacks on the stage, which first became prominent

[1] The more important recent discussions of these topicalities are by R. A. Small, *The Stage-Quarrel Between Ben Jonson and the So-Called Poetasters* (1899); Sir Edmund Chambers, *The Elizabethan Stage* (1923), 1.380-81 and *passim*; J. Dover Wilson, introduction and notes to *Hamlet* (1934); and Alfred Harbage, *Shakespeare and the Rival Traditions* (1952), especially pp. 114-15 and 292-5.

about 1577 and continued until the absolute prohibition of all professional dramatic entertainment in 1642, have been often described and need only a brief review.[2] At first only 'common' plays, that is those performed publicly by professionals for money, were attacked, while those performed by schoolboys, University students, and other amateurs were allowed. But as the attacks continued the distinction between amateur and professional performances was abandoned, and the opponents declared that all playing was by its very nature sinful. The principal objections, laid down in Munday's *Second and third blast of retrait from plaies and Theaters* (1580) and Gosson's *Playes Confuted* (1582), were that plays were a waste of time and a waste of money; that they were inciters to sin and teachers of vice; that acting was counterfeiting and so was a species of lying; and that the playing of women's parts by boys was prohibited by the Bible, because *Deuteronomy* (22.5) forbade men to dress in women's apparel. These arguments were repeated in later pamphlets directed against the social abuses of the age, though after the 1580's the frequency of the literary attacks to some extent subsided. But they flared up with renewed violence with the publication of John Rainolds's *Overthrow of Stage-Playes* in 1599 and its reissue the following year. This work received special attention because of the prestige of Rainolds himself, who was president of Corpus Christi College, Oxford, and one of the most eminent and respected theologians of the day, and because even his particular opponent, the academic dramatist William Gager, though he upheld the legitimacy of amateur performances, was unwilling to defend the professional theater.

Rainolds, both by argument and by citation of an impressive array of authorities, sought to prove that no dramatic performances of any kind should be allowed in an honest civil state. He objected more to acting than to the dramatic texts themselves, for "it is one thing to recite, another thing to play," and he quoted Juvenal, Pliny, and Scaliger, "who dispraised not Poets for reciting comedies, yet thought a man ought rather choose to dye then play them" (p. 22). He asserted that all actors, both amateur and professional, had been counted infamous from ancient times to the present; he of course noted the prohibition of *Deuteronomy*, arguing that it was absolutely binding and admitted of no exceptions; but he principally dwelt upon the corrupting influence of dramatic performances upon the morals of both spectators and actors, concluding that "it is unlawfull to imitate and resemble any misbehaviour" (p. 119).

[2] Chambers gives a convenient summary in Chapters 8 and 9 of *The Elizabethan Stage,* and prints extracts from the more important documents in Appendices C and D.

This last point, concerning the effect and legitimacy of dramatic imitation and representation, was the nub of the matter. While these printed attacks were being launched, the public theaters were also the subject of legislation by the Lord Mayor and Aldermen of London and the Queen's Privy Council. Though the earlier enactments of the London authorities were regulatory rather than repressive, by 1582 they had ordered that all "Enterludes in publique places, and the resort to the same shall wholy be prohibited as ungodly" (*The Elizabethan Stage,* 4.291), and by 1596 they had succeeded in banishing professional dramatic performances from all areas under the city's jurisdiction. Meanwhile the Mayor and Aldermen continued to urge the Privy Council to suppress the theaters outside the city limits, and in response to this pressure the Privy Council in 1597 peremptorily ordered that all playhouses outside the city should be "plucked downe" (*ibid.,* 4.322). The players apparently rallied their friends at Court, and the Privy Council responded on 22 June 1600 with a substitute decree which, instead of complete extirpation, imposed severe limitations on playing by stipulating that only two companies (the Lord Admiral's and the Lord Chamberlain's) be allowed to perform in two theaters (the Fortune and the Globe), and that they perform only twice a week and not at all during Lent (*ibid.,* 4.331).

While the pamphleteers and legislators were trying to eliminate or restrict the practice of playing, the friends of the professional actors circulated a few defenses of the stage by word of mouth or in print. They based their main argument upon the didactic value of the drama, an argument represented by the often-reported assertion that a person could be as well edified by a play as by a sermon.[3] The earliest published defense was Lodge's *Honest Excuses,* printed in 1579 in reply to Gosson's *Schoole of Abuse* but suppressed by the authorities. This was a slight

---

[3] In the prose tale *Mary of Nemmegen* (c. 1518, see note 6 below) the heroine had said, "I have harde my unkyll say often tymes that a play were better than a sermant to some folke" (sig. B5v). The argument reappeared in 1577, when John Northbrooke in his *Treatise* observed that some people "shame not to say, and affirme openly, that playes are as good as sermons, and that they learne as much or more at a playe, than they do at God's worde preached" (ed. Collier, p. 92). It was repeated by Anthony Munday, *A second and third blast* (1580, ed. Hazlitt, p. 139); Phillip Stubbes, *The Anatomie of Abuses* (1583, ed. Furnivall, p. 143); the printer of Rainolds's *Overthrow* (1599, sig. A3v); and Henry Crosse, *Vertues Common-wealth* (1603, sig. Q2). Thomas Freeman made it the subject of a humorous epigram, "In Phaedram," in his *Rub and a Great Cast* (1614):

> Now, by her troth, she hath been, Phaedra says,
> At a play far better edified
> Than at a sermon ever in her days.
> Phaedra, 'tis true, it cannot be denied;
>   For stage-plays thou hast given ear to many,
>   But sermons, Phaedra, never heardst thou any.

piece, chiefly notable for its citation, at third hand by way of Badius Ascensius, of the Ciceronian definition of comedy as an imitation of life, a mirror of manners, and an image of truth. This definition may derive ultimately from Cicero's *Pro Sexto Roscio Amerino,* 16.47:

> Etenim haec conficta arbitror esse a poëtis, ut effictos nostros mores in alienis personis expressamque imaginem nostrae vitae cotidianae videremus.

But the form in which it was universally known during the Renaissance was that given by Donatus in his *De comoedia,* which was printed or quoted in most sixteenth-century editions of Terence:

> Cicero ait Comoedia est imitatio vitae, speculum consuetudinis, et imago veritatis.[4]

This definition continued to be a mainstay of the defenders of the stage, for it was paraphrased by Sidney, referred to by Spenser (*Teares of the Muses,* 199-202), and quoted by Jonson (*Every Man out of his Humour,* 3.6.204-8), Heywood (*Apology for Actors,* sig. F1v), and others. Drama, the defenders asserted, was not counterfeiting or lying, but an image of truth that was an effective force in the improvement of morals.

Of considerably more importance than Lodge's pamphlet was Sidney's *Defence of Poesie,* composed in the early 1580's but first published in two editions in 1595 and reprinted with the 1598, 1599, and later editions of his *Arcadia,* a work that Shakespeare knew thoroughly. Sidney also based his defense on didactic considerations, arguing that poetry and drama were more effective than any of the other arts in moving men to virtuous action. Comedy, he said, is "an imitation of the common errors of our life, which he [i.e. the poet] representeth in the most ridiculous and scornfull sort that may be: so as it is impossible that any beholder can be content to be such a one." High and excellent tragedy, he said,

> openeth the greatest woundes, and sheweth forth the Ulcers that are covered with Tissue, that maketh Kings feare to be Tyrants, and Tyrants manifest their tyrannicall humours, that with sturring the affects of Admiration and Comiseration, teacheth the uncertaintie of this world, and uppon how weak foundations guilden roofes are builded: that maketh us know,
>
> > Qui scaeptra saevus duro imperio regit,
> > Timet timentes, metus in authorem redit.

---

[4] Ed. Wessner, 1.22. The Furness Variorum note to *Hamlet* 3.2.22 quotes Silberschlag's observation (1860) that a similar definition appears in Cervantes' *Don Quixote,* 1.48, and Kittredge quotes *Pro Sexto Roscio Amerino;* neither writer notes the source in Donatus or the frequent repetition of the definition by defenders of the stage.

But how much it can move, Plutarch yeeldeth a notable testimonie of the abhominable Tyrant Alexander Pheraeus, from whose eyes a Tragedie well made and represented, drew abundance of teares, who without all pittie had murthered infinite numbers, and some of his owne bloud: so as he that was not ashamed to make matters for Tragedies, yet could not resist the sweete violence of a Tragedie. And if it wrought no further good in him, it was, that he in despight of himselfe, withdrew himselfe from hearkening to that which might mollifie his hardened heart. (*Works,* ed. Feuillerat, 3.23-4)

Sidney's anecdote about the tyrant Alexander of Pherae was drawn from Plutarch's *Lives* (293F), which Shakespeare had also studied, and *Morals* (334A); in both places Plutarch says that Euripides was the author of the tragedy and that the sufferings of Hecuba were the action that caused the tyrant to weep and withdraw from the theater. The anecdote was often referred to in the sixteenth century; for example, it was repeated from Plutarch in Brusonius's often-reprinted *Facetiarum exemplorumque libri VII* (1559), 4.21, and a variant version from Aelian's *Varia historia,* 14.40, appeared in the chapter "De crudelitate" of Lycosthenes' popular *Apophthegmata* (1551).

The moral efficacy of the drama was also upheld by Case, Puttenham, Harington, and others. Nashe's argument in *Pierce Penilesse* (1592) is typical, and his last phrase makes a new point:

> In Playes, all coosonages, all cunning drifts over-guylded with outward holinesse, all stratagems of warre, all the cankerwormes that breede on the rust of peace, are most lively anatomiz'd: they shewe the ill successe of treason, the fall of hastie climbers, the wretched end of usurpers, the miserie of civill dissention, and how just God is evermore in punishing of murther. (*Works,* ed. McKerrow, 1.213)

The players were also active in their own defense, and inserted scenes in their productions which pointed out the moral value of their performances. One of the earliest of these is a scene inserted in a morality, R. W.'s *Three Ladies of London* (c. 1581), which upheld the didactic value of comedies.[5] Of considerably greater importance is a scene in *A Warning for Faire Women,* an anonymous play acted by Shakespeare's company and printed in 1599. This is a domestic tragedy showing how the culprits in an actual murder case of some years earlier had been brought to justice. When the identity of the murderer is surprisingly revealed by the testimony of a dying man, those in attendance remark

---

[5] It is not preserved in the text printed in 1584 but is described in Gosson's *Playes Confuted,* ed. Hazlitt, p. 185.

that "God's justice hath bin stil miraculous" and tell anecdotes of other revelations, one of which is:

> A woman that had made away her husband,
> And sitting to behold a tragedy,
> At Linne, a towne in Norfolke,
> Acted by Players travelling that way,—
> Wherein a woman that had murtherd hers
> Was ever haunted with her husband's ghost,
> The passion written by a feeling pen,
> And acted by a good tragedian,—
> She was so mooved with the sight thereof,
> As she cryed out, 'the play was made by her,'
> And openly confess[ed] her husband's murder.[6]

The difference in point of view between the attackers and the defenders of the stage comes out clearly in the correspondence and legislative enactments of the London authorities and the Privy Council. In the

[6] Lines 1077-87; ed. Richard Simpson, *The School of Shakspere* (1878), 2.311—first cited by Todd. Thomas Heywood repeated the anecdote in *An Apology for Actors* (1612, sigs. G1v-2—first cited by Steevens), and identified the company as "the then Earle of Sussex players acting the old History of Fryer Francis." Henslowe recorded performances of a play called *Friar Francis* by Sussex's Men, probably at the Rose, in January 1594 (*Henslowe's Diary*, ed. Greg, 1904-8, 1.16). Heywood's factual elaboration of the story may have been no more than Pooh-Bahesque corroborative detail, though I. G. in his *Refutation of the Apology for Actors* (1615, sig. F2v) did not question its historicity. The anecdote must have been current among English players at the turn of the century, for in *Der bestrafte Brudermord* Hamlet, instead of referring in general terms to "guilty creatures sitting at a play," recounts a specific episode: "In Germany, at Strasburg, . . . A wife murdered her husband by piercing him to the heart with an awl. Afterwards she buried the man under the threshold, she and her paramour. This deed remained hid full nine years, till at last it chanced that some actors came that way, and played a tragedy of like import; the woman who was likewise present at the play . . . began to cry aloud (her conscience being touched) alas! alas! you hit at me for in such manner did I murder my innocent husband." (Translated by Georgina Archer in Albert Cohn's *Shakespeare in Germany*, 1865, p. 268—discussed by Simpson, 2.212-16). The remote origin of this anecdote may be the anonymous *Mary of Nemmegen*, a Dutch morality play that was adapted as an English prose narrative early in the sixteenth century. The heroine, who had been seduced by the Devil and had lived with him as his paramour for seven years, came to a town where preparations were being made for the annual production of a play. "Than went Emmekyn and harde the playe and the playe was of synfull lyvynge and there she sawe hyr lyvyng played before hyr face than she began to be sory and take repentance/ than called the dyvell hyr for he wolde have hyr here it nat oute/ But she wolde nat come/ for by the play she was all hole turned fro hyr mysselyvynge and sayde. O good lorde have mercy on me pore wretche and synner/ I am nat wordy to trede upon the erthe and I am afrayde that I have ronne to ferre/ than sayde the dyvyll to his selfe all my laboure is loste she taketh unto hyr hole repentance" (sigs. B5v-6). The Dutch play in which this anecdote was represented (perhaps the earliest occurrence of a play-within-a-play) was printed at Antwerp about 1518 but was not reprinted until 1608. The English prose tale, also printed at Antwerp about 1518, survives in a unique copy in the Huntington Library and was not again reproduced until the present century. It is unlikely that either Shakespeare or his contemporaries had direct knowledge of this older version of the story.

letter which led to the 1597 order that all theaters be plucked down, the Lord Mayor and Aldermen asserted that "neither in politie nor in religion they [i.e. plays] are to be suffered in a Christian Commonwealth," because they portray "lascivious matters, cozeninge devises, and scurrilus beehaviours, which are so set forth as that they move wholie to imitation and not to the avoydinge of those faults and vices which they represent" (*The Elizabethan Stage*, 4.321). But the Privy Council in its order of 1600 allowing performances by two companies twice a week, held that the performance of plays, "not beinge evill in yt self, may with a good order and moderacion be suffered in a well governed estate," especially because "hir Majestie beinge pleased at some times to take delighte and recreacion in the sight and hearinge of them, some order is fitt to bee taken for the allowance and mainteinance of suche persons, as are thoughte meetest in that kind to yeald hir Majestie recreacion and delight" (*ibid.*, 4.330). Though the players had won a temporary reprieve through being partly befriended at Court, strong forces threatening their very existence were arrayed against them. It was in this state of affairs that Shakespeare, sometime around the turn of the century, began a new work for the beleaguered players, his *Tragedy of Hamlet Prince of Denmark.*

The controversy concerning the stage, which had reached a new peak of intensity at the very time he was composing this play, certainly provided material for, and may even have suggested the inclusion of, Hamlet's two scenes with the players. Whether Shakespeare himself invented these scenes, or whether he developed them from suggestions in the *Ur-Hamlet,* remains uncertain.[7] The important point for our present purpose is the way he related the scenes to the current controversy and how, in so doing, he prepared his audience to expect the psychological breakdown of Claudius during the play-within-the-play.

When we examine these two scenes with the details of the stage controversy in mind, various words and phrases take on added meaning. When Rosencrantz remarks, "To thinke my Lord if you delight not in man, what Lenton entertainment the players shall receave from you" (2.2.329), we realize that "Lenton entertainment," in addition to its

---

[7] All we know certainly about the *Ur-Hamlet* is that it was in existence by 1589 and that it contained a ghost who cried "Hamlet, revenge." There is no play-within-a-play in Belleforest and no need for one, because Fengon (Claudius) kills Hamlet's father in full view of the members of the court. The literature of the stage controversy suggests that the argument that "guilty creatures sitting at a play" will proclaim "their malefactions" developed gradually, from the assertion in 1577 that a person can be edified as well at a play as at a sermon, to the statement in 1592 that plays show how just God is in punishing murder, to the anecdote first printed in 1599 of the woman confessing a murder at a play in Norfolk.

ordinary meaning of meager fare, may also mean no reception at all, for by the Privy Council order of 22 June 1600 dramatic performances had been prohibited during Lent (*The Elizabethan Stage*, 4.331). When Rosencrantz further reports that the tragedians of the city are forced to travel because "their inhibition, comes by the meanes of the late innovation" (2.2.345), we are reminded that from at least 1596 onwards all professional players had been "banished by the Lord Mayor from playing within the Cittie by reason of the great inconveniences and ill rule that followeth them" (*ibid.*, 4.320). When reference is made to "common Stages" and "common Players" (2.2.358 and 364, in F only), we are reminded of the distinction between professional and amateur performers which was a major issue in the controversy between Gager and Rainolds (*Th' Overthrow*, pp. 4-8 and 153). When Polonius says he will treat the players "according to their desert," and Hamlet replies, "use every man after his desert, and who shall scape whipping, use them after your owne honor and dignity" (2.2.552-5), we are reminded of the charge of infamy leveled at the actors by opponents of the stage (and by Rainolds especially, pp. 61-73), and of the Elizabethan statute, re-enacted in 1598, which proclaimed that "All Fencers Bearewardes common Players of Enterludes and Minstrelles wandring abroade (other than Players of Enterludes belonging to any Baron of this Realme) . . . shalbe taken adjudged and deemed Rogues Vagabonds and Sturdy Beggers, and . . . shall uppon their apprehension . . . be openly whipped."[8] And when Hamlet says that by having the players present something like the murder of his father before Claudius, "Ile tent him to the quicke" (2.2.626), we are reminded of Sidney's metaphor of tragedy as a probe that "openeth the greatest woundes, and sheweth forth the Ulcers that are covered with Tissue," an image that had also been repeated at the conclusion of *A Warning for Faire Women*:

> Here are the launces that have sluic'd forth sinne,
> And ript the venom'd ulcer of foule lust.
>
> (1693-4)

But these are minor details. Of more significance is the fact that the two scenes contain elements that were suggested by, or that restate, the more important arguments used by defenders of the stage. When the players arrive the audience is shown the respect accorded professional actors and the esteem in which their art is held by members of the Danish

---

[8] 39 Elizabeth c.4, printed by Chambers, 4.324, and referred to by Rainolds, p. 154. Dover Wilson in his note to this passage refers only to the earlier statute of 1572.

court. The King and Queen grace the performance of a play with their presence, and the old councilor Polonius is proud of having been "accounted a good Actor" in his younger days at the University. Prince Hamlet greets without demur the boy who takes a woman's part (he obviously does not accept the literal application of *Deuteronomy*, 22.5), plays the actor himself by reciting the beginning of a speech and the playwright by composing part of a scene, and shows himself a sufficient student of the theater to deliver a lecture on the art of acting. Acceptance by the rulers and nobles of the realm was the main argument the Elizabethan actors used to justify their profession. So long as the Queen was pleased "to take delighte and recreacion in the sight and hearinge" of plays, lesser citizens could not properly object to the players' being maintained and allowed.

When Hamlet calls for "a passionate speech" as a sample of the player's art, we may wonder why he chose one that emphasized the woes of Hecuba. The destruction of Troy was an obvious choice, for it had been cited as an example of fall from fortune and the ultimate in pathos for centuries; but the accounts available to the Elizabethans—Lydgate's *Troy Book*, Caxton's *Recuyell of the historyes of Troye,* and Virgil's *Aeneid* (2.506-58), which Shakespeare by his reference to "Aeneas' tale to Dido" appears to have had specifically in mind—focus upon Priam and do not mention the reactions of Hecuba to her husband's death.[9] Some years earlier, in the *Rape of Lucrece* (1443-91), Shakespeare had reimagined the fall of Troy and had singled out Hecuba,

> Staring on Priam's wounds with her old eyes,
> Which bleeding under Pyrrhus' proud foot lies,

as an example of "all distress and dolour"; but he may also have been led to dwell upon her grief in this scene by recollection of Plutarch's anecdote,[10] which Sidney had cited in defending the drama, of how the

[9] Sackville, in lines 435-76 of his "Induction" to the *Mirror for Magistrates* (1563), also described the destruction of Troy as an episode which more than any other in history made his "eyes in very tears consume"; but he did not mention Hecuba. In Marlowe and Nashe's *Tragedie of Dido* (printed 1594), 2.213-64, which is based almost entirely upon the *Aeneid* and which Steevens suggested Shakespeare may have had in mind when composing the player's speech, Hecuba is only briefly referred to. She is described as being with Priam before the altar, as in the *Aeneid*, and when Pyrrhus cuts off her husband's hands (a detail not in Virgil) she scratches him with her nails until,

> At last the souldiers puld her by the heeles,
> And swong her howling in the emptie ayre.

[10] The passage from the *Lives* only, without reference to Sidney or the other occurrences, was cited by R. Sigismund, *SJ,* 17 (1882), 288-90, and G. E. Marindin, *Athenaeum,* 11 April 1896, pp. 487-8.

tyrant Alexander of Pherae left a play in perturbation at her woes. The episode, in illustrating the effect of the actor's art upon Hamlet himself, may also reflect upon Rainolds's argument that though it is proper to recite a text it is improper to represent it in a performance. The words of the player's speech only describe the miseries of Priam and Hecuba and so are not in themselves dramatic, and though Hamlet savors their mannered artifice he is not especially moved by them alone. It is the action, the simulated emotion of the player as he recites, that causes Hamlet to look within himself and meditate upon his own condition:

> What's Hecuba to him, or he to Hecuba,
> That he should weepe for her?

Words and action combined are more effective than either alone.

In Hamlet's soliloquy after the players' speech Shakespeare draws further material from the stage controversy:

> I have heard,
> That guilty creatures sitting at a play,
> Have by the very cunning of the scene,
> Beene strooke so to the soule, that presently
> They have proclaim'd their malefactions:
> For murther, though it have no tongue will speake
> With most miraculous organ.
>
> (2.2.617-23)

This was the latest of the current arguments in defense of the drama, used in the anecdote about the woman of Norfolk in *A Warning for Faire Women*. Two scenes later Shakespeare again emphasizes the moral effectiveness of dramatic representations when he has Hamlet explain the purpose of playing,

> whose end both at the first, and nowe, was and is, to holde as 'twere the Mirrour up to nature, to shew vertue her feature; scorne her own Image, and the very age and body of the time his forme and pressure. (3.2.22-6)

This is the definition of Donatus, which had been a mainstay of the defenders of the stage during the past twenty years. And in the immediately following play-within-the-play, which causes Claudius to leave the room in perturbation when the murder he has committed is acted out before him, the players are finally vindicated (and Rainolds and the other attackers refuted) by this illustration that a dramatic representation of misbehavior can produce beneficial results.

But Shakespeare does not, like R. W. in *The Three Ladies of London,* introduce these topicalities merely as an extraneous argument in defense of the drama; instead he makes them essential structural elements of his play, which continue to perform their function and remain important even after the controversy concerning the stage is forgotten. Having decided to make the play-within-the-play the first major crisis of his plot, Shakespeare knew that he would have to work upon the psychology of his audience in a way that would lead them to expect, and render them willing to accept, Claudius's reaction. This he accomplishes by a deliberate pattern of repeated hints and foreshadowings illustrating the effect that a dramatic representation may have upon the conscience of its spectators. He first gives his audience a preview of the crisis by showing them how the player's speech leads Hamlet himself to introspection. Then by the direct explanation that "guilty creatures sitting at a play . . . have proclaim'd their malefactions," he indicates that the play will "catch the conscience of the King." And finally, immediately before the performance, by having Hamlet repeat Donatus's definition of comedy he reminds his audience that a play is a mirror in which one may see and by which one may judge himself. By these means he prepares the members of his audience to accept Claudius's psychological breakdown during the ordeal of the play-within-the-play, indeed convinces them ahead of time that Claudius will break down.

But though Shakespeare used some of the arguments of contemporary defenders of the drama, he did not carry them to the same conclusion. All the Elizabethan defenders of acting posited their arguments upon a naive didacticism; they all, like Sidney, asserted that dramatic representations would move men to virtuous action by making virtue attractive and vice odious, for if the errors of our life are represented in a ridiculous manner "it is impossible that any beholder can be content to be such a one." Shakespeare followed his contemporaries in asserting that a play is an image of truth, but he also was aware that knowledge of the right does not necessarily lead a person to righteousness. Though Claudius, tented to the quick, withdraws in perturbation from "The Murder of Gonzago" and admits to himself that his offense is rank and smells to Heaven, he is Claudius still, his thoughts remain below, and instead of confessing his crime he sets about devising yet another murder. Though *Hamlet,* like all Shakespeare's great tragedies, is concerned with the problems and limitations of human knowledge, it is even more concerned with the greater mysteries of the will.

HAMLET'S FIFTH SOLILOQUY, 3.2.406-17

by FREDSON BOWERS

O F THE SOLILOQUIES in *Hamlet,* the twelve lines at the end of 3.2 beginning " 'Tis now the very witching time of night" seem, on the
surface, to be the least interesting. In this brief fifth soliloquy no 'philosophy' is being propounded, no consideration of the world and its ways
or of Hamlet's internal anguish is forthcoming. In the hurried action
that follows on the success of the Mousetrap stratagem, these lines (3.2.406-
17) bridge the gap between, on the one hand, Hamlet's excited dismissal
of Rosencrantz and Guildenstern (3.2.55-6) followed by his exasperating
encounter with Polonius (3.2.103-11), and, on the other, the prayer
scene (3.3) that is prelude to the climactic closet scene (3.4).

All of the immediately preceding action has anticipated this closet
scene in which Gertrude is primed to sift her son to discover his dangerous secret. The scheme for the interview has been set on foot before the
play-within-a-play, and it is one of the many ironies that this strand of
the counter-action that is to lead to the play's climax has automatically
followed its prescribed course as earlier planned between the Queen and
Polonius, though to Claudius the information they hopefully looked for
from the interview is no longer necessary. Hamlet's secret is not now an
enigma to the King.

But Claudius is the only one who has recognized the significance of
"The Murder of Gonzago." In the disorder following his retreat he has
either forgotten to cancel the projected meeting between Hamlet and
Gertrude or he has chosen not to expose himself to questioning by the

213

issue of such an order. Thus the plans for what would be an essentially futile meeting go forward as originally proposed. At Gertrude's instance Rosencrantz and Guildenstern summon Hamlet, Polonius seconds them to make sure that the son will obey, and Hamlet starts towards the Queen's apartments after his short soliloquy at the end of 3.2. In the meantime Claudius has made his own plans to dispose of Hamlet. Rosencrantz and Guildenstern are commissioned for England and dismissed; and only then, when the matter is unimportant to him, is Claudius told by Polonius that Hamlet is on his way to his mother. At this crucial moment, when the slayer of the father has set in motion a plan to destroy the son, Claudius makes his last attempt to escape the consequences of his initial crime; but he fails. And, ignorant that Claudius's heart has not been softened by grace, Hamlet spares him and moves on to the interview.

In this sequence the fifth soliloquy looks both backwards and forwards. Hamlet's "Now could I drink hot blood" sums up the effect on his resolution of his success with the Mousetrap and the certainty that this has brought. These opening lines are the serious counterpart to the feverish jests with Horatio:

> For if the King like not the comedy,
> Why then, belike he likes it not, perdy.

His bloody resolution is clearly directed against Claudius, for the interjection "Soft! now to my mother!" introduces another line of thought. But his new resolution carries over into the next part of the soliloquy when he must caution himself against allowing his bloody frame of mind to influence his actions against his mother. He intends no harm to her, and only in words will he pierce her with daggers.

The first part of the soliloquy corresponds roughly to the general use made of the other soliloquies in that it opens a window into Hamlet's mind. The audience can interpret his preceding jocularity in the light of what is now revealed to be his inner seriousness, and this revealed determination will help to interpret his subsequent action in the prayer scene. In this particular respect the soliloquy looks two ways.

The remainder is of a different order, however. In a relatively crude manner the second part acts as a signpost to direct the audience to what the dramatist wants them to understand in a scene that is to follow. Such obvious manipulation is unique in the soliloquies of this play and is not characteristic of Shakespeare elsewhere, though the "I know you all" soliloquy in *1 Henry IV* is an even more egregious example of the same kind. The shift in the dramatic technique is manifest. Ordinarily the audience is given two sorts of evidence: Hamlet's words and actions in relation to other people, and (in the soliloquies) his verbalized moods and thoughts. The connection between these, the way in which they interrelate, and their significance, are left up to the audience to determine for themselves from the evidence thus dramatically presented.

On the contrary, in the second part of this soliloquy, under the palpably thin pretext of talking to himself about his future intentions, Hamlet steps out of the dramatic framework to warn the audience not to misinterpret his actions in the scene that is being anticipated. The crudeness of the device must reflect what Shakespeare felt to be an unusually urgent need to guide the audience's reactions in what was about to be presented. When a dramatist so patently refuses to allow an audience to judge a scene without special direction, he makes us curious about the danger he anticipates. Hence an investigation of the alternative may give us a valuable insight into Shakespeare's general as well as his specific intention.

For the moment let us pass by the kneeling Claudius and come to the closet scene (3.4). Mother and son are immediately embroiled in a bitter contest for domination, in which Hamlet's high words are so startling to Gertrude, accustomed to his filial respect, that she does not know how to deal with his unnatural metamorphosis. In obvious anger at his blunt attack, which operates as a refusal to hear her and thus to recognize her authority, she threatens him, "Nay, then I'll set those to you that can speak." Since she herself has been unable to "speak" to Hamlet, the "those" must be persons who will have the power to force Hamlet to hear them. We have every reason to believe that Gertrude is proposing to call in a guard which will arrest him. (That imprisonment as a public danger is a risk Hamlet runs has been emphasized shortly before, at 3.2.194-5, where Polonius in proposing the interview to Claudius has remarked casually that if Gertrude does not discover the cause of Hamlet's melancholy the King may send him to England, "or confine him where Your wisdom best shall think.")

It seems evident that Gertrude has received Hamlet seated, that she has risen to her feet at his threat and taken a step towards the door, and that Hamlet has forced her back into her chair. (There is no authority for the bed that has become traditional in modern productions.) This unexpected physical violence must be made so extreme in the action as to cause her to fear for her life at the hands of an insanely antagonistic son. In her bewilderment, turning to panic, she interprets his violence as a murderous attempt on her, and abandoning all pretense of reasoning she calls wildly for help.

It is a profound irony that she is not in danger of her life. (The audience knows this secret because they have overheard Hamlet's intentions in the fifth soliloquy.) Her mistake therefore reveals the hidden presence of Polonius whom, in a final irony, Hamlet mistakes for the King. The impulsive murder seals Hamlet's own doom.[1]

It is clear that Shakespeare felt that this scene posed a real danger if the audience were permitted to be in any doubt about the outcome of the action. Obviously, the difficulty was that an unwarned audience would be as alarmed as Gertrude and would take it that Hamlet was, in fact, assaulting his mother in such a frenzy that her life was endangered; in other words, that Hamlet's control had become so shattered that an initial violent act (his thrusting her back into the chair) had opened the door to a murderous impulse.

In retrospect it is easy for us to see that an audience might readily make such a mistake if Hamlet had not previously revealed that he planned to be violent in his actions, but that he had no intention of becoming a matricide and that though he would "speak daggers to her" he would "use none." Without this vital information the audience might well take it that the reaction from the success of the Mousetrap, the exasperation of dealing at this critical time with Rosencrantz, Guildenstern, and Polonius, the fixed bloody resolve, the tension from sparing the life of Claudius at prayer—all these, it might be feared, had culminated in an emotional unhinging when his mother rose from her seat to betray him to prison in his moment of triumph. The pent-up hatred for his father's murderers (for Gertrude is an accomplice, he seems to think) might easily under these conditions lead him to retaliatory violence that in its consequences would go beyond his conscious intention.

If this is so, it is proper to inquire what is so wrong with such a conception that Shakespeare could not permit his audience to entertain it even for the moment that the swift action was in progress. It is, after all, inherently a situation of enormous suspense, and when a dramatist (for whom suspense is a stock in trade) deliberately keeps the audience from enjoying this uncertainty, and feels he must cut the ground out from under any such possible interpretation, he must have some powerful

---

[1] The question of the choice that Hamlet made in killing the eavesdropper, and its tragic consequences, is worked out in my "Hamlet as Minister and Scourge," *PMLA*, 70 (1955), 740-49.

reason.[2] It is not enough to point out that Shakespeare scorns the sort of titillation that Beaumont and Fletcher would have enjoyed extracting from the scene. The overwrought son in frustration turning against his guilty mother is a sound enough dramatic concept. True, one part of the irony would be lost if Polonius were slain protecting a Gertrude who was in authentic peril; but this irony could be spared, perhaps, in the interest of the heightened drama of the scene.

The fact is that the grand design of *Hamlet* was too important to endanger by allowing the audience the normal leeway here in the interpretation of action dramatically (which is to say, objectively) presented. The Ghost lays upon Hamlet two injunctions: (1) revenge the murder; but (2) in the pursuit of this revenge do not contrive any plot against your mother (1.5.84-8). In itself the latter injunction need not have led Hamlet to a conviction of Gertrude's innocence in the murder. The Ghost could have been sparing his son the crime of matricide by reminding him of Heaven's promise to revenge all crime ("Leave her to heaven"; that is, "Vengeance is mine saith the Lord, I will repay").[3]

However, a very important statement remains. The Ghost forbids Hamlet to "taint" his mind, and he must not plan harm to his mother. The syntax is just loose enough to admit a query, but there can be little doubt that "Taint not thy mind" refers to Gertrude and not to the method of pursuing "this act" of destroying the marriage. Thus the command about Gertrude is in two parts: (1) do not allow your mind to become tainted in respect to your mother; (2) do not punish her. In conjunction with the total lack of evidence for Gertrude's complicity in the

[2] Just so, in the "I know you all" soliloquy, Shakespeare deliberately removes the suspense the audience would have enjoyed throughout the play if they had been permitted to feel that Prince Hal was actually uncommitted. This device should lead the critic of *1 Henry IV* to discover what greater benefit Shakespeare had in mind for such an expensive sacrifice.

[3] In fact, it is not altogether certain that the Ghost is calling for blood-revenge on Claudius, even though Hamlet so interprets the injunction. *Revenge* need not be equated exactly with *blood-revenge*: for example, the English were accustomed to calling a legal suit for murder a revenge, and the public revenge against a tyrant or usurper was accounted meritorious. (See my *Elizabethan Revenge Tragedy*, 1940, pp. 7-8, 36-7.) When the Ghost finally gets down to business and lays his solemn commands on Hamlet, he urges him not to allow the royal bed of Denmark to be a place for lasciviousness and incest; "But howsoever thou pursuest this act" (i.e., the cleansing of the royal couch by the separation of Claudius and Gertrude), do not harm thy mother. By implication, Claudius is not to be left to Heaven, and thus may be punished by earthly justice; but this is still a long way from any literal command to murder. That Hamlet cannot see how else to take revenge on Claudius, given the secrecy of the murder, is another matter. There is nothing in the Ghost's orders that would not be satisfied by Hamlet's exposing Claudius to legal justice or leading an armed national uprising against a murdering usurper.

Ghost's detailed narrative of his death, the warning not to taint his mind seemingly was intended to convey to Hamlet that his mother was not an accomplice to the murder either before or after the fact, and that he must not corrupt his mind by thinking her so.[4] Yet from 3.4.27-30 it seems possible that Hamlet had indeed gnawingly suspected his mother of prior knowledge of his father's murder.[5]

Nevertheless, at no time do Hamlet's thoughts run to matricide, and from the conduct of the action it is evident that he scrupulously tries to adhere to the Ghost's distinction between earthly justice for Claudius and heavenly for Gertrude.

The Ghost had ordered that Gertrude be left to Heaven, "And to those thorns that in her bosom lodge To prick and sting her." Patently, the thorns represent her conscience. It follows that if these thorns rankle enough, she will be led to a repentance and a change in her life that will allow Heaven to temper justice with mercy.

Adultery was a mortal sin, and deliberate incest at least its equal. If Gertrude does not repent (and repentance involves action as well as thought), her soul will be damned for eternity. The Ghost has forecast the possibility (perhaps even the start) of repentance that will enable Gertrude to throw herself on heavenly mercy instead of suffering earthly justice. Yet by the time of the interview, Hamlet has seen no evidence whatever of Gertrude's thorns of conscience. It is of the utmost importance that after Polonius's murder he devote the minutes of freedom left to him to breaking down his mother's stubborn will and forcing her to repentance by his passionate eloquence. In this act he is indeed following the Ghost's instructions. For a son to be oblivious of the fate of his mother's soul under the weight of mortal sin would be unnatural, and it is clear that Hamlet recognizes the paramount importance of assuring Gertrude some degree of mercy by 'converting' her to a repentant way of life in which her deeds will match her new thoughts. So far as he can know at the time, this is the last gift he can make his mother. Although

---

[4] In this context, "Leave her to heaven" signifies that her sins of adultery and incest will be dealt with there and are not to be Hamlet's concern to punish.

[5] The lines "A Bloody deed—almost as bad, good mother, As kill a king, and marry with his brother. . . . Ay, lady, it was my word" are the sole evidence for Hamlet's suspicion, and it is remarkable that this is the first time the audience has been told that he has associated his mother with knowledge of the murder. The oddity of Shakespeare's withholding this information, and the fact that so little is made of it in the closet scene (even if Gertrude's reply shows Hamlet he was mistaken), leads to the query whether this accusation is not a spur-of-the-moment trial—a sort of fishing expedition. If so, then the weight of believing that his mother has guilty knowledge of the murder has not been a contributing cause of Hamlet's melancholia. On the whole, however, the traditional explanation of these lines seems to be justified.

we cannot wholly ignore the very real sexual disgust in his rhetoric, and indeed perhaps even the jealousy, the force of this disgust is aimed at awakening her to a sense of sin and shame: "I must be cruel, only to be kind."[6]

It is of singular importance for us to recognize that this breaking-down of Gertrude's stubborn will and her restoration to a state of grace is not a fortuitous accident resulting from the slaying of Polonius and a seized opportunity to assail her in a moment of weakness. The Queen is not in the least softened by the shock of Polonius's death, for when Hamlet immediately returns to the attack on her, she answers with a contemptuous stubbornness equal to that at the beginning of the scene: "What have I done that thou dar'st wag thy tongue In noise so rude against me? . . . Ay me, what act That roars so loud and thunders in the index?" And it takes a long and disgustingly detailed speech from Hamlet before she is beaten down and overcome with a conviction of her sin. Only then, softened at last, she moans, "O Hamlet, speak no more!"

The plain fact is that the murder of Polonius only momentarily interrupts an interview that Hamlet has controlled from the start and that has had from the start only one purpose—the separation of Gertrude from Claudius by awakening shame and repentance in her. This we know in part from the very beginning of the scene when Hamlet thrusts his mother back into her chair:

> Come, come, and sit you down. You shall not budge!
> You go not till I set you up a glass
> Where you may see the inmost part of you.

The exordium he later delivers would then have followed even if the Queen had not mistaken his abrupt violence and called for help.

The soliloquy ending 3.2 shows clearly that when he obeyed his mother's summons Hamlet had planned on forcing her to repentance, through fear if necessary:

> Let me be cruel, not unnatural;
> I will speak daggers to her, but use none. . . .
> How in my words somever she be shent,
> To give them seals never, my soul, consent!

It follows that the violence of his action that provoked the Queen's out-

---

[6] This scene is greatly vulgarized in Q1 (1603), where the Queen vows she knew nothing about the murder and Hamlet swears her to assist him in the revenge as a means of wiping out her infamy. This is the obvious stuff that a hack would add.

cry was part of this plan. Gertrude had summoned no wearily passive son who happened to seize a sudden and unexpected chance to force his will into domination over hers. There is no evidence that Hamlet has been alone with his mother since the audience saw the assembled court in Act 1. Thus when her summons afforded him the opportunity for a private meeting, a determined Hamlet went to his mother's closet with a fixed end in view, which he fulfilled despite, rather than because of, the murder of Polonius. That he succeeds here means, in effect, that he has successfully concluded one part of the Ghost's injunctions. In separating Gertrude from Claudius and bringing her to repentance in thought and action,[7] he has accomplished the first of the two revenges allotted him.

In our interest in following the conflict between Hamlet and his mighty opposite Claudius, we must not lose our awareness of the fact that Gertrude and her fate are included in the Ghost's commands for the revenge, and that they form an important balance in the play.[8] It is a significant irony that Hamlet's fatal misstep that later requires his death-in-victory for his second revenge is made in the very scene in which he succeeds in his first revenge. It is also an irony that Hamlet's misinterpretation of Claudius's attempt at repentance balances his success with Gertrude.

Hamlet tells the audience two things in the fifth soliloquy: in respect to Claudius I am prepared for blood; on the other hand, I must first put into effect my plan to force my mother to repent by separating her from her husband.

The first lines have an obvious bearing on the prayer scene (3.3) that immediately follows. It is part of the rich density of *Hamlet* that Shakespeare consistently refuses to permit us to pin the characters down to a single precise motive for action: by this means he prevents us from supplying a limited answer that would too easily serve to satisfy our curiosity by 'explaining' Hamlet. Thus Hamlet's refusal to kill the kneeling King may be in some part the honest revulsion of a civilized man when faced with blood. Although his bloodthirsty explanation is in some part

---

[7] It is clear that her partly sacrificial death in Act 5, and her warning to Hamlet of the cup, confirms her repentance in Act 3. Modern sentimentalism forgets the Elizabethan insistence that words must be accompanied by deeds if they are to be taken as valid.

[8] We may not interpret "Leave her to heaven" as an order to leave Gertrude alone. Instead, in his action Hamlet is not to plot against her or to enforce retributive justice on her, as on Claudius. It is the ultimate judgment resulting from Heaven's own retribution that Hamlet must leave to a greater power that will, in this case, repay. Hamlet in no manner has been forbidden to 'convert' his mother in the process of cleansing the royal bed; instead, he has been forbidden to punish her.

a face-saving device, yet we must not discount its partial validity and its considerable value in enabling him to rationalize his withdrawal.[9]

To the various explanations for Hamlet's action in sparing Claudius at prayer we may perhaps add one more: the pending interview with his mother and the importance of its purpose. That the interview is coming has been adduced previously as one of the complex of reasons for his failure to act, but critics have tended to misinterpret the motive, taking it that Hamlet weakly clung to his previous engagement (in a manner of speaking) as an excuse for avoiding action.

The soliloquy indicates the contrary. The time has come to carry out an important part of the revenge as it applies to Gertrude. In the soliloquy (before the prayer scene) this is given precedence over the part that applies to Claudius. The following action thereupon confirms the soliloquy. It is not, I think, fantastic to suggest that, to Hamlet, Gertrude's fate is at least as important as his revenge on Claudius, and that her fate depends wholly (so far as he can see) upon his forcing her to a recognition of her sin.[10] This he has determined on, as Shakespeare takes some pains to inform us. We should take this hint from the playwright and accept the order of events that Hamlet proposes for his double revenge, especially in view of the less-than-perfect circumstance for meting out justice to Claudius that chance thrusts upon him and that he rejects.

When we now at the last return to the original query suggested by this soliloquy, the answer is reasonably clearcut. The grand plan for *Hamlet* comprised a double action for the Ghost-directed protagonist: justice for Claudius; and the separation of his mother from her incestuous marriage, an act that was to include the awakening of her conscience as a means of saving her from the consequences of her mortal sin. The redemption of Gertrude is firmly planned. We hear of it in the soliloquy at the end of 3.2, we follow its course in Hamlet's rejection of an opportunity to mur-

---

[9] That the killing of one's victim's soul as well as his body was an Elizabethan shocker type of story associated with the vilest depths of Italian treachery (as in Nashe's *Unfortunate Traveller*) undoubtedly helped Shakespeare's audience to recognize its face-saving function in *Hamlet*.

[10] Whether too fine-spun or not, the point must be made, also, that the circumstances of repentance had, for the Elizabethan, much to do with the grace that might follow. That is, Gertrude sorrowing over the death of Claudius could repent her sin with greater facility when the opportunity to enjoy its perquisites was no longer in existence. On the other hand, the sincerity of her repentance can be vouched for when, expecting herself and Claudius to continue living, she removes herself from the royal bed, which obviously she has enjoyed. We need not suppose that such limited considerations governed Hamlet's sparing of Claudius for the moment, as we can supply a motivation for it. The strength of his purpose to reform and thereby to save his mother is sufficient on general grounds when added to the other reasonable suggestions that critics have offered.

der Claudius while supposedly in a state of grace as yet denied to Gertrude, and we see it crowned with success despite Gertrude's initial violent opposition and the resulting murder of Polonius. Its importance is attested by the arrangement of the events leading up to Gertrude's death in Act 5.[11]

Any exploitation of the sensational in the closet scene would necessarily detract from the audience's understanding of Hamlet's purpose and the firm manner in which he carried it out under the gravest difficulties. Indeed, it was so important for the audience to recognize that Hamlet was acting a part for a fixed purpose in his violence to his mother that Shakespeare could not permit any question on this score lest the audience lose sight of or else misinterpret the mainspring of Hamlet's actions. This rigorous control of the audience's reactions to a scene could not be managed by normal dramatic means. Hence the special quality of the fifth soliloquy, which points forward to the order of the succeeding events and unmistakably enforces the desired interpretation. When the Queen sobs, "O Hamlet, speak no more," Hamlet's purpose has been achieved and the soliloquy has been justified.

[11] I have discussed Shakespeare's concern with the fates of his characters in "The Death of Hamlet," in *Studies in the English Renaissance Drama in Memory of Karl Julius Holzknecht,* ed. Josephine W. Bennett, Oscar Cargill, and Vernon Hall, Jr. (1959), pp. 28-42.

'GREEKS' AND 'MERRYGREEKS': A BACKGROUND TO *TIMON OF ATHENS* AND *TROILUS AND CRESSIDA*

by T. J. B. Spencer

A FEW YEARS AGO, in a book which demonstrates the contribution of the classics to the literatures of modern Europe, an eminent classical scholar described Shakespeare's *Troilus and Cressida* as a "distant, ignorant, and unconvincing caricature of Greece." *Timon of Athens* is still more outrageous as a representation of society in that city at the height of its civilization, when it was the "educator of Hellas." One can sympathize with the discomfort or indignation which has been felt by those whose ears and eyes are full of the glory of Homer and Plato and Thucydides, when they meet the rather objectionable personages of Shakespeare's plays. The difficulty is felt less and less, of course, as fewer Shakespeare critics are brought up on Homer and the rest. Most students nowadays gain their impressions of the tale of Troy divine primarily from *Troilus and Cressida*. Those are the impressions that count, just as Shakespeare's historical plays are indelibly the sources of their information about English politics and personalities in the fourteenth and fifteenth centuries. The usual reply to the above-quoted opinion of Gilbert Highet (in *The Classical Tradition,* 1949, p. 197) would be something about the 'medieval tradition,' with mention of Chaucer, Lydgate, and Caxton.

This was, in essence, Matthew Arnold's explanation. "The Greeks in Shakespeare's *Troilus and Cressida,*" he said in his lectures *On Trans-*

lating Homer, "are no longer the Greeks whom we have known in Homer, because they come to us through a mode of representation of the romantic world." A more novel view was propounded by a better-informed classical scholar, J. A. K. Thomson, in his *Shakespeare and the Classics* (1952): that Shakespeare was writing in reaction against "the schoolmasters' worship of antiquity" (p. 224).

These explanations are unnecessary and misguided, because they are anachronistic. Our idealization, our emotional approval, of the Grecians and their civilization is a comparatively recent attitude; and to build up this mood of admiration, and sometimes of nostalgia, many influences have been at work: Winckelmann, Chénier, the Elgin marbles, the *Ode on a Grecian Urn,* Matthew Arnold's "Hellenism," the works of Victorian anecdotal painters, the sharp focus on the culture of fifth-century Athens in nineteenth-century educational institutions—these, and many other things, have played their part. On the whole, in spite of all that modern cynics, anthropologists, and economic historians have said, a distinctly favorable impression persists regarding the glory that was Greece, "land of lost gods and god-like men." This vision of Grecian life is shared by the unliterary, as is occasionally revealed by modern advertisements and travel brochures.

It is quite misleading to expect to find something resembling our admiring attitude towards the ancient Greeks in the literature of the Renaissance. This was written with a different background. It is true, of course, that Greek literature then had a great reputation (being fairly well known in Latin translations) and that certain Greek sages were regarded with admiration and awe. But this respect was not transferred to the ancient Greeks as a whole, to their national character, or to their way of living. The reason is simple. Latin literature was much more familiar than was Greek literature; and the opinion about the ancient Greeks which prevailed in the sixteenth century, and for some time afterwards, was, broadly speaking, that of the Romans of the Republic and the Empire. It was derived from a reading of the favorite Latin writers; and the prejudices thus acquired were, in most cases, far from favorable. Of course, the Greeks were the inventors of the arts and the sciences, the civilizers of the human race, and so forth. But, as *men?* . . . *Excudent alii!*

We learn from Plutarch, in a passage in his life of Cicero, that, as terms of contempt, *"Graecian* and scholler . . . are the two wordes, the which the artificers, (and such base mechanicall people at Rome), have

ever readie at their tongues ende" (North's translation, 1579). One Roman opinion, perhaps plebeian, of the Greeks was clearly revealed in
Roman comedy, and was therefore well known in the Renaissance.[1] In
Plautus the verb *pergraecari* had come to mean 'to spend the hours in
mirth, luxurious drinking and eating, and general dissipation':

> dies noctesque bibite, pergraecaminei,
> amicas emite, liberate: pascite
> parasitos: opsonate pollucibiliter.
> *(Mostellaria, 21)*

Likewise, *congraecare* meant 'to squander one's money in luxury and fast
living.' In the *Bacchides* the young man pretends that he has no intention of wrongly using his father's money, "quod dem scortis quodque in
lustris comedim, congraecem, pater" (743). 'To play the Greek' *(graecari)*
meant to live luxuriously and effeminately; and Horace's rustic sage,
Ofellus, sneers at those who, having become accustomed to the loose ways
of living of the Greeks, find Roman field-sports to be too exhausting and
therefore prefer ball-games: "Romana fatigat militia assuetum graecari"
(Satires, 2.2.10).

The convivial, dissipated Greek might be pardoned or tolerated; but
the perfidious Greek was not to be endured. To the Romans, 'Greek
faith' was proverbial, like the Greek Calends, and meant no faith at all.
When in Plautus's *Asinaria* the bawd Cleareta informs the eager young
lover, "Graeca mercamur fide" (199), she is referring to purchases for
ready cash, no credit being allowed. We must also take into account the
strongly anti-Greek bias of the *Aeneid,* probably the most widely read
and highly esteemed work of Latin literature during the Renaissance.
There, the hostile comments on Greek conduct, though of course dramatically appropriate in the poem, were capable of being given a wider
application.

> accipe nunc Danaum insidias et crimine ab uno
> disce omnes.
> (2.65)

Most famous of all was the proverbial "timeo Danaos et dona ferentes"
(2.49), which could be construed as a general condemnation of Greek
double-dealing.

---

[1] I have borrowed some of these examples from my *Fair Greece, Sad Relic* (1954),
where I have used them for another purpose: to show how in the early centuries they
affected opinions about the modern Greeks, the contemporary inhabitants of the
southern Balkan peninsula.

Cicero, who brought so much Greek culture to Latin literature and philosophy, wrote disparagingly of the *graeculus* on many occasions, and the Romans of the Empire declared their contempt, dislike, or derision of the Greeks, often in highly vituperative terms, which made a deep impression upon the habits of thought of the men of the Renaissance. Everybody knows Juvenal's superb and scathing passage of indignation at the insinuating Greek in Rome: "non possum ferre, Quirites, Graecam urbem," the poet exclaimed (3.60-61). Pushing, versatile, quick-witted, and utterly unscrupulous, the Greek wormed his way into the confidence of great men.

> ingenium velox, audacia perdita, sermo
> promptus et Isaeo torrentior. ede quid illum
> esse putes; quemvis hominem secum attulit ad nos.
>
> (73-5)

He is ready to play any part, physician or professor, acrobat or soothsayer, what you will; "omnia novit Graeculus esuriens" (77-8). The brilliant phrase stuck. Other Roman writers were equally emphatic. The elder Pliny wrote of the "portentosa Graeciae mendacia" (5.1.4) and the "Graeciae fabulositas" (12.5.11); and likewise Livy, Seneca, Quintilian, and others sneered at the failings of the Greeks, their impudence, venality, mendacity, vanity, and servility. There were very few good Greeks; and *they* were all dead. Tacitus records the rebuke of the proud Roman Piso to Germanicus, the romantic Hellenist, for his honoring "non Athenienses, tot cladibus exstinctos, sed conluviem illam nationum" (*Annales,* 2.55.1).

Even stronger and more convincing testimony to the bad qualities of the Greeks (at least, of some of them) was provided by St. Paul. Writing to Titus, whom he had left in Crete as the first bishop there, he warns his friend that he is likely to run into difficulties, owing to the evil disposition of the Cretans. For, did not one of their own sages (supposed to be Epimenides) declare that his countrymen were always liars, vile beasts, and idle gluttons? "Dixit quidam ex illis proprius ipsorum propheta: Cretenses semper mendaces, malae bestiae, ventres pigri. Testimonium hoc verum est" (1.12). As regards the lying propensities of the Cretans, St. Paul thus corroborated Ovid's opinion ("mendax Creta") in his *Ars amatoria* (1.298). Furthermore, in his first epistle to the Corinthians (6.9 ff.) St. Paul gives a lengthy catalogue of vices and depravities of the Greeks, which will keep them out of the Kingdom of Heaven.

Here then was weighty testimony against the Greek character; and it was this Roman and scriptural point of view that, on the whole, dominated the writers of the Renaissance. Erasmus clearly understood the situation and expressed it with his accustomed simplicity:

> Graecorum gens mala audit passim apud poetas Latinos, et item apud Ciceronem, non solum quasi voluptatibus addicta, et effoeminata delitiis, verum etiam quasi lubrica fide.

But Erasmus in his *Adagia* (from which this is quoted, 4.1.64) incorporated all these Roman prejudices; and so words and phrases such as *pergraecari* and *fide graeca* and *Cretiza cum Cretensi* (". . . id est, adversus mendacem mendaciis utere") were given authority in the numerous editions, epitomes, adaptations, and translations of Erasmus's great garnering of flowers of speech, elegant aphorisms, and figurative and proverbial expressions in the Latin tongue. Every schoolboy could learn to sneer at the Greeks.[2]

This helps to explain why the word *Greek* appeared in sixteenth-century English as a common noun in derogatory senses. There were two usages, both based upon Roman precedent.

First, the word *Greek,* generally preceded by an epithet like 'mad' or 'merry,' became an ordinary conversational expression meaning a person of loose and lively habits, a boon companion, a fast liver. The name of the well-known character Mathewe Merygreeke in *Roister Doister* (about 1553) is obviously related to Plautus's use of *pergraecari.* Nashe mentions "one *Dick Litchfield,* the Barber of *Trinity Colledge,* a rare ingenuous odde merry Greeke, who (as I have heard) hath translated my *Piers Pennilesse* into the Macaronicall tongue" (ed. McKerrow, 3.33). "Its a good mery greke," says Orgelus to Sir John in *Misogonus* (1560-77, 2.4). In John Cooke's play *Greene's Tu Quoque, or The City Gallant* (printed 1614), Pursenet says of Spendall:

> This is the captain of brave citizens,
> The Agamemnon of all merry Greeks.
> (Collier's Dodsley, 7.34)

In Thomas Heywood's *Edward IV* (printed 1599), Spicing exclaims to Falconbridge: "My brave *Falconbridge,* my mad *Greeke,* my lusty Neville!" (ed. Shepherd, 1.26). The phrase is common in Ben Jonson who in his prefatory contribution to *Coryats Crudities* in 1611 ("the Character of the famous Odcombian") gave his testimony of the author: "Hee is a mad *Greeke,* no lesse than a merry" (ed. Herford and Simpson, 8.377; see also 3.63, 164, 6.432). There are instances in Dekker, Fletcher, Mas-

---

[2] Some evidence for the currency of proverbs based upon these is given in M. P. Tilley's *Dictionary of the Proverbs in England in the Sixteenth and Seventeenth Centuries* (1950), C822, F31, M901.

singer, and others;[3] and the phrase is, of course, familiar in Shakespeare. "I prithee, foolish Greek, depart from me," says Sebastian to Feste in *Twelfth Night* (4.1.19), when he begins to lose patience with what he supposes to be the clown's unseasonable jests and licentious solicitations on behalf of some 'lady.' "Then she's a merry Greek indeed," says Cressida of Helen, on hearing an anecdote of her wanton conduct (*Troilus and Cressida*, 1.2.118); and when she parts from her Troilus, she laments that she will be "A woeful *Cressid* 'mongst the merry Greeks" (4.4.58).

There was a widespread opinion that the Greeks were remarkable for their persistent indulgence in drunkenness, a view which (in spite of the *Symposium*) hardly colors *our* estimate of the countrymen of Sophocles and Pericles. To drink *graeco more,* according to Cicero, referred to the continued drinking of healths; and so the opinion was encouraged by the scholars of the period. The humanist Nicolaus Leonicus, for example, included in his volume of serious essays on classical themes a discussion "de variis bibendi consuetudinibus apud Graecos."[4] Rabelais (*Pantagruel,* 2.1) casually declares that those fine fellows the Greeks were eternal drinkers: "Gregoys, Gentilz, qui furent buveurs eternelz." In *Les Serées* of Guillaume Bouchet (1584) we read:

> Les Grecs estans plus grands biberons que les Romains ne laissans gueres leurs vins en repos. Que cela soit vray, quand on veult parler de bien boire . . . on dit *graecari* & *pergraecari.* (ed. C. E. Roybet, 1873-83, 1.51)

This conviction about Greek inebriety may have been, in part, encouraged by the popularity of Greek wines in western Europe; every reader of Elizabethan literature is familiar with their reputation. In *The Old Law* by Middleton, Massinger, and Rowley, there is a comic scene of dissipation in which the Drawer cries: "Here, gentlemen, here's the quintessence of Greece; the sages never drunk better grape." And the Cook replies: "Sir, the mad Greeks of this age can taste their Palermo as well as the sage Greeks did before 'em." The arrival of some new revelers is, naturally, greeted with: "Here's a consort of mad Greeks" (4.1). In *A Hermeticall Banquet drest by a Spagiricall Cook, for the better Preservation of the Microcosme* (1652), the poets are given various duties in the family of Eloquentia: Shakespeare, butler; Ben Jonson, clerk of the kitchen; and "Homer because a merry Greek, Master of the Wine-Cellars" (p. 35).

---

[3] Further examples can be extricated from E. H. Sugden, *A Topographical Dictionary to the Works of Shakespeare and his Fellow Dramatists* (1925), p. 235.
[4] *N. Leonici Thomaei de varia historia libri tres* (Basel, 1531), 3.93.

In brief, to do things after the high Roman fashion was very different from behaving like a frivolous or dissolute Greek. It is Ben Jonson who gave expression most neatly to the contrast between Roman gravity and Greek levity, between (say) Lucan's "victrix causa deis placuit sed victa Catoni" and Plautus's "pergraecaminei." Mosca exclaims to Volpone, at the moment when their plot has failed and they are both in extreme danger of exposure and punishment:

> Let's die like *Romans,*
> Since wee have liv'd like *Grecians.*
> (3.8.14)

The second common meaning of the word *Greek,* which developed during the sixteenth century, was based upon the opinion of Greek wickedness, rather than of Greek dissoluteness. A 'Greek' meant what we should call a 'twister,' that is, a sharper, a cheat, a crook, any kind of confidence-trickster; it meant, in fact, all that was implied in the proverb *fide graeca.* This popular usage received full support and encouragement from learning and literature. In *The Civile Conversation of M. Steeven Guazzo,* as translated by George Pettie (1581), Annibal declares "touching conditions you knowe that the Greekes though singular in learning and eloquence, yet are they disloyal and faythles, and therefore it is proverbially saide, The Greekish fayth" (Tudor Translations, 1.64). In Lyly's *Euphues, The Anatomy of Wit* (1578) and its continuations and imitations, this attitude to the Greeks is a commonplace. When Philautus fears that his friend Euphues has robbed him of his love Lucilla, he soliloquizes:

> Is this the curtesie of *Athens,* the cavillyng of schollers, the craft of *Grecians?* Couldest thou not remember *Philautus* that Greece is never without some wily *Ulisses,* never void of some *Synon,* never to seeke of some deceitfull shifter? Is it not commonly saide of *Grecians* that crafte commeth to them by kinde, that they learne to deceive in their cradell? (ed. Bond, 1.232)

In lists of national characteristics, it is this derogatory view of the Greeks that is introduced as a matter of course. Euphues, "being demaunded of one what countryman he was, he answered, what countryman am I not? if I be in *Crete,* I can lye, if in *Greece* I can shift, if in *Italy,* I can court it" (1.186). Almost the same words are used in *Euphues and his England* (1580), where one of the characters says: "If I met with one of *Creete,* I was ready to lye with him for the whetstone. If with a *Grecian,* I could dissemble with *Synon* . . ." (2.24). And in *Euphues and his Ephoebus,* the

Elizabethan reader was told that "of olde it was sayde to a *Lacedemonian*, that all the *Grecians* knewe honesty, but not one practised it" (1.275). In like manner, in *Greenes Mourning Garment* (1590) the Greeks are notorious:

> In *Creete* thou must learne to lye, in *Paphos* to be a lover, in *Greece* a dissembler, thou must bring home pride from *Spaine*, lascivousnesse from *Italy*,

and so on (ed. Grosart, 9.136). In the anonymous play, *The Statelie Tragedie of Claudius Tiberius Nero* (printed 1607), the ambitious Sejanus declares that "He that wil clime, and aime at honours white" must be able to accommodate himself to all temperaments,

> Drink with the Germain, with the Spaniard brave:
> Brag with the French, with the Ægiptian lie,
> Flatter in Creet, and fawne in Graecia.
>
> (683)

Donne in one of his epigrams jeers at the *Mercurius Gallo-Belgicus*, a periodical publication of the early seventeenth century which gave news of events in Europe, some of it apparently untrustworthy:

> Change thy name: thou art like
> *Mercury* in stealing, but lyest like a *Greeke*.

And the seventeenth-century traveller John Josselyn, who first came to America in 1638, took the proverb to the New World and applied it to the inhabitants: "No trading for a stranger with them, but with a Grecian faith, which is not to part with your ware without ready money" (*An Account of two Voyages to New England*, 1674, ed. 1875, p. 181).

With this background, it is easy to see how, from the early sixteenth century onwards, the word *Greek* had the meaning, by antonomasia, of a 'crook.' It was widespread for three centuries.[5] A favorite use of the word was for a sharper at cards, but it could be applied to any kind of cheat. For example, in Greene's *Defence of Conny-Catching* (1592) we are told "A pleasant Tale how a holy brother Conny-catcht for a Wife." A sly rogue hears of a young lady who has an ample portion in her own right; so "to this girle goeth this proper Greek a wooing, naming himself to be a Gentleman of *Cheshire* . . ." (ed. Grosart, 11.80).

It needs to be added that the women of Greece had a reputation that

---

[5] In French *grec* was similarly used and apparently still survives. See Littré, s.v.; also Kastner and Marks, *A Glossary of Colloquial and Popular French* (1929), s.v. For the sixteenth-century history of the word see E. Huguet, *Dictionnaire de la langue française du seizième siècle* (1949), 4.366-7.

corresponded to the men's, the complement of rogue with whore having long been usual. Juvenal had deplored the grecizing libidinous habits of the women of his time. Every provincial girl wanted to be a 'maid of Athens.'

> Nam quid rancidius, quam quod se non putat ulla
> formosam, nisi quae de Tusca Graecula facta est,
> de Sulmonensi mera Crecropsis?
>
> (6.186)

The fame of the Grecian women for venery was widespread in the literature of the sixteenth and seventeenth centuries. Antique fables about Cythera and Paphos, memories of Corinthian revels, of Phryne and Lais, of the Grecian courtesans celebrated in Roman poetry—these could not be forgotten. The 'Greek vice,' too, was of course a byword, and Shakespeare deliberately introduces this Renaissance notion in relation to Achilles and Patroclus: "Thou art thought to be Achilles' male varlet," says Thersites to Patroclus. "Male varlet, you rogue! What's that?" "Why, his masculine whore" (5.1.19).

Thus it came about that, in England, France, Italy, and elsewhere, during Shakespeare's lifetime, *Greek* was a household word for a voluptuary or a crook. The Greeks were, clearly, a bad lot. There was little to resist the influence of the prevailing Roman attitude to the Greeks, namely, that they were licentious, luxurious, frivolous, bibulous, venereal, insinuating, perfidious, and unscrupulous.

The fact that some of these qualities are both inconsistent among themselves and inconsistent with the reverence and admiration owed to the civilizers of mankind, the glorious creators of philosophy, science, and art, need not perplex us; for the existence of such contrary opinions at the same time, even in the same mind, is common enough.

Furthermore, in one of Horace's most famous poems ("Troiani belli scriptorem, Maxime Lolli," *Epistolae,* 1.2), we have an interesting account of the Roman moralistic attitude to Homer, which is entirely appropriate to the general Roman attitude to the Greeks. It was the source of the characteristic Renaissance attitude to Homer as an ethical poet who in the *Iliad* expounded the evils of quarrelsome and unreasonable conduct among rulers ("quidquid delirant reges plectuntur Achivi"). In Horace's poem the lofty Homer of our imagination is scarcely recognizable. The story of the *Iliad,* says Horace, concerns wicked conduct both inside and outside the walls of Troy, including intrigue, double-crossing, lechery, and quarrelsomeness:

seditione, dolis, scelere atque libidine et ira
Iliacos intra muros peccatur et extra.
(15-16)

This may not, to our notions, fit the *Iliad*. But is it not an accurate and pithy description of most of *Troilus and Cressida*? Of course, it need not be supposed that Shakespeare had read this *Epistle* of Horace; it is, however, a curious coincidence that one of the few verbal quotations from Latin literature in Shakespeare's mature works should be taken accurately from this very poem (62). In *Timon of Athens* Timon describes Apemantus: "They say, my lords, *ira furor brevis est*; but yond man is ever [F "Verie"] angry" (1.2.28). Still, whether or not Shakespeare had had a look at the poem or some Horatian friend had talked to him about it, it was an important, influential, and accessible opinion of Homer. It was not Chapman's attitude; but it was the orthodox attitude which would have been expounded to Shakespeare (if he needed it) by Ben Jonson or any other Horatian. Chapman, obsessed with the importance of Homer and a desire to defend him against his Scaligerian detractors, tried to make out Achilles to be an epitome of all virtues and an image of the Earl of Essex. But Horace in his *Ars poetica* had given the Roman view of Achilles, and therefore the usual Renaissance view:

impiger, iracundus, inexorabilis, acer,
iura neget sibi nata, nihil non arroget armis.
(121-2)

This is Horace's Achilles, and it is Shakespeare's Achilles; and Swinburne was under a misapprehension when he supposed that Shakespeare "set himself as if prepensely and on purpose to brutalise the type of Achilles . . . an enterprise never to be utterly forgiven by any who ever loved from the birth of his boyhood the very name of the son of the sea-goddess" (*A Study of Shakespeare*, 1880, p. 201). This is eloquently and touchingly written, for Swinburne loved his Homer; but he ignored the history of opinion about Homer.

Are the Greeks of *Timon of Athens* and *Troilus and Cressida* any different from what we should expect, if we can disentangle ourselves from merely modern classical prejudices and see the Greeks as they were seen in the Renaissance? Shakespeare does not merit the regrets of our classical scholars, nor is there need for subtle explanations of his attitude to these Greek stories—least of all that he was writing in reaction against "the schoolmasters' worship of antiquity." We should be equally cautious of the facile explanation that Shakespeare was writing under the influence of medieval habits of telling the tale of Troy; these habits were in many respects as remote from *Troilus and Cressida* as *Troilus and Cressida* is from the *Iliad*. As for *Timon of Athens,* we should certainly be thinking anachronistically if we were to regret that the chaste Doric beauties of the Parthenon and a Sophoclean or Socratic elevation of thought do not provide the background to Timon's life. Rather, he exists (appropriately, by Renaissance ideas of the ancient Greeks) in a world inhabited by Alcibiades with his 'beagles,' Phryne and Timandra, and by perfidious friends like Lucullus and Sempronius. In fact, Timon and his circle 'live like Grecians.' Similarly, Achilles, Diomedes, and the rest of the Grecian host, do not represent an attempt by Shakespeare's ignorant or disordered imagination to deny, distort, debunk, or calumniate the nobility of the Homeric heroes. They—and the wanton Cressida and Helen as well—are merely 'Greeks.'

RECOGNITION IN *THE WINTER'S TALE*

by NORTHROP FRYE

IN STRUCTURE *The Winter's Tale*, like *King Lear*, falls into two main parts separated by a storm. The fact that they are also separated by sixteen years is less important. The first part ends with the ill-fated Antigonus caught between a bear and a raging sea, echoing a passage in one of Lear's storm speeches. This first part is the "winter's tale" proper, for Mamillius is just about to whisper his tale into his mother's ear when the real winter strikes with the entrance of Leontes and his guards. Various bits of imagery, such as Polixenes' wish to get back to Bohemia for fear of "sneaping winds" blowing at home and Hermione's remark during her trial (reproduced from *Pandosto*) that the emperor of Russia was her father, are linked to a winter setting. The storm, like the storm in *King Lear,* is described in such a way as to suggest that a whole order of things is being dissolved in a dark chaos of destruction and devouring monsters, and the action of the first part ends in almost unrelieved gloom. The second part is a tragicomedy where, as in *Cymbeline* and *Measure for Measure,* there is frightening rather than actual hurting. Some of the frightening seems cruel and unnecessary, but the principle of 'all's well that ends well' holds in comedy, however great nonsense it may be in life.

The two parts form a diptych of parallel and contrasting actions, one dealing with age, winter, and the jealousy of Leontes, the other with youth, summer, and the love of Florizel. The first part follows Greene's *Pandosto* closely; for the second part no major source has been identified. A number of symmetrical details, which are commonplaces of Shake-

235

spearian design, help to build up the contrast: for instance, the action
of each part begins with an attempt to delay a return. The two parts are
related in two ways, by sequence and by contrast. The cycle of nature,
turning through the winter and summer of the year and through the age
and youth of human generations, is at the center of the play's imagery.
The opening scene sets the tone by speaking of Mamillius and of the
desire of the older people in the country to live until he comes to reign.
The next scene, where the action begins, refers to Leontes' own youth
in a world of pastoral innocence and its present reflection in Mamillius.
The same cycle is also symbolized, as in *Pericles*, by a mother-daughter
relationship, and Perdita echoes Marina when she speaks of Hermione
as having "ended when I but began." In the transition to the second part
the clown watches the shipwreck and the devouring of Antigonus; the
shepherd exhibits the birth tokens of Perdita and remarks, "Thou mettest
with things dying, I with things new-born." Leontes, we are told, was to
have returned Polixenes' visit "this coming summer," but instead of that
sixteen years pass and we find ourselves in Bohemia with spring imagery
bursting out of Autolycus's first song, "When daffodils begin to peer."
If Leontes is an imaginary cuckold, Autolycus, the thieving harbinger of
spring, is something of an imaginative cuckoo. Thence we go on to the
sheep-shearing festival, where the imagery extends from early spring to
winter evergreens, a vision of nature demonstrating its creative power
throughout the entire year, which is perhaps what the dance of the
twelve satyrs represents. The symbolic reason for the sixteen-year gap is
clearly to have the cycle of the year reinforced by the slower cycle of
human generations.

Dramatic contrast in Shakespeare normally includes a superficial resemblance in which one element is a parody of the other. Theseus remarks in *A Midsummer Night's Dream* that the lunatic, the lover, and
the poet are of imagination all compact. Theseus, like Yeats, is a smiling
public man past his first youth, but not, like Yeats, a poet and a critic.
What critical ability there is in that family belongs entirely to Hippolyta,
whose sharp comments are a most effective contrast to Theseus's amiable
bumble. Hippolyta objects that the story of the lovers has a consistency
to it that lunacy would lack, and everywhere in Shakespearian comedy the
resemblance of love and lunacy is based on their opposition. Florizel's
love for Perdita, which transcends his duty to his father and his social
responsibilities as a prince, is a state of mind above reason. He is advised,
he says, by his "fancy":

                              If my reason
        Will thereto be obedient, I have reason;
        If not, my senses, better pleased with madness,
        Do bid it welcome.

Leontes' jealousy is a fantasy below reason, and hence a parody of
Florizel's state. Camillo, who represents a kind of middle level in the
play, is opposed to both, calling one diseased and the other desperate.
Both states of mind collide with reality in the middle, and one is anni-
hilated and the other redeemed, like the two aspects of law in Christianity. As the Gentleman says in reporting the finding of Perdita, "They
looked as they had heard of a world ransomed, or one destroyed." When
Leontes has returned to his proper state of mind, he echoes Florizel when
he says of watching the statue,

            No settled senses of the world can match
            The pleasure of that madness.

The play ends in a double recognition scene: the first, which is reported only through the conversation of three Gentlemen, is the recognition of Perdita's parentage; the second is the final scene of the awakening of Hermione and the presenting of Perdita to her. The machinery
of the former scene is the ordinary *cognitio* of New Comedy, where the
heroine is proved by birth tokens to be respectable enough for the hero
to marry her. In many comedies, though never in Shakespeare, such a
cognitio is brought about through the ingenuity of a tricky servant.
Autolycus has this role in *The Winter's Tale,* for though "out of service"
he still regards Florizel as his master, and he has also the rascality and
the complacent soliloquies about his own cleverness that go with the role.
He gains possession of the secret of Perdita's birth, but somehow or other
the denouement takes place without him, and he remains superfluous to
the plot, consoling himself with the reflection that doing so good a deed
would be inconsistent with the rest of his character. In *The Winter's Tale*
Shakespeare has combined the two traditions which descended from
Menander, pastoral romance and New Comedy, and has consequently
come very close to Menandrine formulas as we have them in such a play
as *Epitripontes.* But the fact that this conventional recognition scene is
only reported indicates that Shakespeare is less interested in it than in
the statue scene, which is all his own.

    In *Measure for Measure* and *The Tempest* the happy ending is brought
about through the exertions of the central characters, whose successes

are so remarkable that they seem to many critics to have something almost supernatural about them, as though they were the agents of a divine providence. The germ of truth in this conception is that in other comedies of the same general structure, where there is no such character, the corresponding dramatic role is filled by a supernatural being—Diana in *Pericles* and Jupiter in *Cymbeline*. The *Winter's Tale* belongs to the second group, for the return of Perdita proceeds from the invisible providence of Apollo.

In *Pericles* and *Cymbeline* there is, in addition to the recognition scene, a dream in which the controlling divinity appears with an announcement of what is to conclude the action. Such a scene forms an emblematic recognition scene, in which we are shown the power that brings about the comic resolution. In *The Tempest*, where the power is human, Prospero's magic presents three emblematic visions: a wedding masque of gods to Ferdinand, a disappearing banquet to the Court Party, and "trumpery" (4.1.186) to entice Stephano and Trinculo to steal. In *The Winter's Tale* Apollo does not enter the action, and the emblematic recognition scene is represented by the sheep-shearing festival. This is also on three levels. To Florizel it is a kind of betrothal masque and "a meeting of the petty gods"; to the Court Party, Polixenes and Camillo, it is an illusion which they snatch away; to Autolycus it is an opportunity to sell his "trumpery" (4.4.608) and steal purses.

An emblematic recognition scene of this kind is the distinguishing feature of the four late romances. As a convention, it develops from pastoral romance and the narrative or mythological poem. The sheep-shearing festival resembles the big bravura scenes of singing-matches and the like in Sidney's *Arcadia,* and *The Rape of Lucrece* comes to an emblematic focus in the tapestry depicting the fall of Troy, where Lucrece identifies herself with Hecuba and Tarquin with Sinon, and determines that the second Troy will not collapse around a rape like the first one. In the earlier comedies the emblematic recognition scene is usually in the form of burlesque. Thus in *Love's Labours Lost* the pageant of Worthies elaborates on Don Armado's appeal to the precedents of Solomon, Samson, and Hercules when he falls in love; but his appeal has also burlesqued the main theme of the play. The allegorical garden episode in *Richard II* represents a similar device, but one rather different in its relation to the total dramatic structure.

In any case the controlling power in the dramatic action of *The Winter's Tale* is something identified both with the will of the gods, especially Apollo, and with the power of nature. We have to keep this association of nature and pagan gods in mind when we examine the imagery in the play that reminds us of religious, even explicitly Christian, conceptions. At the beginning Leontes' youth is referred to as a time of paradisal innocence; by the end of the scene he has tumbled into a completely illusory knowledge of good and evil. He says:

> How blest am I
> In my just censure, in my true opinion!
> Alack, for lesser knowledge! How accurs'd
> In being so blest!

Or, as Ford says in *The Merry Wives,* "God be praised for my jealousy!" The irony of the scene in which Leontes is scolded by Paulina turns on the fact that Leontes tries to be a source of righteous wrath when he is actually an object of it. Hermione's trial is supposed to be an act of justice and the sword of justice is produced twice to have oaths sworn on it, but Leontes is under the wrath of Apollo and divine justice is his enemy. The opposite of wrath is grace, and Hermione is associated throughout the play with the word grace. During the uneasy and rather cloying friendliness at the beginning of the play Hermione pronounces the word "grace" conspicuously three times, after which the harsh dissonances of Leontes' jealousy begin. She also uses the word when she is ordered off to prison and in the only speech that she makes after Act 3. But such grace is not Christian or theological grace, which is superior to the order of nature, but a secular analogy of Christian grace which is identical with nature—the grace that Spenser celebrates in the sixth book of *The Faerie Queene.*

In the romances, and in some of the earlier comedies, we have a sense of an irresistible power, whether of divine or human agency, making for a providential resolution. Whenever we have a strong sense of such a power, the human beings on whom it operates seem greatly diminished in size. This is a feature of the romances which often disappoints those who wish that Shakespeare had simply kept on writing tragedies. Because of the heavy emphasis on reconciliation in *Cymbeline,* the jealousy of Posthumus is not titanic, as the jealousy of Othello is titanic; it expresses only a childish petulance about women in general: "I'll write against them, Despise them, curse them." Similarly Leontes (as he himself points out) falls far short of being a somber demonic tyrant on the scale of Macbeth, and can only alternate between bluster and an uneasy sense of having done wrong:

> Away with that audacious lady! Antigonus,
> I charg'd thee that she should not come about me.
> I knew she would.

This scaling down of the human perspective is in conformity with a dramatic structure that seems closely analogous to such Christian conceptions as wrath and grace. But the only one of the four romances in which I suspect any explicit—which means allegorical—references to Christianity is *Cymbeline.* Cymbeline was king of Britain at the birth of Christ, and in such scenes as the Jailer's speculations about death and his wistful "I would we were all of one mind, and that mind good," there are hints that some far-reaching change in the human situation is taking place off-stage. The play ends on the word "peace" and with Cymbeline's promise to pay tribute to Rome, almost as though, as soon as the story ended, another one were to begin with Augustus Caesar's decree that all the world should be taxed.

No such explicit links are appropriate to *The Winter's Tale,* though it is true that the story does tell of a mysterious disappearing child born in the winter who has four father-figures assigned to her: a real one, a putative one who later becomes her father-in-law, a fictional one, Smalus of Libya in Florizel's tale, and a shepherd foster-father. This makes up a group of a shepherd and three kings, of whom one is African. The first part of *The Winter's Tale* is, like *Cymbeline,* full of the imagery of superstitious sacrifice. Leontes, unable to sleep, wonders if having Hermione burnt alive would not give him rest. Antigonus offers to spay his three daughters if Hermione is guilty, though he would prefer to castrate himself. Mamillius, whom Leontes thinks of as a part of himself, becomes the victim necessary to save Leontes, and the exposing of Perdita is attended by a sacrificial holocaust. Not only is Antigonus devoured by a bear, but the ship and its crew were "Wrecked the same instant of their master's death and in the view of the shepherd; so that all the instruments which aided to expose the child were even then lost when it was found." In contrast, the restoring of Perdita to her mother is an act of sacramental communion, but it is a secular communion, and the "instruments" aiding in it are the human arts. The main characters repair to Paulina's house intending to "sup" there, and are taken into her chapel and presented with what is alleged to be a work of painting and sculpture. Hermione, like Thaisa in *Pericles,* is brought to life by the playing of music, and references to the art of magic follow. Art, therefore, seems part of the regenerating power of the play, and the imagination of the poet is to be allied with that of the lover as against that of the lunatic.

Apart from the final scene, at least three kinds of art are mentioned in the play. First, there is the art of the gardener who, according to Polixenes' famous speech, may help or change nature by marrying a gentler scion to the wildest stock but can do so only through nature's power, so that "the art itself is nature." This is a sound humanist view: it is the view of Sidney, who contrasts the brazen world of nature with the golden world of art but also speaks of art as a second nature. Sidney's view does not necessitate, but it is consistent with, his ridiculing of plays that show a character as an infant in one act and grown up in the next, and that mingle kings and clowns in the same scene. It is also the view of Ben Jonson who, recognizing a very different conception of nature in Shakespeare's romances, remarked good-humoredly that he was "loth to make nature afraid in his plays, like those that beget tales, tempests, and suchlike drolleries." We note that Polixenes' speech entirely fails to convince Perdita, who merely repeats that she will have nothing to do with bastard flowers:

> No more than, were I painted, I would wish
> This youth should say 'twere well, and only therefore
> Desire to breed by me. . . .

—a remark which oddly anticipates the disappearance of the painted statue of Hermione into the real Hermione. It also, as has often been pointed out, fails to convince Polixenes himself, for a few moments later we find him in a paroxysm of fury at the thought of his own gentle scion marrying the wild stock of a shepherd's daughter. Whatever its merits, Polixenes' view of art hardly seems to describe the kind of art that the play itself manifests.

Secondly, there is the kind of art represented by Julio Romano, said to be the painter and sculptor of Hermione's statue, a mimetic realist who "would beguile Nature of her custom, so perfectly is he her ape." But it turns out that in fact no statue has been made of Hermione, and the entire reference to Romano seems pointless. We do not need his kind of art when we have the real Hermione, and here again, whatever Romano's merits, neither he nor the kind of realism he represents seems to be very central to the play itself. The literary equivalent of realism is plausibility, the supplying of adequate causation for events. There is little plausibility in *The Winter's Tale,* and a great deal of what is repeatedly called "wonder." Things are presented to us, not explained. The jealousy of Leontes explodes without warning: an actor may rationalize it in various ways; a careful reader of the text may suspect that the references to his youth have touched off some kind of suppressed guilt; but the essential fact is that the jealousy suddenly appears where it had not been before, like a second subject in a piece of music. "How should this grow?" Polixenes asks of Camillo, but Camillo evades the question. At the end of the play Hermione is first a statue, then a living woman. The explanations given do not satisfy even Leontes, much less us. He says:

> But how, is to be question'd; for I saw her,
> As I thought, dead, and have in vain said many
> A prayer upon her grave.

As often in Shakespeare, further explanations are promised to the characters, but are not given to the audience: Paulina merely says, "it appears She lives."

Thirdly, though one blushes to mention it, there is the crude popular art of the ballads of Autolycus, of which one describes "how a usurer's wife was brought to bed of twenty money-bags at a burden." "Is it true, think you?" asks Mopsa, unconsciously using one of the most frequently echoed words in the play. We notice that Shakespeare seems to be calling our attention to the incredibility of his story and to its ridiculous and outmoded devices when he makes both Paulina and the Gentlemen who report the recognition of Perdita speak of what is happening as "like an old tale." The magic words pronounced by Paulina that draw speech from Hermione are "Our Perdita is found," and Paulina has previously said that the finding of Perdita is "monstrous to our human reason." And when one of the Gentlemen says "Such a deal of wonder is broken out within this hour that ballad-makers cannot be able to express it," we begin to suspect that the kind of art manifested by the play itself is in some respects closer to these "trumpery" ballads than to the sophisticated idealism and realism of Polixenes and Romano.

My late and much beloved colleague Professor Harold S. Wilson has called attention to the similarity between Polixenes' speech and a passage in Puttenham's *Arte of English Poesie* (1589), which in discussing the relation of art and nature uses the analogy of the gardener and the example of the "gillyvor."[1] Puttenham also goes on to say that there is another context where art is "only a bare imitator of nature's works, following and counterfeiting her actions and effects, as the Marmoset doth many countenances and gestures of man; of which sort are the arts of painting and carving." We are reminded of Romano, the painter and carver who is the perfect "ape" of nature. The poet, says Puttenham, is to use all types of art in their proper place, but for his greatest moments he will work "even as nature her self working by her own peculiar virtue

---

[1] "'Nature and Art' in *Winter's Tale* 4.4.86 ff.," *SAB*, 18 (1943), 114-20.

and proper instinct and not by example or meditation or exercise as all other artificers do." We feel that Puttenham, writing before Shakespeare had got properly started and two centuries earlier than Coleridge, has nonetheless well characterized the peculiar quality of Shakespeare's art.

The fact that Leontes' state of mind is a parody of the imagination of lover and poet links *The Winter's Tale* with Shakespeare's 'humor' comedies, which turn on the contrast between fantasy and reality. Katharina moves from shrew to obedient wife; Falstaff from the seducer to the gull of the merry wives; the King of Navarre and his followers from contemplative pedants seeking authority from books to helpless lovers performing the tasks imposed on them by their ladies. Similarly when Florizel says that his love for Perdita

> cannot fail but by
> The violation of my faith; and then
> Let nature crush the sides o' th' earth together
> And mar the seeds within! . . .

—he is supplying the genuine form of what Camillo describes in parallel cosmological terms:

> you may as well
> Forbid the sea for to obey the moon,
> As or by oath remove or counsel shake
> The fabric of his folly, whose foundation
> Is piled upon his faith.

Puttenham begins his treatise by comparing the poet, as a creator, to God, "who without any travail to his divine imagination made all the world of nought." Leontes' jealousy is a parody of a creation out of nothing, as the insistent repetition of the word "nothing" in the first act indicates, and as Leontes himself says in his mysterious mumbling half-soliloquy:

> Affection, thy intention stabs the centre!
> Thou dost make possible things not so held,
> Communicat'st with dream—how can this be?
> With what's unreal thou coactive art,
> And fellow'st nothing.

A humor is restored to a normal outlook by being confronted, not directly with reality, but with a reflection of its own illusion, as Katharina is tamed by being shown the reflection of her own shrewishness in Petruchio. Similarly Leontes, in the final scene, is "mocked with art," the realistic illusion of Romano's statue which gradually reveals itself to be the real Hermione.

In the artificial society of the Sicilian court there are Mamillius, the hopeful prince who dies, and the infant Perdita who vanishes. In the rural society of Bohemia there are the shepherdess Perdita who is "Flora Peering in April's front," and Florizel who, as his name suggests, is her masculine counterpart, and the Prince Charming who later reminds Leontes strongly of Mamillius and becomes Leontes' promised heir. Perdita says that she would like to strew Florizel with flowers:

> like a bank for love to lie and play on,
> Not like a corse; or if, not to be buried,
> But quick and in mine arms.

The antithesis between the two worlds is marked by Polixenes, who is handed "flowers of winter" and who proceeds to destroy the festival like a winter wind, repeating the *senex iratus* role of Leontes in the other kingdom. But though he can bully Perdita, he impresses her no more than Leontes had impressed Hermione. Perdita merely says:

> I was not much afeard; for once or twice
> I was about to speak and tell him plainly
> The selfsame sun that shines upon his court
> Hides not his visage from our cottage but
> Looks on alike.

There is a faint New Testament echo here, but of course to Perdita the god of the sun would be Apollo, who does see to it that Polixenes is outwitted, though only by the fact that Perdita is really a princess. As always in Shakespeare, the structure of society is unchanged by the comic action. What happens in *The Winter's Tale* is the opposite of the art of the gardener as Polixenes describes it. A society which is artificial in a limited sense at the beginning of the play becomes at the end still artificial, but natural as well. Nature provides the means for the regeneration of artifice. But still it is true that "The art itself is nature," and one wonders why a speech ending with those words should be assigned to Polixenes, the opponent of the festival.

The context of Polixenes' theory is the Renaissance framework in which there are two levels of the order of nature. Art belongs to human nature, and human nature is, properly speaking, the state that man lived in in Eden, or the Golden Age, before his fall into a lower world of physical nature to which he is not adapted. Man attempts to regain his original state through law, virtue, education, and such rational and conscious aids as art. Here nature is a superior order. In poetry this upper level of nature, uncontaminated by the sin and death of the fall, is usually symbolized by the starry spheres, which are now all that is left of it. The starry spheres produce the music of the spheres, and the harmony of music usually represents this upper level of nature in human life.

Most Shakespearian comedy is organized within this framework, and when it is, its imagery takes on the form outlined by G. Wilson Knight in *The Shakespearean Tempest* (1932). The tempest symbolizes the destructive elements in the order of nature, and music the permanently constructive elements in it. Music in its turn is regularly associated with the starry spheres, of which the one closest to us, the moon, is the normal focus. The control of the tempest by the harmony of the spheres appears in the image of the moon pulling the tides, an image used once or twice in *The Winter's Tale*. The action of *The Merchant of Venice*, too, extends from the cosmological harmonies of the fifth act, where the moon sleeps with Endymion, to the tempest that wrecked Antonio's ships. In *Pericles*, which employs this imagery of harmony and tempest most exhaustively, Pericles is said to be a master of music, Cerimon revives Thaisa by music, Diana announces her appearance to Pericles by music, and the final recognition scene unites the music and tempest symbols, since it takes place in the temple of Diana during the festival of Neptune. Music also accompanies the revival of Hermione in the final scene of *The Winter's Tale*. All the attention is absorbed in Hermione as she begins to move while music plays; and we are reminded of Autolycus and of his role as a kind of rascally Orpheus at the sheep-shearing festival: "My clown . . . would not stir his pettitoes till he had both tune and words; which so drew the rest of the herd to me that all their other senses stuck in ears. . . . No hearing, no feeling, but my sir's song, and admiring the nothing of it." Here again Autolycus seems to be used to indicate that something is being subordinated in the play, though by no means eliminated.

In another solstitial play, *A Midsummer Night's Dream*, the cosmology is of this more conventional Renaissance kind. In the middle, between the world of chaos symbolized by tempest and the world of starry spheres symbolized by music, comes the cycle of nature, the world of Eros and Adonis, Puck and Pyramus, the love-god and the dying god. To this middle world the fairies belong, for the fairies are spirits of the four natural elements, and their dissension causes disorder in nature. Above, the cold fruitless moon of Diana, whose nun Hermia would have to be, hangs over the action. While a mermaid is calming the sea by her song and attracting the stars by the power of harmony, Cupid shoots an arrow at the moon and its vestal: it falls in a parabola on a flower and turns it "purple with love's wound." The story of Pyramus is not very coherently told in Peter Quince's play, but in Ovid there is a curious image about the blood spurting out of Pyramus in an arc like water out of a burst pipe and falling on the white mulberry and turning it purple. Here nature as a cycle of birth and death, symbolized by the purple flower, revolves underneath nature as a settled and predictable order or harmony, as it does also in a third solstitial play, *Twelfth Night,* which begins with an image comparing music to a wind blowing on a bank of violets.

But in *The Winter's Tale* nature is associated, not with the credible, but with the incredible: nature as an order is subordinated to the nature that yearly confronts us with the impossible miracle of renewed life. In Ben Jonson's animadversions on Shakespeare's unnatural romances it is particularly the functional role of the dance, the "concupiscence of jigs," as he calls it, that he objects to. But it is the dance that most clearly expresses the pulsating energy of nature as it appears in *The Winter's Tale,* an energy which communicates itself to the dialogue. Such words as "push" and "wild" (meaning rash) are constantly echoed; the play ends with the words "Hastily lead away," and we are told that the repentant Leontes

> o'er and o'er divides him
> 'Twixt his unkindness and his kindness; th' one
> He chides to hell and bids the other grow
> Faster than thought of time.

Much is said about magic in the final scene, but there is no magician, no Prospero, only the sense of a participation in the redeeming and reviving power of a nature identified with art, grace, and love. Hence the final recognition is appropriately that of a frozen statue turning into a living presence, and the appropriate Chorus is Time, the destructive element which is also the only possible representative of the timeless.

REPEATED SITUATIONS IN SHAKESPEARE'S PLAYS

by MATTHEW W. BLACK

NO LONG ACQUAINTANCE with the plays of Shakespeare is needed to make the reader aware that beneath the poetry and the seemingly effortless generation of lifelike and memorable characters he manifested to a considerable extent the bourgeois virtue of economy. The man who plowed his profits back into playhouse property, who purchased a "praty howse of brike and tymbar" and retired to it at a time of life when almost all of his confreres in the profession were destined for penury, displayed the same ingrained conservatism toward valuable plot-material as toward money.

So obvious a fact has of course been remarked on. As early as 1910 William Allan Neilson (*Shakespeare's Complete Works*, p. xvii) had commented: "In the mechanics of his plays, he repeated himself freely. When a device, a situation, a contrast of character, proved successful on the stage, he did not scruple to use it again and again, displaying in the variations he worked on it abundant cleverness, but at the same time an economy of invention, in striking contrast to his lavish prodigality in thought and imagery."

In addition to innumerable comments on particular repetitions by the editors of individual plays, two publications—an article and a book— have considered this complex matter in part or as a whole. D. T. Starnes ("Repeated Themes and Situations in Shakespeare's Comedies," *The Texas Review*, 6, 1920-1) points out such repeated themes as the separation and reunion of parents and children, education, unrequited love,

247

marriage-for-money, wife- or husband-hunting, overhearing, mistaken identity with or without disguise, substitution (in *Much Ado, All's Well,* and *Measure for Measure*), and certain repeated situations: the girl disguised as a page who acts as a go-between for lovers, one woman falling in love with another, discussion of suitors by mistress and servant, clowns' soliloquies, shipwreck and its consequences.

In 1941 appeared Paul V. Kreider's volume, *Repetition in Shakespeare's Plays.* Part 1 takes up the mechanics of repetition as displayed in disguise and devotes particular attention to the introduction, character, and motivation of the villain, his relation with his fellows, his system of self-defense, and the destruction of his victim. Part 2 takes up several types of repetition: repetition of idea ("Macbeth and Sleep"); of the theme of blindness and sight ("Gloucester's Eyes"); of atmosphere (in *As You Like It*); of satire on romantic conventions in drama (in *As You Like It*). An appendix attempts the formidable task—which Kreider would be the first to characterize as incomplete—of listing specific repetitions in Shakespeare and organizing them according to the backgrounds of Elizabethan life in which they arise: sports, social organization; beliefs, literary customs; banishment, bereavement, and grief, atrocities, death; concealed identity and disguise; disruption of families and civil war; low or clownish characters; villains.

It need hardly be said that this tabulation is invaluable and that it is the starting-point of the present article. Does it, in fact, leave room for this or any further discussion of the subject? The answer, as it seems to me, is that there is room and need for examination of the situations and devices repeated in several plays, with a view to showing that in a number of typical instances the successive stages of a situation or device are developed and transformed rather than simply repeated. Rarely would a spectator who might have seen all the plays in order of their appearance be conscious of the repetition—surely the point of chief importance in the theater. Such an examination may modify to some extent the emphasis placed by the three critics cited on Shakespeare's own consciousness of what he was doing, on his lack of scruple, on his "abundant cleverness," as Neilson puts it. It seems more likely that these situations and devices merely hovered on the edge of consciousness in that teeming and burgeoning brain, coupled with an emotional impression of favorable audience response. Then when the action of some scene in a new play suggested it, the elementary form of the situation or device would be furnished with new characters and new dialogue, almost invariably improved and elaborated, sometimes changed from a comic to a tragic tone, and sometimes varied by being combined with a new theme or device. There is no evidence that the earlier text was ever consulted. The re-use is natural and instinctive, like that of the recurrent images. The 'repetitions' simply share in Shakespeare's general development as playwright and poet, and a study of them in their order highlights that development in a special and valuable way.

Let us take as a first illustration what Kreider (p. 283) calls the "enumeration and ridicule of suitors," citing *The Two Gentlemen of Verona,* 1.2.1-33, and *The Merchant of Venice,* 1.2.30-148. In *The Two Gentlemen* (1594) the review of the suitors is a very brief prologue to a longer scene in which the waiting-woman Lucetta urges on her mistress Julia a passionate letter from Proteus, for which Julia pretends to reprove her: "Now, by my modesty, a goodly broker!" It is noteworthy that in this first use of the situation it is the mistress who enumerates and the waiting-woman who mocks with pert comment; and that only three suitors are mentioned, the third being the favored lover. With its artless directness and frequent stichomythy, the episode is typical early work. "Of all the fair resort of gentlemen That every day with parle encounter me, In thy opinion which is worthiest love?" asks Julia. "Pray you repeat their names, I'll show my mind According to my shallow, simple skill," replies Lucetta. "What think'st thou of the fair Sir Eglamour?" "As of a knight well-spoken, neat and fine; But were I you he never should be mine." Lucetta gives no other but a woman's reason, and Sir Eglamour remains a shadowy figure. Again Julia asks, "What think'st thou of the rich Mercatio?" Lucetta answers, "Well of his wealth; but of himself, so so." With the next question—"What think'st thou of the gentle Proteus?"— Lucetta changes her tune, reveals that she bears a letter from Proteus to Julia, and falls into the role of go-between and favorer of the match.

It is, as indicated, a brief and elementary handling. Yet something in it—at a guess, Lucetta's mockery of Sir Eglamour and Mercatio, delivered with gusto, may have gotten laughs—implanted it in the dramatist's subconscious as something that went well with an audience. Its first flowering is the brilliant dialogue between Portia and Nerissa in *The Merchant* (1596)—also, it may be noted, in the second scene of the piece. It is too well known to require quotation here, but attention may be called to several points about the 'repetition.' For one thing, it is about four times as long as the Julia-Lucetta review, and the last-mentioned gentleman, the true love, is the seventh instead of the third in order. For another, it is now the waiting-woman who enumerates, the mistress who comments. Also, whereas Julia's "fair resort of gentlemen" is only mentioned, the wooers of Portia are an integral part of the casket plot and two more of them, in addition to Bassanio, actually appear later. But the greatest increment is the little vignettes of the suitors themselves, the variety of types, the satire on national traits, and Portia's dazzling wit playing about them. The Italian prince who can talk of nothing but his horse; the overserious County Palatine; the capering French lord ("God made him, and therefore let him pass for a man"); the insular Englishman with his array of foreign fashions; the testy Scot; the drunken German—in an age when certain conventionalized ideas about foreigners were fixed in the public mind, these thumbnail sketches must have brought down the house. Indeed they are human enough to bring it down still. Small wonder if a putative Elizabethan playgoer at *The Merchant* who had already seen *The Two Gentlemen* should feel that he was seeing a review of the suitors for the first time.

But the idea of Lucetta as a broker must have remained on the fringe of Shakespeare's consciousness and inspired one more enumeration, tabulated by Kreider under heading of "the go-between" and actually a combination of the two devices. It is in *Troilus and Cressida* (1602) and once more in the second scene of the play (192-297). This time the principals are the wanton Cressida and Pandarus, who has taken upon himself the bringing together of Cressida and Troilus. To be sure, the warriors here —except Troilus—are not suitors of Cressida; but Pandarus praises each as a man, almost as though he were a suitor, to exalt his own candidate. And the procedure is suggestive. A retreat of the Trojans has been sounded. "Shall we stand up here, and see them as they pass toward Ilium?" says Pandarus. "I'll tell you them all by their names as they pass by; but mark Troilus above the rest." Aeneas passes. "One of the flowers of Troy," cries Pandarus, "but mark Troilus, you shall see anon." Cressida, like Julia, is coy and difficult. Antenor passes, to the accompaniment of praise of him and Troilus by Pandarus, which is mocked by his niece. Hector, Paris, Helenus pass. Then comes Troilus. But while her uncle is momentarily distracted Cressida spies Troilus and asks, "What sneaking fellow comes yonder?" Pandarus embarks on a flustered paean of praise of Troilus which Cressida interrupts to plague her uncle further by seeming to disregard completely the one real suitor, whom Pandarus —and the audience—naturally takes to be the end of the procession. The forces, that is the common soldiers, pass, and "Here come more" cries Cressida. "Asses, fools, dolts! . . . porridge after meat," is the indefatigable old bawd's comment, but in the end he has to admit that Cressida is one too many for him. "You are such another." In sharpness and subtlety of characterization and in the richly ludicrous turning of the tables on Pandarus the scene is a little masterpiece of sophisticated comedy. Its complete change of character and tone as compared with the scenes from *The Two Gentlemen* and *The Merchant* illustrates the adaptability of the review to another purpose, as well as the persistence in Shakespeare's mind of a device the stage acceptability of which had already been established. It may be added that the scene employs a further ramification in that the warriors, instead of merely being enumerated like those in *The Two Gentlemen* and the first group in *The Merchant,* pass over the stage in procession, a device which recurs in *Pericles* (2.2).

Another example of vast improvement in effect, together with the combination of two devices, is the use of twins in *The Comedy of Errors* and *Twelfth Night.* Though some of the improvement must here be attributed to Shakespeare's choice of source, the choice was his and the result—our present concern—was his. It will be remembered that in adapting Plautus's *Menaechmi* as *The Comedy of Errors* (1592-3) he added the servant of Antipholus the Citizen, making him the twin of the Traveller's servant, and thereby more than doubled the possibilities of mistaken identity. The result is a play still actable and enjoyable though perhaps somewhat mechanical in its progress. Thus in 1.2 we meet Antipholus of Syracuse and Dromio of Syracuse in the mart. This Antipholus bids his Dromio bear his money to the Centaur where they are lodged while he, Antipholus, walks about the town. His Dromio departs. In the course of his walk the stranger Antipholus encounters Dromio of Ephesus, and each mistakes the other. "Where is the gold I gave in charge to thee?" asks Antipholus. "My charge was but to fetch you from the mart Home to your house . . . to dinner," is the reply. "What, wilt thou flout me thus unto my face Being forbid? There, take you that, sir knave." Antipholus beats him and Dromio takes to his heels, to report at home that his master has struck him and will not come.

In 2.2 Antipholus of Syracuse meets his own Dromio and beats *him* because he denies any previous encounter. As they walk along, Adriana and Luciana, the wife and sister-in-law of Antipholus of Ephesus, meet them and take them to be husband/brother-in-law and his servant. "I know you not," says the stranger Antipholus, and his Dromio of course denies having been sent to fetch his master. Finally Antipholus decides to go with his 'wife': "I'll say as they say and persever so And in this mist at all adventures go." Dromio is to be porter and keep the gate.

In 3.1 and 3.2 the cream of the jest is achieved when Antipholus of Ephesus finds his own door barred against him while, within, the stranger Antipholus amazes his 'sister-in-law' by proffers of love and his Dromio encounters a sluttish wench to whom the other Dromio is engaged. The Goldsmith, Angelo, delivers a chain ordered by Antipholus of Ephesus, of course to the wrong brother.

In 4.1 Antipholus of Ephesus, returning from a visit to the Courtesan, to whom he had gone when his own house was locked against him, is met by the Goldsmith with a request for payment for the chain, which had been wrongly delivered. When Antipholus declares he has not received it, the Goldsmith has him arrested. Also, having sent his own Dromio for a rope to beat his household with, Antipholus of Ephesus is met by the other Dromio with news that he has taken passage on a bark of Epidamnum, and in amazement sends him back to his wife for money to bail him out. The money being given to Dromio of Syracuse, he delivers it to his master—the wrong Antipholus—who is wandering about the town, amazed that everyone greets him, including the Courtesan. In 4.4 Dromio of Ephesus returns to his master, also in the street, bringing the rope for which he had been sent, only to be beaten for not bringing the money, which the other Dromio had received and delivered to *his* master. Adriana and Luciana then appear with Doctor Pinch, a conjurer, to deal with Antipholus of Ephesus as mad. He is in fact seized and shut up in a dark room, like Malvolio later. The stranger Antipholus and his Dromio now appear with drawn swords, and Adriana, Luciana, the Officer, and the Courtesan run away. Antipholus of Syracuse is now resolved to take ship. In 5.1 the stranger Antipholus and his Dromio are mistaken for their brothers and take refuge in a priory, pursued by Adriana and Luciana and others, who tell the Abbess that master and servant are mad; they are given sanctuary by the Abbess. Meantime Antipholus of Ephesus and his Dromio have escaped and finding Adriana with the Duke appeal to him for justice. The old father Aegeon, who is in the Duke's custody, recognizes them. The Abbess brings in the other pair and the 'recognition' scene begins. Even when all the mistaken identities have been explained, Dromio of Syracuse still mistakes Antipholus of Ephesus for his master.

After the high point in 3.1 and 3.2, when Antipholus of Ephesus finds his own house locked against him and is told that he himself is already within, the action—involving the Goldsmith, another mis-identification by Antipholus of Ephesus of the wrong Dromio and another beating, the Courtesan, Adriana, Luciana, Dr. Pinch, and the Officers—becomes a little too complicated in reading and even in performance. It imposes too much of a strain on 'the willing suspension of disbelief' and though presented by Shakespeare with unfailing zest, verges on the stale, flat, and unprofitable. Perhaps the dramatist, with his fast-growing feeling for his craft, became conscious of this danger. At any rate he hurries on to the finale—and *The Comedy of Errors* is the shortest of all the plays.

Far more delightful to an audience is the handling of twins in *Twelfth Night* (1600-1), and this improvement is achieved not only by the inclusion of other stories but chiefly by combining mistaken identity with another successful device, the girl-boy disguise, reducing the number of twins from a cumbersome four to two, and these two not identical twins but a girl and boy. This of course also reduces the number of mis-identifications to such an extent that the audience easily understands and eagerly awaits them, and it avoids the undesirable repetition of the Antipholus-Dromio and Dromio-Antipholus mistakes. Moreover the girl-boy deception and the employment of the 'boy' as love-messenger, introduced late (4.2) and somewhat conventionally worked out in *The Two Gentlemen,* are here extended through most of the play and are piquantly complicated when the loved one falls in love with the messenger. Viola as Cesario deceives the Duke from 1.4 until 5.1.215, when he first sees her and her brother together and exclaims, "One face, one voice, one habit, and two persons!" Olivia is similarly deceived from 1.5 until the recognition scene. Sebastian's brief appearances in 2.1 and 3.3 with his rescuer, the sea-captain Antonio, reveal the existence of the pseudo-identical twins to the audience who, perceiving the confusions that are to come, are held in long but pleasant suspense while being entertained by other complications. Viola's disguise as Cesario deceives Malvolio, Feste, Sir Toby, Sir Andrew, Fabian, and Maria and leads to the highly entertaining challenge and the duel between two reluctant adversaries. The mistaking of Sebastian for Cesario by the Clown, Aguecheek, and Toby similarly leads to the amusing chastisement of Aguecheek and the duel between Sebastian and Toby when a supposed coward turns out to be a fire-eater. Olivia's mistaking of Sebastian for Cesario begins in 4.1, when the countess interrupts the armed encounter of Sebastian and Toby, and is complicated only once when Cesario enters with the Duke in 5.1, by which time the recognition scene is imminent. The only other complication is Antonio's mistaking of Cesario for Sebastian in 3.4 and asking Viola for the money he had entrusted to Sebastian. Antonio's natural outburst—"O how vile an idol proves this god"—has the additional effect of convincing Toby and Aguecheek that Sebastian (actually Cesario) is a coward. The total effect of the combination of devices in *Twelfth Night* is one of clarity, of pleasurable suspense, and of economy of means as compared with the somewhat geometrical pattern of *The Comedy of Errors.*

Another example of the adaptability and improvement of a device is the episode of a father's prying into secret writings possessed by his son (Kreider, p. 262). In *The Two Gentlemen* (1.3.45-59) Proteus has received a love-letter from Julia which he is afraid to show his father lest the latter object to their love. Antonio, the father, asks "What letter are you reading there?" Proteus replies that it is "a word or two Of commendation sent from Valentine" (the friend of Proteus who has gone to take service with the Duke of Milan). Antonio is not quite satisfied: "Lend me the letter; let me see what news." Proteus embroiders on his lie: "There is no news, my lord, but that he writes How happily he lives . . . ; Wishing me with him, partner of his fortune." This sends Antonio off on another tack: "And how stand you affected to his wish?" Proteus answers dutifully: "As one relying on your lordship's will," whereupon Antonio reveals that he has resolved that Proteus shall follow in Valentine's footsteps, thereby unwittingly separating him from his Julia.

It is somewhat difficult to imagine what was especially entertaining to an audience in the brief episode of Proteus's deceiving his father about the contents of the letter, though of course the suspicious and curious parent and the smoothly-lying son are stageworthy as far as they go. Perhaps the chief attraction of the scene was the father's turning the tables on the son without knowing that he had done so. The nimble-witted Proteus sees the irony of it at once: "With the vantage of mine own excuse Hath he excepted most against my love."

At any rate Shakespeare remembered the device of father and son and in *Richard II* (1595) turns it to far more dramatic use (5.2.56-117). Aumerle, a nobleman loyal to Richard, has entered into a conspiracy to overthrow the usurper Henry Bolingbroke and restore the deposed Richard to the throne. His copy of the indenture, signed and sealed by a dozen conspirators, is concealed in his bosom, but one of the seals escapes the confining garment and dangles out where it can be seen. His father, the Duke of York, who has given his loyalty to the new king and is indeed bound over on pain of death to guarantee the loyalty of his son, perceives the telltale seal. "What seal is that that hangs without thy bosom?" he demands. Aumerle shows fear. "Yea, look'st thou pale? Let me see the writing," the testy father continues. Aumerle answers that it is nothing, but the Duke is not to be put off: "No matter then who see it: I will be satisfied; let me see the writing." Aumerle parries feebly enough: "I do beseech your grace to pardon me: It is a matter of small consequence,

Which for some reasons I would not have seen." "Which for some reasons, sir, I mean to see," the father insists. After a lame explanation has
been offered by Aumerle's irate mother and scornfully rejected by York,
the Duke plucks the document out of Aumerle's bosom, reads it, and at
once orders his horse saddled so that he may ride to the King and de-
nounce his son as a traitor.

Once again this repetition is longer than its predecessor in *The Two
Gentlemen*; it is far more spirited and contains more action. The characters are better defined, especially that of the Duchess, whose presence
adds a touch of feminine illogicality and pathos and who endears herself
to us by her spirited determination to plead with the King for her son's
life: "After, Aumerle! mount thee upon his horse; Spur post, and get
before him to the king, And beg thy pardon ere he do accuse thee. I'll
not be far behind; though I be old, I doubt not but to ride as fast as
York." This episode, with its sequel, the near-comic successful pleading
of the Duchess for Aumerle's life, lends variety and bustle to a serious
play which is somewhat wanting in action. That it transcends the brief
interchange in *The Two Gentlemen* is self-evident.

Shakespeare's third use of the suspicious father and the son who conceals a letter converts the device into preparation for a grim tragedy. It
is in *King Lear* (1605), at 1.2.27-95. The son here is a villain of Iago's
dye, the father, Gloucester, a weak and credulous old man. Moreover the
device is combined with another borrowed from Iago himself—that of
the reluctant witness whose pretence of concealment causes his evidence
to be accepted without question. It will be remembered how successfully
Iago plays this part in *Othello* (1604), at 3.3.92-277. He begins with a
seemingly casual question about Cassio's involvement in Othello's wooing of Desdemona. Told that Cassio was privy to the whole affair, Iago
says "Indeed." "Discernest thou aught in that? Is he not honest?" asks
Othello. "Honest, my lord!" is the answer, and Othello's noble simplicity
begins to take the bait: "By heaven, he echoes me As if there were some
monster in his thought Too hideous to be shown." Iago proceeds with
faint praise of Cassio: "I think Cassio's an honest man." Urged by Othello
to "speak to me as to thy thinkings," Iago virtuously replies that he is
not bound to utter his thoughts, but quickly adds, "Say they are vile and
false." He continues his tactics of innuendo and refusal until, after he
has gone, Othello is almost entirely deceived: "This honest creature
doubtless Sees and knows more, much more than he unfolds." Even then
Iago, to strengthen the impression he has made, returns to ask that
Othello think no more about what he has said and hold Desdemona free

of suspicion. By this time Othello's mind is possessed and he goes still further toward belief in his wife's falseness: "This fellow's of exceeding honesty. . . . If I do prove her haggard, Though that her jesses were my dear heartstrings I'ld whistle her off and let her down the wind To prey at fortune." Such, in outline, is the technique of the 'reluctant witness,' and it is this that Edmund employs in dealing with his father.

Edmund has forged a letter in his brother Edgar's hand, the purport of which is to invite Edmund to join him in murdering Gloucester and enjoy half his revenue forever. Gloucester comes in while Edmund has the letter in his hand. "How now! what news?" he asks. "So please your lordship, none," replies Edmund, thrusting the letter into his pocket. Gloucester's suspicions are aroused: "What paper were you reading?" "Nothing, my lord." "What needed, then, that terrible dispatch of it into your pocket? The quality of nothing has not such need to hide itself." Edmund proceeds with Iago's technique of refusal and hint, but finally turns over the letter, at the same time feebly trying to excuse it: "I hope, for my brother's justification, he wrote this but as an essay or taste of my virtue." Gloucester reads the letter, convinced of its genuineness. He does question his son a little further, how the letter came ("I found it thrown in at the casement of my closet") and whether it is in Edgar's handwriting ("It is his hand, my lord; but I hope his heart is not in the contents"). Edmund feels it safe to interpolate one out-and-out lie: "I have heard him oft maintain it to be fit, that, sons at perfect age, and fathers declining, the father should be as ward to the son, and the son manage his revenue." At this Gloucester, completely deceived, execrates Edgar: "Oh, villain, villain! His very opinion in the letter! . . . I'll apprehend him, abominable villain! Where is he?" Thereupon, Iago-like, Edmund suggests that his father suspend his indignation until further evidence can be obtained. Gloucester falls into more execration of Edgar and woeful reverie about the evils of the age. Here, then, is another father prying into a document possessed by a son, but the episode has now the atmosphere of tragedy and Edmund's technique is carried over from that of Iago in *Othello*. Again we have a repeated device transformed and combined with another.

A further example of the transformation of a device from comedy to tragedy is the situation in which an unscrupulous character borrows money from a dupe on the illusory promise of preferment with a mistress. This is handled with a light, sure touch in *Twelfth Night*, where Sir Toby Belch has Sir Andrew Aguecheek in tow. Aguecheek is of course a simpleton but he does occasionally see the truth of his position and threaten to withdraw. At 1.3.111 he says, "Faith, I'll home tomorrow, Sir

Toby: your niece will not be seen; or if she be, it's four to one she'll none of me: the count himself here hard by woos her." Sir Toby's reply has truth in it: "She'll none of the count"; it also has prevarication and implied flattery: "she'll not match above her degree, neither in estate, years, nor wit; I have heard her swear't. Tut, there's life in 't, man." Aguecheek's reply is revealing: "I'll stay a month longer. I am a fellow o' the strangest mind i' the world; I delight in masques and revels sometimes altogether." The fact of it is that, with Sir Toby for company, he is enjoying himself in Olivia's house, and while he is driven by no passion for the lady, and no real hope that she will marry him, he knows very well that life at home would seem dull, and so stays on. His second protest comes in 3.2.1-69: "No, faith, I'll not stay a jot longer." Toby and Fabian ask him his reason and it is a sound one: "Marry, I saw your niece do more favours to the count's servingman than ever she bestowed upon me." This calls for strategy on Toby's part, but he and Fabian are equal to the occasion: "She did show favour to the youth in your sight only to exasperate you, to awake your dormouse valour, to put fire in your heart and brimstone in your liver." And so they prompt him to the comic challenge and duel, and he remains with Sir Toby for all that that worthy has been dear to him "some two thousand strong, or so."

Iago's handling of Roderigo is in a different key. Roderigo is not a fool except in his hopeless passion for Desdemona. Iago is the consummate villain, adept in every art of deception including the making of acute and true observations on life when it suits his purpose. His manipulation of Roderigo begins with the first scene of the play when Roderigo suspects Iago of keeping from him the news of Desdemona's marriage to Othello: "Tush! never tell me, I take it much unkindly That thou, Iago, who hast had my purse As if the strings were thine, shouldst know of this." For the moment Iago need tell nothing but truth: "If ever I did dream of such a matter Abhor me." Roderigo is still suspicious: "Thou told'st me thou didst hold him in thy hate." "Despise me if I do not," answers Iago, and pours forth the tale of his being passed over for promotion in favor of Cassio. Roderigo is convinced and indignant, whereupon Iago slips for a moment into the part of the stoic philosopher suffering injustice (one of his most potent weapons is his superb ability as an actor), and when Roderigo says "I would not follow him then," Iago explains at some length his own duplicity: "In following him, I follow but myself. . . . I am not what I am." He takes quick advantage of his transference of Roderigo's indignation from himself to Othello: "Call up her father, Rouse him; make after him, poison his delight." This the dupe, with a little help from Iago, who keeps in the background, proceeds to do. After a dignified and gentlemanly speech of Roderigo has convinced Brabantio of his daughter's elopement and marriage, the senator calls up his retainers and, while Iago discreetly withdraws, Brabantio takes Roderigo with him in the search for Desdemona, even going to the length of saying to Roderigo, "Would you had had her!" When Brabantio's party encounters Othello's, Iago calls to Roderigo, "Come sir, I am for you," intending a harmless exchange of thrusts and so cementing their secret alliance.

After the marriage of Desdemona has been confirmed in the senate and Othello ordered to Cyprus, Roderigo and Iago have another exchange of dialogue. This time Iago is the loyal friend ("What say'st thou, noble heart?") and worldly-wise counselor when Roderigo announces that he will incontinently drown himself. "Why, thou silly gentleman! . . . Ere I would say, I would drown myself for the love of a guinea hen, I would change my humanity with a baboon." When Roderigo meekly confesses that he has not the virtue to amend his fondness, Iago launches into brilliant speeches of advice. "We have reason to cool our raging motions, our carnal stings, our unbitted lusts, whereof I take this that you call love to be a sect or scion. . . . Come, be a man. . . . I have professed me thy friend. . . . I could never better stead thee than now. Put money in thy purse." All that is needed, he implies, is a waiting game—and money. Both Desdemona and Othello are fickle. "She must change for youth." There follows the promise that Iago's wits will upset the frail vows and Roderigo shall enjoy Desdemona, coupled with more raillery at Roderigo's threat of drowning himself. "Wilt thou be fast to my hopes?" asks the wretched Roderigo, partially convinced by Iago's bewildering flood of casuistry and flattery. "Thou art sure of me: . . . I hate the Moor: . . . There are many events in the womb of time which will be delivered." Finally Roderigo, after further raillery, is completely won over and parts with the wild promise "I'll go sell all my land," leaving Iago to soliloquize, "Thus do I ever make my fool my purse."

The next step in the deception is an outright lie. In 2.1 after Othello and Desdemona have left the quay, Iago begins to move Roderigo to jealousy of Cassio. "I must tell thee this," he says to Roderigo, "Desdemona is directly in love with him" (that is, Cassio). Roderigo's common sense has reawakened: " 'Tis not possible." There follows another outpouring of cynical worldly wisdom and casuistry from Iago. Desdemona has loved the Moor with violence "but for bragging and telling her fantastical lies," and "her eye must be fed." She will turn to "some second choice," and who so likely as Cassio, "a slipper and subtle knave, a finder of occasions"? Roderigo once more reneges: "I cannot believe that in her; she's full of most blessed condition." Iago ridicules this and supports his position by interpreting Desdemona's courtesy to Cassio as lechery. Then, as later with Othello, he desists from argument and proposes a plan of action by which Roderigo and he, working together, will bring about the displanting of Cassio and for Roderigo "a shorter journey to your desires by the means I shall then have to prefer them." To this Roderigo gives a qualified assent. But after the plan has been carried out he is again in need of Iago's masterly brand of applied psychology and gets it in a brisk lecture on patience which sends him back to his lodgings. But again in 4.2 Roderigo returns to the charge that Iago is bilking him and reveals the magnitude of the fraud:"The jewels you have had from me to deliver to Desdemona would half have corrupted a votarist." This also makes it clear that Roderigo, unlike Aguecheek with Olivia, has been gulled into supposing that he is bribing Desdemona herself. Again Iago—this time by admitting the justice of the charge, then turning to flattery and adroit use of the news that a commission has come from Venice to depute Cassio in Othello's place—bewilders the wretched dupe and entraps him into the scheme to murder Cassio which leads to Roderigo's death at Iago's own hand. Taken together, the Iago-Roderigo scenes constitute a play-within-the-play, in length and in a display of villainous versatility second only to the duping of Othello himself.

To my thinking, then, the detailed comparison, in the generally accepted order of their composition, of a few examples of 'repetition' as they come to mind de-emphasizes the element of conscious repetition and highlights the enrichment of the dramatist's art as he passes from apprenticeship into maturity. Another example equally telling, if space permitted its inclusion, is the amateur theatricals in *Love's Labours Lost* and *A Midsummer Night's Dream*. To be sure, instances readily occur which seem to point in the opposite direction: Parolles in *All's Well* is a somewhat faint echo of Falstaff, and Leontes' jealousy in *The Winter's Tale* is sudden and unmotivated compared to the realism of Othello's. But perhaps these could be explained with reference to the total picture in each case; certainly the second is counterbalanced by the superb handling of the statue scene in *The Winter's Tale* as compared with the 'death' and return of Hero in *Much Ado*. On balance, and especially considering the thoroughness and excellence of recent work on Shakespeare's handling of his sources, it may be in order to suggest that yeoman service remains to be done on his borrowings from himself.

STAGE IMAGERY IN
SHAKESPEARE'S PLAYS

by Clifford Lyons

"THIS PLAY IS THE IMAGE of a murder done in Vienna"—so Hamlet tells the questioning King Claudius during the performance by the visiting players at Elsinore (3.2.248). Here "image" means the whole representation, the play itself; it includes all that the actors say and do, in dialogue, dumbshow, gesture, and action. This usage suggests that in our study of imagery it may be helpful (and sobering) to remember that the whole play is a dramatic 'image' which actors on a stage body forth, project for an audience. And it is rewarding to study the kinds of imagery which are parts of the inclusive image. We may divide dramatic imagery into two main categories, 'language' imagery and 'stage' imagery: that is (1) all that the spectators hear the actors speak, and (2) all that the spectators see on the stage, together with all that they hear other than the spoken lines—music and sound effects.

Language imagery may be considered under two heads, 'literal' imagery and 'figurative' imagery. The latter first. Figurative imagery here means the auxiliary metaphors and similes which are tied to literal statement or literal image. They are, to use the terminology of I. A. Richards, 'vehicles,' secondary images for stated 'tenors,' the primary literal (*The Philosophy of Rhetoric,* 1936, p. 96). H. W. Wells's 'minor and major term' (*Poetic Imagery,* 1924), S. L. Bethell's 'oblique and direct reference' ("The Diabolic Images in *Othello*," *Shakespeare Survey,* 5, 1952), and R. A. Foakes's 'subject and object matter' ("Suggestions for a New Approach to Shakespeare's Imagery," *ibid.*)—these various terms make the

261

same basic distinction. In Sonnet 73 Shakespeare compares "that time of life in me" (the tenor) to autumn, to twilight, and to a dying fire (vehicles). Macbeth uses the autumn metaphor: "My way of life Is fallen into the sere, the yellow leaf." But direct reference, more literal speech follows the figurative:

> And that which should accompany old age,
> As honour, love, obedience, troops of friends,
> I must not look to have; but, in their stead,
> Curses, not loud but deep, mouth-honour, breath,
> Which the poor heart would fain deny, and dare not.
>   (5.3.24-8)

Here is imagery—old age, troops of friends, repressed curses—but not the imagery of similitudes. Such a passage we may call 'literal imagery-discourse,' that is, actors' lines which are direct statements, involving both 'sensible' and non-concrete narrative realities. Such a passage is literal story-fact. One would not contend that it is less dramatically effective or less poetic than the figurative.

Terminology can create difficulties. The term 'literal' may imply factual rather than fictional, prosaic and unpicturesque, or without symbolic significance. No such implications are here intended. Literal means fictive-literal. A literal stage prop such as a crown may be worn by a monarch in the play; may be the subject of meaningful and colorful discourse; may be a symbol of kingship, of kingly care or of kingly ambition; and it may even be the tenor of a simile: "Now is this crown like a deep well" (*Richard II*, 4.1.184). One of the most intensely dramatic scenes in literature, the sleep-walking scene in *Macbeth* (5.1), is almost completely without figurative imagery. In that scene we have, almost entirely, literal imagery-discourse; and we have the visible imagery of stage, actors, and acting: the Waiting Gentlewoman and the note-taking Doctor of Physic, the sleep-walking Lady Macbeth, the simulated washing of hands and revulsion from the smell of blood, deep sighs, an allusion to a bell striking, the burning taper, appropriate costumes. Thus the whole scene, in language and stage presentation, is an image of sleepless guilt, "that within which passeth show."

The scene in *Macbeth,* except for the Doctor's concluding lines, is in prose; many other scenes and long passages, like Antony's funeral oration in *Julius Caesar,* are, as a quick examination will show, almost completely literal imagery-discourse. In other extended passages in the plays where figurative images are more frequent and prominent—even where there may be, as G. Wilson Knight contends, "solid gems of poetry which lose little by divorce from their context" (*The Wheel of Fire*, 1930, p. 98) —they are generally a small percentage of the total context. This is not to deny that they may be excellent in themselves and significantly functional. Figurative imagery is important and worthy of study for more than one valid purpose. But we may reasonably doubt whether the auxiliary similes and metaphors of a play, considered singly or cumulatively, are the soundest or the only guides to story, mood, or theme. If we collect them and heap them together by subject-matter categories, they may, thus weighted and divorced from their dominant and controlling literal contexts, tempt us to unwarranted and wayward conclusions.

It is the purpose of this essay to call attention to the literal imagery of Shakespeare's plays, primarily to the interplay of the imagery-discourse with the stage imagery, what the spectators hear the actors speak with what they see on the stage. (Here I should like to call attention to such relevant contributions as Foakes's article already cited; and to Alan S. Downer, "The Life of our Design: The Function of Imagery in the Poetic Drama," *The Hudson Review*, 1949.) For readers of the plays, this interplay involves imagined staging as a constituent part of the printed play-script. For editors, the implicit interplay requires consideration of stage-directions additional to those of 'substantive' textual sources —how many, what kinds, where placed in the text; and consideration of notes on stage implications which supplement and clarify the text (there is relatively little editorial annotation of this sort). Nothing in this paper is meant to imply that staging outweighs the importance of the word-text, the dialogue. The lines, the 'poetry,' are, of course, the primary carrier of story and theme. Yet they were written to be spoken by actors, who in part convey, clarify, emphasize, supplement, condition the meaning of the lines with appropriate speaking, gestures, actions, props, positioning and groupings, stage areas and furnishings, sound effects.

Elizabethan dramatic art is stage-conscious, audience-conscious; it does not try to conceal the actors' working space with realistic illusion, nor sharply differentiate the performance and audience by theater construction and lighting: both in dramatic technique and dialogue the plays frankly acknowledge the existence of stage and audience. Thus it is desirable and prudent that readers, editors, and commentators think in terms of stage imagery—as directors, actors, and audiences must. Not only is critical and scholarly practice thus in accord with the nature of drama; but, furthermore, there may be protection against irrelevancies and distortions which spring from thinking only in terms of the story-fact which the play represents—as if it were fiction unlimited. The circumstances and meanings of theatrical representation are an integral and defining part of the play, of the dramatic 'imitation.'

Although we may not be able to settle satisfactorily the argument between those who prefer reading a play and those who prefer seeing it performed, we can probably agree that the closet reader must in some measure supplement the lines by imagining essential 'stage-business.' For example, Falstaff's line—"This is the right fencing grace, my lord; tap for tap, and so part fair"—is pointless if we fail to reconstruct the tit-for-tat incident which precedes his line (2 Henry IV, 2.1.179-206). Falstaff tries to enter the conversation between Gower and the Lord Chief Justice, who ignores his insistent questions, on the stage doubtless keeping his back to the in-thrusting Knight. As the Chief Justice starts to leave, inviting Gower to go with him, Falstaff seizes the chance to come between them; and now keeping his back to the Chief Justice he ostentatiously and repeatedly addresses a dinner invitation to Gower, exclusively stressing his name. Then, turning impudently to the Chief Justice, he gives tap for tap with words and a fencing gesture. He has scored a palpable hit. From Theobald on (1733) there has been scattered notice of the little comic scene (see the New Variorum edition of 2 Henry IV, by Matthias A. Shaaber, 1940). J. Dover Wilson comments on it in The Fortunes of Falstaff (1944, p. 103), though in his edition (as in editions generally) there is no helpful stage-direction or note. Is clarification here less relevant than notes and directions elsewhere, some of which explain the obvious? At any rate, the theater provides clarifying stage imagery; texts or readers may not.

The stated or implied staging is sometimes readily imaged; it is therefore no less important. In the great reunion scene between Lear and Cordelia (4.7) the essential effect would be impoverished if there were no stage imagery: the music, the old Lear in a chair with fresh garments on him (his costume and quiet sleep contrasting with the distraught violence of his previous stage appearance disheveled in mind and garb); Lear pricking his finger to assure himself of reality; Cordelia kneeling for Lear's benediction and then gently restraining her father as he himself tries to kneel; Lear touching Cordelia's cheek to know if her tears are real tears; the Doctor and the loyal Kent standing by—the whole a setting for the height of it all, Cordelia's moving cry, "No cause, no cause."

Our assumptions about the Elizabethan stage and Elizabethan acting will necessarily condition our re-creation of scenes and how we take the lines. The more we can know about these matters the better; we can be thankful for the illuminating attention given to Elizabethan stage and stagecraft in our time. It may be useful, however, to make a distinction between general knowledge, interesting and desirable in itself, and a concern with what is meaningful and functional in specific scenes. Sometimes the particular 'how' of stage technique may not matter much to the story; sometimes it does. The concern here is with what is clearly functional in story or theme. Following are several illustrations of stage images which fulfill the play-script. The selection of instances is not intended to be representative in variety and range.

Beginning with Rowe in 1709, editors have added a stage-direction in 3.3 of *Othello* (there is none in Q or F) to indicate the dropping of the handkerchief when Desdemona attempts to bind Othello's forehead. Rowe has *"she drops her handkerchief"*; Capell (1768) has *"he puts the handkerchief from him and she drops it"*; and a common slight variation of this is *"he puts the handkerchief from him and it drops."* All three versions are used by recent editors. The manner of the dropping does not matter—except that it must be wholly unnoticed by either Desdemona or Othello. Indeed, it does not matter greatly if the audience fails at the moment to pay particular attention to the inadvertent loss. As soon as Desdemona and Othello leave the stage Shakespeare makes unmistakably clear what is important for the story: Emilia picks up the handkerchief where it has fallen ("I am glad I have found this napkin") and then proceeds to emphasize that it is a very special handkerchief given to Desdemona by the Moor.

There need be no quarrel with the various stage-directions as such; but there may be, justly, with the positioning of the direction in the text, where for readers, perhaps actors, it may lead to a misreading of the line "Let it alone," with consequent evocation of an erroneous stage image. Customarily the direction is inserted between lines 287 and 288:

> *Othello.* Your napkin is too little:
>   [*He puts the handkerchief from him; and it drops.*]
> Let it alone. Come, I'll go in with you.

With the direction thus interposed, the comment of the second line appears to be subsequent to the action described in the direction, and the antecedent of "it" in "Let it alone" seems to be "it," the handkerchief of the direction (in all three versions). So taken, the sentence seems to mean something like, "Let it lie there; don't pick it up"—curious indeed since later Desdemona and Othello remember nothing about its loss. That many readers do in fact so understand the line can be readily determined by a few inquiries. (Our present use of the phrase is nearer to the misreading than to Shakespeare's usage: as in "Don't touch it; let it alone.") Very few editors comment (Neilson and Kittredge have notes, though they keep the direction where it is). In "Let it alone" the antecedent of "it" is the forehead or the action of binding the head. Othello is saying, "The napkin is too little; don't bother, don't try to bind my head," and brushes it aside. It may be lost unobtrusively as they start off stage. And a direction can easily be devised and placed so as to avoid the possibility of ambiguity. The visual stage image here is an essential element in the story.

Editorial punctuation, often a semihidden form of emendation, may conceal the meaning of a passage through misapprehension of the implicit stage imagery. An example, of no great importance in itself, occurs at 5.1.26 of *Antony and Cleopatra*. After the stage-direction *"Enter Dercetas, with the sword of Antony"* (4), Dercetas reports to Caesar and his generals Antony's death and the manner of his death. Here are his concluding lines and Caesar's response:

> *Dercetas.* . . . This is his sword;
> I robb'd his wound of it; behold it stain'd
> With his most noble blood.
>   *Caesar.*   Look you sad, friends?
> The gods rebuke me, but it is tidings
> To wash the eyes of kings.
>
>   (24-8)

The punctuation as here cited, which follows Theobald (1733) and Hanmer (1744), is widely accepted by modern editors: "Look you sad, friends?" This makes good sense, alone and in context; yet we may question the correctness of the punctuation. Consider the stage picture. Dercetas is holding forth, for all to see, the sword of Antony: "behold it stain'd With his most noble blood." The attention of actors and audience is on the sword, the sign and proof of Antony's death. Caesar's words, almost in themselves a gesture, are in accord:

> Look you, sad friends;
> The gods rebuke me, but it is tydings
> To wash the eyes of kings.

And he turns aside because he cannot restrain his tears.

The line is so punctuated, with the comma after "Look you," in F3, F4, Rowe (1709), and Pope (1725). In F1 (the substantive text) the line reads: "Look you sad Friends, . . ." A somewhat parallel line occurs in this same scene (5.1.48), punctuated in the same ways: in F1, "Heare me good Friends"; and in F3-4, "Hear me, good Friends." No editor doubts that in this line "good Friends" is direct address. Moreover, "Look you" as a gesture imperative is paralleled by Mark Antony's words in *Julius Caesar* as he pulls back the bloody mantle to reveal Caesar's body, marred by traitors: "Look you here" (3.2.200).

Implied stage images may in part account for a puzzling passage in *Measure for Measure* (3.1.172-83). In the folio, the sole textual source, there are only four stage-directions: the initial *"Enter Duke, Claudio, and Provost"*; *"Enter Isabella"* (line 47); *"Exit"* (Provost, 183); and *"Exit"* (Isabella, 281). Editors have wisely recognized the desirability of additional directions to indicate other movements in this scene. After the Duke (disguised as a friar) has attempted to reconcile Claudio to certain death, Isabella enters to speak with her brother; the Provost (line 52) withdraws to conceal the Duke where he may overhear their conversation (whether on stage or off is not clear). Isabella sharply reproves her brother for pleading that she save him from death by shamefully yielding to Angelo. As she is about to leave, the Duke comes forward; she agrees to speak with him in a moment and steps aside (remaining on stage). The Duke has a few words with Claudio, whom he again advises to prepare for death. Except for the final *Exit* there are no stage-directions in the folio text of the following passage; those bracketed are representative of editorial tradition:

> Duke. . . . go to your knees and make ready.
> Claudio. Let me ask my sister pardon. I am so out of love with life that I will sue to be rid of it.
> Duke. Hold you there; farewell.   [*Exit Claudio.*]

Then we have this passage:

> Duke. . . . Provost, a word with you!
>   [*Re-enter Provost.*]
> Provost. What's your will, father?
> Duke. That now you are come, you will be gone. Leave me awhile with the maid; my mind promises with my habit no loss shall touch her by my company.
> Provost. In good time.   Exit [*Provost. Isabella comes forward*].
>   (3.1.172-83)

At first glance the Duke's words to the Provost seem rather pointless. Why should the Provost enter only to be told to leave again? And why should the Friar-Duke reassure the Provost about his staying unattended with Isabella? Is it not possible that one function of this brief dialogue may be to draw the Duke aside and leave the stage focally to Claudio and Isabella? Most editors add a direction, as here cited, to indicate that Claudio exits immediately after the Duke's "Farewell." But Claudio's "Let me ask my sister pardon" in the preceding line evokes audience anticipation which no dialogue fulfills. A brief tableau, however, can effectively cap the Isabella-Claudio prison scene. Claudio approaches Isabella and in mime asks pardon of his sister; she lovingly responds, giving her blessing to a brother penitently kneeling and now prepared for death. Such a tableau would provide good theatrical contrast with the preceding image of the kneeling Claudio begging his unbending sister to buy his life with her honor (133-52). It would also fulfill the Duke's admonition, "go to your knees and make ready." And such a tableau would be a fitting dramatic climax to that dominant movement of the play which treats of Angelo's attempt to seduce Isabella.

Here, then, is a tentative reconstruction of the action of 3.1.172-83. After the Duke's "go to your knees and make ready," Claudio joins his sister (waiting on stage to speak with the Duke); the Duke moves upstage, near a door. The tableau, downstage, requires only a few effective moments. Then the Duke calls to the Provost, who enters immediately; they converse briefly while the brother and sister take silent leave of one another. Claudio exits with the Provost—with whom (and the Duke) he had first entered, at the beginning of the scene. The Duke approaches Isabella, who stands watching her brother depart in custody of the officer, presumably to assured death. The Duke and Isabella converse—and here begin a new mood and a new movement in the play. As to the Friar-Duke's curious statement to the Provost that his mind and friar's habit promise no harm to Isabella (181-2), may it not have some point (in part humorous) because the spectators know him to be not a friar but actually the Duke, having already observed (in the case of the Duke's deputy) the danger to Isabella of private conference with a man? At any rate, the Duke-Provost passage, however slight in substance, provides helpful supporting clues to significant stage images of penitent resignation and of loving reconciliation and leave-taking.

A stage image to which only the lines point, such as the Claudio-Isabella tableau, may be as effective as words. Says the Gentleman reporting Leontes' and Camillo's response to the discovery of Perdita's identity: "There was speech in their dumbness, language in their very gesture" (*The Winter's Tale*, 5.2.14). And when Hermione is reunited with Leontes, when she steps forward to her husband, "embraces him," and "hangs about his neck," they speak no words to each other (5.3.111-12). It is almost as though Shakespeare explicitly emphasizes Hermione's silence (as he does, 113, 118) in order that he may commit this climactic moment entirely to a stage image, to a moving tableau.

In Act 5 of *1 Henry IV*—just before the battle of Shrewsbury—we have the following stage-direction and lines:

> *Enter a Messenger.*
> *Messenger.* My lord, here are letters for you.
> *Hotspur.* I cannot read them now.
> O gentlemen, the time of life is short!
> To spend that shortness basely were too long. . . .
> (5.2.79-83)

A Messenger coming on the stage with letters which Hotspur has no time to read is in itself a slight touch which adds to the scene a sense of urgency. But the incident has a more emphatic significance prepared for previously in the play by lines, stage actions, and props—the reading of letters, the delivery of letters, the sending of letters. Scene 3 of Act 2 opens with the stage-direction: *"Enter Hotspur, solus, reading a letter."* The letter brings bad news, the refusal of an unnamed lord to participate in the conspiracy, expressing doubts of its success. At 4.1.12 the stage-direction is *"Enter a Messenger with letters."* More bad news: Hotspur's father is grievous sick and has been unable to raise a force to join with Hotspur. This, Hotspur recognizes as "A perilous gash, a very limb lopp'd off." In 4.4 the Archbishop of York hands to Sir Michael a letter for delivery to the northern confederates, the Lord Marshall and Scroop. There are grave fears for the outcome at Shrewsbury: not only is Northumberland sick, but the promised forces of Glendower and Mortimer are both absent. Thus when a messenger enters with letters for Hotspur, just before the King's onset, the audience knows what the stage image means —bad news. The effect, a forecast of disaster, is preconditioned and cumulative, especially in the theater where stage imagery tellingly reinforces the spoken lines.

There is in *Antony and Cleopatra* a similar (but more significant) cumulative effect, in this instance made possible by a reiterated manner of address in words and bodily attitude. Cleopatra several times wins Antony, or tries to do so, by assuming a humble, penitent, submissive attitude, addressing him as "courteous lord," "my lord," "good my lord": when Antony, angered by her mockery, is firm for return to Rome (1.3.86); when Antony blames her for his flight from Actium (3.11.54); when Antony is enraged by her warm reception of Caesar's envoy

(3.13.109); when Antony is maddened by the yielding of her fleet to Caesar ("Why is my lord enraged against his love?"—4.12.31). Is it not reasonable to suppose that the boy-actor playing Cleopatra might in each instance accompany the words with a submissively ingratiating posture? And in these contexts, and others, do not the words "my lord" bear implications of a special personal relationship? For instance as Antony dies, Cleopatra cries out: "O, see, my women, The crown o' the earth doth melt. My lord!" (4.15.62-3). (The question mark of the folio may suggest more effectively than the usual editorial exclamation point a tone and gesture of affectionate, pleading dismay.)

When Cleopatra's fleet defects to Caesar, Antony in his fury harshly speaks of her as "a triple-turn'd whore" (4.12.13). The meaning is clear: from Pompey to Caesar, from Caesar to Antony, from Antony to Octavius Caesar. For those who see in the play, especially after Antony's death, only Cleopatra's steadfast love and fidelity, it may be difficult to admit the possibility that in 5.2.111-90 Cleopatra is represented as attempting another conquest. (We should remember her alluring submission to Caesar's envoy, arousing Enobarbus's disgust and Antony's fury; and she has just won Dolabella, who betrays to her Caesar's purposes.) In Plutarch, Cleopatra is "naked in her smock," and "marvellously disfigured," her hair plucked, her face scratched, her eye sunken with blubbering; although her comeliness is not entirely defaced she is in "an ugly and pitiful state" (Skeat, *Shakespeare's Plutarch,* 1875, p. 225). There is in Shakespeare no hint that she is without her customary charms; appropriately she is not wearing her queenly robe and crown (see 5.2.283). When Caesar enters Cleopatra kneels, all submission, rising at his bidding: "My master and my lord, I must obey" (115-16). To Cleopatra's coy confession of feminine frailties, Caesar responds with promises of leniency but with threats against her children if she oppose him or take Antony's course. He then starts to leave, but Cleopatra hastily detains him, handing him the inventory of her treasures—"Here, my good lord" (136). Seleucus spoils this act of ingratiating humility by bluntly declaring the accounting to be false. Her fury against Seleucus spent, she is again all self-excusing submission. When Caesar soothingly reassures her, Cleopatra makes her last 'play,' winningly assuming an attitude and using words significantly familiar to the audience (190): "My master— and my lord." But Caesar is not Antony. His response is brief and final. "Not so. Adieu."

The stage picture and action in the opening scene of *Antony and Cleopatra* dramatically emphasize Antony's contempt for Roman responsibilities and for Caesar. Philo's scornful words about the general's dotage, his "Look where they come" and "Behold and see," point to the entrance of the Egyptian Queen, *"with Eunuchs fanning her,"* and Antony, "The triple pillar of the world transform'd Into a strumpet's fool." The immediate effect of the stage image and Antony's excessive declarations is dramatic verification of Philo's choric introduction. The rest of the scene which Shakespeare has contrived reinforces the initial effect. It is built around the arrival of Messengers, ambassadors from Rome and Caesar, to whom Antony, wholly fettered by the charms of Cleopatra, by "the love of Love and her soft hours," refuses to listen. The effect can be especially telling if Antony scorns the Roman representatives standing on stage, mute, not permitted to speak one syllable. Antony's last words as he sweeps off stage with Cleopatra and their train are "Speak not to us" (55). Editors commonly ignore the issue posed by these words or indicate in text or note (Kittredge, Dover Wilson, Ridley) that they are addressed to the Attendant who reports (18) the arrival of Messengers from Rome. This is unlikely. The Attendant is not the bearer of news; in announcing the off-stage presence of Messengers he has already spoken his speech. Editors are quite right to substitute, in the direction at line 18, Attendant for Messenger (F). (There is in the play an exact parallel at 3.13.36-7. After the folio direction *"Enter a Servant,"* the Servant announces: "A messenger from Caesar.")

The annoyed Antony wants only the gist of the news. Cleopatra is insistent that he hear the Messengers themselves: "Nay, hear them, Antony" (perhaps with a gesture toward the door?). She seizes the occasion to taunt Antony about mandates from his wife and the scarce-bearded Caesar. Then Cleopatra speaks these lines:

> Where's Fulvia's process? Caesar's I would say? both?
> Call in the messengers. As I am Egypt's Queen,
> Thou blushest, Antony; and that blood of thine
> Is Caesar's homager: else so thy cheek pays shame
> When shrill-tongued Fulvia scolds. The messengers!
> (1.1.28-32)

Cleopatra's "Call in the messengers" is a command to the Attendant, a clear indication that the Messengers are not yet on stage. The last words, "The messengers," may be delivered in one of two ways: as a reiterated, peremptory command to the lingering Attendant; or as an acknowledgment of the entrance of the Messengers and her mocking presentation of them to the reluctant Antony. The editorial exclamation point, instead of the folio period, seems to stress the first reading to the exclusion of the second. In any case, it is clear that the Messengers here come on stage, in costume identifiable as Roman, and wait upon Antony. Not only do the lines justify the inference, but the deliberately aroused audience anticipation of their entrance and the theatrical effect of their presence in this dramatic context demand it. Antony's response to the presence of these Roman representatives, with a gesture toward them, is extravagant disdain:

> Let Rome in Tiber melt, and the wide arch
> Of the ranged empire fall.

Then, turning away from them and once again to Cleopatra, he declares: "Here is my space" (33-4). Antony and Cleopatra are centered in a stage picture which is framed by his scornful soldiers on one side and the scorned Roman envoys on the other. When Antony, interested only in further pleasures, continues to ignore the waiting Messengers—"Let's not confound the time with conference harsh"—Cleopatra (with a gesture toward them) is mockingly insistent: "Hear the ambassadors." But Antony will have "No messenger—but thine" (with gestures this is another visual antithesis). He leads his Queen out to Egyptian pastimes, dismissing the ambassadors with an abrupt "Speak not to us."

This insulting treatment of the Roman representatives gives dramatic force to Demetrius's astonished words: "Is Caesar with Antonius prized so slight?" The visual emphasis also gives special point to Caesar's reference twice later in the play to Antony's reception of his messengers: "hardly gave audience, or Vouchsafed to think he had partners" (1.4.7-8), "with taunts Did gibe my missive out of audience" (2.2.73-4). Although Antony a second time scorns an ambassador from Caesar, when he orders the whipping of Thyreus (F "Thidias," 3.13), it is in the opening scene of the play that Shakespeare, in dialogue and staging, strikingly introduces his basic theme of antithesis between Egypt and Rome.

As a concluding instance, Othello's speech at 5.2.259-82, may serve to illustrate several kinds of dramatic imagery. After recognition of his murderous error, Othello has these lines when Montano disarms him:

> I am not valiant neither,
> But every puny whipster gets my sword:
> But why should honour outlive honesty?
> Let it go all.
>
> (243-6)

Left alone on stage, he finds "in this chamber" another weapon and demands that Gratiano, who guards the door, come in; and Gratiano enters, sword in hand. Othello delivers a rather long speech of twenty-three lines, which divides into four roughly equal sections and a brief concluding lament. Flourishing his battle sword, Othello confronts Gratiano:

> Behold, I have a weapon;
> A better never did itself sustain
> Upon a soldier's thigh: I have seen the day,
> That, with this little arm and this good sword,
> I have made my way through more impediments
> Than twenty times your stop: . . .
>
> (259-64)

Then the mood changes: despairingly resigned, he lowers the sword:

> . . . but, O vain boast!
> Who can control his fate? 'tis not so now.
> Be not afraid, though you do see me weapon'd;
> Here is my journey's end, here is my butt,
> And very sea-mark of my utmost sail.
> Do you go back dismay'd? 'tis a lost fear;
> Man but a rush against Othello's breast
> And he retires. Where should Othello go?
>
> (264-71)

There is figurative imagery in the passage: Othello compares his present plight to a journey's end, to an archery target, and, elaborating the first figure, to the uttermost destination of a sea voyage. At first glance archery may seem out of place with the other two 'journey's-end' images; but it is not, for a butt is the place where an arrow-flight stops. (May not image-collecting, which leads to inferences from subject-matter categories, unduly neglect the functioning of varied subject-matter images in the same literal context?) The figurative images here are vehicles with concord of function, serving the tenor: Othello's recognition that for him this is the end. Also supplementing the literal dialogue is literal stage imagery: Othello, the great general, lowers and then lays aside or drops his sword. This self-disarming intensifies the effect of the disarming by Montano; and it is tragic verification of Othello's agonized response earlier in the play (3.3.348-57) to doubts of Desdemona's fidelity, his farewell to the "pride, pomp, and circumstance of glorious war." What only seemed true then is indeed true now: "Farewell! Othello's occupation's gone." (A moment later when Iago is brought in a prisoner, Othello, snatching up his sword, wounds him, and is again disarmed (lines 283-8). The last weapon he ever takes in hand is the dagger which ends his story.) Then remorsefully he turns to the bed where Desdemona lies:

> Now, how dost thou look now? Oh ill-starr'd wench!
> Pale as thy smock! when we shall meet at compt,
> This look of thine will hurl my soul from heaven,
> And fiends will snatch at it. Cold, cold, my girl!
> Even like thy chastity.
>
> (272-6)

There are two similes here, in this case both drawn from the literal: the first compares Desdemona's paleness to the whiteness of her garment; the other compares her bodily coldness to her virtue (he touches her hand or cheek). Her look of innocence and death moves Othello to turn away and invoke devils to bring him deserved and terrible punishment:

> Whip me, ye devils,
> From the possession of this heavenly sight!
> Blow me about in winds! roast me in sulphur!
> Wash me in steep-down gulfs of liquid fire!
>
> (277-80)

Although there are no similitudes here, some readers may think these lines more figurative than literal. They express an intense inner reality; to what extent they are taken as literal may depend upon assumed beliefs. Othello turns again to Desdemona with a despairing cry:

> O Desdemona! Desdemona! dead!
> Oh! Oh! Oh!
>
> (281-2)

In its entirety, the speech is chiefly literal imagery-discourse; the proportion of figurative imagery is reasonably typical. An actor on a stage with other actors projects the whole for an audience—by appropriate speaking of the lines, by gestures, actions, movements. In this play the actor uses a sword which serves not only the immediate story context, but which also has prepared-for, heightened significance. In all of Shakespeare's dramatic scripts, stage imagery has important implications of meaning and delight for the reader as well as for the hearer-observer-participant in the theater; for it is a functional part of that total 'image' which is the play.

ENGAGEMENT AND DETACHMENT
IN SHAKESPEARE'S PLAYS

by MAYNARD MACK

THIS ESSAY IS AN EFFORT to summarize some of the ways in which
Shakespeare makes his profit as a practicing playwright from the familiar psychological principles that I have called in my title engagement and detachment. These principles underlie to some extent our experience of any art,[1] and the drama notably; but Shakespeare's handling
of them seems to me characteristically many-sided, as he explores their
implications for the audience-play relationship, applies them to individ-
ualize and evalute his characters, incorporates them as aspects of his
style, and even, I am inclined to think, sets going at certain moments
under his surface dialogue a kind of brooding debate between them, to
which we are also meant to listen, as in a passacaglia to the figured bass.
The subject is a large one and deserves a book. All that I can hope to
do here is to touch on some of the signs of what I take to be Shakespeare's interest and sophistication in these matters.

[1] For an interesting account of engagement as the painter sees it, see Alberti's
On Painting, ed. J. R. Spencer (1956), pp. 56 ff. L. A. Heydenreich notes in his
Leonardo da Vinci (1954), 1.38, that even the table linen and cutlery in Leonardo's
Last Supper were modeled on those actually used in the refectory where the monks,
seated at their table, looked up to see the disciples seated at theirs. A related point
about Taddeo Gaddi's *Last Supper* and Girlandajo's is made in Eve Borsodi's *Mural
Painters of Tuscany* (1960), pp. 15, 131-2, and plate 13; pp. 31, 158-9, and plate 79.
I am grateful to my sister, Mrs. Andrew Bongiorno, for the above references.—Sir
Kenneth Clark in *The Nude in Art* (1956), p. 130, makes the point about Titian that
I wish to make about Shakespeare: that "he could maintain that balance between
intense participation and absolute detachment which distinguishes art from other
forms of human activity."

1.

Detachment and engagement are of course crucial in a theater audience's experience. Engaged by what is taking place before him, the spectator is in some sense rapt out of himself, snatched by the poet "To Thebes, to Athens, when he will and where"—as Pope says, translating Horace in *To Augustus* (347). As engagement increases, the spectator's passions become "raised"—I quote now from James Shirley's preface to the first folio of Beaumont and Fletcher (1647)—and "by such insinuating degrees" that he "shall not chuse but consent, and go along with them," till at last he finds himself "grown insensibly the very same person" he sees. (Shirley says "reads," but he is writing after the closing of the theaters.) If such *ekstasis* intensifies, the spectator may discover that he is advising the personages on-stage in tones audible throughout the theater, like Partridge at Garrick's *Hamlet* in *Tom Jones* (16.5). The maximum possibilities of engagement do not stop there. A radio audience in the thirties, it will be recalled, panicked when listening to an Orson Welles program dramatizing an invasion from Mars; several spectators are reported to have been carried out in a dead faint from Peter Brook's production of *Titus Andronicus* at Stratford-upon-Avon in 1955; and we are told that at the performance of Aeschylus's *Eumenides* in 458 B. C. the sight of the chorus of Furies caused several women with child to give birth right in the theater of Dionysus. The theoretical absolute of such responses is probably the case where a member of the audience leaps on-stage and wrings the villain's neck.

These are curiosities. But they remind us that the playwright's task is not simply to create illusion: he must know how to control it too. Several reasons spring to mind. Sartre urged one of them in his address before the Sorbonne in 1959, in which he said (deploring what he called a bourgeois debasement of the theater) that if drama does no more for us than encourage unmitigated identification, it becomes an exercise in narcissism—a means not to self-knowledge, but to self-indulgence.[2] This is a criticism applicable to much of Hollywood's and Broadway's annual product. Brecht makes a related but different point with his *Verfremdungseffekt*, his 'alienation' principle, which he declares a necessary counterweight to engagement.[3] When one is carried away, he points out, one is no longer reflective: we have the experience, but we miss the meaning, as Mr. Eliot would say. Therefore in any kind of drama where

---

[2] I paraphrase loosely from accounts of the address appearing in French and English newspapers of the time.

[3] *Kleines Organon für das Theater* (*Brecht Versuche*, 12, 1948), par. 40.

events not only exist as events but figure forth a meaning, as events do in poetic drama (witness Lear's storm, Hal's victory over Hotspur, Malvolio's imprisonment in darkness), an appreciable degree of detachment is imperative. Finally, for testimony of a third sort, we may turn again to Shirley's preface, which goes on to add that in the same moment you find yourself grown insensibly the person you behold, you also "stand admiring the subtle Tracks of your engagement."[4] The essential condition of dramatic experience, and in fact the Renaissance view of art generally, has rarely been better put. The work, though composed to be experienced as a Second Nature, is likewise to be experienced as art; the mirror remains a mirror, and our pleasure in the face we see in it comes as much from the fact that we know it to be a reflection as from the fact that it is a face we know.

What the modern theater seeks to recapture in the work of a few advanced dramatists, Shakespeare's theater had as free gift from its history, structure, and conventions. This is not the place to rehearse the commonplaces about the Elizabethan stage. The crux of the matter, as we all know, is that this stage and the style of drama played on it enjoyed a system of built-in balances between the forces drawing the spectator to identify with the faces in the mirror and those which reminded him that they were reflections. There was the bare stage itself, if nothing else, the open daylight, the jostling visible crowd, a style of acting that, however we may describe it on the basis of meager information, had "more of recitation" in it than ours, as Coleridge apprehended long ago[5]—not to mention two hazards that Shakespeare himself periodically deplores, the huffing actor who is only for a part to tear a cat in, whose conceit lies in his hamstring, and the timid actor, "a little o'erparted," as Costard says of Nathaniel (5.2.589), "Who with his fear is put beside his part" (Sonnet 23). All these factors must have pulled enormously in the direction of detachment. No wonder that a situation which came readily to Shakespeare's mind in his early days should be that of the audience whose detachment has got altogether out of hand: the young lords and ladies watching "The Nine Worthies" in *Love's Labours Lost*; Theseus, Hippolyta, and the lovers watching "The most lamentable comedy and most cruel death of Pyramus and Thisbe" in *A Midsummer Night's Dream*; Christopher Sly beginning to nod at *The Taming of the Shrew*.

On the other side, pulling manfully toward engagement, were the

[4] I owe this reference to my friend and colleague, Professor E. M. Waith.
[5] *Select Poetry and Prose*, ed. Stephen Potter (1933), p. 342.

"well-grac'd actor," to borrow the phrase that York applies in *Richard II* (5.2.24), a few props, some splendid costumes, and the power of a poet's imagination to involve the imaginations of others. An unequal contest, one would say—yet the imagination evidently held its own, and if we recall *A Midsummer Night's Dream* we can see that Shakespeare knew perfectly well why. *A Midsummer Night's Dream* has qualities that prompt one to regard it as a loving and perhaps even fully conscious study of what the imagination can and cannot do. In the play itself, we are allowed to contemplate its operations at their most persuasive, drawing us to accept the corporeal solidity of invisible and indeed imaginary presences like Puck, Oberon, and Titania, and to view them, at the poet's will, as vast meteorological forces, pert mischievous mannikins, and onstage actors of the normal human-family size. On the other hand, in the play-within-the-play and the preparations for it, we are shown how imagination can be trammeled by not trusting it, as the mechanicals do not trust it when they look in the almanac for moonshine and decide to use a man to present a wall. For them, as for Sir Philip Sidney and all champions of the unities of place and time, play and reality are so far from being distinguishable, the spectator's engagement is presumed to be so complete, that a moonlit night at "Ninny's Tomb" requires a moonlit night in Athens (or still another actor), place must be constrained not simply to one city but to approximately six feet on either side of a wall, and if a lion appear on-stage, he must be accompanied by a prologue to tell he is not a lion, or else stick his actor's head out of the lion's mouth to reassure the ladies. One wonders whether Bottom's play is not in part a wry retort to some of those "lisping fantasticoes" and other formalists (like Tybalt), who doubtless sometimes sat on Shakespeare's stage or near it and complained that things did not go by the book. It is quite possible that Bottom's asshead was not invented for him alone.

All of Shakespeare's plays show him keenly aware of the processes of audience engagement, and in a few instances he seems actually to make the nature of those processes part of the subject matter of his scene. At the extreme end of his career, we have, for instance, Miranda. Watching the great tempest and the "brave vessel . . . Dash'd all to pieces" before her eyes (1.2.6), she clings to the assurance, as we do too when sitting at an exciting play, that this is only the work of a great magician: "If by your art, my dearest father, you have Put the wild waters in this roar, allay them." Yet she responds to what she sees with emotions whose reality she cannot doubt: "O, I have suffer'd With those that I saw suffer!

... O, the cry did knock Against my very heart. Poor souls, they perish'd.
... O, woe the day!"

In the middle of Shakespeare's career, we have Claudius at "The Murder of Gonzago" (3.2). He too identifies, feels real emotions set astir by what he knows is only an image in a mirror; but because in his case it is his own image, he is so gripped by the thing it is and the question how it came there that he breaks the audience-play relation altogether and rushes from the room clamoring for light. Whenever the identity to which the theater engages us concurs nearly with some part of the identity we bring to it, engagement is at a peak. Probably most of us can think of plays that at some time in our lives have held for us this status of semirevelation.

Finally, toward the beginning of Shakespeare's career, we have Sly in *The Taming of the Shrew*. Even in the anonymous play *A Shrew,* but much more in Shakespeare's version, we confront in Sly's experience after being thrown out of the alehouse what appears to be an abstract and brief chronicle of how stage illusion takes effect. Sly, having fallen briefly into one of those mysterious sleeps that Shakespeare elsewhere attributes to those who are undergoing the power of a dramatist, wakes to find the identity of a rich lord thrust upon him, rejects it at first, knowing perfectly well who he is ("Christopher Sly, old Sly's son, of Burtonheath. . . . Ask Marian Hacket, the fat alewife of Wincot, if she know me not"), then is engulfed by it, accepts the dream as reality, accepts also a dressed-up players' boy to share the new reality with him as his supposed lady, and at last sits down with her beside him to watch the strolling players put on *The Taming of the Shrew*. Since Sly's newly assumed identity has no result whatever except to bring him face to face with a play, it is tempting to imagine him a witty paradigm of all of us as theatergoers, when we awake out of our ordinary reality of the alehouse, or whatever other reality ordinarily encompasses us, to the superimposed reality of the playhouse, and find that there (at any rate, so long as a comedy is playing) wishes are horses and beggars do ride. Sly, to be sure, soon disengages himself from the strollers' play and falls asleep; but in Shakespeare's version—the situation differs somewhat in *A Shrew*[6] —his engagement to his identity as a lord, though presumably broken when the play ends, stretches into infinity for anything we are ever told.

This way of considering Sly is the more tempting in that the play as a whole manipulates the theme of displaced identity in a way that can

---

[6] In *A Shrew*, Sly wakes up resolved to try out what he has gleaned of the play's purport before falling asleep, and tame his own shrew at home.

hardly be ignored. For what the Lord and his Servants do in thrusting a temporary identity on Sly is echoed in what Petruchio does for Kate at a deeper level of psychic change. His gambits in taming her are equally displacements of identity: first, in thrusting on himself the rude self-will which actually belongs to her, so that she beholds what she now is in his mirror, and he (to quote his man Peter) "kills her in her own humour" (4.1.183); and second, in thrusting on her the semblance of a modest, well-conducted young woman—

> 'Twas told me you were coy and rough and sullen,
> And now I find report a very liar,
> For thou art pleasant, gamesome, passing courteous—
>   (2.1.245)

so that she beholds in another mirror what she may become if she tries, in the manner of Hamlet's advice to his mother:

> Assume a virtue, if you have it not.
> That monster, custom, who all sense doth eat
> Of habits evil, is angel yet in this,
> That to the use of actions fair and good
> He likewise gives a frock or livery
> That aptly is put on.
>   (3.4.160)

Petruchio's stratagem is thus more than an entertaining stage device. It parodies the idolatrousness of romantic love which, as Theseus says, is always seeing Helen in a brow of Egypt; but it also reflects love's genuine creative power, which can on occasion make the loved one grow to match the dream. Lucentio, possibly because identity for him is only skin-deep, as the nature of his disguises seems to show, takes the surface for what it appears to be (like Aragon and Morocco in *The Merchant of Venice*), and though he wins the girl discovers he has not won the obedient wife he thought. In Geoffrey Bullough's words, he falls victim to "the last (and richest) 'Suppose' of all."[7]

2.

One of the most notable conventions of the Elizabethan theater for fostering a balance of engagement and detachment was that which proclaimed the stage to be the world and the world to be a stage. Shakespeare constantly alludes to this interplay of fact and dream, as the critics have pointed out. Sometimes he uses it to supply the distancing

---

[7] *Narrative and Dramatic Sources of Shakespeare* (1957), p. 68.

that enables us to enjoy an action without qualms, as when he reminds us (through Fabian) that this is only a stage play just before Malvolio's humiliation in the dark room—"If this were play'd upon a stage now, I could condemn it as an improbable fiction" (3.4.141). Or, in line with Brecht's thinking, he will use it to make us sit back and reflect on the meaning of what we see. Thus when Brutus and Cassius, their bloody hands contrasting absurdly with their cries of Peace, tell each other that as often as future ages re-enact this lofty scene, "So often shall the little knot of us be call'd The men who gave their country liberty" (3.1.117), the allusion invites us to remember what kind of liberty in fact ensued. Or, he may use it to draw attention to a manifest implausibility and so sterilize its power to annoy. Edmund's scornful comment at the approach of Edgar (whom he is about to gull with implausible success)— "and pat he comes, like the catastrophe of the old comedy: my cue is villainous melancholy" (1.2.146)—functions in this propitiatory way.

However used, the effect of the stage and world comparison is to pull us in both directions simultaneously, reminding us of the real world whose image the playhouse is, but also of the playhouse itself and the artifice we are taking part in. If the traveling players in *Hamlet* solidify the realism of the play by the lesser realism of the fictions they bring to it, they also nourish our sense of the play as an artful composition made up of receding planes where almost everybody is engaged in some sort of 'act' and seeks to be 'audience' to somebody else. Conversely, if we sit looking down with detached superiority on the lovers watching Bottom's play in *A Midsummer Night's Dream,* because they in turn look down with detached superiority on the antics of Pyramus and Thisbe without realizing that they are watching the very image of their own antics the night before, we are forced by Theseus's remark about the best in this kind being but "shadows," and the worst no worse "if imagination amend them" (5.1.214), to understand that there is another play afoot, in which we are actors as well as spectators, and embraced by a still larger irony than our own: Puck's—Shakespeare's—the Comic Spirit's—perhaps even that "high heaven's" before whom, we are told in a later comedy, we play such fantastic tricks "as makes the angels weep" (2.2.121).

Strongly supporting such verbal allusions to the metaphor of stage and world were the stratagems of the Elizabethan theater for narrowing the psychic distance between tiring-house and yard-and-galleries. On the one hand, to varying degrees, the audience could be involved in the play. If the play were written for a private occasion, this might be brought about by merging the occasion in some way with the content, as Shakespeare is generally believed to have done in *A Midsummer Night's Dream*, where the blessing of the fairies on the house of Theseus probably fell also on the house in which the play was played, and on the real bridal couple, or couples, whose nuptial, like his, had been celebrated by the play-within-the-play. Something analogous takes place in *Troilus and Cressida*, when Pandarus at the end dissolves the barriers between the onstage and the playhouse audiences; and this sort of effect could be obtained at almost any moment in a theater which took for granted the relation of personage to spectator implied in the soliloquy and the aside. Coriolanus, and the tribunes in *Julius Caesar*, vilifying the Roman mob; Henry V before Harfleur haranguing "You noblest English" (3.1.17); King Lear scourging a social system that only his offstage audience could be supposed to have experienced; Prospero reminding others than Ferdinand and Miranda that we are such stuff as dreams are made on—at every such moment, it can have required nothing more ingenious from Shakespeare than optimum use of the spatial relations of his theater to bring the audience to that alert sense of participation and revelation which Joyce calls epiphany.

And over and through all this, as we know, still floated the traditional theatrical notion of man (proud man!), on his little space of earth, working out his destiny between the painted Heavens of the canopy and the Hell opened into by the trap. A variant of this notion was already present in the architecture of the Roman theater, if we may believe Vitruvius, who saw in its circularity an emblem of cosmic harmony that included "the twelve celestial signs, which astrologists calculate for the music of the stars" (*De architectura*, 6.1). It was more deeply and centrally embedded in the mystery plays, whose subject was precisely the salvation of men, including those who came to watch and those who took part, and whose spectators, on at least one occasion (recorded in Jean Fouquet's *Martyrdom of St. Apollonia*), occupied the same scaffolds with the angels, thus dramatizing their common involvement in the unfolding story. Perhaps the efficacy of the architectural symbolism of the Elizabethan theater had weakened by Shakespeare's time; but the sense of the player as universal man, suffering and acting as epitome of the race, was evidently still strong enough to support and give special poignancy to those invocations (and sometimes, apparitions) of the extra-human audience in which his plays abound: "Angels and ministers of grace, defend us!" (1.4.39). "O heavens, If you do love old men . . ." (2.4.192). "Come to my woman's breasts And take my milk for gall, you murd'ring ministers" (1.5.49). "Behold, the heavens do ope, The gods look down, and this unnatural scene They laugh at" (5.3.183).

This was one way of bridging the gulf between tiring-house and audience: to bring the audience into the play. Another way was to bring the tiring-house and all that it represented into the play. What I refer to is the recapitulation on-stage, as part of the drama, of elements which derive from the conditions under which plays are prepared for performance. For example, the actor's impersonation of another than himself becomes, if moved into the play and supported there by make-up box and wardrobe, the disguised character. The actor's speaking as if he were unconscious of his auditors, moved into the play, becomes the overhearing episode. In the plot of *Much Ado*, Shakespeare has seven such overhearings, acted or described, and the play as a whole may be viewed as a comic study of the psychology of perception: how the eye and ear may be tricked, and how they may trick themselves.

Though any play has the option of drawing into itself these elements of the theatrical situation, it is notoriously the Elizabethans who exploit them with gusto, and Shakespeare most of all. One is struck, for instance, by how often he places among his dramatis personae an author surrogate —either a commentator like Edgar, Enobarbus, or Menenius, or a stage-manager like Oberon, Rosalind, the Friar-Duke Vincentio, Prospero, Richard III, Prince Hal, or Hamlet (to mention only a handful)—who assumes within the play the explanatory and choral functions, or else the incentive and implicating ones, which are properly the author's. In *1 Henry IV*, these onstage evocations of life behind the tiring-house facade are extended to include the casting process, when Hal objects to Falstaff's impersonation of the King; and in *Love Labours Lost,* to include an actors' quarrel, when Hector and Pompey, played by Armado and Costard, almost come to blows about Jaquenetta's pregnancy during the performance of "The Nine Worthies." In view of the probably topical nature of *Love's Labours Lost,* Shakespeare may be glancing in this latter circumstance at some particular altercation as well known to his contemporaries as the stage tussle of Cuzzoni and Faustina was to John Gay's, when he fixed it forever in the amber of *The Beggar's Opera*. And then there are all the versions of rehearsal in Shakespeare's plays. In *1 Henry IV* alone, Falstaff rehearses Hal for the next day's encounter with the King, Hal rehearses Poins for the little joke on Francis, and Bardolph and his crew have been rehearsed for their part in the great fib, even to the point of hacking their swords and slubbering their garments with nosebleed. Often the variants of the rehearsal motif are less overt. In

As You Like It, Rosalind manages to rehearse Orlando in a romantic lover's attitudes and speeches while pretending to cure him of love. Iago's manipulations of Roderigo, while not rehearsals, have something of rehearsal in them. Edmund all but rehearses Edgar in the bloody farce they are to act before Edgar flees. And Cleopatra, like any modern director, perhaps like Shakespeare with Burbage, teases, cajoles, insults, and comforts Antony, until he warms and swells and rises to the roles her mind cuts out for him. "Still he mends," she says to Charmian in his hearing at 1.3.83:

> But this is not the best. Look, prithee, Charmian,
> How this Herculean Roman doth become
> The carriage of his chafe.

There are even a few places in the plays where our attention is drawn explicitly to the most vexing problem of the Elizabethan acting company's art: how to mime reality in its grander forms without riveting attention on the inadequacy of the means. One can hardly read, for instance, the Chorus's caveat in *Henry V*—

> Where—O for pity!—we shall much disgrace
> With four or five most vile and ragged foils,
> Right ill dispos'd in brawl ridiculous,
> The name of Agincourt . . .
>
> (Chorus, Act 4)

—without thinking of Hal's reflection as he watches Falstaff gird for his part as Henry IV: "Thy state is taken for a join'd-stool, thy golden sceptre for a leaden dagger, and thy precious rich crown for a pitiful bald crown" (2.4.418). So, in an age prolific of regal and martial grandeur, it must have often seemed to other spectators than Hal.

And then came the other half of the process. After the putting-on, the taking-off; from being Henry V or Antony or Richard II to being simply Richard Burbage. In More's treatise of the Four Last Things, there is a touching passage on this subject, comparing the man of proud estate, soon to be snatched by death from all his comforts, with the actor exchanging at the play's end his lordly costume for the shabby clothes in which he came:

> If thou shouldest perceive that one were earnestly proud of the wearing of a gay golden gown, while the lorel playeth the lord in a stage play, wouldest thou not laugh at his folly, considering that thou art very sure that when the play is done he shall go walk a knave in his old coat. Now thou thinkest thyself wise enough while thou art proud in thy

player's garment, and forgettest that when the play is done, thou shalt go forth as poor as he. Nor thou rememberest that thy pageant may happen to be done as soon as his.[8]

In the world that was a theater and the theater that was a world, such sudden metamorphoses came often into Shakespeare's meditations, as we know from comments put into the mouths of Richard II, Hamlet, Prospero, and the King in *All's Well,* who comes forward in the epilogue to tell us: "The King's a Beggar now the play is done." One is driven to speculate whether we may not possibly have a relic of such another meditation in the great scene in *Lear* where the old king is moved to strip off his robe to become like naked Poor Tom:

> Thou owest the worm no silk, the beast no hide, the sheep no wool, the cat no perfume. Ha! here's three on 's are sophisticated. Thou art the thing itself. (3.4.108)

Even if these words owe nothing to the reversal of butterfly into worm— the poor bare forked animal that Shakespeare saw about him every afternoon at the Globe—they must have brought a shock of recognition to the actor who spoke them first, as they have to audiences ever since.

By bringing into the play itself the actor's as well as the audience's world, the Elizabethan theater could hold a fine poise between elements making for engagement and those making for detachment. Not simply because devices that drew the audience into the play were matched by others that insisted on the consciousness of artifice, but because devices on either side could be used so as to exert an influence in both directions. Use of disguised characters, for instance, which tends to stress dramatic artifice, made it possible for boys who were acting girls to become boys again, and so intensify realism. Soliloquy, which insists that we acknowledge the presence of an actor, has yet such psychological intimacy that it encourages maximum identification of spectator with persona, as Shakespeare's tragedies amply prove. While in the conditions we have been discussing, the ineradicable awareness of a man moving on a scaffold could be made to merge at chosen points with awareness of a larger scaffold, so that the dream one watched melted imperceptibly— for the time being—into the dream one lived.

---

[8] *English Works* (1557), fol. fg2v. More bears interesting witness to the sophistication of the Renaissance mind with respect to illusion. In his life of Richard III, he has a very fine passage on how the spectators at a stage play well know "that he that playeth the soldan is perchance a souter," i.e. a shoemaker (More is evidently thinking of a guild performance), yet if anyone should venture to address him in that identity, "one of his tormentors might hap to break his head, and worthy for marring the play" (*ibid.,* fol. elv). I have modernized More's spelling in both passages.

3.

If it should ever come to pass that an actor experienced the absolute degree of engagement to his role—say, the role of Macduff in *Macbeth*— he would presumably come back onstage at 5.1.53 with a real head on his pike, that of the actor playing the usurper. He would have become so 'lost' in his part that he failed to differentiate it from fact. This is the condition attributed to Don Quixote by Cervantes, and the condition parodied in Beaumont and Fletcher's Ralph, who is so subdued to his idea of himself as Knight of the Burning Pestle that he takes the appurtenances of a barber-surgeon to be those of a cruel destroying giant. The incident is hilarious, and the moral we are evidently to draw from it, as from *Don Quixote*, Part 1, is the usual lesson of comedy: that overengagement to any obsessive single view of oneself or the world is to be eschewed. In Theseus's words in *A Midsummer Night's Dream,* once a man gets into the grip of his imagination, "How easy is a bush suppos'd a bear" (5.1.122). Yet the problem is not so simple as Theseus thinks. Ralph's mad mistaking of the barber-surgeon's professional identity, again like Quixote's mistaking of the nature of his world, makes a point about the barber-surgeon at a deeper level of identity, as his romance-name Barbaroso seems intended to confirm. Thus through misconception and even self-deception we may stumble into truth, and find the beginnings of wisdom in an intensity of vision the world calls mad.

Some such speculations on the narrowness of the gulf that separates comic from tragic writing are in order as we turn to consider Shakespeare's manipulation of engagement and detachment as aspects of character in action. His tragic persons, on the whole—Brutus, Othello, Lear, Timon, Macbeth, Antony, Coriolanus—are exemplars of engagement. They have an heroic, single-minded commitment to some absolute in themselves or in the sum of things, or both, to which their hyperbolic speech is vehicle; and against them, characteristically, are ranged all the personalities and forces which favor a less intransigent address to life, the tempters representing orthodoxy or expediency, for whom, also, something is to be said, and who say it in a correspondingly lesser idiom, often in Shakespeare a racy understating prose.[9] Even Hamlet, the least engaged of all the Shakespearian heroes, because disengagement is in a sense his problem, is made to seem heroically engaged when placed

[9] This is a point of view developed at length in my essay "The Jacobean Shakespeare: Some observations on the construction of the Tragedies", in *Jacobean Theatre* (Strat-ford-upon-Avon Studies, 1, 1960), pp. 10-41.

against the extreme detachment of Horatio; though Hamlet's detachment is likewise placed favorably against the too easy engagement of Fortinbras and Laertes. That Hamlet does not manifest the extreme engagement of Othello and the rest, but seems to stand back, withholding something, a man of multiple not single directions, is perhaps the reason that our feelings about him (he is, I think, alone among the tragic heroes in this) contain no jot of patronage. He is never anyone's dupe; there are no springes he does not finally uncover. He is, in fact, partly an *eiron* figure, to use the terminology that Northrop Frye has lately restored to general circulation;[10] and his language shows it. The other heroes, hyperbolists, use the language of the *alazon,* the eiron's reversed image in the comic mirror; but Hamlet's speech is mixed. All but its most inflated resonances have an undertone of *eironeia,* the eiron's native tongue. For the most part, too, the other heroes support ironies that are thrust upon them; Hamlet, though sometimes thrust upon, knows how to return the thrust: he mines beneath the mines of others and hoists them with their own petard.

In Shakespearian comedy, the characters most sympathetic are those who, like Hamlet, combine both principles. But the total moral weight of comedy inclines generally toward the detached man, as that of tragedy inclines toward the man engaged. One is somewhat higher in the comic scale if one is Jaques, say—even though detachment, as his Seven-Ages speech and his role in general show, has made him a type of comic vampire feeding curiosity on the acts and feelings of those more vital than himself—than if one is simply Silvius, engrossed by a single convention. Or again, one is higher in the scale if one is Feste than if one is the Orsino or Olivia of the opening scenes of *Twelfth Night*; if one is Puck rather than Demetrius; Costard rather than Armado; Benedick rather than Claudio. But only somewhat higher. What is really high in Shakespearian comedy is to be Rosalind, who both indulges love and schools it; Biron, who can commit himself to the folly of Navarre without failing to recognize it for what it is; Duke Theseus, who is sympathetic with imagination even while skeptical about its influence; Viola, who is man enough to please Olivia, woman enough to marry Orsino; the Benedick of the end of *Much Ado,* who has learned to eat his scoffs at love and marriage with a grin. To this group belongs notably the Fool Touchstone, who can ridicule the life of nature as wittily as the life of nurture—

[10] See especially "Characterization in Shakespearean Comedy," *SQ,* 4 (1953), 271-7.

> That is another simple sin in you, . . . to offer to get your living by
> the copulation of cattle; to be bawd to a bellwether, and to betray a
> she-lamb of a twelve-month to a crooked-pated old cuckoldy ram, out
> of all reasonable match. If thou beest not damn'd for this, the devil
> himself will have no shepherds— (3.2.82)

and who, though he sees Audrey for what she is, can accept her like
a prince in a fairy tale (like Bassanio, in fact, choosing the leaden casket):

> A poor humour of mine, sir, to take that that no man else will. Rich
> beauty dwells like a miser, sir, in a poor house, as your pearl in your
> foul oyster. (5.4.61)

Touchstone is a good reminder that Shakespeare's plays exhibit foolery
of two kinds, the dry and the sly.[11] This has often been noted, and the
change from Bottom and Dogberry to Touchstone and Feste and the
Fool in *Lear* credited to the replacement of Will Kempe in Shakespeare's
company by Robert Armin. There is no reason to quarrel with this
speculation, so long as we are aware that both styles of fooling appear in
Shakespeare's plays of every date, and would almost necessarily appear
there even if Armin and Kempe had never lived, for the reason that they
represent the two bases of all humor, the intentional and unintentional.
Dogberry's humor, obviously unintentional, is dry. It arises from an
engagement to present self and present purposes so single-minded as
to inhibit freedom of intellectual and emotional maneuver, and its
badge in Shakespearian comedy is normally malapropism. This need not
be of the glaring type illustrated in Bottom's "There we may rehearse
most obscenely and courageously" (1.2.111), or Dogberry's "If I were as
tedious as a king, I could find it in my heart to bestow it all of your
worship" (3.5.23). Juliet's Nurse manifests malapropism of a subtler
kind when, in her effort to reproduce the indignation of a great lady at
sexual insult, she drops into the treacherous idiom of: "And thou must
stand by too, and suffer every knave to use me at his pleasure!" (2.4.164).
Much of the humor of Mistress Quickly comes from ringing the changes
on this style of malapropism, as she walks repeatedly into semantic traps:
"Thou or any man knows where to have me, thou knave, thou!" (3.3.147).
Still more sophisticated is the form malapropism takes in Malvolio, who
does not misuse language like Dogberry (though he does use it at least
once with unrealized equivocations—2.5.95—like Quickly and the Nurse),
but abuses it by wrenching it, in the letter laid out for him by Maria, to
mean what he wants it to mean:

---

[11] For an account of this contrast from a different point of view and using somewhat
different terms, see W. H. Auden's valuable "Notes on the Comic," in *Thought*, 27
(1952), 57-71, to which I am indebted.

"I may command where I adore." Why, she may command me: I serve her; she is my lady. Why, this is evident to any formal capacity. There is no obstruction in this. And the end, what should that alphabetical question portend? If I could make that resemble something in me! Softly, M, O, A, I. . . . This simulation is not as the former; and yet, to crush this a little, it would bow to me, for every one of these letters are in my name. (2.5.126)

The deception to which Malvolio here falls victim, by 'crushing' the simulation a little, is not far different from that which victimizes Macbeth, when he too crushes to his will the riddling speeches of the Witches; or what King Lear allows to happen when he reads duty in the flattering phrases of his elder daughters, ingratitude in the blunt speaking of Cordelia; or what takes place in Othello when his whole vocabulary begins to shift and slide, as from some hidden rock-fault, under the erosion of Iago's insinuations. Here again the attributes of the comic alazon and the tragic hero throw light on one another.

At the opposite pole from Dogberry's, stands Touchstone's humor, which is intentional and 'sly.' It therefore has for its badge the pun, which is a voluntary effect with language, as malapropism is involuntary. Instead of single-mindedness, pun presupposes multiple-mindedness; instead of preoccupation with one's present self and purposes, an alert glance before and after; and instead of loss of intellectual and emotional maneuverability, a gain, for language creatively used is freedom. Whereas the alazon shows his innate hybris by using words and the concepts they represent without regard for their properties, like a bad artist—

Dost thou not suspect my place? Dost thou not suspect my years? O that he were here to write me down an ass! But, masters, remember that I am an ass; though it be not written down, yet forget not that I am an ass. No, thou villain, thou art full of piety, as shall be prov'd upon thee by good witness. I am a wise fellow, and, which is more, a householder, and, which is more, as pretty a piece of flesh as any in Messina, and one that knows the law, go to; and a rich fellow enough, go to; and a fellow that hath had losses, and one that hath two gowns and everything handsome about him. Bring him away. O that I had been writ down an ass! (4.2.76)

—the eiron, on the other hand, honors his materials and, circling them with the golden compass of his wit, marks out a world:

Therefore, you clown, abandon—which is in the vulgar leave—the society—which in the boorish is company—of this female—which in the common is woman; which together is, abandon the society of this female; or, clown, thou perishest; or, to thy better understanding, diest; or, to wit, I kill thee, make thee away, translate thy life into death, thy liberty into bondage. I will deal in poison with thee, or in bastinado, or in steel. I will bandy with thee in faction; I will o'er-run thee with policy; I will kill thee a hundred and fifty ways: therefore tremble, and depart. (5.1.54)

The intellectual action of Shakespearian comedy may frequently be read as a continuing debate between sly and dry voices, complicated, in the so-called romantic comedies, by a third voice, that of romantic convention. The pattern appears at its simplest in *A Midsummer Night's Dream*, where the lovers speak the convention, Bottom and his companions run riot through language like those dry fools of the cinema who find themselves in a house where everything they touch comes apart in their hands, and Theseus, though no jester, shows the disengaged catholicity that belongs to 'slyness.' For these groups in *Much Ado* may be substituted Claudio and Hero, Dogberry and Verges, and those virtuosi of language, Beatrice and Benedick. *As You Like It* has Rosalind, Touchstone, and, within limits, Jaques, for its sly voices, Audrey and William for its dry ones, and for its conventionalists the hyperconventional Silvius and Phebe (who are themselves a species of dry fool), as well as the more moderate Celia and Orlando. *Twelfth Night's* dry fools are Aguecheek and Malvolio, who share common failings despite their differences in temperament and status and are both on the make; Feste, and in some respects Toby, Maria, and Fabian, are its sly fools; Orsino and Olivia are the conventionalists (but again with a list toward the 'dry').

After the 1590's, dry and sly continue to appear—almost as often in the tragedies as in the comedies—but usually occupy a lesser role. For example, the counterpoint of Autolycus and the Clowns in *The Winter's Tale,* dramatizing, one supposes, some familiar notions about the inadequacies of 'Art' (meaning among other things the life of courts) and 'Nature' (meaning among other things the life of the country) if either is taken singly, is obviously related to the themes of a play which finds its summing up and resolution in a figure—the 'statue' of Hermione—that is *both* Nature and Art; yet it is certainly not so crucial to the working out of these themes as the counterpoint of Malvolio and Feste in *Twelfth Night,* or of Bottom and Theseus in *A Midsummer Night's Dream,* or of Armado and Costard in *Love's Labours Lost.* And the same is true of those episodic antiphonies of sly and dry which echo between Hamlet and Polonius, Pompey and Escalus, Thersites and Ajax, Lavatch and Parolles, the Fool and King Lear, even the Witches and Macbeth.

Patterns in plays, like patterns of nerves in the body, reward study, since they can bring to us a clearer understanding of how the organism works. But they need to be studied *in situ* as well as in abstraction, and when one puts them back into context, one usually finds them to be more perplexed than one supposed. None of the groupings just mentioned, for example, will quite stand. Beatrice and Benedick, though they have the language skills of sly fooling, become dry fools during the arbor trick. Claudio and Pedro, who participate in the slyness of that occasion, go dry when tricked by Borachio. Dogberry and the Watch, the apparently unredeemable dry fools, manage for all their maladroitness to deviate into sense: they really have, to tell truth, "comprehended" the villains, and the villains really are "aspicious" (3.5.50) for a happy ending. Similar readjustments must be made for the other plays. Nor may we even claim, always, that the voice of the eiron strikes a more responsive note in us than the alazon with his dunderhead. Aguecheek could hardly be a 'dryer' fool, as Maria insists, yet there is so endearing an enthusiasm in his candidacy for the role (2.5.85) that the heart goes out to him, as it does yet more to Bully Bottom, whose dedication to something deeper than fool—to the sheer delight of being unself-consciously and exuberantly what one is, and of asserting what one is with aplomb and complacence right in the face of the forces that are making a fool of one—offers once again a comic version of the experience of the tragic hero.

As if to make the pattern still more complicated, Shakespeare sometimes claps both voices into one man's speech. The obvious case is Falstaff. Falstaff ought to be an alazon. He has all the classic symptoms, apart from being fussed by language, and during most of the first two acts of *1 Henry IV* he is 'engaged' with his fellow rascals in an enterprise which purposes to expose him. Poins and Hal plainly have the eiron's position at the puppet strings as they wait for Falstaff to reach the inn, and Hal etches this fact on our attention by his sly fooling at the expense of Francis. But the joke on Francis turns out to be inconclusive—in fact, falls flat and turns against its proposer; for while Francis is confused and says what Hal has predicted, his touching deference to the Prince and generosity in the matter of the pennyworth of sugar move our sympathy. *Mutatis mutandis,* the process repeats itself in the jest that follows. The trap is sprung: Falstaff utters the lies that have been predicted, but again the result is inconclusive. Our usual way of acknowledging its inconclusiveness has been to take sides in the still unsettled argument as to whether or not Falstaff suspects the trick. An alternative way of acknowledging it would be to admit that, whatever the truth about Falstaff's consciousness, this is not what the scene shows Shakespeare to be interested in. Shakespeare is interested in the dramaturgical effect of thwarted expectancy, acted out in terms of a situation that derives ultimately from behind the tiring-house facade, like those we considered earlier: the actor who will not act the role set down for him, but insists on remaking it, to the ruin of the play. All begins well enough. Falstaff enters swaggering, as a good *miles gloriosus* should, and apparently, with his bluster about cowards and his appeal for confirmation to his confederates (for he too has a play outlined in his mind, in which, though he has rehearsed his company, he is to find their performance unsatisfactory), is about to make an easy prey. But then, as those stage-managers Hal and Poins do not at first understand, the play goes wrong. They make the comments called for in the script as they understand it:

> What, fought you with them all?
>
> Pray God you have not murd'red some of them.
>
> What, four? Thou saidst but two even now.
>
> Seven? why, there were but four even now.
>
> Prithee, let him alone; we shall have more anon.
>
> So, two more already.
>
> O monstrous! eleven buckram men grown out of two! (2.4.203)

And if the alazon would only play his part, the effect on the theater audience would be a resounding discomfiture for him, like the discomfiture of Pistol or Parolles. But the part as Falstaff plays it has no such effect. On the contrary, Hal's and Poins's speeches seem prosy, lame, literalistic, like Hal's formerly with Francis; while Falstaff, with the conscious virtuosity of the great artists of mendacity ("Do so," he says at one point in his story, "for it is worth the listening to"), soars off into the world of pure comic romance so long as the lovely vision lasts— where he will be joined by Don Quixote later.

It is as though Shakespeare were dramatizing Hal's frustrated sense of what has happened to his triumph, when he makes him abruptly close his intended toying with the victim in an explosion of abuse— comic abuse, but still abuse:

> These lies are like their father that begets them; gross as a mountain, open, palpable. Why thou clay-brain'd guts, thou knotty-pated fool, thou whoreson, obscene, greasy tallow-ketch . . . . (2.4.249)

The joke has recoiled on the joker—for *of course* the lies were open, palpable: that was the cream of the jest; and to register it now so stridently, without irony, in epithets of stupidity that are never relevant to Falstaff and least of all right now, is to admit how completely he has lost the comic initiative. Nothing that happens later, not even Falstaff's shamefaced "Ah, no more of that, Hal, an thou lov'st me," can quite restore it to him either. The game is a draw, because the part that was intended for the alazon in Falstaff was played by the eiron in him; and the eiron in him goes on to take over the play *ex tempore,* makes Henry appear as outrageous an ass as Bottom, and meets the comic homiletics of the Old Order spoken by the 'King'—

> Why dost thou converse with that trunk of humours, that bolting-hutch of beastliness, that swollen parcel of dropsies, that huge bombard of sack; that stuff'd cloak-bag of guts— (2.4.495)

with a handsome appeal to charity and forbearance spoken by the champion of the New Order, the 'Prince':

> If sack and sugar be a fault, God help the wicked! If to be old and merry be a sin, then many an old host that I know is damn'd. If to be fat be to be hated, then Pharaoh's lean kine are to be lov'd. No, my good lord, banish Peto, banish Bardolph, banish Poins; but for sweet Jack Falstaff, kind Jack Falstaff, true Jack Falstaff, valiant Jack Falstaff, and therefore more valiant, being as he is old Jack Falstaff, banish not him thy Harry's company . . . . (2.4.517)

It took Shakespeare all of *2 Henry IV* to overcome the effects of this, and it is still questionable whether he succeeded.

1 Henry IV furnishes as good an illustration as can perhaps be found of the complex ways in which Shakespeare makes detachment and engagement evaluative factors in characterization throughout an entire play. In the largest design, we have the obsessively engaged Hotspur, an exceedingly refined and sympathetic redefinition of the alazon, who can trick himself just as effectively in the reading of *his* letter as Malvolio does, but more attractively. Over against him, Falstaff, whose status as *miles gloriosus* and engagement in the robbery mirror Hotspur's status as honor-seeker and engagement in the conspiracy; but whose escape from the role of others' dupe in the tavern scene, and detachment from the war—a detachment no more adequate, however, as total response than Hotspur's love of carnage—mark him as a more complicated type. Over against both of these, Hal, the inclusive man, as everyone has said, who can be detached from the Court, yet engaged to its problems when the need arises, can exhibit both detachment and engagement on the field of battle, can praise his enemy as well as conquer him. Such is apparently Shakespeare's general scheme. But the configurations of it alter repeatedly. Falstaff, as we have seen, is both alazon and eiron; Hal, an eiron in conception, sometimes plays alazon to Falstaff's eiron, not only in the tavern scene, but during the battle when it turns out that what "will sack a city" in Falstaff's pistol-case is a bottle of sack; Hotspur, bickering with Glendower, becomes momentarily eiron to Glendower's alazon; the King adds a new twist to the eiron's habitual linguistic dexterity by what amounts to a sartorial and coinage pun: he has many "counterfeit" Henries "marching in his coats"; Sir Walter Blunt, dead, gives a new dimension to engagement, like the tragic hero's ("Sir Walter Blunt. There's honour for you!"). Worcester and Vernon, deciding not to tell Hotspur of "the liberal kind offer of the king," make plain the quicksands that lie in an excess of detachment; and Falstaff, leaning over Blunt's corpse, as later taking on his back the body of Hotspur, further deepens the drama of ambiguity and pathos that the play is making with these terms by simplifying them to mean simply life versus death:

> Counterfeit? I lie. I am no counterfeit. To die is to be a counterfeit, for he is but the counterfeit of a man that has not the life of a man; but to counterfeit dying, when a man thereby liveth, is to be no counterfeit, but the true and perfect image of life indeed.

It should not be overlooked that, like the lying after the robbery, this speech is an instance of Falstaff's departing from the role assigned him. Hal utters his epitaph for a dead Falstaff, and Falstaff promptly rises to wound the dead Hotspur in the thigh. But this time the audience's sympathy stays with Hal.

4.

If I may turn for my conclusion to the optative mood, I should like to express a hope that interpretation may soon take more serious account than it recently has of Shakespeare's conventions for controlling engagement and detachment in the one area I have not mentioned here. I refer to the area of style. Shakespeare's dramatic style, as we all know, comprises a range of idioms and stage techniques whose poles are, on the one side, the decisively 'emblematic' moment, illustrated in such scenes as the garden scene in *Richard II* and in such vocabularies as the Gentleman's description of Cordelia's tears in terms of holy water and pearls from diamonds dropped; on the other side, the moment of decisively 'psychological' truth, which occurs, for instance, when Lear exclaims, confusing the two persons he has loved most, "and my poor fool is hang'd" (5.3.305), or when Othello's tortured mind turns on its tormentor with a demand that only underlines how far its corruption has gone: *"Prove my love a whore"* (3.3.359). The actual writing of any given Shakespearian play moves back and forth along the line determined by these extremes, inclining, especially in the tragedies, toward the psychological end, yet rarely touching either pole.

The emblematic style is of course an instrument of detachment. Insisting on artifice, it increases our 'distance' from the stage and makes us reflect on meaning, as Brecht desires. Conversely, the psychological style serves the ends of engagement, tends to draw us in and make us share the experiences we watch, become the person we behold. I can think of no better instance of the two styles in perfect congruence than Falstaff's speech on honor in *1 Henry IV*. It is a revealing expression of Falstaff's nature, or to put the matter the other way round as an audience must, we may read the speech straight back into the man, since there is nothing in it that the rest of the play does not confirm. At the same time, it is highly emblematic in that it accords with a scheme of definitions of honor which, lying quite outside Falstaff's individual awareness, permeates the play as a whole. Not that the styles are always in such balance as this, nor need they be. In a speech like Hamlet's "O what a rogue and peasant slave am I," we are swung sharply toward the psychological pole. The lines are *more* important for what they tell us about Hamlet's inner life since it was divulged to us last than for their relations to the play's larger pattern—though these should not be missed. On the other hand, with Hamlet's most famous speech, "To be or not to be," we are drawn back toward the emblematic pole. This speech too is profoundly expressive of Hamlet's inner life, but if we begin to read back from it as though it were exclusively a record of that life, we find ourselves entangled in such a pointless question as when Hamlet experienced "the law's delay" or "the spurns That patient merit of the unworthy takes," and so on. Clearly Shakespeare judged it more important at this juncture to expand our sense of Hamlet to that of universal figure, making us hear in his words the still sad music of humanity in all times and places, than to focus narrowly on the experience of young Hamlet the Dane.

These distinctions are obvious, embarrassingly hackneyed. Yet we seem unready to draw the necessary conclusion. By mistaking the emblematic mode for the psychological, scholars and critics of surprising repute have during the last four decades set out to prove Hamlet either a villain or a dramatized version of the death-wish, Othello a miserable egomaniac who spends his last moments cheering himself up, Edgar and Cordelia a couple of nauseous prigs, and Prospero an irascible old tyrant, with—so it is asserted in some quarters—an unnatural interest in his daughter's chastity.

No one will deny that there are episodes and situations in Shakespeare where determination of the dominant mode has to be extraordinarily nice. Just how far, for instance, shall we read Hamlet's obscenities back into his character? Or how far regard them as expressions of a pervasive theme, of which he is one mouthpiece? Is Cordelia, at the opening of *Lear,* to be judged stubborn, even a trifle self-righteous, a true chip off the old block? Or is she already an emblematic figure of Patience under affliction and of Charity which "suffereth long and is kind"?

These are tricky questions, which will never be easy to resolve. But certainly our best chance of meeting them with the right weapons is to keep resolutely in view that whole arsenal of artifices and devices, so congenial to the Elizabethan stage, whose relation to detachment and engagement is that of turbine to the lamp by which we read.

FRANCIS BACON ON THE DRAMA

by PAUL H. KOCHER

LEAVING ASIDE the chimeras of the Shakespeare-Bacon controversy, the present essay confines itself to humbler and more accessible questions. What sorts of dramatic or semidramatic 'devices' is Bacon himself known to have written? What were his opinions about the theater, courtly or professional? And how do these opinions fit into the remainder of his philosophy? Perhaps the best method of approach will be to analyze the nature of the 'devices' themselves; then, to consider Bacon's direct references to the theater in his other works; next, to connect these with his general theory of poetry; and, finally, to show how this theory of poetry in turn relates to his view of the right functioning of the Imagination not only in poetry but also in natural science, religion, ethics, and rhetoric. Such a treatment should give us a summary idea both of what Bacon thought about the stage and why he thought it. Considerations of space, unhappily, forbid extended discussion, but the relevant kinds of evidence will be indicated in each case.

Following James Spedding, Bacon's great editor, we may accept Bacon's authorship of parts of three semidramatic 'devices.'[1] In 1592 he wrote, on behalf of Essex for presentation before Queen Elizabeth, a speech "In Praise of Knowledge" and another "In Praise of the Queen." Then, in early 1595, as one feature of the Christmas festivities at Gray's Inn, he contributed to *Gesta Grayorum* speeches by six counselors on the true aims and ends of a political state. And later in the same year, again for Essex at Court, he penned a debate between four speakers on the topic

---

[1] The G. Spedding, R. Ellis, and D. Heath edition of Bacon's *Works*, 7 vols., and *Letters and Life*, 7 vols. (from 1857), is here cited as a continuous single set of 14 vols., referred to as *Works*. Bacon's three protodramatic devices are at 8.123, 332, and 375 ff.

of self-love as opposed to love of the Queen. Definitions of drama may vary, but at least it is clear that these three 'devices,' entertainments, protodramas, or whatever they may be called, make little or no attempt at characterization or plot.

The two speeches of 1592, for example, are not attributed to any particular speakers and are not set in any atmosphere of a conflict of issues. They are merely orations flattering the Queen and setting forth, in the manner of exposition, many of Bacon's most cherished ideas on the reform of the natural sciences. The speeches in *Gesta Grayorum* move only slightly further towards plot. This work presents a mock meeting of a Privy Council in which six counselors sit at a table on a dais before a Prince's throne. He asks their advice regarding "the scope and end" to which he should direct his government (*Works*, 8.332). Each counselor then speaks in turn, the first advising the Exercise of War, the second the Study of Philosophy, the third Fame by Buildings and Foundations, the fourth Absoluteness of State and Treasure (including defense of the royal prerogative against popular liberties), the fifth Virtuous Government, and the sixth Pastimes and Sports. In the end the Prince, by way of graceful transition to a continuation of the evening's festivities, accepts the suggestion of the sixth counselor, without however commenting in any way on the speeches of the preceding five. No real issue has been set up, since the speeches do not necessarily contradict one another, and no real decision has been made. Indeed it is evident that Bacon has merely been seizing the opportunity to promote some of his favorite programs, for the oration of the second counselor, on Philosophy, is obviously a preliminary sketch of the ideas later to be advocated in *The New Atlantis,* while the oration on Virtuous Government embodies Bacon's constant propaganda for law reform. In short, there is no effort to characterize any of the counselors as a distinctive person; each is only Bacon delivering an oration on a set theme. We are not here in a situation even like that in *Gorboduc,* where the arguments are sharply opposed, the issues are moral and political, and the outcome is tragic. Rather we are met with a series of orations loosely organized around a central theme and designed as vehicles for the exposition of ideas. The dramatic or even fictional element is at a minimum.

The same observation is roughly true of the November 1595 device presented at Court, though its plot element is stronger (8.375). Here three emissaries come from Philautia (Self-love) to persuade Erophilus (Essex) to love himself and to follow his own interests instead of the Queen's. These emissaries are "an Heremite or Philosopher, representing Contemplation; the second like a Captain, representing Fame; and the third like a Counsellor of Estate, representing Experience" (8.377-83). Each gives a persuasive speech but is answered conclusively by Erophilus's Squire, who argues instead for love of the Queen. Bacon makes it plain that the three emissaries are morally and politically wrong and that their speeches represent an evil temptation. The theme is therefore somewhat like that of a morality play. But the great want, from this point of view, is that Erophilus himself, who should be the central personage, never appears or speaks a word, or wavers between right and wrong like Everyman or Mankind. This lack of a focal character in whom to centralize the conflict leaves the device, again, merely a series of loosely connected speeches on preordained topics, designed primarily for the presentation of ideas. Nor are the three emissaries and the Squire individualized as persons. Each still represents only a Baconian point of view, and the total effect is still only that of rival lawyers arguing a case.

One may speculate about the reasons for Bacon's failure or refusal to give more plot and characterization to these three devices. He cannot have lacked opportunity to see plays in the public or private theaters, or at Court, or at the inns of court or universities. Indeed, only six days before the presentation in 1594 of *Gesta Grayorum* at Gray's Inn, where Bacon was in residence, Shakespeare's *Comedy of Errors* had also been staged there, a play which is nothing if not plot. Nor is it likely that Bacon can have lacked ability to invent a plot on some kind of pedestrian level, if he had wished. The more probable explanation is that he did not so wish. It seems altogether likely that he preferred to maintain what he regarded as the more dignified and aristocratic manner of undiluted oration and statecraft and, as we shall see, to omit the element of fiction from his writing as tending to distort and falsify his ideas. The ideas were important to him, not the drama. At any rate, after the 1590's he wrote nothing more that can be remotely connected with the stage. In 1613 he financed two masques at Court, one for the Princess Elizabeth and one for Robert Carr, Viscount Rochester, but he had no hand in composing either (11.343, 393). And when, in 1625, he wrote Essay 37, "Of Masques and Triumphs," his opening sentences were: "These things are but toys to come amongst such serious observations. But yet, since princes will have such things, it is better they should be graced with elegancy than daubed with cost" (6.467). That he knew a good deal concerning the court masque is shown by his detailed recommendations about both dancing and acting to song, scene-changes, costumes, antimasques, and the like. But although he could and did write about such courtly trifles, he never elected to write an essay about tragedies or comedies or histories, the more popular and profound theatrical fare of his day.

Of course Bacon was not unaware of the existence of such things. A reader who perseveres in reading through the full fourteen volumes of his writings in the standard Spedding and Ellis edition will discover some direct references to drama. But such a reader will also discover, I am sure, that such references are scanty (perhaps about three or four per volume), that they are usually incidental and unimportant, that they are so general in character as not to mention any specific plays, playwrights, or theaters, and that they tend to be in tone either indifferent or unfavorable. A few examples must suffice. In the *De augmentis scientiarum* Bacon compared the machinations of rival political factions to "stage plots and a number of like fables" (5.43), and similarly in his *History of Henry VII* he likened to "stage-plays" the impersonations of Lambert Simnel and Perkin Warbeck as heirs to the throne (6.45, 46, 59, 132, 191). Essay 18, "Of Travel," enumerates for young Englishmen traveling abroad some twenty sights worth visiting in each country. Far down on the list (number nineteen, to be exact) are "comedies, such whereunto the better sort of persons do resort" (6.417). We notice the qualifying clause. Elsewhere in the *De augmentis* Bacon put his stage-reference in a parenthesis. The Cyrenaics and Epicureans, he says, placed felicity in pleasure "and made virtue (as is used in some comedies, wherein the mistress and the maid change habits) to be but a servant, without which pleasure cannot be properly served and attended" (5.8). At least twice, in Essay 10, "Of Love," and in the *De augmentis,* Bacon remarks that "the stage is more beholding to Love, than the life of man. For as to the stage, love is ever matter of comedies, and now and then of tragedies; but in life it doth much mischief" (6.397, 4.487). In other words, the theater is scarcely true to life. He complains that the Martin Marprelate debate is being "handled in the style of the stage," like a comedy or satire (*Of the Controversies of the Church,* 8.76). His single specific reference to a contemporary play, so far as I am aware, occurs in his *Charge Against Oliver St. John* (1615), St. John having been a trouble-maker for King James: "And for your comparison with Richard II I see you follow the example of them that brought him upon the stage and into print in Queen Elizabeth's time. . . . And this I would wish both you and all to take heed of, how you speak seditious matter in parables, or by tropes or examples" (12.145). The political notoriety of Shakespeare's play had evidently not escaped Bacon, who was interested in such matters. And in another legal case, the *Charge Against the Countess of Somerset* (1616), Bacon indulged in a complicated metaphor describing that lady's plots as being hatched in a vault beneath the stage on which they were finally enacted, at first concealed by the curtain of God's Providence (12.299)—all of which displays some knowledge on his part of the physical structure of the contemporary stage, presumably that to be found in the regular theaters.

References like this scattered thinly through a vast body of writing over the period of a lifetime inevitably leave an impression of Bacon's superficial acquaintance with, and virtual indifference to, the noncourtly drama of his day, rather than one of real familiarity or enthusiasm. This impression is verified by the brevity and condescension with which he treats dramatic art (he calls it Representative Poetry) in that section of *The Advancement of Learning* and its later expanded Latin translation, *De augmentis scientiarum,* in which he deals with Poetry, a section itself quite brief and ambiguous in evaluation. The earlier work merely says of the drama, in one sentence, that it "is a visible history, and is an image of actions as if they were present. . ." (3.344; cf. 4.314-35, especially 316). At the end of the section on Poetry, Bacon warns that "it is not good to stay too long in the theater" and hastens on to philosophy, "the judicial or palace of the mind, which we are to approach and view with more reverence and attention" (3.346, 4.335). When he came to enlarge and translate this section on Poetry into Latin in the *De augmentis,* seventeen years later, Bacon retained this ending. He even made the transition to the ensuing section on Philosophy by adding a caveat against the dreamlike, impractical quality of all poetry, including the dramatic, and contrasting it with the value of history and philosophy:

> All History, excellent King, walks upon the earth, and performs the office rather of a guide than of a light; whereas Poesy is as a dream of learning; a thing sweet and varied, and that would be thought to have in it something divine; a character which dreams likewise affect. But now it is time for me to awake, and rising above the earth, to wing my way through the clear air of Philosophy and the Sciences. (4.336)

Bacon also felt the need, in the Latin translation of the main section on Poetry, to say something more than one sentence about the drama. He therefore amplified his comments into a brief paragraph of some six sentences, still saying considerably less therein than about the other two kinds of poetry, the narrative and the parabolical. The drama, he now declares, "would be of excellent use if well directed. For the stage is capable of no small influence both of discipline and of corruption. Now in corruptions of this kind we have enough; but the discipline has in our times been plainly neglected" (4.316). Modern states esteem the drama only a toy; but the ancients used it as a means of moral education. A few remarks upon the power of the stage to move men's minds for good or evil, especially in crowds, conclude the paragraph.

From this discussion it seems clear that Bacon was interested in plays primarily as a means towards good ethics and politics, and that he was dissatisfied with the modern drama on this score. This is typical enough Renaissance criticism, though rather on the Puritanical side. But the paragraph is almost more notable for what it omits than for what it includes. Missing are the usual Renaissance debates about the nature of imitation, the unities, decorum, mixture of tragedy with comedy, and so forth, fundamental in Aristotle, Horace, Scaliger, Castelvetro, and the rest.[2] Missing also are allusions to any particular dramas or dramatists, ancient or modern, such as one finds in Gosson or Sidney. Bacon, in short, is not writing a *Poetics* or engaging in current controversies about the stage, but is restricting himself rather sharply to classification and incidental evaluation.

Why? Because, I would suggest, Bacon was not genuinely interested in poetry (including drama) as poetry, but rather in its relations with the absorbing topics of natural science, politics, history, religion, rhetoric, and right conduct. That is, he wanted to show how poetry might help or harm or contrast with these (to him and to most of his contemporaries) more important fields of human thought and behavior. As we shall see, philosophically this problem reduced itself to the problem of the proper relationship between Imagination, the source of poetry, and Reason, Will, and the Passions, which were primarily responsible for those other fields. For the moment, however, let us take a closer look at the remaining portions of Bacon's overt discussion of Poetry in *The Advancement* and the *De augmentis*.

In comparing poetry with history, under the heading of narrative poetry, Bacon is most struck by the fictional, picture-building capacity of poetry to create human beings and human worlds more pleasing than those which actually exist. It can "feign acts more heroical," provide new varieties of events, make virtue conquer vice as it often fails to do

---

[2] See J. E. Spingarn, *A History of Literary Criticism in the Renaissance* (1908), *passim,* and J. W. H. Atkins, *English Literary Criticism: The Renaissance* (1951), especially those parts dealing with Bacon, pp. 264-72. Looking for the possible sources of Bacon's literary views (a thankless and rather useless task) is no part of the function of this essay. I might suggest, however, that Bacon seems to owe little to Aristotle, Sidney, or the Italian Renaissance critics, somewhat more to Plato, but most of all to his own political and scientific orientation.

in real life, and in general feed man's soul with satisfactions not common on earth (3.343-4, 4.315-16). But is this necessarily a good thing? At this particular point in both *The Advancement* and the *De augmentis*, Bacon seems definitely to say that it is. Man's soul is capable of these grander, clearer visions which cannot be realized in his daily life. A divine longing is in question, and the art of poetry which ministers to it therefore "may be fairly thought to partake somewhat of a divine nature." Yet we should be cautious in taking this as Bacon's final, unequivocal estimate. As noted above, only a few pages after thus glorifying poetry, Bacon, at the start of the section on philosophy, speaks unflatteringly of "staying too long in the theater," praises history as mankind's guide upon the earth, describes poetry as a dream "that would be thought to have in it something divine," and concludes that it is time for him to wake up and discuss philosophy. Further on in the *De augmentis* he argues that a study of men's different dispositions is a necessary foundation for a sound system of ethics. And where shall we find the materials for such a study? Here history is superior to poetry because of the exaggerations practiced by the latter: ". . . among the poets (heroic, satiric, tragic, comic) are everywhere interspersed representations of characters, though generally exaggerated and surpassing truth. . . . But far the best provision and material for the treatise is to be gained from the wiser sort of historians. . ." (5.21).[3] In the *History of Henry VII*, history is praised as most useful for man's life and "nearest allied unto action," whereas those who study poetry "as they attain to great variety, so withal they become conceited" (6.18). Here "conceited" seems to mean 'too imaginative.'

Some clearing up of these apparent confusions is supplied by a fundamental distinction which Bacon draws in *A Description of the Intellectual Globe,* a distinction between knowledge and play. History affords the primary material of knowledge. With this material

> the human mind perpetually exercises itself, and sometimes sports. For as all knowledge is the exercise and work of the mind, so poesy may be regarded as its sport. In philosophy the mind is bound to things; in poesy it is released from that bond, and wanders forth, and feigns what it pleases. (5.503) [4]

[3] Compare Bacon's statement in the *De augmentis* (4.310), that "it not a little embases the authority of a history to intermingle matters of lighter moment, such as triumphs, ceremonies, spectacles, and the like, with matters of state."
[4] This view of poetry as a mere relaxation or sport of the imagination is present also in Bacon's discussion of the functions of this faculty, in which he states that although imagination may be an aid to reason it cannot originate any useful sciences of its own: ". . . I find not any science that doth properly or fitly pertain to the Imagination. . . . For as for Poesy, it is rather a pleasure or play of imagination, than a work or duty thereof" (*The Advancement*, 3.382).

This may sound like a neutral enough distinction, leaving to history and philosophy the sphere of reality and to poetry the sphere of play. But considering Bacon's own serious and hard-working character and the intensity of his desire to promote philosophic truth, it is already weighted against poetry (including drama), an activity which escapes into feigned worlds of its own.

Moreover—and this was the crucial point in Bacon's thinking—the private and public fantasies associated with poetical imagination were perpetually bursting through their appointed bounds of fiction and invading and corrupting the search for knowledge of the real world. Under this aspect they were Idols, the Idols of the Theater being prominent among them. No reader of Bacon needs to be told how often he inveighed against the Idols of the Theater and how fatal he considered them to the formation of a true natural science. They had turned the past history of the philosophy of science into one long procession of false systems bearing little or no relation to reality. So he wrote in the *Novum organum*, typically: ". . . in my judgment all the received systems are but so many stage-plays, representing worlds of their own creation after an unreal and scenic fashion. . . . many more plays of the same kind may yet be composed and in like artificial manner set forth." This comparison of all other philosophies to mere theatrical designs occurs over and over in Bacon's writings and bears eloquent witness to his belief in the dangers of the theatrical imagination to the search for truth (Aphorism 44, *Works*, 4.55; see also Aphorisms 45-65).[5]

Furthermore, the theatrical imagination was not only deceptive but also proud and irreligious when operating illegitimately in the sphere of natural science. To yield to the temptation to create a universe of science for ourselves like the argument of a play, Bacon wrote passionately in *A Natural and Experimental History*, is to fall again like Adam, who tried to rival God. For in this

---

[5] Further citations of this ubiquitous Baconian outlook seem unnecessary. Wherever Bacon condemns an ancient, medieval, or modern philosophical system he is starting from this premise. Such, for example, is his condemnation of the schoolmen (in Book 1 of *The Advancement*, 3.285), who, "knowing little history, either of nature or time; did out of no great quantity of matter, and infinite agitation of wit, spin out unto us those laborious webs of learning which are extant in their books." The spider image and the theater image here coincide. Such also is his censure of Pythagoras in Century 10 of *Sylva sylvarum* (2.640): "The philosophy of Pythagoras (which was full of superstition) did first plant a monstrous imagination; which afterwards was, by the school of Plato and others, watered and nourished. It was that the world was one entire living creature. . . ." Pertinent here also is Bacon's overall disrespect for Alchemy, Natural Magic, and Astrology, those sciences which "have had better intelligence and confederacy with the imagination of man than with his reason . . ." (3.289 ff.).

. . . we copy the sin of our first parents while we suffer for it. They wished to be like God, but their posterity wish to be even greater. For we create worlds, we direct and domineer over nature, we will have it that all things are as in our folly we think they should be, not as seems fittest in the Divine wisdom, or as they are found to be in fact. . . . Wherefore our dominion over creatures is a second time forfeited, not undeservedly. (5.132) [6]

In narrative and dramatic poetry, clearly ticketed and labeled as such, therefore, it may be divine to build new worlds of fiction to satisfy our longings for better things; but it is pride and insolence, anything but divine, to foist such creations of our own upon the actual world with which God has surrounded us. Indeed an early passage on Hope in the *Meditationes sacrae* (1597) condemns man's world-building propensities under any circumstances:

> Moreover the mind suffers in dignity, when we endure evil only by self-deception and looking another way, and not by fortitude and judgment. . . . Therefore all hope is to be employed upon the life to come in heaven: but here on earth, by how much purer is the sense of things present, without infection or tincture of imagination, by so much wiser and better is the soul. (7.248)

Such an outlook would not favor the comforting self-deceptions of stage-plays described in *The Advancement* and the *De augmentis*. Perhaps Bacon outgrew this earlier attitude. Or perhaps, rather, he continued to waver between earth and Heaven, as did many Christians of his time, reflecting his waverings in successive evaluations of the creative imagination. But the main drive of Bacon's life was always towards the search for truth in natural science, philosophy, and law.

From this point of view it is understandable why Bacon's estimate of the imagination, with its outgrowths in narrative poetry and the stage, remained always grudging, suspicious, and condescending. For him, imagination played no really constructive role in scientific method. Its dangers were spread upon the pages of history. The only remedy was to root out its fantasies, adopt a rigorously inductive approach, and restrict imagination as a servant of reason in science. The function of imagination must be merely to collect, organize, and report sense impressions accurately to reason, its master. Imagination must remain a conduit and receptacle rather than an independent fabricator.

To follow the complicated involutions of Bacon's theory of imagina-

---

[6] See also Raleigh's Preface to *Sylva sylvarum* (2.337): "I will conclude with an usual speech of his lordship's; That this work of his Natural History is the world as God made it, and not as men have made it; for that it hath nothing of imagination."

tion in other areas of human thought and interest is of no direct concern in the present essay.[7] We may summarize by saying, however, that he always tries to keep it a useful and obedient servant instead of a self-legislating equal or master. His favorite type of poetry is the parabolical, in which reason feeds ideas to the imagination and the latter clothes them in images and tropes for the better understanding of the vulgar. Bacon wrote a whole treatise, *Of the Wisdom of the Ancients,* to exemplify this concept in its application to physical science. Similarly in religion, reason and divine inspiration often use imagination as a help in clarifying difficult ideas to the apprehension of the people, whereas if imagination tries to work independently it merely produces harmful superstitions.[8] Again, in rhetoric imagination should be a useful ally of reason, enlisting the emotions of the auditors in favor of the true and the good (see *Works,* 4.455). Allowed to run wild, imagination would delude these emotions, enslaving and inundating the sovereign reason. Its function in ethics is essentially the same. And while on this topic we may note in passing that what Bacon says in *The Advancement* and the *De augmentis* about the power (much abused in the plays of his day) to induce virtue verges on the perfunctory. Other passages in these works as well as in the *Novum organum* strongly suggest that Bacon himself believed contemporary conventional moral standards were in need of overhauling and redefinition. He had schemes for collecting data about human nature which would show what men really were, not what they thought they were—schemes which would therefore provide a basis for revising the rules as to what men could expect themselves to become.[9] All this would have little to do with fanciful dreams of ideal worlds for ideal men, expressed in narrative poetry or drama.

There was a poet somewhere in Francis Bacon. His own tremendous

---

[7] The task has been undertaken, with divergent results, by Murray W. Bundy, "Bacon's True Opinion of Poetry," *SP,* 27 (1930), 244-64, and by John L. Harrison, "Bacon's View of Rhetoric, Poetry, and the Imagination," *HLQ,* 20 (1957), 107-25.

[8] For Bacon's ideas on the proper role of poetry in religion see the key sections on poetry in *The Advancement* (3.344) and the *De augmentis* (4.316-17), as well as his main section on the function of the imagination (3.382). His fear of imagination as a source of superstition in religion may be seen in Essay 17, "Of Superstition" (6.415), and more especially in Book 1, Aphorism 65, of the *Novum organum* (4.65), decrying modern attempts to found philosophy on Scripture by "tumid and half poetical" uses of imagination from which "there arises not only a fantastic philosophy but also an heretical religion." Bacon's whole effort to keep science and religion apart results from his dread of the interweaving operations of imagination between the two fields.

[9] A large subject, but see for suggestions *The Advancement* (3.434, 453, 456), and the statement in the *Novum organum,* Book 1, Aphorism 127 (4.112), that ethics should be made the subject of inductive investigation. I doubt that Bacon had clarified all his ideas on this difficult problem.

visions for the betterment of science and law show plainly that imagination, in a more Coleridgean sense, was one of his strongest qualities. And the sheer magnificence of his style looks in the same direction. But we are not now discussing that question. Caught in a philosophy which regarded literature as inferior since it was fiction, rather than fact, and himself dedicated with all his energies to a lifelong search for fact, Bacon relegated narrative and dramatic art to a category of play, which was insulting enough. But there, at least, such art could disport itself harmlessly. If it trespassed outside the bounds of that category it became potentially one of the acutest of perils and might be tolerated, watchfully, only if it kept on its good behavior as a servant of thought and action. The world was objectively real; poetry dealt with the unreal. There can be no doubt where Bacon's conscious, continuous allegiance lay. There might be moments when he grew weary of the world and lamented, in the words of the Psalm, that he was but a pilgrim here. At such moments the unreal worlds of the theater might seem to him closer to man's true goal in Heaven.[10] But the moods passed, and Bacon resumed with characteristic determination his campaign for a better place for himself and for deluded humanity in the here and now. This, I suggest, explains such minor waverings as may appear in his estimate of literature (including drama) and, above all, the dominant condescension, bordering on suspicion and contempt, with which he treated it in most of his work.

[10] Those who are interested in psychological associations (as I am) will note that in his moods of world-denial and depression Bacon frequently chose an image from the theater, describing himself on one occasion as "knowing myself by inward calling to be fitter to hold a book than to play a part." See his Letter to Sir Thomas Bodley (1605), in *Works* (10.253), and my article, "Francis Bacon and His Father," *HLQ,* 21 (1958), 133-58.

THE REVENGER'S TRAGEDY
AND THE VIRTUE OF ANONYMITY

by ALLARDYCE NICOLL

1.

EXACTLY FIFTY YEARS AGO, in 1911, E. H. C. Oliphant declared that in his opinion *The Revenger's Tragedy* was "the greatest work of its period of that prolific writer ANON," and that "the establishment of the identity of the author" should be regarded "as one of the chief problems to be tackled by students of the Elizabethan drama" ("Problems of Authorship in Elizabethan Dramatic Literature," *MP*, 8, 1910-11). With this pronouncement and with his subsequent ably-argued attempt to assign the play to Middleton ("The Authorship of *The Revenger's Tragedy*," *SP*, 12, 1926), he set in motion something which—erratically and with many spurts and flurries—has been lumbering on ever since.

The primal impetus reached a temporary peak during the years 1930-31 in a debate between the proponents of Middleton and Tourneur within the pages of *The Times Literary Supplement*, but even at that time strength was being gathered for a further advance, inspired by the wish to apply to the problem other considerations than the 'parallel-passage' technique which up to then had been popular and dominant. As a result, the past three decades have witnessed as active an attention to the question as had the two decades preceding them.

Somewhat ironically (and appropriately so for a drama so ironic as *The Revenger's Tragedy*), the progress of the Tourneur-Middleton controversy has been marked time and again by the simultaneous appearance of confident statements wholly opposed to each other and hence mutually contradictory. Thus, for example, in the 1930's both Marco Mincoff and Una Ellis-Fermor conceived the idea of examining the play's imagery in an endeavor to determine, if possible, the interests and identity of its author. Mincoff came to the conclusion that the playwright was a man of the city, almost certainly Middleton ("The Authorship of *The Revenger's Tragedy*," *Studia historico-philologica Serdicensia*, 2, 1939). Miss Ellis-Fermor, on the other hand, found evidence which convinced her that the playwright was a countryman, undoubtedly Tourneur ("The Imagery of *The Revenger's Tragedy* and *The Atheist's Tragedy*," *MLR*, 30, 1935). (The later-appearing study was prepared without knowledge of the earlier.) Some twenty years after this, in 1955, Samuel Schoenbaum, while admitting that he was dealing with "probabilities," did not hesitate to refer to *The Revenger's Tragedy* as "Middleton's play," as though the question of authorship had been finally settled (*Middleton's Tragedies*, 1955). During the same year Inga-Stina Ekeblad, with equal emphasis, declared that "internal evidence of structure, themes, moral attitude, etc. speak against Middleton's authorship" ("A Note on *The Revenger's Tragedy*," *N&Q*, 2, 1955). And three years after that, in 1958, R. H. Barker alluded to *The Revenger's Tragedy* as assuredly by Middleton, stating positively that Oliphant "was right after all" (*Thomas Middleton*, 1958), within a month or so of the publication of Henri Fluchère's considered opinion, in the introduction to his translation, that this play and *The Atheist's Tragedy* were produced by the same hand (*La tragédie du vengeur*, 1958).

This is neither the place nor the occasion to make a complete survey of the numerous contributions to this theme or to examine in detail the several arguments which have been adduced in support of the one view or the other. What has been said, however, is sufficient to demonstrate two basic facts—that interest in *The Revenger's Tragedy* has by no means weakened during recent years, and that the authorship issue has loomed large in critical discussions precisely because of this interest. The inherent (though somewhat puzzling) macabre power possessed by the drama is amply attested by the anxious endeavors of Middleton enthusiasts to bring it within the compass of that author's works; indeed, one of these enthusiasts, after pointing out its kinship with several Middleton plays, goes so far as to admit that "it is more imaginative than any of them" (Barker, p. 64). Despite William Archer's attempt to dismiss it as a barbaric work offering nothing save "hideous sexuality" and a "raging lust for blood" (*The Old Drama and the New*, 1923), there can be no doubt but that almost all critics have sensed in it a tantalizing vigor and a stark impressiveness. The reputation of *The Revenger's Tragedy* has definitely increased rather than diminished with the passing of the years.

2.

Clearly, the main task before us is to determine, so far as we may, the nature of this play's hold over us; and that task is by no means easy. In one sense, Archer was right: *The Revenger's Tragedy* exhibits many crudities and at moments it may appear almost absurd; if it were put upon the stage today, unless it received such a production as Peter Brook gave to *Titus Andronicus* in 1955, some of its scenes would probably arouse among the spectators not tragic terror but merely nervous laughter. And yet, even while we fully recognize its weaknesses, the play still clutches us in its skeletal grip and still displays a keen dramatic, 'theater' sense on the part of its creator. Assuredly, then, our prime business should be to analyze its structure, language, and characters with the specific object of ascertaining the secrets of its power.

Just as soon as we admit this, however, we realize that the focus of discussion upon the question of authorship has tended to distract attention from the central issue and thus to prove a thwarting force. In general, so far as matters of critical assessment are concerned, we must agree that the contributions of real value have come either from Middleton-Tourneur debaters at moments when they could turn their attention from the authorship problem to a consideration of other matters or, more particularly, from writers not concerned with the authorship problem at all. Furthermore, it would appear that, so far as the first group is concerned, the proponents of Middleton, because they are necessarily engaged in attempting to prove a case, have had less opportunity for escaping from the specific issue than those who, accepting Tourneur's authorship, have been called upon to adopt little more than a defensive position. It is true that the attribution to Tourneur rests on no very sure external evidence, but after all the play is given to him in the Archer playlist of 1656 and it agrees with *The Atheist's Tragedy* in being a King's Men's play; absolutely no external evidence for a Middleton ascription exists, if we except the attempt to identify it with *The Viper and her Brood* which Middleton in 1606 declared he had given to Keysar—a hazardous thesis in view of the facts that *The Viper* was evidently designed for the Company of the Queen's Revels and that *The Revenger's Tragedy* shows signs of having originally been calculated for a Globe production. (See W. D. Dunkel, "The Authorship of *The Revenger's Tragedy*," *PMLA*, 46, 1931, and Inga-Stina Ekeblad, "A Note on *The Revenger's Tragedy*," *N&Q*, 2, 1955.) However slim their external support, therefore, the Tourneur proponents are less actively compelled to preach a new creed and thus can more easily take a wider view. Thus, for example, R. A. Foakes's acute comments on the nature of the verse-style in the drama and his remarks on the significance of the characters' Italianate names, though they appear in an article entitled "On the Authorship of *The Revenger's Tragedy*" (*MLR*, 48, 1953) and are contributory to his argument, have a value which goes considerably beyond that of the troublesome and somewhat barren area of parallel-passages and the like. Similarly, Inga-Stina Ekeblad's discussion of the play's imagery, in which she demonstrates how it has been designed to support and amplify the central *exemplum horrendum* and thus has been fashioned to serve an essentially dramatic function, while certainly aiding the 'Tourneur' argument, gives us an insight into the creative core of the work such as we had not been given in preceding imagery studies planned rather to prove a thesis than to explore dramatic values ("An Approach to Tourneur's Imagery," *MLR*, 54, 1959).

The truth of this observation is emphasized when we turn to those essays wherein the issue of authorship has been completely, or almost completely, set aside. Most important among these are several articles which have concentrated upon the cardinal question of the 'thought,' or the intellectual-emotional concept, out of which the drama has arisen. Rightly, it seems, the emphasis here has, in the main, been laid upon an attempt to demonstrate that the older view, culminating in the judgments of T. S. Eliot (*Selected Essays*, 1932) and Una Ellis-Fermor (*The Jacobean Drama*, 1936), which saw in *The Revenger's Tragedy* an 'affirmation of evil,' was in fact a misreading of its purpose. A series of studies, from that of Harold Jenkins in 1941 on through those of Robert Ornstein and others in the 1950's, have interestingly revealed an entirely different picture.[1] This picture shows an author of a Puritan, Calvinistic trend of mind, a man whose roots are to be found in the mid-sixteenth century, one whose reflections on life readily cast themselves in such forms as had been revealed in the morality plays. Opinions differ in detail, but John Peter seems to be expressing an attitude which is coming to receive a large amount of general acceptance when he declares that "to brand him [i.e. the author] as a cynic or nullifidian is at best to obliterate the key-signature on his score." Schoenbaum's demonstration

---

[1] Jenkins, "Cyril Tourneur," *RES*, 17 (1941); Ornstein, "The Ethical Design of *The Revenger's Tragedy*," *ELH*, 21 (1954) and "*The Atheist's Tragedy* and Renaissance Naturalism," *SP*, 51 (1954). Other contributions to this theme include: L. G. Salingar, "*The Revenger's Tragedy* and the Morality Tradition," *Scrutiny*, 6 (1938); Peter Lisca, "*The Revenger's Tragedy*: A Study in Irony," *PQ*, 38 (1959); John Peter, "*The Revenger's Tragedy* Reconsidered," *Essays in Criticism*, 6 (1956); Samuel Schoenbaum, "*The Revenger's Tragedy*: Jacobean Dance of Death," *MLQ*, 15 (1954); and H. H. Higgins, "The Influence of Calvinistic Thought in Tourneur's *Atheist's Tragedy*," *RES*, 19 (1943).

of the influence exerted upon the playwright by the concept of Death's Dance helps us to appreciate his work. And perhaps the most penetrating comment is that by Ornstein, who discerns in *The Revenger's Tragedy* the "intense, but only temporary, disillusion of a very orthodox and very conservative mind." This suggestion of the sudden surging-up of a molten horror, "immortalized in Italianate metaphor," unquestionably helps us to a keener perception of the inner nature of the drama's shaping force.

The facts that nearly all these contributions towards an understanding of the 'thought' which inspired *The Revenger's Tragedy* have come during the past few years and that they are largely unconnected with the authorship debate, or at least have only an indirect association with it, may well lead us to hope that adequate attention will now be directed towards other significant aspects of the play—particularly the quality of its characterization and the secrets of the impact made upon us by its verse. Maybe, in the end, these two elements are really one. Hitherto, the few comments made upon the persons of the tragedy have tended to suggest that they are monstrous "caricatures" or "laboratory specimens," figures at whom we look from the outside and for whom we never feel. Such, indeed, they appear when we compare them with Shakespeare's 'living' characters; and yet the fact remains that hardly anyone can escape captivation by these grotesques; they come to assume in our imagination a queer, vibrant existence of their own. Unquestionably, the paradox has to be explained largely by reference to the intensity of the verse, but it is also bound up with the dramatic structure and technique of the play as a whole. Symbolic of this structure is the opening scene wherein, on the one hand, we watch the terrible procession of Duke, Duchess, and prodigious brood while, on the other, we are ourselves led onto the stage by Vendice and, intoxicated by his words, become involved in the action. In this particular combination of remoteness and nearness, of objective presentation and direct engagement, of unreality and reality, of the artificial and the emotionally intense, appears to reside the ultimate secret of the drama's quality. At the same time, this quality is subtle and complex; only careful and detailed analysis can explain or reveal it fully.

3.

The chance that deviation from discussion of the authorship of *The Revenger's Tragedy* may encourage the exploration of some basic critical questions leads us, inevitably, towards a final consideration which goes far beyond the realm of Tourneur or Middleton. Obviously the debate about this play does not stand alone; it is accompanied by scores of similar discussions concerning other plays, and it falls into the general pattern of research into the lives of the playwrights of this time. When we consider such investigations as a whole, we must, of course, agree that every addition made to our knowledge of Elizabethan and Jacobean drama must be heartily welcomed. We may agree further that the more we know about the authors of the time the better, and that for biographers discussion of authorship questions, even those that cannot be settled absolutely or with universal acceptance, are of essential import. Anyone engaged in surveying the work of Ford or Massinger, for example, must take into account the fact that these authors began their careers by writing plays in collaboration with others; as a result, every attempt has to be made to determine, if possible, the dramas in whose writing they shared. The inquiry here is without doubt both right and proper.

Nevertheless, we may well be justified in asking ourselves whether this orientation is the one best calculated to produce the most effective results if our objective is to demonstrate the essential qualities in the dramatic literature of the time. We might, indeed, put two questions. Do we really gain so much by discussing the theater of this age in terms of authors? And, May not emphasis upon authorship tend to close our eyes to other and more significant considerations? Thus, for instance, the concentration on the Tourneur-Middleton issue has led us to relate *The Revenger's Tragedy* almost exclusively either to *The Atheist's Tragedy* or to such works as *The Phoenix* and *Your Five Gallants*. It was left for H. H. Adams to note the connection between the two 'Tourneur' plays and the tragedies of Chapman ("Cyril Tourneur on Revenge," *JEGP,* 48, 1949); and it was further left for Clifford Leech to draw significant conclusions from this fact (*"The Atheist's Tragedy* as a Dramatic Comment on Chapman's *Bussy* Plays," *JEGP,* 52, 1953).

Such an example suggests that maybe the Elizabethan and Jacobean drama can, in general, best be explored by regarding individual plays as independent entities—and in this connection it may be observed that, even within the limited range of Shakespeare's work, Kenneth Muir has recently expressed the opinion that we should do much better to consider the tragedies separately than to think in terms of 'Shakespearian tragedy' (*Shakespeare and the Tragic Pattern,* 1958).

For the most part, general accounts of the drama during the 'Elizabethan' period take shape as critical-historical surveys in which the names of authors, from Lyly and Marlowe on to Massinger, Ford, and Shirley, provide the chapter-headings. Perhaps a more effective image of dramatic development during these years might be secured if the total contributions of separate playwrights were made less prominent. After all, despite Shakespeare's majesty and Jonson's aggressive individualism, the habit of collaboration was common and the writers were working in a commonly accepted tradition.

This thought brings to mind the monumental *Bibliography of the English Printed Drama* of Sir Walter Greg, so recently, and for us so fortunately, completed. I recall vividly my first conversation with him. We met (in the 1920's) as we sat together watching a Phoenix Society production of *The Country Wife*; at its conclusion we went to a nearby restaurant for a chat. At that time I was engaged in searching for information about Tourneur, while he was patiently gathering material for his great volumes. When he told me that he had decided to deal with his subject chronologically by plays and when he further remarked that he was "trying to forget that these plays had authors at all," I freely confess that (with his useful short-title handlist in mind) I was both surprised at and somewhat doubtful about the wisdom of his decision. But of course Greg was absolutely right.

Although it is quite true that, with a few exceptions, he had firmly established printing-dates at his command whereas numerous production-dates are entirely conjectural, still we may reasonably wonder whether an approach similar to his towards the dramatic literature of these years might not stimulate exploration of divers significant aspects which are apt to be neglected when attention is focused upon the questions of authorship. Between the 1580's and the 1620's theatrical time was moving with extraordinary rapidity, and it is this element of accelerated time, made visible in the plays, which sometimes tends to become lost when we think exclusively in terms of Shakespeare's work or Jonson's, Dekker's or Heywood's, Fletcher's or Massinger's. We certainly want to know all we can about the dramatists' careers, but we also need to divorce ourselves at times from them.

These thoughts therefore lead to the suggestion that "for students of the Elizabethan drama" "the establishment of the identity of the author" of *The Revenger's Tragedy* is not today "one of the chief problems to be tackled." *The Revenger's Tragedy* stands as an achievement in its own right, and I would suggest that we may come to understand it best, not by contrasting and comparing it only with *The Atheist's Tragedy* or with Middleton's works, but by focusing attention upon its position in the larger contexts of dramatic and theatrical history. We shall be fully justified in pursuing the authorship problem still further, just as we are justified in exploring the lives of all the playwrights of the time, so long as, in doing so, we keep our minds open to the consideration of other approaches—especially that which would appreciate the plays themselves in their dramatic and theatrical interrelationships, without thought of the particular dramatists responsible.

ITALIAN *FAVOLE BOSCARECCE* AND JACOBEAN STAGE PASTORALISM

by JOHN LEON LIEVSAY

IT IS NOW A LITTLE MORE than a half a century since the publication of Sir Walter Greg's admirable *Pastoral Poetry and Pastoral Drama* (1906). In the main outline of the relationship between Italian and English pastoralism there traced singularly few changes have been necessary, and the amount of new information supplied by subsequent investigators has not been great. Certainly I do not flatter myself that I shall in these few pages be able to add much factual information to Greg's scholarly survey. It is hard gleaning after such a master. Nevertheless, I believe that the time has now come when the whole matter of the dramatic pastoral may be profitably re-examined. What is offered here, then, are some detached observations and speculations looking toward such re-examination of the particular connections between the firmly established and widely cultivated Italian *favola boscareccia* and the English drama of the late-sixteenth and early-seventeenth centuries.

At the outset it should be made clear that the Italians draw no essential distinctions among *favole pastorali, favole boscarecce,* and *favole silvestre.* Even the *favole pescatorie* are insufficiently differentiated to constitute them a separate type. When I use the term *boscareccia,* therefore, I mean the pastoral drama in general, exclusive of simple dramatic eclogue; and I do so because the plays which I have examined for the present purpose, with the exceptions of Ongaro's *Alceo,* Guarini's *Pastor fido,* and Bonarelli's *Filli di Sciro,* are all specifically designated *favole boscarecce* on their title-pages. The term *favola boschereccia* (or, commonly,

317

boscareccia), as Greg points out (p. 437), was used at least as early as c. 1545 for the *Mirzia* of Epicuro de' Marsi, though it was undoubtedly its use by Tasso for his *Aminta*, "supremo ed unico modello della boschereccia poesia,"[1] which gave it its later widespread currency. After the publication of the *Pastor fido*, with its tragicomic hybridization and its further impetus to the diffusion of the pastoral drama, Alessandro Turamini could say, in his *Sileno* (Napoli, 1595):

> Le Fauole boscareccie spiegate in verso non humile, ritrouamento assai leggiadro de' Poeti di nostri tempi, sono state in Italia, e da Principi, e dalla gente mezana conueneuolmente gradite, e tenute care. Et in esse per auuentura, più che nelle Comedie Cittadine, si hà con il diletto congiunta l'vtilità, perchè più felicemente per lo mezo della compassione in questo accostandosi alla Tragedia (ilche quelle non fanno) da loro i nostri affetti si purgano. (sigs. †4v-†5)

Such an Horatian fusion of the *dulce et utile*, assuming for the moment that Turamini is right, should have appealed quite as much, one would think, to the English as to the Italians. That it apparently did not, judging from the relatively slender cultivation of the form in England, is one of those quirks of public taste connected with the pastoral drama which I consider to be in need of further exploration.

Turamini's other point, involving the "verso non humile" and tragic affinities of the *boscarecce* is also worthy of attention. In the better Italian specimens of the form there is a high incidence of elevated and dignified verse, not to mention a scattering of exquisite lyrics. And, although the roles of the sexes are often reversed, there lies in the basic plot-formula of the pastoral an inherent approximation to what may be called the Hippolytus theme: a 'nymph,' a proud and disdainfully cold virgin, vowed to Diana, is ardently beloved of a shepherd votary of Venus.[2] Or it may be the other way around. The description of Nice, the beloved of Coridone in Ranieri Totti's *Amanti furiosi* (Venetia, 1597), is typical of many an icy 'nymph' in these forest pastorals:

> E tu per proua ben sai, che lei
> (E già non puoi di non saperlo)
> Assai rigida più d' Alpina selce,
> Più fallace, che 'l vento,
> Di sua bellezza altera, conoscendo,
> Che ne l' auorio & ostro del bel uiso,

---

[1] P. A. Serassi, "Discorso sopra l' *Aminta*"; see *L' Aminta e l' Amor fuggitivo di Torquato Tasso, il Pastor fido del Cavaliere Batista Guarini* (1824), p. 14.

[2] A pointed illustration of this Diana-Venus conflict may be seen in the *Andromeda tragicomedia boscareccia* (Venetia, 1587) of Diomisso Guazzoni.

E ne' begli occhi suoi s' annida Amore,
Sdegnosa sprezza ogn' uno? e solo ha gusto
Di seruir a Diana . . . .

(fol. 2v)

The art of the pastoralist—together with such suspense as a play with a prescribed happy ending is capable of—then consists in pushing this ill-assorted pair along the brink of imminent disaster through five acts without once permitting a fatal slip. In the hands of some maladroit practitioners these near-tragic complications sometimes became so snarled that resolution was possible only through resorting to the *deus ex machina*. But that, of course, was a trick not wholly unknown to Greek dramatists. Certainly there was, on the part of some Italian writers in this genre, a deliberate attempt to make their readers (or spectators) aware of any resemblances between their plays and those of the ancient tragic poets. Guarini's own elaborate notes to the *Pastor fido,* for instance, constantly illustrate the incidents and speeches of his play by comparisons with the Greeks. So cluttered with classical echoes, indeed, is the *Pastor fido* that there is left little room for a living voice to produce them. The prologue spoken by Diana in Francesco Partini's *Califfa* (Venetia, 1597), as another instance, is clearly an intentional parallel to that spoken by Aphrodite in the *Hippolytus* of Euripides. And, of course, the almost universal retention by the Italians of a chorus, used after the ancient manner, strongly reinforces the suggestion of a link between the *boscarecce* and Greek tragedy.

Now this is just such learned bait, one might suppose, as would lure so whopping a classical fish as Ben Jonson, especially if one remembers that the pedantic Ben was content to supply his *Sejanus* and even some of his masques and entertainments with the lumber of ponderous classical source-notes. But did he take the bait? Not so much as a nibble. If we accept Greg's thesis, as I think we must, that "the pastoral drama of Italy was the immediate progenitor of that of England" (p. 155), and if we assume that Jonson was familiar with Guarini, as his own statement (in *Volpone,* 3.4) virtually compels us to do, is it not doubly—trebly— anomalous that his unfinished *Sad Shepherd,* one of Greg's three prime examples of English pastoral drama, should be among the least classical, the most un-Italianate, the most roundly English works to come from his pen? To speculate on how Jonson might have completed *The Sad Shepherd* is futile; but it is clear that his play was not headed in the direction of the *favola boscareccia.*

Nor was Ben the only Englishman to wear his pastoral cloak with a difference. The English pastoral drama was, at best, but an imperfectly successful adaptation of its foreign original. Although his statement is not quite without ambiguity, Greg is at least right in the intention of his declaration that "with Daniel begins and ends in English literature the dominant influence of the Italian pastoral drama" (p. 262). The popularity in England of the *Aminta* and the *Pastor fido* is amply attested by the numerous translations and adaptations; but in creating their own pastoral plays the English (Daniel excepted) showed little willingness to follow at all closely the pattern set for them by Tasso and Guarini. They were content, mainly, to forgo the chorus; they treated love less philosophically, and less satirically, than did the Italians;[3] they shied away from the type-cast satyr and, after the time of Lyly, from an admixture of classical mythology. So far as I am aware, not a single English pastoral play introduces the *intermedii* ubiquitous in Italian *boscarecce*. And even though they could not quite abandon a tendency to moralize, it seems to me that the English were a trifle less self-consciously sententious than the Italians.[4]

It is somewhat misleading to speak, as I have done above, of "the English pastoral drama." There were a *few* English pastoral dramas, isolated and not particularly successful. Even Fletcher's *Faithful Shepherdess,* the play most likely to come to mind when one thinks of English pastoral drama, was a failure on its first performance—in my opinion justly so, for aside from its pretty versification it is a confused and feeble play. So confused, in fact, that the reader is perfectly justified in asking who *is* the faithful shepherdess, Clorin or Amoret? Beyond its title and the resemblance of the character of Cloe to that of Corisca, it shows little specific indebtedness to Guarini. The Sabrina-like figure of Clorin, for instance, while parallels are to be found in other *favole boscarecce,* has no counterpart in Guarini's well-knit plot; and the mawkish goody-goodiness of the Satyr is a far cry from any satyr-depiction that would have passed muster in the Italian pastoral plays.[5] When all the English examples have been taken into consideration, the fact remains that there never was in England, as there was in Italy, a true vogue of the theatrical pastoral. And this is the more surprising when it is considered that the Eng-

---

[3] The greater seriousness of the Italians on this score may be seen in Carlo Noci's *La Cinthia* (1596), where Dameta's long plea to Laurinia (4.2, pp. 111-19) virtually summarizes Renaissance doctrines of love.

[4] It was a common practice among the Italian pastoralists to print proverbs, adages, and other sententious 'purple passages' within quotation marks.

[5] Satyrs and pretended satyrs appear in Thomas Goffe's (?) *Careless Shepherdess* (c. 1629). The plot and machinery seem to indicate some connection between this play (which I have not seen) and the Italian pastoral drama. See Greg, pp. 347-51.

lish were loaded to the gunwales with other manifestations of the pastoral mode—witness the poetical miscellanies—just at the time of the greatest Italian incidence of pastoral plays.

Hardly less strange is the fact that, whereas the English pastoral plays were undeniably a direct response to what was currently popular in Italian literature, the same responsiveness to contemporary literary fashion was not reflected in any apparent awareness of Gabriello Chiabrera, certainly then reputed the best of the Italian poets between Tasso and Marino. Indicative of this neglect is the absence in Greg of any mention of Chiabrera's three *boscarecce, Gelopea* (1604), *Meganira* (1608), and *Alcippo* (1614). Not that these pieces are any grand prize. All are brief and uncomplicated, like the *Aminta*, their obvious model, though their competent, somewhat sweetish versification is far removed from the melodic spontaneity of Tasso. But one marked feature of Chiabrera's plays, the moralistic, should have appealed to the 'moral' English. We have no evidence that it did.[6]

In his discussion of Jonson's *Sad Shepherd* (and elsewhere in his study) Greg recognizes in the English play the presence of features more congenial to English audiences than "would have been the oracles, satyrs, and other outworn machinery of regular pastoral tradition" (p. 315). In addition to the oracles and satyrs, and the chorus (concerning which I shall presently have more to say), what were the most conspicuous parts of this "outworn machinery"?

One of them, certainly, consists of the masquelike *intermedii*, frequently turning on mythological subjects, presented between the acts and, in the printed plays, normally grouped together following the text. Another is the practice of using the prologue for purposes of exposition of the plot, a practice not without ancient precedent. Similarly, in the epilogue the appeal[7] to the audience for its applause, inherited from classical comedy, might be considered a fairly normal mechanism in the *boscarecce*. One of the most troublesome cogs of the machine, happily

---

[6] Nor, until the eighteenth century, were the English apparently any better acquainted with his lyrics. See A. Lytton Sells, *The Italian Influence in English Poetry from Chaucer to Southwell* (1955), p. 111.

[7] A pleasant illustration is provided by the *Amanti furiosi* of Ranieri Totti, already cited. Sprilla, the clown, speaks the epilogue—in character:

> Non aspettate Spettatori fuore
> Più nessun de noi altri,
> Andateui con Dio, perche vogliamo
> Andar à far le Nozze, io non v' inuito
> Perche poi per dirla,
> Non ci vò mangiator, doue son' io,
> E in tanto se piaciuta,
> Questa Fauola è datene segno,
> Con il rumoreggiare.

absent from most of the English plays, is the overdependence upon solution through the *deus ex machina* or, more frequently, through the intervention of some local witch or mage. And though they may not, strictly, qualify as 'machinery,' certain other features were of fairly regular occurrence in the Italian pastoral plays. After Tasso, for instance, one might expect to find in almost any *boscareccia* a set piece on the Golden Age, another contrasting Arcadian simplicity with courtly sophistication,[8] and still another built around the Dantean theme, "Amore a null' Amato amar perdona." The echo-scene[9] was also practically *de rigueur*, though commonly managed with more mechanical ingenuity than sense. Stock names, too, recur with wearisome persistence: Tirsi, Ergasto, Coridone, Aminta, Montano, Selvaggio, Clori, Silvia, Amarilli, Dorinda. Strangely, however, stock characters, where they begin to emerge, are not identified by any special stock name as were the characters in the *commedia dell' arte* or the *commedia erudita*. Among the type characters, the rustic clowns and bumpkins often use dialect for their comic scenes, a practice noticeably missing from English pastoral plays.[10] If this machinery of venerable conventions sometimes groaned and creaked a bit, its complaints must surely have drawn but little attention in a type of drama whose whole atmosphere and essence is that of cloudcuckooland.

I have already remarked upon the disuse of the chorus in English pastoral drama; but Samuel Daniel's *Queenes Arcadia* (1605, printed 1606) offers an important exception. True, no members of a chorus figure among "The Names of the Actors" prefixed to the play. They are nonetheless present, interestingly, in the persons of Melibaeus and Ergastus, described as "two ancient *Arcadians*." In 1.1 these two ancients, unseen spies upon the other persons of the drama, speak what may be regarded either as prologue or as the opening chorus. Thereafter, as in Tasso, Guarini, and scores of other Italian writers, this chorus *à deux* comes forward to make the final comment and moralization at the end

---

[8] In Illuminato Perazzoli's *Filleno* (Venetia, 1596) even Cupid (Amore), speaking the prologue, succumbs to this motif (p. 5):

> Satio son di mirar Palagi, e Torri,
> E di veder sete fregiate d' oro;
> Assai son stato ascoso
> Nei seni ad arte releuati, e gonfij,
> E di crin simulati in rizzi schiui,
> Hor vagheggiar fra questi boschi bramo
> Vn bel cotturno acconcio a gentil piede
> Di vaga Ninfa, e fra le poma acerbe
> Di bianco sen quiui annidarmi spesso. . . .

[9] Greg, p. 343, considers the echo-scene in *The Maid's Metamorphosis* (anonymous, 1600) the earliest of the rare uses of this device in English pastoral plays.

[10] Ben Jonson's *Sad Shepherd* is an exception in this, as in other respects.

of each of the first four acts. In the fifth act, where they assume in addition something of the resolving function of *dei ex machina,* they slip out of their role of primary (intercalary) chorus of detached observers and, following the distinction so carefully drawn in Guarini's own notes to the *Pastor fido,*[11] become a semichorus speaking directly to the other Arcadians. Appropriately, Melibaeus, as choragus for this semichorus, is allotted the final speech in the play. Incidentally, one marked feature of *The Queenes Arcadia,* negligible in the *Pastor fido* which it so closely follows, is the satiric motivation. An explanation of this, possibly, is that satire, not then at its liveliest in Italy, was just at the turn of the century a flourishing commodity in English letters.

Daniel's second attempt at the form, *Hymens Triumph* (1615), affords in the speech of Dorcas (2.1.506) the nearest approach among English pastoral plays to an equivalent for Tasso's "O bell' età dell' oro." Even so, the likeness is in theme only: Daniel's lines have nothing of the exquisite lyricism of their original. As in *The Queenes Arcadia,* Daniel again preserves the chorus. For the first three acts, however, the chorus is merely a musical voice; only in the final two acts does it become, as semichorus, an active participant in the dialogue. It may be noted, in passing, that the versification of *Hymens Triumph* represents a distinct improvement in smoothness over that of *The Queenes Arcadia.* While Daniel's main indebtedness to Guarini remains unquestioned, the

---

[11] See *Il Pastor fido tragicommedia pastorale del Cavaliere Battista Guarini con annotazioni* (1807), pp. 85, 294-5. The second of these passages deserves quotation in full: "Il Coro, che viene in Scena qui [i.e. in 4.3], è il medesimo che ha tramezzato la favola in ciascun Atto; perciocchè due son gli ufficij del Coro; l'uno è di cantare in fine di ciascun Atto, l'altro di favellare come istrione con tutti gli altri. Il primo si chiama Coro intercalare, perchè divide le parti secondo i Greci, e secondo i Latini, e moderni tragici gli Atti della tragedia. Il secondo dai Latini e dai nostri fu ed è chiamato Semicoro: ma quanto bene io nol so; perciocchè questo secondo ufficio non si distingue dal primo per quantità di persone, ma solo per qualità di operazione, come si vede chiaro in tutte le antiche e moderne favole; e chiaramente c' insegnò Arist[otile] il qual disse: *che il Coro intercalare tutto cantava e saltava, e che il Coro istrione, ancora che in quantità fosse il medesimo, un solo nondimeno parlava in vece di tutti.* Oggi il Coro intercalare non salta, e le più volte non canta, nè sta continuamente in Scena come stava quello de' Greci, la quale usanza è stata con gran giudizio dismessa dai nostri tragici, che in questo veramente hanno veduto assai più degli antichi; e ciò per molte ragioni, che non è luogo qui da recare. Vien dunque il Coro in questa Scena come istrione: e come quello, che non dee mai comparire (quando è ben maneggiato) se non per cosa grave, appartenente al negozio pubblico della favola; avendo inteso che Silvio ha liberato l'Arcadia da quel fiero cignale, che la infestava, gli va contra per onorarlo, e qui si vuole avvertire un particolare molto importante; cioè che quando il Coro è venuto fin qui tre volte in Scena per tramezzare, come s' è detto, gli Atti, non ha parlato mai se non di quel negozio, che tanto preme a tutti, cioè delle nozze di Silvio e d' Amarilli, e dell' amor di Mirtillo, che son le parti principali di questa favola. Ma ora che tratta di onorare Silvio per un particolare spettante all' episodio, che è la caccia, non l' ha serbato nel canto intercalare, ma viene come istrione a trattarne in mezzo dell' Atto."

amorous complications of the central situation somewhat resemble those of Shakespeare's *Twelfth Night*.

In Randolph's *Amyntas* (printed 1638)—which, despite the title, is not derived from Tasso—the scene, as is the case with occasional Italian pastoral plays, is laid in Sicily rather than in Arcadia. A chorus of "Priests, Shepherds, Nymphs" listed among the dramatis personae appears on two occasions only, in the final act, and then only to sing songs. Being thus almost nonfunctional, it is completely negligible. The last scene (5.8) uses an only moderately successful echo-passage to resolve one of the two enigmas upon which the plot confusedly hinges. The clowning of the minor rustics (Jocastus, Mopsus, Bromius, Dorylas), though it has some parallels (needing further investigation) in scattered Italian *boscarecce,* especially those containing dialect roles, has none in the *Pastor fido* and is more nearly akin to that in Shakespeare's *Midsummer Night's Dream*[12] or Jonson's *Sad Shepherd*. And while Guarini undoubtedly provides the main complication, the Damon-Alexis rivalry for the love of Laurinda seems also to reflect the "doppio amore" of Bonarelli's Celia.

Randolph's *Amyntas* having taken us, technically at least, beyond the immediate concern of this discussion, for a few final remarks on the English pastoral let us return to an earlier play. Phineas Fletcher's *Sicelides* (performed 13 March 1614/15, printed 1631), though nominally a piscatory and though having obvious links with antecedent native productions, nonetheless vies with Daniel's two pastoral plays for the dubious honor of being the English original play (as contrasted with mere translation) best to exemplify the spirit and form of the Italian *boscareccia.* How little significance is to be attached to the difference in label and to the transferral of the scene from the woods and mountains of Arcadia to the coast of Sicily is attested by the speech of Perindus in the opening scene:

> Shepherd or fisher, I am still the same,
> I am a sea guest not for gaine, but game.

All the other paraphernalia remain unchanged. Here are the disdainful 'nymphs'[13] and their wooers, love at cross-purposes, the envious and

---

[12] Cesare Simonetti's *Amaranta* (Padova, 1588), 3.3, provides a curious parallel to the enamorment of Titania and Bottom. Amaranta, scornful of love, and the conventional devotee of Diana, is by way of penalty made to become infatuated with Sbardella, a lumpish clown who searches the woods for his lost donkey.

[13] The reader will undoubtedly have perceived that whereas the satyrs of the *boscarecce* remain the sylvan creatures of mythology, the *ninfe* are simply shepherdesses.

scheming 'wanton,' oracles, disguises, the sacrificial virgin, inexorable priests, monsters (replacing satyrs), timely rescues and unexpected reunions, a rascally witty servant, doltish fishermen-dupes (replacing clodhoppers), a chorus—used, for once, in the Italian manner—and the inevitable happy hymeneal ending.

Such life as there is in *Sicelides* lies wholly in the farcical underplot. Nothing could salvage the play from its ingrained puerilities; and the frigid, stilted couplets that predominate in the versification serve only to emphasize the artificiality of a form already conventionalized beyond possibility of acceptance by any save the most inveterately uncritical addict of drama in whatsoever form. F. S. Boas, in the preface to his edition of the Fletchers, speaks of *Sicelides* as "a very long play" (*The Poetical Works of Giles and Phineas Fletcher,* 1908, 1.17). As compared with the typical Italian *boscareccia* it is perhaps so, though I am inclined to believe that the tedium of the familiar pattern only makes is seem so. Certainly it is much longer than the *Aminta* or the three pastorals of Chiabrera; but as compared with the interminable *Pastor fido* it is a mere drop in the bucket.

Having begun with Greg, let us return to him for our last word. *Pastoral Poetry and Pastoral Drama* devotes much space to Anglo-Italian literary ties. On the English side its coverage is thorough, judicious, and well-nigh definitive for the areas it attempts to survey. Where it is weak, if that is a permissible adjective for so excellent a study, is on the Italian side. Greg's tacit assumption that the relationship between the two national dramas could be satisfactorily determined from an examination of only the most conspicuously successful or well-known of the Italian plays is simply not defensible. The whole corpus[14] of the Italian

---

[14] Italian pastoral plays exist by the hundreds, and those specifically designated as *boscarecce* (or *silvestre*) by the scores. As a starting-point for anyone who may wish to pursue the subject further, I append here a list of such of the latter as have come to my attention. Since my interest in examining them was in their form, and not their history or bibliography, I cannot vouch that the dates are those of first editions.

Nicola degli Angeli, *Ligurino* (Venetia, Guerigli, 1594); Guidobaldo Benamati, *La Pastorella d' Etna* (Venetia, Muschio, 1627); Gasparo Bonifacio, *Amor venale* (Venetia, Ciotti, 1616); Alessandro Calderoni, *L' Esilio amoroso* (Ferrara, Baldini, 1607); Maddalena Campiglia, *Flori* (Vicenza, heredi di Brunelli, 1588); [G. B. Casotti], *Gratiana* (Venetia, Alberti, 1599); Gabriello Chiabrera, *Gelopea* (Mondovì, de' Rossi, 1604), *Meganira* (Firenze, Caneo, 1608), *Alcippo* (Genova, Pavoni, 1614); Cesare Cremonini, *Le Pompe funebri, overo Aminta, e Clori* (Ferrara, Baldini, 1590), *Il Ritorno di Damone, overo la sampogna di Mirtillo* (Venetia, Ciotti, 1622); Giovanni Battista Donzellini, *Boscerecci amori* [n.p., 1600?] (I have not seen this work, which is possibly not a play).

Faconio Ostianese [pseudonym?], *Erminia* (Brescia, Bozzòla, 1617); Piergirolamo Gentilericcio, *I Sospetti* (Venetia, Combi, 1608); Cesare Gonzaga, *Procri, favola bosche-*

pastoral drama needs to be examined—preferably by someone with Greg's acumen and knowledge of the English drama. And that combination will be hard to find. It was, of course, no part of Greg's task to concern himself with nondramatic instances of English adaptations from Italian pastoral drama; but future investigations of Italian influence upon English letters, such as that promised in A. Lytton Sells's continuation of his recent study (see note 6 above), might do well to follow the path already indicated by Obertello in the notes to his *Madrigali italiani in Inghilterra* and by Hyder Rollins in the notes to his edition of the Davisons' *Poetical Rhapsody*.

In drama, the pastoral represents a variety of intellectual *rigor mortis*. After Tasso and Guarini, nothing was left to be said. But, in Italy at least, it continued to be said—*ad nauseam*. It is perhaps just as well that English attempts to naturalize this foreign hothouse plant resulted in one of the more signal failures of Elizabethan and Jacobean drama.

---

reccia in tre atti (ed. Marco Pellegri, 1958); Diomisso Guazzoni, *Andromeda. Tragicomedia boscareccia* (Venetia, Imberti, 1587); Giovanmaria Guicciardi, *Il Sogno* (Ferrara, Baldini, 1601); Pietro Lupi, *I Sospetti* (Firenze, Sermartelli, 1589); Muzio Manfredi, *La Semiramis boscareccia* (Pavia, Bartoli, 1598); Pietro Michiele, *Favole boscherecce di Pietro Michiele* (Venetia, Guerigli, 1643); Carlo Noci, *La Cinthia* (Venetia, Compagnia Minima, 1596); Francesco Partini, *Califfa* (Venetia, Prati, 1597).

Illuminato Perazzoli, *Filleno* (Venetia, Moretti, 1596); Bernardino Percivallo, *L' Orsilia boscareccia sdrucciola* (Bologna, Rossi, 1589); Luigi Rusca, *Il Pastor infido* (Pavia, Rossi, 1622); Cesare Simonetti, *Amaranta* (Padova, Cantoni, 1588); Pietro Antonio Toniani, *Dameta* (Vicenza, Amadio, 1616); Giovanni Paolo Trapolini, *Tirsi, egloga boschereccia tragicomica* (Trevigi, Deuchino, 1600); Ranieri Totti (or Trotti), *Gli Amanti furiosi* (Venetia, Brugnolo, 1597); Alessandro Turamini, *Sileno* (Napoli, Stigliola, 1595); Francesco Vinta, *Il Rapimento di Corilla* (Venetia, Ciotti, 1605); Viviano Viviani, *L' Ortigia tragicomedia boscareccia* (Venetia, Pulciano, 1606).

THOMAS HEYWOOD'S DRAMATIC ART

by ARTHUR BROWN

THE VERY USE OF THE WORD 'art' in connection with Thomas Heywood may cause at least a slight raising of the eyebrows on the part of some readers. A dramatist who could claim, with no indication of being ashamed of the fact, that he had "had either an entire hand, or at the least a maine finger" in some 220 plays (epistle to the reader, *The English Traveller*, 1633); who has been called by one modern critic (T. S. Eliot) "a facile and sometimes felicitous purveyor of goods to the popular taste," and by another (Fredson Bowers) "an assembly-line dramatist" —such a one, it may be felt, is automatically out of court so far as any consideration of dramatic art is concerned. On the other hand one often has the suspicion that much of the modern tendency to sneer at Heywood arises in the first place as a reaction against Lamb's over-enthusiastic term "prose Shakespeare," and in the second place from the general inaccessibility of almost all his works except *A Woman Killed with Kindness*. We do well to remind ourselves that Webster could write, in his preface to *The White Devil* (1612), of "the right happy and copious industry of Master Shakespeare, Master Dekker, and Master Heywood, wishing what I write may be read by their light," and that even Eliot, in the essay from which I have already quoted, righted the balance by referring to the fact that "verse which is only moderately poetical but very highly dramatic" is by no means singular in Heywood's work, going on to add that "undeniably Heywood was not without skill in the construction of plays" (*Elizabethan Essays*, 1934, p. 108).

Other considerations call for comment. Heywood deserves credit for not, so far as we know, attempting anything which he knew to be beyond his capabilities. We have no example from his pen of tragedy as it was practiced by Shakespeare or Webster or Tourneur, nor of comedy in, for example, the Jonsonian manner. In the prologue to *A Woman Killed with Kindness* (1607), his nearest approach to tragedy of any kind, he can write, "Looke for no glorious State, our Muse is bent Vpon a barren subiect, a bare Scene," and in his "Address to the Reader" in *2 The Iron Age* (1632) he can muse somewhat wistfully on the possible reception of plays no longer in fashion: "I know not how they may bee receiued in this Age, where nothing but *Satirica Dictaeria,* and *Comica Scommata* are now in request: for mine owne part, I neuer affected either, when they stretched to the abuse of any person publicke, or priuate." Part of a dramatist's art lies in his choice of subject matter, and I shall say more about Heywood in this respect; for the moment it may be noted that in these two instances, as well as elsewhere in his plays, he was himself aware of making a deliberate choice.

He imposed a further limitation upon himself—the word is used in no derogatory sense—in his attitude towards the publication of his plays. He was himself an actor, he was alone among his fellow-playwrights in writing at considerable length on the actor's art (in his *Apology for Actors,* 1612), and his prefaces, prologues, and addresses to readers make it clear beyond all possible doubt that for him the play lived on the stage and that its appearance in print was at best a poor substitute which the true dramatist should neither hope for nor fully approve: "It hath beene no custome in mee of all other men (curteous Readers) to commit my plaies to the presse . . . for though some haue vsed a double sale of their labours, first to the Stage, and after to the presse, for my owne part I heere proclaime my selfe euer faithfull in the first, and neuer guiltie of the last" (epistle to the reader, *The Rape of Lucrece,* 1608). Similar comments are easy enough to find in the rest of his works, but one other is worth quoting here for the note of disdain which creeps into Heywood's voice as he contemplates his fellows' shortcomings in this respect: "True it is, that my playes are not exposed vnto the world in Volumes, to beare the title of *Workes* (as others), one reason is, that many of them by shifting and change of Companies, haue beene negligently lost, Others of them are still retained in the hands of some Actors, who thinke it against their peculiar profit to haue them come in print, and a third, that it neuer was any great ambition in me, to bee in this kind Voluminously read" (epistle to the reader, *The English Traveller*). Heywood wrote for the theater; the presentation of his play by actors was his main concern; if, by accident, a play eventually came into print, he could usually summon up enough concern to acknowledge it with a preface. But there is very little evidence indeed, if any, to suggest that the printed version received any polishing or revision at his hands.

We have in Heywood, therefore, a dramatist who wrote easily and quickly, if not always thoughtfully, who knew his own limitations and kept well within them, who had no particular social, moral, or religious axe to grind (at least not to the extent of turning his plays into treatises —"studious for thy pleasure and profit" seems to sum up quite well his attitude towards his audience), who had an intimate knowledge of and respect for the acting profession, and who was concerned above all things with writing for the stage, not for the study. With this picture of him in mind we are in a better position to examine and assess his methods.

Of the 220 plays which Heywood himself mentions, only some two dozen can now be identified with certainty and little can be conjectured about the rest. The survivors exhibit considerable variety in subject matter, and on his choice of material Heywood makes a few significant comments. In the prologue to *The Four Prentices* (1615), for example, he remarks: "Our authority is a manuscript, a booke writ in parchment; which not being publique, nor generall in the world, wee rather thought fit to exemplifie to the publique censure, things concealed and obscur'd, such as are not common with euery one, than such Historicall Tales as euery one can tell by the fire in Winter. Had not yee rather, for nouelties sake, see *Ierusalem* yee neuer saw, then *London* that yee see howerly?" This emphasis on novel or little-known themes occurs again in the epilogue to *The Brazen Age* (1613), spoken by Homer:

> All we haue done we aime at your content,
> Striuing to illustrate things not knowne to all . . . ;

and one of Heywood's main arguments in defense of the stage in *An Apology for Actors* is that plays "haue made the ignorant more appre-hensiue, taught the vnlearned the knowledge of many famous histories, instructed such as cannot reade in the discouery of all our English Chronicles . . . ." The purpose behind this deliberate choice of little-known material is, of course, a didactic one, but Heywood also gives a very clear impression that he preferred it too for its own sake. All was grist to his mill: "our English chronicles" gave him material for *If You Know Not Me,* a chance to glorify not only the Protestant Elizabeth but also his beloved London in the account of Sir Thomas Gresham and the building of the Royal Exchange; possibly they gave him material for *Edward IV*, though his authorship of this play is uncertain. Classical sources provided him with material for the *Four Ages,* a series of dramatized myths and stories from the establishment of the pagan gods to the destruction of Troy, *The Rape of Lucrece,* and *Love's Mistress,* in which the Cupid-Psyche, Midas, and Apuleius stories gave him a chance not only to teach the unlearned but also to poke fun at things which he elsewhere took very seriously. Romantic adventure stories, in which the scene shifted with bewildering rapidity from one exotic part of the world to another, and in which the Englishman (or woman) could be shown triumphant over foreign enemies, provided material for *The Four Prentices, A Maidenhead Well Lost, The Royal King and the Loyal Subject* (comparable with the 'Patient Griselda' type of story of which Dekker was so fond), *A Challenge for Beauty,* and *The Fair Maid of the West,* with its seemingly unending series of Eastern courts, piracy, murder, sea-fights, brigands, and chastity in peril. Finally, Heywood's interest in the contemporary scene, and in particular in the domestic scene, produced *A Woman Killed With Kindness* and *The English Traveller,* both laying stress on the domestic virtues of patience and fidelity, and *The Late Lancashire Witches* and *The Wise Woman of Hogsdon.* A selective principle may not be immediately obvious in this welter of material; yet if we consider the work of his fellow-dramatists we shall see that there were a great many things which Heywood did *not* attempt, and what remains is indicative of a deliberate choice by a man working with a firm principle in mind—the edification and entertainment of the citizen audiences of the public theaters.

Before such an audience and in such a theater the method of opening a play must have been very important. Heywood seems to have been aware of this and to have given the problem some thought. *Edward IV* opens with a fierce argument between the King and the Duchess of York about the former's marriage to a young widow at the very moment when his ambassadors are engaged in arranging a match for him with the daughter of the French king; *The Fair Maid of the West* has a quarrel over a pretty barmaid, a tavern brawl, and a murder, all in the first few minutes; *Fortune by Land and Sea* repeats the tavern brawl and the murder; *A Woman Killed with Kindness* opens cheerfully enough with the celebration of Frankford's marriage but moves swiftly through a series of scenes in which dramatic irony and foreboding are the keynotes —Sir Charles's arrest for a double murder (committed, of course, on the stage), Frankford's soliloquy on his own happy estate in the possession of a virtuous wife, the announcement of the arrival of Wendoll (the eventual cause of the tragedy), which pleases Frankford ("I haue preferr'd him to a second place In my Opinion, and my best regard"), Wendoll's report of the murders, and Nick's doubts about Wendoll's character ("I do not like this fellow by no meanes. . . , The Deuill and he are all one in my eye"); *A Challenge for Beauty* loses no time in setting the story in motion by the banishment of Bonavida; in *The Royal King and the Loyal Subject* ominous threatenings from the discontented Lords Chester and Clinton against the honors heaped upon the Lord Marshal appear in the first seventy lines; *The Wise Woman of Hogsdon* opens with a gambling scene; *A Maidenhead Well Lost* reveals in its opening lines the plot of the villain Stroza to be revenged for his alleged injuries by spreading slander about his enemies. The list could be continued, but it seems fair to say that in only a few cases, and those in plays which do not reveal Heywood at his best on any count, does he fail to open the action dramatically and reveal the essential strands of the plot as quickly as possible. In this respect his art is very much that of the professional dramatist, aware of the necessity of getting off to a good start.

Once the play has started, Heywood seems to have no objection to using any and every stage device in the manipulation of his plot, and it is on this ground, I feel, that the most serious accusations may be leveled against him as a dramatic artist. Writing about the aims of a popular Elizabethan dramatist with particular reference to Dekker, George F. Reynolds once remarked: "Poetry, Speed, strong Emotional Scenes to give the actors the greatest opportunities for stirring their audiences, Sharp Contrasts, do pretty well sum up what the Elizabethan romantic plays actually do offer. . . . There is nothing about decorum, nothing about the unities, no regard for the different Kinds, no hint of trying to improve the audience, but only the main motive of stirring their emotions" (*Renaissance Studies in Honor of Hardin Craig*, 1941, p. 151). This is perhaps not altogether fair to Dekker and is certainly not altogether true of Heywood, yet the fact remains that the latter was often too readily dependent on swift changes of location, coincidence, accident, disguise, nonrecognition between closely related characters, dumbshow, and all the other paraphernalia by means of which a plot could be kicked along if it showed signs of flagging. In *The Fair Maid of the West* (1631) Spencer, Bess's lover, flees from a charge of murder resulting from a tavern brawl, and the entire plot depends upon an incorrect report of his death arising from the quite incredible confusion between him and another man of the same name. Once this initial coincidence has been perpetrated, there is no holding Heywood. Bess goes to sea to bring home Spencer's body and is wooed by Mullisheg, King of Fesse. By another coincidence Spencer has arrived at the same court and is wooed by the Queen of Fesse. This tricky situation is overcome by falling back on the time-honored 'exchanged-beds' routine, but Spencer has the misfortune to be captured while trying to escape. Incredibly heroic virtue and fidelity in the face of overwhelming odds seem to be bringing their own reward, but the dramatist still has time for more adventures and the play is moved on by the separation of Bess and Spencer by pirates. Bess is rescued by the Duke of Florence, who proceeds to woo her. Inevitably Spencer turns up and, not recognizing Bess, solemnly promises Florence to help him gain her love! All notions of a well-constructed plot are irrelevant in the face of this kind of composition; on the other hand, so infectious is Heywood's enthusiasm both for his incidents and for his characters that he almost succeeds in making us feel that we are to blame for raising such considerations.

The Four Prentices relies still more on accident, coincidence, and lack of recognition, resulting in a bewildering pattern of interchanges between the major characters. Once the Old Earl has assumed, on fairly flimsy ground, that he has only one son, Charles, left alive, the way is left open for a flood of the most improbable situations. The four sons are scattered—Godfrey in Boulogne, Guy in France, Charles in Italy, and Eustace in Ireland—and meet in rapidly changing pairs, while the movements of their sister Bella Franca complicate matters still further. Eustace and Charles meet, do not recognize each other or their sister, and fight for her love. They join the army of Tancred, Prince of Italy, while he 'looks after' Bella Franca. Meanwhile Guy and Godfrey, not recognizing each other, join the army of Robert of Normandy. In the ensuing trouble between Tancred and Robert, Charles is matched against Godfrey, Eustace against Guy. Eustace and Guy are banished; Guy rescues Robert and Charles, Eustace rescues Tancred and Godfrey. So the play goes on, ending only when just about every possible permutation and combination of characters has been tried. One feels with Heywood, however, that for the play as a whole there is no natural and inevitable end, only one dictated by the length of time that an audience would be prepared to devote to it. The introduction of a new set of adventures at almost any point could extend it indefinitely, and we have the example of the second part of *The Fair Maid of the West* to show that he was perfectly capable of doing this.

Yet there is another side to the coin, for not everything is to be entered to the debit side of Heywood's account. The two plays described above are extreme examples of Heywood's use of a multitude of stock devices and situations; furthermore, to read them in summary, even to read them in full, is to miss what was for Heywood the most important thing: their impact on a theater audience. In puzzling out the complications while reading the plays, one is in grave danger of overlooking at least two things at which Heywood frequently excelled: speed and timing. It is perhaps true to say that Heywood's ability in these two respects shows up to better advantage when he applies it to a smaller area than an entire play; *The Fair Maid of the West* and *The Four Prentices* may be astonishing *tours de force,* but our reactions are quickly numbed by repeated blows on exactly the same spot. Still using accident and coincidence, and even nonrecognition, Heywood displayed his gifts of speed and timing much more satisfactorily in such episodes as the Jupiter-Amphitrio-Alcmena tangle in *The Silver Age* (1613), with the principals balanced by their servants Ganimede and Socia, and in the disposal of the body of the murdered Friar John in *The Captives* (c. 1624). The former incident is well enough known to Elizabethan scholars, not only from Heywood and Plautus but from the interlude of *Jack Juggler;* it calls for a good deal of care in staging but was just the kind of situation in which Heywood delighted and which he could handle with considerable skill. In the second incident, part of the subplot of *The Captives,* Friar John has been murdered by the jealous d'Averne and his man Denis, and the body put over the wall into the grounds of the neighboring monastery; knowing the ill-feeling among the inmates of the monastery, d'Averne is confident that one of the monks will be blamed for the murder. John is discovered by his old enemy, Friar Richard, who, receiving no reply to his greetings, hits him with a stone and, seeing the body fall, thinks that he has killed him. He puts the body back over the wall into d'Averne's garden! Here John is rediscovered by Denis; he and d'Averne dress the body in armor, place it astride an old stallion, and drive it out of the gates "to seek his fortune." Richard meanwhile has decided to flee from the scene of his 'murder,' borrowed a mare from the baker, and set out just at the moment that John is being driven out on the stallion; the stallion, bearing John's body, chases the mare, bearing Richard. The text suggests that the mounting of John on the stallion was done on the stage (Malone Society Reprint, 2728-32); possibly the mare appeared on the stage too (2740). The chase took place off-stage, but the stage-directions at this point give plenty of scope for 'noise' and 'trampling of horses,' and for the rapid reporting of events by one character after another, and the resultant confusion must have been very satisfying to an Elizabethan audience. Certainly the episode borders on farce, but handled in production in the way Heywood no doubt saw it could be handled, there could be no question but that it would succeed.

Two other instances may be singled out to demonstrate Heywood's successful use of speed and timing on a more extended scale: much of the subplot of *The English Traveller,* and a number of the 'wise-woman' scenes and the denouement of *The Wise Woman of Hogsdon* (1638). Eliot says that "it was in *The English Traveller* that Heywood found his best plot" (*Elizabethan Essays*, p. 111). He is referring, of course, to the main plot, which he finds "especially modern" among Elizabethan plots, but one might add that Eliot's condemnation of the subplot (p. 110) as "a clumsy failure to do that in which only Jonson could have succeeded" is less than just to Heywood. It is true that the notion of an empty house taken over by a gang of rascals, led by a trusted servant, is much more fully developed in *The Alchemist*; but Heywood was not making an entire play out of it, and for his purpose the 'sharp contrast' with his main theme was all he required. Contrast with what Eliot calls (p. 111) "the refinement of agony of the virtuous lover who has controlled his passion and then discovers that his lady has deceived both her husband and himself" is certainly present, and in popular drama of this kind we should not expect anything more subtle. In addition there is plenty of scope for the actor taking the part of Reignald as he tries desperately to stave off disaster when confronted by the "usuring rascal" from whom he has borrowed money to support his riotous behavior, and by his newly-returned master who requires some explanation for the strange state of his house.

The Wise Woman of Hogsdon is more elaborately conceived, and in it Eliot suggest (p. 110) that Heywood "succeeds with something not too far below Jonson to be comparable to that master's work; the wise woman herself, and her scenes with her clientele, are capitally done, and earn for Heywood the title of 'realist' if any part of his work can. The scene of the unmasking of Young Chartley must be excellent fun when played." Almost casually Eliot has, I think, touched on the essential quality of Heywood's art in the words "excellent fun when played." Heywood cries out to be played; all his efforts were directed towards the construction of scenes which could be played and which must be played before they really come to life. Speed, emotional scenes, contrast, dependence on skillful timing—all are there in abundance; but we cannot expect to savor them to the full on the printed page, for which Heywood himself had a certain contempt. One can only begin to imagine what his reaction would have been to the almost condescending "excellent fun when played"; certainly bewilderment would form a considerable part of it! In any consideration of Heywood's art, the sharp distinction which he drew between writing for a theater audience and writing for a reader cannot be overemphasized. This, no doubt, was one reason for his popularity as a writer of pageants for the Lord Mayor's shows, and a remark made in *Londini speculum* (1637), after the speech of St. Katherine from the water, neatly sums up his position: "These few following Lines may (and not impertinently) be added vnto *Jupiter's* message, delivered by *Mercury,* which though too long for the Bardge, may perhaps not shew lame in the booke, as being lesse troublesome to the Reader than the Rower."

Heywood's art of characterization would be accorded no more than cautious praise by the most ardent of his admirers, yet a variety of scholars have made an exception in the case of his clowns. Some, indeed, have found the 'Heywood clown' so distinctive a figure that they have not hesitated to attribute to the dramatist certain anonymous plays in which such a figure appeared. Without sharing their enthusiasm, one may nevertheless agree that this clown had certain prominent traits, many of which contributed in no small measure to Heywood's dramatic art. His fondness for juxtaposing violently contrasting scenes has already been mentioned, and in this respect the clown is a very useful figure: he appears in *The Rape of Lucrece,* immediately before and immediately after Tarquin's crime; interspersed between the more serious scenes of *The English Traveller* and *Fortune by Land and Sea*; in the person of Clem, presenting the antics of a country yokel in the exotic court of an eastern potentate in *The Fair Maid of the West*; in the person of Gallus, set to watch while Mars and Venus sleep together in *The Brazen Age*; and as Jupiter's attendant, called upon to distract Danae's keepers while Jupiter makes love to her in *The Golden Age.* Not only does the clown in these and other plays help to effect contrast in the action; for all his clowning he is also allowed to pass shrewd comment on the action as it unfolds. With an earthy realism of speech, a fondness for bawdy jests, and a considerable skill in wordplay, he allows very little to be said or done without bringing to bear upon it the caustic judgment of the man who has no illusions. Lauretta and her mother, in *A Maidenhead Well Lost,* may bewail their wretched state and indulge in the romantic notion of "better dye staru'd than basely begge"; but for their servant, "all the Ladies of *Florence* shal neuer make mee of that beleefe. I had rather begge a thousand times, than starue once. . . . I'le make all the highwayes ring of me with 'For the Lords sake.' I haue studied a Prayer for him that giues, and a Poxe take him that giues nothing . . . ," and so on. Nick, the nearest character to a clown in *A Woman Killed with Kindness*, is clearer sighted than his master in his assessment of Wendoll and, when Anne is dying at the end of the play, withdraws himself from the rest when they express a wish to die with her, remarking, "So will not I, Ile sigh and sob, but by my faith not dye." The Clown in *Fortune by Land and Sea* who, his loyalties divided, will show himself "a true Citizen and stick to the stronger side," will nevertheless find several ways of helping the weaker side and will sum up Old Hardcastle very well while expressing grief at his death: "O my Master . . . the kind churl is departed, never did poor hard-hearted wretch part out of the world so like a lamb; alas for my poor usuring, extortioning Master . . . my sweet, cruel, kind, pittiless, loving, hard-hearted Master . . . my sweet, vild, kind, flinty, mild, uncharitable Master." Furthermore the Clown will be the mouthpiece for the antiromantic trait in Heywood's nature, in *Love's Mistress* (1636), for example, reducing Cupid to the status of "king of cares, cogitations and coxcombs, viceroy of vows and vanities, prince of passions, prate-apaces and pickled lovers . . . ," a "princox" maintained in his "pontificalibus" by "a company of pitifull fellows called Poets"; and as a prime example of burlesque, dealing with the story of Troy in the following terms: "This Troy was a village of some twenty houses; and Priam as silly a fellow as I am, only loving to play the good fellow, hee had a great many bowsing lads, whom he called sonnes. . . . By this Troy ranne a small brook, that one might stride over; on the other side dwelt Menelaus, a farmer, who had a light wench to his wife call'd Hellen, that kept his sheep, whom Paris, one of Priams mad lads, seeing and liking, ticeth over the brooke, and lies with her in despight of her husbands teeth: for which wrong, he sends for one Agamemnon his brother, that was then high Constable of the hundred, and complaines to him: he sends to one Vlisses, a faire-spoken fellow, and Towne-clarke, and to divers others, amongst whom was one stout fellow called Ajax, a butcher, who, upon a holy-day brings a payre of cudgells, and layes them downe in the midst, where the two hundreds then met, which Hector, a baker, another bold lad of the other side seeing, steps forth, and takes them up; these two had a bowt or two for a broken pate. And here was all the circumstance of the Trojan warres."

To which the listening swain may well reply: "To see what these Poets can do!"

The rapid interchange of serious matter and broad comedy, indeed buffoonery, is a prominent feature of Heywood's art, and it is interesting to note that although he had no illusions about the capabilities of those in the audience who preferred the second element, he nevertheless acknowledged their right to be supplied with this kind of entertainment and in some measure approved of it. *Love's Mistress* is full of scenes in which the classical stories are interpreted in terms suited to the 'meaner intelligences.' In his preface to the reader he remarks that "the Argument is taken from *Apuleius,* an excellent Morrall, if truly understood, and may be called a golden Truth, contained in a leaden fable, which though it be not altogether conspicuous to the vulgar, yet to those of Learning and judgement, no lesse apprehended in the Paraphrase, than approved in the Originall: of which, if the perusers hereof were all *Apuleians,* and never a *Midas* amongst them, I should make no question . . . ." Heywood gets over his difficulties in the plot by letting Apuleius represent the learned, Midas the unlearned, and by making use of the subplot to explain for the vulgar the finer points of the main one. He did not often, unfortunately, deal with this problem so neatly, as we shall see. A statement in his pageant *Londini speculum* makes his attitude clear: "The third Pageant or Show meerly consisteth of Anticke gesticulations, dances and other Mimicke postures, devised onely for the vulgar, who are better delighted with that which pleaseth the eye, than contenteth the eare, in which we imitate *Custome,* which carrieth with it excuse: neither are they altogether to be vilefied by the most supercilious and censorious, especially in such a confluence, where all Degrees, Ages, and Sexes are assembled, every of them looking to bee presented with some fancy or other, according to their expectations and humours: since grave and wise men have beene of opinion, that it is convenient, nay necessitous, upon the like occasions, to mixe *seria iocis;* for what better can set off matter, than when it is interlaced with mirth?"

Heywood's intention of killing two birds with one stone may have been admirable; but it must be confessed that the methods he adopted were not always successful, especially from the point of view of dramatic art. The dumbshow, that only too readily available device of the Elizabethan dramatist troubled with a surfeit of plot-materials, had no more fervent admirer, especially in *The Four Ages;* and when it could not be conveniently used in these plays there was a second line of defense in the character of "blind Homer" who, acting as a commentator, could be brought on to speak fifty lines or so in order to explain the action or change the scene. Long allegorical interpretations appear in, for example, *The Brazen Age,* to extract the last ounce of 'benefit' from the stories of the Golden Fleece and the Labors of Hercules. And in the same play, lest any member of his audience should be in doubt about the Golden Fleece story, Heywood allows Absyrtus to invite his sister Medea to explain matters: "Discourse, fair sister, how the golden fleece First came to *Colchos.*" It is an invitation which no woman could resist, and the action of the play comes to a full stop until she has finished. Similarly in *2 The Iron Age* Heywood feels it necessary to insure that there are no misunderstandings about the origins and habits of the Amazons before he allows the play to proceed. Yet it may be noted, in fairness to Heywood, that these highly undramatic devices or episodes occur for the most part in his plays on historical and classical subjects, in which, in common with many of his fellow-dramatists, he gave way to the temptation of trying to handle too much material. If his history plays tend to be chronicles of ill-digested facts, and his *Ages* a series of pageants rather than well-constructed plays, he was at least erring in good company. To such an extent were some of the journeymen-dramatists of the period uninterested in dramatic construction for its own sake that the impatience voiced by Heywood at the end of *The Brazen Age* was probably not unique to him:

> He that expects fiue short Acts can containe
> Each circumstance of these things we present,
> Me thinkes should shew more barrennesse than braine.

There is no arguing with a dramatist who conceives it his duty to overcome a disadvantage of his chosen medium by resorting to methods which do not belong to it, and who feels, besides, that this is a perfectly legitimate thing to do! Certainly we find far less of this inability to choose and shape material, with its accompanying reliance on any and every undramatic trick, in his romantic adventure plays, or in the field which he really made his own, his plays on domestic themes.

An examination of Heywood's art places him fairly and squarely in the company of those Elizabethan and Jacobean dramatists, some known, many others anonymous, who, while having a flair for the theater, rarely rose to the heights of great drama, often plumbed the depths of bad drama, but in general managed to keep to the broad road of drama which could at least be relied upon to provide a company with its bread and butter. They could never become specialists in any kind, for the simple reason that they were called upon to write all kinds. Having no particularly profound outlook upon life, they would tend inevitably to produce work which in the last resort could be called uninspired. Speaking of Heywood's "sense of pity" Eliot remarks (p. 116) that "it is genuine enough, but it is only the kind of pity that the ordinary play-goer, of any time, can appreciate. Heywood's is a drama of common life, not, in the highest sense, tragedy at all; there is no supernatural music from behind the wings. He would in any age have been a successful playwright; he is eminent in the pathetic, rather than the tragic." The same might also be said of his comedy: lacking the driving force of Jonson's satire, he is content with a range from the belly-laugh to the amusing. All the evidence that we have points to his interest in the production of his plays before a not-too-critical audience. He is concerned to entertain the greatest possible number, and as a result many of his plays exhibit what Eliot (p. 106) calls "the minimum degree of unity." He has a wide range of subject matter, yet all too often little control over it. He is adept at all the available stage tricks, yet often gives the impression of not knowing when to stop. He has an infectious enthusiasm for his stories, a considerable sympathy for many of his characters, yet seems to lack the discipline which would enable him to make them more memorable. None of these criticisms, however, would have caused him much concern; in the epilogue to *A Woman Killed with Kindness* he speaks of "an honest crew" drinking in a tavern, each with a different opinion of the wine he is tasting:

> Vnto this wine do we allude our play;
> Which some will iudge too triuiall; some too graue:
> You as our guests we entertaine this day,
> And bid you welcome to the best we haue:
> Excuse vs then; good wine may be disgrast,
> When euery seuerall mouth hath sundry tast.

MASSINGER THE CENSOR

by PHILIP EDWARDS

MASSINGER SEEMS TO HAVE been one of the reluctant dramatists of his age: a gentleman in reduced circumstances who became a playwright as gentlewomen later became governesses. That he would have preferred to be a lord (of the old school) seems a safe guess. What he might have done, as a nobleman, to educate his family, his tenants, his neighbors—and, indeed, his king and his country—he had to do in his plays. Everyone who writes on Massinger recognizes him as a moralist, a sage and serious man determined to indicate what behavior was acceptable and what was not. Yet the kind of dramatic romance he chose to write, or felt he had to write, seems preposterously unsuitable for preachments and sermons. The incongruity has often been noticed. Massinger's latest biographer, T. A. Dunn, has no doubt that the moralist sabotaged the dramatist. "For him," he says, "artistic conscience always succumbs to the conscience of the moralist" (*Philip Massinger,* 1957, p. 74). I do not think this is easily granted. A square peg in a round hole Massinger may have been, but he made a very determined effort to make his art both popular and moral, to present convincing theatrical action which should at the same time be the figured language of morality. Finding himself a dramatist by necessity, and being a moralist by nature, he tried to make 'two distincts, division none.' To watch him at work, bending an unlikely form of play to its moral mold, is perhaps to find a better artist and a more interesting moralist than has sometimes been recognized.

It may seem odd that Massinger should have been so set on wooing the public with the Fletcherian kind of play. He had served his apprenticeship, and more than his apprenticeship, in collaborating with Fletcher in the very popular tragicomedies and romantic tragedies; he seems dedicated to the view that these were the plays which the drama's patrons wanted. Fletcher had not conceived his plays as disquisitions on conduct, and the risks which Massinger later ran are his own responsibility. Massinger chases the consequences of moral choice as Fletcher had fled from them. The sense of strain in continuing to write what his friend and master had shown to be popular is often evident. Though he was a leading writer for the King's Men for a long period, the public does not seem to have been very fond of his plays. In his commendatory verses (1630) to *The Renegado,* Shirley implies that there was a positive dislike and says, with a touch of defiance,

> Yet I commend this poem, and dare tell
> The world I liked it well.

William Singleton mentions "detraction" in his verses (1632) for *The Emperor of the East.* The prologue to the same play says frankly that "Many are apt to wound his credit in this kind." W.B. (in his verses, 1624, to *The Bondman*) goes so far as to claim that Massinger was indifferent to detraction: "his own best way Is to be judge, and author of his play . . . Nor does he write to please, but to endure." It is not likely that Massinger was unmoved by unpopularity. The tone of the prologue to the late play, *The Guardian,* is embarrassingly humble. It speaks of the failure of two plays, a two-year silence, and a reputation for playwriting lost. The author fears his "strengths to please," and submissively asks to know his errors, that he may reform them. Not all of this can be explained as the perfunctory obeisance of a prologue.

Yet Massinger could write other kinds of play. His two comedies of social satire, *A New Way to Pay Old Debts* and *The City Madam,* show that he can excel in that kind. The liveliness of the invention and of the verse carries both plays along with wonderful vigor. It is hard to explain why he wrote only two. Such satires are necessarily built round a moral spine, and seem to perform just what he asked of drama. His patrician contempt for mercantilism, and his dislike of frivolity in women and servility in men, can show themselves in the very material of the plot. The outwitting of Overreach and (in the other play) the ingenious double discomfiture of Luke and the women, are as excellent theatrically as they are 'edifying.' But there are only the two plays. In the dedication (1633) to *A New Way to Pay Old Debts,* Massinger asks the Earl of Carnarvon, by accepting "this trifle," to encourage him to present "some laboured work, and of a higher strain." Such a work Massinger had written, probably soon after *A New Way*, and already published, namely *The Roman Actor* (1626). In that play is a startling example of the uselessness of satire. To cure Philargus of his avarice, Paris the actor puts on a play, "The Cure of Avarice," confident that Philargus,

> looking on a covetous man
> Presented on the stage, as in a mirror
> May see his own deformity, and loath it.
> (2.1.97-9)

But it doesn't work. Philargus 'identifies,' but despises the repentance of the stage miser. "An old fool, to be gull'd thus!" Correction by satire does not work. There are two other playlets in *The Roman Actor*. While watching the first, Domitia is so aroused by Paris, who is acting the part of a lover, that she afterwards seduces him. In the second, Paris acts the part of the servant wooed by his master's wife—a mirror scene of the actual situation he is in—and the emperor, playing the role of the master, kills him in earnest. The moral of the three playlets seems clear. Drama reflects the passages of real life, drama has power to move the audience into 'identification,' even into confusing simulated action with reality. But satire cannot amend the vicious, and the vicious may find cause for vice even in a virtuous play.

It is possible that Massinger had no faith in the usefulness of portraying Overreach and Luke, and preferred to use the moving power of drama to strengthen the potentially virtuous rather than to try to cure the wicked. This is speculative, but it is certain that social satire gave him less scope than the more romantic drama for portraying nobility and (his forte) near-misses at nobility. Had he been left to himself, with no audience to please, he would no doubt have worked entirely in the 'higher strain' of *The Roman Actor*. "I ever held it the most perfect birth of my Minerva," he wrote in 1629. It is as well he was not left to himself; the play is rather wooden and lifeless, too carefully worked to an austere pattern of excellence. *Believe As You List* is much better, easily his best tragedy, but the misfortunes which attended that play show the cost of writing political tragedies. At every point, he seems driven to the Fletcherian mode.

A Very Woman, a late play, seems to be not merely in the Fletcherian mode, but actually a revision of one of Fletcher's plays. It is a failure, perhaps because of the difficulties of reworking, but its weaknesses are instructive. It contains the favorite romantic components of a death which is not a death and a lover in disguise. The last act will bring the dead man back on to the stage and reveal the lover. The familiar components are used to portray, not violent passions and dreadful miscalculations, but insufferable conduct—a defect in nobility and courtesy which Spenser might have been interested in. A strong first act shows the intolerable manners of the lovers, Almira and Cardenes, in slighting the respectful, rejected suitor Antonio. The outcome of their rudeness is a fight and the 'death' of Cardenes. Massinger goes on to test his two flawed characters. Cardenes, dangerously ill, is somewhat tediously brought to repent of his discourtesy. Almira, the "very woman," is tested by the return (brought about by pirates) of Antonio in disguise. She falls in love with the interesting "slave" whom, as a prince, she had spurned. Her lightness is incurable. Antonio is properly disgusted. But there is a woeful happy ending. Cardenes being no longer interested in women, Almira chooses the slave; and when he is revealed as the prince—*he accepts her.* Here indeed the moralist has been betrayed by a miserable devotion to the conventional marriage-ending. It makes no sense at all. This is the only play in which I feel that the artist and moralist have been tugging in different directions, and that the work of art is the poorer because the moralist has lost.

The weakness of *A Very Woman* helps us to judge the strength of two other plays, *The Bondman* and *The Maid of Honour.* Each of them deals, more or less centrally, with defective honor or courtesy. We may take *The Maid of Honour* first, because its ending, though in a way formally 'correct' for tragicomedy, is quite the opposite of that in *A Very Woman* in suiting the moral drift of the play. Camiola, the maid of honor, and Bertoldo, a Knight of Malta and natural brother to the King, are in love. Bertoldo is presented with a wonderful detachment by Massinger. Detachment, even if it arises from some fundamental lack of warmth in the dramatist, is yet a great asset in the dispassionate scrutiny of worth and frailty. One should not make too much of Massinger's heavy-handedness in distinguishing right and wrong. He had the talent to let deeds speak for themselves, as the present play shows. Bertoldo has all the appearance of nobility. In the matter of sending troops to aid their ally in distress, he is all fire and honor, and is opposed to the prudent, self-interested, and somewhat crooked caution of the King (usually supposed to be an image of James, hesitant about aid to the Elector Palatine). But there can be no doubt that the war is a bad cause; the ally has been rash and dishonorable, and the King is right not to support him, even if he acts from the wrong motives. With a pleasant cunning,

Massinger makes it harder for us to see Bertoldo's imperfections by giving him the attractive qualities of impulsiveness and warmth and setting him against a cold, self-regarding monarch (and, of course, by making Camiola love him). His impulsiveness is, in fact, a wanton rashness. His words about "the glory of the war," and "redeeming our mortgaged honours," seem hollow indeed when we eventually get to the scene of the war. Bertoldo's fellow-officers are carpet knights who thought that

> To charge, through dust and blood, an armed foe,
> Was but like graceful running at the ring
> For a wanton mistress' glove.
>
> (2.5.23-5)

They put up no kind of a showing and, worst of all, the war is against a woman. In undertaking it, Bertoldo is breaking his vow as a Knight of Malta. This is the understanding of Bertoldo which Massinger slowly reveals. But we must come back to Camiola's opinion of him. She loves him, but she will not consent to marry him for two reasons: first because their ranks are too disparate, and secondly because marriage means the abandonment of the vows of his order to celibacy. These are the obstacles which honor puts in the way of love. The question of rank, incidentally, was decisive for Massinger, who had a respect for the niceties of stratification which seems unhealthy to us. Camiola has money, but she is not an aristocrat.

The action of the first half of the play, up to the capture and disgrace of Bertoldo in the field, is to reveal the essential shallowness of Bertoldo and the constant honor of Camiola in his absence. Now occurs a scene which seems to have no direct significance. A suitor of Camiola's, Adorni, a gentleman who "had dependence" on her father, fights and wounds the King's favorite for his insulting behavior to Camiola. In the most delicate way, he hints that his protection of her name deserves the reward of her affection. With equal indirection, she firmly puts him in his place. Protection of her name would have been fitting in one in a position to make her his wife, "a height, I hope, which you dare not aspire to." The importance of this scene is that it mirrors and explains the crux of the play—Camiola's ransoming of Bertoldo.

The King has refused to ransom his brother. Camiola, with magnificent generosity, pays the huge sum. She does more than this; by the emissary, she withdraws her previous refusal to marry him, says indeed, in a jesting way, that her granting of his suit shall be the price *he* shall pay for the ransom. But this great act, of generosity and love, is a fall.

It is coming down to the level of Bertoldo and Adorni. It is coming down to Bertoldo's level because she is now prepared to waive her previous refusal and to think as little of his vows as he has done. It is coming down to Adorni's level because she imagines she is erasing inequality of rank through an act of generosity. Her refusal to allow Adorni to buy equality with courage now condemns her own actions. If she previously believed that the disparity in rank between herself and Bertoldo was an insurmountable obstacle, it must always be so.

The reward for the misguided compromise which her love and good intentions lead her into are frightful. Bertoldo reveals his full lightness and inconstancy, by yielding, as soon as he is free, to the attentions of his equal in rank, the princess Aurelia. In the last act, when all is revealed, Aurelia gives up Bertoldo to Camiola. Bertoldo is entirely penitent. What shall Camiola do? She forgives him—but she will not marry him. She will marry no one now, and retires into a convent. If there is to be no compromise with honor, her commerce must be with Heaven and not with men. The last act is surprise upon surprise in the best tradition of tragicomedy. And of the last surprise, the audience has no inkling. It is good theater, and it is the better theater for following the logic of the moral attitude. The moral attitude is undoubtedly daunting. The conception of honor is austere and stern—so it always is in Massinger. But at least it is consistent, and Camiola's final firmness is preferable to the complaisance of Antonio in *A Very Woman*.

A much lighter play, *The Picture*, also has a strong ending to underline Massinger's criticism of his characters. For his usual study in frailty, Massinger cleverly uses the absurd folk-tale element of a magic mirror which will announce a wife's infidelity. The husband is an excellent study in masculine self-assurance and confidence, priggishly making sure of his patient wife's behavior in his absence. But it is he who is tempted and very nearly falls. When he returns to the arms of his wife and we expect a yawning passage of tenderness, the wife refuses to have him back until she is convinced that she has exploded his sureness in himself and his doubting of her. Massinger's plays are rather like those 'house-parties' at which candidates for posts live under constant scrutiny for several days on end. They live to be tested.

The best example of a play in which the trappings of romantic drama are used to test character is *The Bondman,* the finest of the more serious tragicomedies. Massinger took great care in planning the play. Taking from Seneca's *Controversiae* the basic situation of a slave who had protected his mistress during a slave's rebellion and of his right, therefore, to marry her, he welded together patches of Sicilian history from different parts of Diodorus, borrowing from Plutarch and others too, to fill out the moral landscape and draw a distinction between true and false nobility and true and false love. And yet the story is essentially only the familiar one of a prince (disguised as a slave) winning his bride after a series of highly-colored incidents, proving himself a fit husband at the end, from the social point of view, by throwing off his disguise.

Massinger sets the scene of a Sicily corrupted by a decadent aristocracy. Its members are as haughty as they are debauched. They are entirely promiscuous in their sexual habits; they are incapable of meeting a threat of invasion; they treat their slaves like dirt. They have to import Timoleon to lead them against the Carthaginians, and it is Cleora alone (the heroine) who sways them to obey him in surrendering their private wealth and in going to war themselves rather than press the peasants and their slaves. Cleora is intended by her father for Leosthenes, who is one of Massinger's most successful characters. (Massinger has not a very robust power of characterization, and he cannot differentiate by language, but he is a perceptive observer of the weaknesses of men and he collects a good gallery of individual portraits.) Leosthenes reveals himself slowly, like other characters. He is a bit like Faulkland in *The Rivals*. Diffident and self-distrustful, he is yet unable to trust others; his only happiness is self-torment about his relations with people. Beneath this self-distrust is a disgusting priggishness and self-righteousness (as there so often is). His speech to Cleora as he goes off to the war (2.1.108-61) is a masterpiece of a man incapable of faith in others yet insisting they should have faith in him. He takes it for granted that she will fall to the first seducer; he suggests that if *he* had wooed her unchastely she would have fallen. Cleora's answer is to bind her eyes and swear to look at no one and speak to no one till he returns (and she keeps her word).

In Leosthenes' absence, the mystery-man stirs up a rebellion of the slaves. Cleora knows him only as a slave who professes love for her but, amid riot and rape, takes no advantage of her helpless position. His magnanimity and belief in her affect her strangely. (She is, by the way, assured he was born a gentleman.) When Leosthenes returns and the revolt is put down, the old jealousy and arrogance are still there; he cannot believe her innocent, and when he learns that a slave has protected her, he has nothing but contempt for the slave. Cleora has had enough, like Camiola; she chooses true nobility, even in rags and in prison; she throws in her lot with the slave—who eventually justifies her choice by revealing himself for what he really is, a gentleman who had paid court to Cleora but had been rudely sent away by her family. The testing of Cleora through her reaction to a lover disguised as a slave is similar to the testing of Almira in *A Very Woman*. Cleora finds the nobility, even in its disguise; but Almira falls in love with the man, as a slave, whose nobility she had spurned when he was himself. *The Bondman* has its weak points, chiefly through the difficulty of making the hero act like Pisander and at the same time like the slave whom the audience supposes him to be. But its revelation of Leosthenes' weakness and Pisander's strength, through the incidents of a wildly romantic plot, is very well done.

Time and again one finds that Massinger's tragicomedies turn upon problems of conduct. No one would suggest that the very gentle *Great Duke of Florence* was primarily a didactic play. Yet the crisis of the play is the favorite's decision to lie to the king about the beauty of Lidia and to get the young hero to cover up as well; the importance of the play from the moralist's point of view is the degradation which deception brings the two men into. And all this is handled within a comedy whose tone is as light as possible. As one reads the plays, one soon gets into the position which Massinger as censor himself seems to take, and one takes a keener pleasure in the plays as plays because of this moral viewpoint. One watches closely for the telltale strokes which give away the flawed man— for, as I have said, Massinger is careful not to broadcast his disapproval at the beginning of the play. It is true that it is much more difficult to identify oneself with Massinger's rigid code of honor, but then there are difficulties in accepting Jane Austen's. *The Fatal Dowry* (before 1620) is a good example of a play which improves greatly when one sees oneself as a juryman. The play tells how the incorruptible Charalois, whom no cruelty could weaken, is destroyed by generosity—the gift of a fortune and a faithless wife. Again Massinger sets his hero in a corrupt society, this time a mercantile society, moved only by money values. Rochfort is so moved by Charalois' nobility in a degenerate age that he frees him from prison, pays his debts, and weds him to his daughter Beaumelle. Charalois finds her in bed with young Novall and kills her. The question which the play sets, taking it over from the source, is whether Charalois should not have pocketed up his wrongs in gratitude to the father Rochfort, who had done so much for him. The audience is asked to judge.

In the initial, lengthy exposition of Charalois' virtue, we have a feeling that he is something too uncompromising. He is a proud man, consciously pursuing nobility, disgusted by the idea of humility or of obtaining his ends by a little flattery and diplomacy. And so, when he discovers Beaumelle's infidelity, he deliberately casts out any feeling except that of honor. Her sorrow and grief are very moving, and he fears her repentance lest it weaken him.

> See, how you force me
> To this, because mine honour will not yield
> That I again should love you . . . .
> How pity steals upon me! Should I hear her
> But ten words more, I were lost . . . .
> That to be merciful should be a sin!
>
> (4.4.65-7, 76-8)

Still in the trance of the demands of justice and honor, he exacts from the wretched father the judgment that the punishment of Beaumelle's sin is legally death and, as his own executioner, he ceremonially stabs her. Rochfort's impassioned reproach seems "mere madness." In the fine court-scene at the end, Charalois maintains that gratitude to Rochfort could not be allowed to obliterate the distinction between right and wrong. His only crime is that he took the law into his own hands. And the court supports him. When he is stabbed in vengeance by the associate of his wife's lover, he sees his own death as a punishment not for his judgment of Beaumelle but for his taking the place of the hangman. His final "Forgive me!" is surely directed to the audience.

I do not think that Massinger meant Charalois to be an awful warning of what may happen when the passion for honor and absolute justice overcomes all feelings of pity, gratitude, and loyalty. He seems so to us. Given that the choice before Charalois was almost an impossible one, Massinger seems to have approved his hero's path as the better way. But he has recognized that a man is not going to be rewarded for preferring honor to compromise. He makes much of the suffering which the unremitting pursuit of justice brings about. He does all he can to move us with pity for Beaumelle and her father. And he shows Charalois' death as a direct result of his own actions. Yet he wants us to assent in the end that if Charalois erred in his virtue, he would have erred more greatly had he compromised. Whether one assents or not, it is certain that the movement of the play can only be appreciated when the center is seen to be the question of the rightness of Charalois' decision. Otherwise the crisis of the plot seems lost between a lengthy portrayal of Charalois' piety towards his dead father and an irrelevant court-scene.

It is impossible that a point of view so bleak as that implied in *The Fatal Dowry* should ever be attractive to more than a few people, and those few unlikely to have been frequenters of the Caroline theater. *The Fatal Dowry* was an early play, and only *The Maid of Honour* comes near to it in severity among its successors. I like to think that Massinger's efforts to make his moral romance popular were crowned with success once, in the late play *The Guardian* (1633) which he was so dejected about in the prologue. It is a much gayer play than Massinger generally wrote, and the farcical mistakes of the night in the middle of the play are excellently plotted. A carefully maintained tone prevents us from taking anything too seriously. There is a lightness which comes near to banter in the pastoral scenes at the close, with their hackneyed ingredients of the banished nobleman as bandit, the discovery that the servant-maid is really a gentlewoman, and the betrothal of the young leads. Besides treating his romantic genre in semiserious fashion, Massinger implies a tolerance in the moral outlook which is something entirely new. The magnificent amorality of the licentious old guardian is never rejected. He is a thoroughly sympathetic character, much more attractive than his overmoral nephew, busy idealizing women and love. Even the typically Massingerian 'cure' of Iolante—a woman in love with the romance of adultery—is carried off in a new, half-ironical way. She literally wriggles out of the constraint her husband has imposed on her, and her protestations of innocence, like her husband's forgiveness, contain unspoken reservations. Yet the play is written by a good moralist. The frailty of the woman is very neatly described, and the 'lessons' are as clear as in any other play. By easing the severity of his attitude, Massinger has increased the buoyancy of the play. Perhaps Massinger himself is running the risk of compromise. It may be only our own weakness that makes us prefer the easygoing attitude of *The Guardian*. But there is no doubt that the moralist and the dramatic craftsman are very happily married in *The Guardian*.

The Guardian is a peak after which there is only decline. Two extant plays are later than *The Guardian*: the failure of *A Very Woman* we have already seen, and in praise of *The Bashful Lover* there is nothing whatever to be said.

In trying to exercise the high office of a poet in so unpromising a medium as Fletcherian tragicomedy, Massinger was inevitably fighting a losing battle. But to say this is not to condemn his moral romances as plays. The plays could not have been more successful if they had contained less morality, for without the moral scrutiny which is at their core they have no reason for existing.

LENTEN PERFORMANCES
IN THE JACOBEAN
AND CAROLINE THEATERS

by G. E. BENTLEY

THE OBSERVATION OF LENT in the London theaters during the Jacobean and Caroline period was apparently less strict than in Elizabethan times, but it is not easy to make out precisely what the practice was.

Even under Queen Elizabeth the restrictions seem to have varied from time to time. An order of the Privy Council on 13 March 1578/9 had forbidden all playing in Lent,[1] and Sir Edmund Chambers notes that Henslowe's records of performances of the Admiral's Men show long intervals for Lent in 1595 and 1596. But in 1597 the company played a good part of the season before Easter (*The Elizabethan Stage,* 1923, 2.141-2), and in 1592 Lord Strange's Men scarcely observed Lent at all (*ibid.,* 1.315-16). In the years 1600, 1601, and 1604 Council orders seem to reflect a strict enforcement of Lenten closing in the theaters (*ibid.*). But again there were wholesale violations of the prohibition in 1615, for on 29 March of that year representatives of all four of the leading London companies were called before the Privy Council for presuming to play despite the order of the Master of the Revels during "this prohibited time of Lent" (*Malone Society Collections,* 1.4-5, 1911, 372).

After 1615 I find no example of a strictly enforced prohibition of play-

[1] John Roche Dasent, *Acts of the Privy Council of England* (1895), 11.73-4.

ing during Lent.[2] Indeed, in January 1618/19 certain of the inhabitants of the district of Blackfriars, in a petition of complaint against the theater in their precinct, recited the nuisances caused by the theater and concluded:

> Theise inconveniences fallinge out almost everie daie in the winter tyme (not forbearinge the tyme of Lent) from one or twoe of the clock till sixe att night. . . . (*Malone Society Collections*, 1.1, 1907, 92)

Perhaps the fact that the first signature to this petition is that of William Gouge, the Puritan minister of St. Anne's Blackfriars, should prompt one to expect exaggeration in the statements about the frequency of the inconveniences caused by the theater. On the other hand, a number of other statements of comparable date indicate that the theaters were usually under some kind of Lenten restriction. Later allusions to the Lenten dejection of the players are not unlike the statement by Stephens in 1615 in his character of "A common Player":

> . . . when aduersities come, they come together: For Lent and Shrouetuesday be not farre asunder, then he is deiected daily and weekely. (John Stephens, *Essayes and Characters*, 1615, sigs. V7v-8)

For example, one of the poems on the death of the great actor Richard Burbage, on 13 March 1618/19 (i.e. during Lent), has the lines:

> And you, his sad companions, to whom Lent
> Becomes more Lenten yn this accident,
> Henceforth your wavering flag no more hang out.
> Play now noe more at all. . . .[3]

Ten years later writers are still assuming that their readers will be familiar with the Lenten troubles of the players, for John Earle writes in one of his characters, "24. A Player":

> . . . Shroue-tuesday hee feares as much as the Baudes, and Lent is more damage to him then the Butcher. (*Micro-cosmographie*, 1628, sigs. E7v-8)

In the following year Francis Lenton notes the same deprivation as it applies to the spectators in his observations on the frivolities of the young Inns of Court man:

---

[2] The annual Privy Council order about Lent, regularly issued from 1616 to 1627, makes no mention of theaters or players or of any restrictions except those concerning butchering and meat-eating. There are numerous records of actions concerning Lenten offenders from 1616 to 1625, but none involves violations other than those concerned with meat-eating. (*Acts of the Privy Council*, volumes for 1615-16 to 1627-8.)

[3] C. C. Stopes, *Burbage and Shakespeare's Stage* (1913), p. 119.

> Your Theaters hee daily doth frequent
> (Except the intermitted time of Lent) .
>
> *(The Young Gallants Whirligigg*, 1629, sig. B4)

William Prynne, in his *Histrio-Mastix: The Players Scourge, or, Actors Tragœdie,* published in 1633 but written, at least in part, several years earlier, speaks of a recent change:

> Thirdly, there are none so much addicted to Stage-playes, but when they goe unto places where they cannot have them, or when as they are suppressed by publike authority, (as in *times of pestilence,* and in Lent till now of late) can well subsist without them. . . . (sig. 5G4v)

All these allusions to the unhappiness of the players during Lent show clearly that in the time of James I and Charles I the London theaters were not open for business as usual during the weeks before Easter, in spite of the fact that there are no records of absolute prohibitions like those of 1579 and 1601. Prynne, however, indicates that there had recently been a change, and he seems to imply some liberalization of the regulations. A century and a half later Edmund Malone, in his *Enlarged History of the Stage,* indicated the probable form which relaxation of the prohibition took:

> Plays in the time of King James the First, (and probably afterwards,) appear to have been performed every day at each theatre during the winter season, except in the time of Lent, when they were not permitted on sermon days, as they were called, that is, on Wednesday and Friday; nor on the other days of the week, except by special license: which however was obtained by a fee paid to the Master of the Revels.[4]

> These dispensations [i.e. for playing in Lent] did not extend to the sermon-days, as they were then called; that is, Wednesday and Friday in each week. (Variorum ed., 3.65, note 7)

> After Sir Henry Herbert became possessed of the office of Master of the Revels, fees for permission to perform in Lent appear to have been constantly paid by each of the theatres. (*ibid.,* 3.66)

Malone did not, unfortunately, document his assertions, but the question is illuminated by scattered quotations from Sir Henry Herbert's manuscripts extracted by others, or used by Malone in other contexts. Several passages record dispensations to the players and managers for Lent. For example:

> "[Received] of the King's players for a *lenten dispensation,* the other companys promising to doe as muche, 44s. March 23, 1616."

[4] In *The Plays and Poems of William Shakespeare,* ed. James Boswell (1821), 3.151-3 (referred to below as "Variorum ed.").

"Of John Hemminges in the name of the four companys, for toleration in the holy-dayes, 44s. January 29, 1618." *Extracts from the office-book of Sir George Buc, MSS. Herbert. (ibid.,* 3.65, note 7)

For the Kings company . . .
M^r. Hemings brought mee for Lent this 1st Apr. 1624—2^li.5

For a daye in Lent from the Cockpitt companye when their tyme was out 10^s. M^r. Biston sent mee for Lent by M^r. Blagrave in the name of the company this 5th April 2^li. (Halliwell-Phillipps, Scrapbook *Appliances,* p. 127)

From Mr. Blagrave, in the name of the Cockpit company, for this Lent, this 30th March, 1624. £2.0.0. March 20, 1626. From Mr. Hemminges, for this Lent allowanse, £2.0.0. *MSS. Herbert.* (Variorum ed., 3.66, note)

After the Restoration, when Sir Henry Herbert was endeavoring to maintain himself in his old office with all the old rights and fees, he asserted in a petition to the Lord Chancellor and the Lord Chamberlain that among his regular fees was "For Lent Fee . . . [£3.0.0.]" *(ibid.,* 3.266). The inflation is characteristic of Herbert's Restoration petitions, but in other instances scattered records usually show that he did exercise before the wars the rights he claimed after the Restoration.

One final example bears on the problem of the allowance of acting during Lent in the Caroline period. We know from Malone's extracts from Sir Henry Herbert's office-book that in the midst of the long plague-closing from May 1636 to October 1637,[6] the theaters were opened for a week near the end of February 1636/7. But the relation of Lent to this short playing period is indicated only by the Earl of Strafford's London correspondent, the Reverend George Garrard, who writes the Earl as follows:

Upon a little Abatement of the Plague, even in the first Week of *Lent,* the Players set up their Bills, and began to play in the *Black-Fryars* and other Houses. But my Lord of *Canterbury* quickly reduced them to a better Order; for, at the next Meeting at Council his Grace complained of it to the King, declared the Solemnity of *Lent,* the Unfitness of that Liberty to be given, both in respect of the Time and the Sickness, . . . concluding that if his Majesty did not command him to the contrary, he would lay them by the Heels, if they played again. . . . [The Lord Chamberlain thereupon objected to the Archbishop's inter-

---

[5] From an independent transcript of Sir Henry Herbert's manuscript, probably made by Craven Ord and now pasted into various volumes of J. O. Halliwell-Phillipps's Scrapbooks at the Folger Shakespeare Library. This extract is from the volume labeled *Kemp,* p. 142.

[6] G. E. Bentley, *The Jacobean and Caroline Stage* (1941, 1956), 2.661-5.

ference.] . . . So the King put an End to the Business by commanding my Lord Chamberlain that they should play no more.[7]

These surviving records seem to me generally to confirm Malone's understanding that so long as the managers paid the proper fee to the Master of the Revels the theaters could remain open during Lent for four days each week excepting Holy Week.

There is further confirmation in Sir Henry Herbert's office-book (though Malone did not note it in this connection) in some of the records of the French troupe which visited London in 1635 during and after Lent (11 February to 29 March). The French players are first noted on 15 and 17 February 1634/5, when they performed before the Queen at Denmark House and then before both the King and Queen at the Cockpit in Whitehall, but of course these performances at Court would not have been governed by the Lenten restrictions applicable to the London theaters. Sir Henry Herbert then records:

> This day being Friday, and the 20 of the same monthe [February], the kinge tould mee his pleasure, and commanded mee to give order that this Frenche company should playe the too sermon daies in the weeke, during their time of playinge in Lent, and in the house of Drury-lane [i.e. the Phoenix, or Cockpit], where the queenes players usually playe.
>
> The kings pleasure I signifyed to Mr. Beeston [manager of the Phoenix] the same day, who obeyd readily.
>
> The house-keepers are to give them by promise the benefit of their interest for the two days of the first weeke.
>
> They had the benefitt of playinge on the sermon daies, and gott two hundred pounds at least; besides many rich clothes were given them.
>
> They had freely to themselves the whole weeke before the weeke before Easter, which I obtayned of the king for them. (Variorum ed., 3.121)

These few records of the French visitors of 1635 fit precisely the interpretation made above that the acting dispensations which the London companies bought gave them four days a week for playing, but not the two sermon days in any week of Lent and not Holy Week. Since these were the very days given to the French players for their performances, it is not surprising that Christopher Beeston, manager of the Phoenix, "obeyd readily," for the days he was graciously granting were days on which Queen Henrietta's Men could not have performed at the Phoenix in any case.

So far Malone's understanding of Lenten regulations in the Jacobean and Caroline period seems confirmed. On the other hand, his under-

[7] *The Earl of Strafforde's Letters and Dispatches,* ed. William Knowler (1739), 2.56.

standing that it was for *plays* that the theaters were open during Lent is not so well sustained by the records that have survived. Malone himself noted exceptions to dramatic fare in Herbert's records:

> The managers however did not always perform plays during that season. Some of the theatres, particularly the Red Bull and the Fortune, were then let to prize-fighters, tumblers, and rope-dancers, who sometimes added a Masque to the other exhibitions. These facts are ascertained by the following entries:

> 1622. 21 Martii. For a prise at the Red-Bull, for the howse; the fencers would give nothing. 10s. *MSS. Astley.*

> From Mr. Gunnel [Manager of the Fortune], in the name of the dancers of the ropes for Lent, this 15 March, 1624. £1.0.0. (*ibid.,* 3.66, note)

There were other Herbert records of a like nature and dated during Lent which Malone found no occasion to copy, but which are known from the extracts of others who saw the manuscript of the office-book. For example:

> For the Kings company.
>   Shankes Ordinary written by Shankes himself this 16th March 1623. (Halliwell-Phillipps, Scrapbook *Kemp,* p. 152)

> a license to Mr. Lowins, on the 18th of February 1630, for allowing of *a Dutch vaulter,* at their Houses [the Globe and Blackfriars].[8]

> From Vincent—For dancing on the Ropes this Lent at ye Fortune by Blagrave 7 March 1634—2ˡⁱ. (Halliwell-Phillipps, Scrapbook *Fortune,* p. 46)

It is clear from these records that the activities which took place in the specially licensed London theaters on their allowed days in Lent were not always performances of plays. Were they ever plays? Was Malone mistaken in his reading of the accounts in Sir Henry Herbert's office-book? W. J. Lawrence contended that he was. In an essay entitled "The Origin of the Substantive Theatre Masque," Lawrence declared that

> playing had long been rigorously prohibited during the period of abstinence, but that a loophole of escape from an intolerable position had been found. Finding that exhibitions of fencing and acrobatics gave little offence in the close time, the Master of the Revels availed of the circumstances to extract an extra fee and make things a trifle less stringent for the players. Though the proceeds of Lenten letting were

---

[8] George Chalmers, *A Supplemental Apology for the Believers in the Shakspeare-Papers* (1799), p. 209.

the prerogative of the theatre owners, they doubtless shared them, by arrangement with the players. . . . The secret is out. After acting in Lent had been regularly prohibited for some years in James's time, the players got out of their difficulty by letting their theatres during Lent to foreign mountebanks. (*Pre-Restoration Stage Studies,* 1927, pp. 329-30)

Lawrence thought that a further step in the development of nondramatic entertainment at the theaters during Lent was the evolution of what he calls the 'substantive theater masque,' of which *The World Tost at Tennis, The Sun's Darling,* and *Microcosmus* are examples. The argument is his familiar combination of winning exuberance, non sequiturs, careless misstatement of fact, irrelevancies, sweeping generalizations from slight evidence, and triumphant conclusion. Nevertheless the account includes, as usual, shrewd observation and cannot be ignored. One may ask, therefore, what evidence not cited by Lawrence exists to show that the Jacobean and Caroline theaters, though allowed to remain open a good part of the time during Lent, did not present plays then.

The various previously noted laments about the poor players are inconclusive, for the acknowledged prohibition during Holy Week and on Wednesdays and Fridays in the preceding five and a half weeks would have involved nearly 50 per cent reduction in the playing time, and a lamentable shrinkage of income even if the companies had performed their usual plays on *all* the allowed days. The licenses for new or newly revised plays which have come down from Herbert's records during his period of activity, 1622-42, suggest restricted activities, but they do not support the assumption of a complete absence of plays in Lent.

There are nearly 140 of Herbert's dated licensing records now known, and it is notable, to be sure, that fewer of them fall in Lent than in other periods of the year. It is perfectly clear that Lent was not a usual time for the production of new plays, as January, May, June, October, and November clearly were (*Jac. & Car. Stage,* 1.101-3). Yet we know of records of performance licenses for five pieces granted by the Master of the Revels during Lent: Dekker and Ford's *The Sun's Darling* for the Lady Elizabeth's Men at the Phoenix, 3 March 1623/4; John Shank's piece, *Shankes Ordinary* for the King's Men, 16 March 1623/4; Massinger's *Emperor of the East* for the King's Men at the Blackfriars and the Globe, 11 March 1630/31; William Heminges's *Coursing of a Hare, or The Madcap* for the company at the Fortune sometime in March 1632/3; and Henry Glapthorne's *Hollander or Love's Trial* for Queen Henrietta's Men at the Phoenix on 12 March 1635/6 (*ibid.,* 3.459-61, 5.1050-51, 4.777-81, 542-3, 482-3).

Of the five, one might argue for Lawrence that *The Sun's Darling* is not a play but one of his 'substantive theater masques,' and therefore a proper Lenten theater production. But though *The Sun's Darling* is allegorical, so is Middleton's *Game at Chess*, and that piece was produced with sensational success as a play at the Globe six months later. *Shankes Ordinary* is more to Lawrence's purpose, for the actor and jig-dancer John Shank is known as a writer only for his songs and jigs, and *Shankes Ordinary* may very well have been some special sort of Lenten entertainment *(ibid.,* 2.562-7, 5.1049-51). Even for Massinger's *Emperor of the East,* Lawrence might have presented a weak case by contending that this was one of the author's plays written in the plague year of 1630, during which we have no Herbert licenses, and was therefore part of an accumulation of unacted plays prepared by the prompter in an idle period for production later *(ibid.,* 4.755, 777-81).

Though the cases I have made to reconcile the Lenten acting licenses of *The Sun's Darling* and *The Emperor of the East* with Lawrence's hypothesis that no plays were acted in the London theaters during Lent do not strike me as very impressive, I can make none at all for William Heminges's *Coursing of a Hare,* licensed for the Fortune sometime in March 1632/3 (in that year all but the first five days of March fell in Lent), or for Glapthorne's *Hollander,* licensed ten days after the beginning of Lent in 1635/6. Lawrence's reconstruction of the Lenten practices of the players must therefore be rejected.

I think one must say, then, that an examination of the extant entries from Sir Henry Herbert's office-book seems to indicate that in the Jacobean and Caroline period the theaters were theoretically closed during Lent, but that upon the payment of a fee to the Master of the Revels the prohibition was enforced only on Wednesdays and Fridays and during Holy Week; and that even on those days an exception was made at least once—in the case of the French players at the Phoenix in 1634/5. On the days when the theaters were open in Lent the entertainment often consisted of fencing, rope-dancing, and vaulting, at least at the Fortune, the Red Bull, and the Globe. Though there were performances of plays, such performances were far fewer than at other times in the spring and autumn, and accordingly the earnings of the players were sufficiently reduced to make Lent an unpopular season with them.

An analysis of "Annals of Jacobean and Caroline Theatrical Affairs"[9]

---

[9] An appendix prepared for Volume 6 of *The Jacobean and Caroline Stage,* listing chronologically dramatic and semidramatic events of the period, including all recorded performances of plays, masques, and shows. I must apologize for referring to an as-yet-unpublished source, but each of the Lenten events cited can be verified in some source already printed.

roughly confirms this impression. Notable is the diary of Sir Humphrey Mildmay, the most consistent theatergoer among private men of the time of whom we have record. Sir Humphrey records in the period of his diary and accounts (January 1631/2 to December 1641) some fifty-four visits to plays, exclusive of Court performances. Only two of the visits fell in the period of Lent, though it must be noted that Sir Humphrey was often out of town at this time of year. The two entries are:

> 20 March 1633/4 "To a base play att the Cocke pitt. . . . this after noone J wente to the Cocke pitt to a playe wth Bor An^th: a fooleishe one. . . .
> 19 February 1634/5 ". . . To a play, & to Supper. . . ." (*Jac. & Car. Stage,* 2.676-7)

Other Lenten activities datable in the "Annals" pertain mostly to Court activities or to licenses, but play performances outside the Court are indicated or suggested in February or March 1622/3 when John Gill was wounded by an actor on the stage of the Red Bull;[10] on 16 February 1634/5 when Herbert committed Cromes to the Marshalsea for lending the Salisbury Court Players the church robe they used in a production in their theater, presumably within the previous three or four days (*Jac. & Car. Stage,* 1.294); in February and March 1634/5 when John Greene saw six plays performed mostly at the Blackfriars and the Phoenix[11] (no specific days are recorded, but all but ten days of these two months fell in Lent); and 24-8 February 1636/7 when the companies all acted for a week between plague closings (*Jac. & Car. Stage,* 2.662).

These activities are not extensive, and some of them do not necessarily indicate Lenten performances, but taken together they would seem to refute Lawrence's contention and to corroborate other evidence that in the Jacobean and Caroline period the London theaters did present a reduced number of plays, as well as variety turns, four days a week during the first five and a half weeks of Lent.

---

[10] J. C. Jeaffreson, *Middlesex County Records* (1886-92), 2.175-6.
[11] E. M. Symonds, "The Diary of John Greene (1635-57)," *English Historical Review,* 43 (1928), 386.

THE RETURN OF THE OPEN STAGE

by GEORGE F. REYNOLDS

SIXTY OR SO YEARS AGO, in discussions of the Elizabethan public-theater stage, emphasis was chiefly on an acting area *behind* an assumed *front* curtain. Today, in many quarters, emphasis has shifted to an acting area *in front of* an assumed *rear* curtain (or even in front of an uncurtained tiring-house wall). The latter acting area was the projecting *proscænium,* or 'stage,' shown in contemporary pictures of the interiors of Elizabethan theaters. It was 'open' on three sides to be viewed by the surrounding audience; on the fourth side in the Swan picture was the front wall of the tiring-house, with doors leading directly into it. (The few spectators in the gallery over the stage in this picture and in the *Roxana* vignette do not affect the essential situation of an open stage.) Thus the Elizabethan public-theater stage was not an 'arena' stage, as Leslie Hotson would have us believe ("Shakespeare's Arena," *Sewanee Review,* 61, 1953); it had always this immediate background, of which the doors are so important a part that they cannot be separated from it. My title, "The *Return* of the Open Stage," means simply to emphasize the greater importance in Elizabethan times of the open stage itself, as compared with the importance of the space immediately behind the stage; and, today, the renewed importance of the open stage after its near disappearance in recent decades.

In the later days of the nineteenth century (and, as I remember, still later) it was common to describe this open stage as 'naked,' a term which made any serious inquiry into Elizabethan theatrical matters almost unnecessary. The term could also occasion all the more praise for the glories of the then-contemporary stage. At that time in the legitimate the-

361

ater realism was rampant, and in the staging of Shakespeare elaborate settings were fashionable. Scenes were furnished not only with properties required by the action but also with anything interesting that conceivably might have been there. Historic examples are the gondolas moving slowly across the back of the stage in *The Merchant of Venice,* Irving's carload of scenery for *Hamlet,* and Beerbohm Tree's live rabbits hopping about in the forest of *A Midsummer Night's Dream.* With Irving this elaboration often resulted in memorably beautiful settings but also caused the gibe (of course exaggerated) that sometimes in his performances the curtain was down longer for the changes of the settings than it was up for the play to be heard. Time-consuming changes of settings necessitated the omission of many of Shakespeare's numerous scenes or their rearrangement to bring those with the same background together even if the logical order of episodes was thus broken up.

In Germany, meanwhile, the publication by Karl T. Gaedertz in 1888 of Van Buchell's notebook with De Witt's description of the Swan Theater, which he had seen in London around 1596, and the accompanying sketch of its interior, had interested scholars (notably Cecil Brodmeier, *Die Shakespeare Bühne,* 1904) in fresh studies of the Elizabethan theater and its stage, and especially of the way in which Shakespeare's plays were given in his own day.

Interpreting the Swan picture as representative of the Elizabethan public-theater stage, and postulating that a curtain was hung between the stage posts supporting the 'heavens,' Brodmeier and others formulated the theory of 'alternation': No two differently 'set' scenes could occur in succession, for each of such scenes would have had to be played on the 'rear' stage, behind the curtain; and accordingly a scene without special setting must have intervened on the uncurtained 'front' stage. This theory seemed to explain the structure of many of the plays, and to spring from a real familiarity with theater custom. In my first year of graduate study at the University of Chicago (1899-1900), I was a student in a course on Shakespeare which considered this theory in connection with every play, and in Part 1 of my doctoral dissertation, "Some Principles of Elizabethan Staging" (*MP,* 2, 1904-5), I undertook to prove the truth of the alternation theory as applied to all Elizabethan plays before 1603. However, my study turned up so large a number of violations that it became rather a disproof of the theory, and consequently I had to turn elsewhere for any positive conclusion.

Other attempts to make the alternation theory acceptable proved no more convincing until in 1942 John Cranford Adams published *The*

Globe Playhouse, and a few years later further illustrated his proposals in "The Original Staging of *King Lear*" (in *Joseph Quincy Adams Memorial Studies,* 1948). In this article Adams categorically stated his basic assumption that "the Elizabethan drama from beginning to end tended to support stage illusion by scenic realism" (p. 330). 'Tended' is a word difficult to pin down; and realistic touches do have a special appeal to most audiences. Adams's statements on the size and uses of his 'inner stage' and 'upper stage' (or 'study' and 'chamber' as he also calls them since thus he can more easily find scenes supposedly requiring their use) are so positive and specific, and his escape from the problem of 'clashes' (by placing one of two or three consecutive scenes supposedly requiring a setting—and hence supposedly also a front curtain—in the upper inner stage or 'chamber') so simple and apparently reasonable, that college and festival theaters have been built in accordance with his plans, and many performances have followed his suggestions. Irwin Smith, in *Shakespeare's Globe Playhouse* (1956), has slightly modified a few of Adams's rules which are especially open to exception, but his approach is generally similar. Both writers ignore plays that do not fit their plan and create directions for which there are no hints in the original texts. Their 'inner stage,' fronted by a curtain and held within definite bounds, is essentially a modern proscenium-arch stage with the addition of a large 'apron' stage (itself essentially an 'open' stage, but because of the inner stage behind it quite different in its uses from the stage shown in the Swan picture). In his article on *King Lear,* Adams supplied his 'study' and 'chamber' with a number of changeable backgrounds designed to characterize scenes more definitely and more realistically. Thus his rationale of staging is, to say the least, considerably more modern than can be justified by proved Elizabethan usage.

Before and during these developments in Germany and America, in Great Britain something quite different was stirring. William Poel, actor and director, sick of the elaborate mutilation of Shakespeare in the Victorian theater, set himself, in the eighties and nineties, to discover and use again the way the plays had been given in Shakespeare's own time. He had no theater continuously at his disposal and therefore had to use various halls and courtyards for his performances; and he received no adequate financial support and only limited public recognition. He was born in 1852 and died in 1934; a few years later the Society for Theatre Research set itself to gain for him the recognition he deserved. Sir Lewis Casson's "William Poel and the Modern Theatre" (*The Listener,* 10 January 1952) provides a summary of Poel's aims and practices, and the

Society later sponsored *William Poel and the Elizabethan Revival* (1954), a detailed and illuminating account by Robert Speaight of Poel's theatrical career. (Further valuable commentary on Poel's work is made by M. St. Clare Byrne in "Modern Production and Theatrical Tradition," *The Listener,* 8 September 1949.) Because of Poel's revolutionary ideas concerning staging, acting, and delivery, and his lack of adequate financial backing, his immediate influence on the theater of his day was admittedly not very great. Nor does he seem to have made much impression on the scholars; for instance, his name does not occur in the indexes to Sir Edmund Chambers's *Elizabethan Stage* (1923) or *William Shakespeare* (1930). Poel visited Harvard in the autumn of 1905 and a little later the University of Chicago, lecturing at both places before he returned to England. (These visits, incidentally, are not mentioned in the chronological appendix of Poel's activities compiled by Allan Gomme for Speaight's book, p. 283.) It was, Casson says, through the young men who came under Poel's influence directly or indirectly—Nugent Monck, Granville-Barker, Bridges-Adams, Robert Atkins, Casson himself, and in more recent years Sir Tyrone Guthrie—that Poel's ideas on staging have profoundly modified many professional productions.

A statement of Poel's basic idea, quoted by Casson, is "that the open platform, or the arena, surrounded—or almost so—by the audience, alone provided the proper setting for plays which were never intended to be realistic or to be spectacles to be gazed at. They were games of 'Let's pretend,' played by the audience on their nursery floor which they could make a ship or a battlefield at will, with soliloquies and asides talked to them with greater personal intimacy than those of George Robey or Danny Kaye." There, as I need scarcely point out, is recognition of the open stage and a definite contrast to insistence on realism. Thus today we have two basically different ways of regarding the Elizabethan stage: Adams's which sees it as "tending to support stage illusion by scenic realism," and Poel's which would create stage illusion through stylized suggestion and the audience's powers of make-believe.

At this point Part 2 of my dissertation may be mentioned (*MP,* 3, 1905-6). Having shown in Part 1 that the alternation theory as stated by Brodmeier and others did not fit the English plays dating before 1603, I had turned for an explanation to their medieval inheritance. This had of course been emphasized already by Creizenach, Jusserand, Matthews, and Chambers himself in *The Medieval Stage* (1903). I pointed out certain medieval practices as continuing on the Elizabethan stage, among them unlocated scenes, journeying scenes in which even a few steps on the stage were accepted as representing a much greater distance, and, as most conspicuous, the retention on the stage, in scenes where they did not belong, of certain properties for convenience or symbolic value. To this convention Chambers, though admitting its use elsewhere and describing it at length, was strongly opposed in the public theaters of Shakespeare's day, insisting that each scene had "full occupation of the stage." He did admit that there were scenes even then where the problem did arise, but thought it could be solved by use of a trap door or by hoisting the incongruous property to the hut over the stage (*The Elizabethan Stage,* 3.88). I suspect that since this condemnation few scholars have accepted the idea of Shakespeare's stage as basically medieval. But it is precisely this use of incongruous properties that directors at once scholarly and practical have now adopted; for instance, Tyrone Guthrie in his *Henry VIII* at Stratford-upon-Avon (1949) did not use the front curtain at all, and the great throne remained in sight throughout the play (as it did also in the whole series of historical plays at Stratford in 1951) for use as a royal seat and as a symbol of what was at stake.

I mention these matters here to suggest that exposure of a very raw graduate student to the medieval background before he had acquired any settled ideas concerning the Elizabethan stage made it easier to understand that stage as one that did not attempt 'realism.' A single sentence from the conclusion of my dissertation shows how close I came to the idea of the open stage: "The stage for the playwright of Shakespeare's day was necessarily only a platform upon which his characters stood, while the scene was anywhere his fancy dictated or his plot required." I admit that in writing that sentence I did not realize all the implications of the open stage, or of the theory that a given scene should have "full occupation" of the stage. (Chambers did not coin that phrase till nearly twenty years later.) My dissertation, published as two magazine articles in April and June of 1905, was naturally never formally reviewed. I was therefore gratified, in the autumn of that year, to learn through a former student of mine who attended Poel's lectures at Harvard that Poel had several times commended my dissertation; and after Poel's visit to Chicago Professor John Matthews Manly wrote me to the same effect.

A basic difference of opinion on the Elizabethan stage concerns the size and importance of the discoverable spaces. The problem is extremely complicated and can be only glanced at here. Adams naturally makes much use of the discoverable space on the level of the stage, as well as of that above. His argument calls for discoverable acting spaces of considerable size, both above and below: at the Globe, for instance, twenty-three feet wide and eight deep. He sees his large inner stage as a means of continually changing 'sets' behind a closed curtain, and of framing action in accordance with the 'fourth-wall' convention; and he argues that the inner stage was normally used several times during each performance. In contrast Richard Hosley finds little evidence for a discoverable acting place at all ("The Discovery-space in Shakespeare's Globe," *Shakespeare Survey,* 12, 1959). What evidence he finds in Globe plays suggests a space no wider than seven feet or deeper than four; and he sees that space as a means of suddenly 'showing' a striking or significant tableau at very infrequent intervals—perhaps as seldom as once or twice a play in every second or third play. Hence he suggests that discoveries were effected in the space behind an open doorway in the tiring-house wall, concealed by hangings. Such a space, he argues, would not have been used, like Adams's inner stage, as an acting area in which special 'sets' were prepared or in which much if any movement took place. Most other theories of the discoverable space below fall between these two, though generally that space is conceived of as a structure (usually temporary) standing on the stage in front of the tiring-house. Among these theories are Tieck's 'pavilion,' of which A. M. Nagler has recently reminded us (*Shakespeare's Stage,* 1958); Nagler's own 'tent'; the curtains I have suggested to be hung on a movable framework in front of the central tiring-house door when the need arises for a discoverable space larger than the one usually provided ("*Hamlet* at the Globe," *Shakespeare Survey,* 9, 1956); and the small 'booth' proposed by C. Walter Hodges in *The Globe Restored* (1953).

The advantages of the open stage have been stated with special insight by Richard Southern in *The Open Stage* (1953), and by Tyrone Guthrie in "Shakespeare at Stratford, Ontario" (*Shakespeare Survey,* 8, 1955) and *My Life in the Theatre* (1959). Most of these advantages are obvious as soon as mentioned. The simple setting does not call attention away from the actor and what he says and does; thus it is especially favorable to poetry. The simplicity of setting requires almost no time for stage arrangement. The actor is close to his audience, and thus can easily establish and maintain an intimacy of acting style. And Southern, like Poel rejecting the notion that realism has anything to do with the creation of stage illusion, says with special force that the open stage, with spectators surrounding it on three sides, reminds each of them that they are all together, actors and spectators alike, taking part in the performance of a play.

So far we have been thinking of the return of the open stage as a great advance in the presentation of Shakespeare. George Kernodle, in his challenging essay "The Open Stage: Elizabethan or Existentialist?" (*Shakespeare Survey*, 12, 1959), on factual and philosophic grounds finds modern emphasis on the open stage (by which term he seems to understand a 'bare' stage) rather the result of "our own loss of faith in a unified vision of a meaningful universe. . . . the open stage was once used as part of a vision of man's central place in a cosmos of dignity and order." Kernodle is quite properly lamenting the loss of symbolic values emanating from what might be called the architectural decor of the Elizabethan stage and its containing theater. But an 'open' stage is not necessarily 'bare' or uninformative. Vivid costumes convey at once the social position of the wearer and go far toward satisfying the eye's natural hunger for pageantry; and simple but essential properties (as Brecht understood so well) go beyond costume in helping the eye (and the mind) to compose a 'scene.' Some stools and a table (with two or three battered tankards) are 'set out,' and the stage becomes a tavern. A bed is 'put forth' or 'thrust out' or 'drawn in,' and we accept the stage as a chamber. A girl comes on stage carrying a pitcher and sets it down beside the open trap door, and we immediately recognize this as a well. These devices are effective in establishing standard 'scenes.' In addition, there were other scenic conventions, among them the use of locality boards, the indicating of a change of scene without a change of setting by an actor's exit at one door and immediate re-entrance at another, and the retention on the stage of sizable properties like the throne or trees during scenes in which, from a 'realistic' point of view, such properties would have been incongruous. But these conventions make up another story altogether.

A BIBLIOGRAPHY OF THE WRITINGS OF HARDIN CRAIG FROM 1940 TO 1961*

compiled by J. M. BRAFFETT

1940 *A Treatise on Melancholie by Timothy Bright.* Introduction by Hardin Craig. The Facsimile Text Society. New York: Columbia University Press. Pp. xxii, xxiii, 285.

1941 *Stanford Studies in Language and Literature.* Edited by Hardin Craig on the Fiftieth Anniversary of the Founding of Stanford University. Stanford University Press. Pp. vi, 387.

Review: Paul V. Kreider, *Repetition in Shakespeare's Plays* (1941). *MLQ,* 2 (December), 648-50.

"Recent Literature of the Renaissance: A Bibliography," *SP,* 38 (April), 271-426.

1942 "Shakespeare's Development as a Dramatist in the Light of His Experience," *SP,* 39 (April), 226-38.

Review: John Erskine Hankins, *The Character of Hamlet and Other Essays* (1941). *MLQ,* 3 (March), 125-6.

Review: Arthur Hobson Quinn, *Edgar Allan Poe: A Critical Biography* (1942). *Virginia Quarterly Review,* 18 (April), 285-90.

"Recent Literature of the Renaissance: A Bibliography," *SP,* 39 (April), 328-486.

---

* Professor Craig's earlier writings are listed by Francis R. Johnson, "Bibliography of the Writings of Hardin Craig from 1901 to 1940," in *Renaissance Studies in Honor of Hardin Craig,* ed. Baldwin Maxwell, W. D. Briggs, Francis R. Johnson, and E. N. S. Thompson (1941).

1943 "The Field of Academic Learning in Relation to the War," *South Atlantic Bulletin,* 9 (April), 1, 5.

"The Universities after the War," *Bulletin of the American Association of University Professors,* 29 (April), 209-17.

Review: Don Cameron Allen, *The Star-Crossed Renaissance* (1941). *JEGP,* 42 (July), 433-6.

"Recent Literature of the Renaissance: A Bibliography," *SP,* 40 (April), 257-366.

1944 *Literary Study and the Scholarly Profession.* Seattle: University of Washington Press. Pp. xiii, 150.

Machiavelli's The Prince: An Elizabethan Translation. Edited by Hardin Craig. Chapel Hill: University of North Carolina Press. Pp. xli, 177.

"Of *The Laws of Ecclesiastical Polity*—First Form," *JHI,* 5 (January), 91-104.

"Shakespeare and the Normal World," *Rice Institute Pamphlet,* 31 (January), 1-49.

"Librarians and Literary Culture," *Pacific Northwest Library Association Quarterly,* 8 (July), 129-36.

"Renaissance Ideal: A Lecture on Shakespeare," *University of North Carolina Extension Bulletin,* 24 (November), 25-35.

Review: Thomas Marc Parrott and Robert Hamilton Ball, *A Short View of Elizabethan Drama* (1943); M. M. Bhattacherje, *Courtesy in Shakespeare* (1940); Oscar James Campbell, *Shakespeare's Satire* (1943); T. W. Baldwin, *William Shakspere's Petty School* (1943). *MLN,* 59 (February), 133-7.

Review: Don Cameron Allen (ed.), *The Owles Almanacke* (1943). *JEGP,* 43 (October), 457-8.

"Recent Literature of the Renaissance: A Bibliography," *SP,* 41 (April), 265-369.

1945 "Recent Scholarship of the English Renaissance: A Brief Survey." In *Studies in Language and Literature,* ed. George R. Coffman. Chapel Hill: University of North Carolina Press, pp. 120-51.

"*The Shrew* and *A Shrew*: Possible Settlement of an Old Debate." In *Elizabethan Studies and Other Essays in Honor of George F. Reynolds,* ed. E. J. West. Boulder: University of Colorado Press, pp. 150-4.

Review: E. M. W. Tillyard, *The Elizabethan World Picture* (1944). *College English,* 6 (January), 236-8.

"Recent Literature of the Renaissance: A Bibliography," *SP,* 42 (April), 271-377.

1946 *Literature and the Community: The Problem of Choice.* Chapel Hill: University of North Carolina Library. Pp. 13.

"The Origin of the Passion Play: Matters of Theory as Well as Fact." In *Studies in Honor of A. H. R. Fairchild,* ed. Charles T. Prouty. Columbia: University of Missouri Studies, pp. 83-90.

"Recent Literature of the Renaissance: A Bibliography," *SP,* 43 (April), 275-460.

1947 Review: F. P. Wilson, *Elizabethan and Jacobean* (1945). *MLQ,* 8 (March), 124-5.

Review: Howard Mumford Jones, *Education and World Tragedy* (1946). *American Literature,* 19 (March), 83-5.

Review: Harley Granville-Barker, *Prefaces to Shakespeare,* volume 1 (1946). *JEGP,* 46 (July), 312-15.

"Recent Literature of the Renaissance: A Bibliography," *SP,* 44 (April), 267-452.

1948 *An Interpretation of Shakespeare.* New York: Dryden Press. Pp. ix, 400.

"Pericles Prince of Tyre." In *If By Your Art: Testament to Percival Hunt,* ed. George Carver and Agnes L. Starrett. University of Pittsburgh Press, pp. 1-14.

"Shakespeare and the History Play." In *Joseph Quincy Adams Memorial Studies,* ed. James G. McManaway, Giles E. Dawson, and Edwin E. Willoughby. Washington: Folger Shakespeare Library, pp. 55-64.

"Shakespeare's Bad Poetry," *Shakespeare Survey,* 1.51-6.

"Pericles and *The Painful Adventures,"* *SP,* 45 (October), 600-605.

Review: Harley Granville-Barker, *Prefaces to Shakespeare,* volume 2 (1947). *JEGP,* 47 (July), 303-4.

"Recent Literature of the Renaissance: A Bibliography," *SP,* 45 (April), 237-417.

1949 *Freedom and Renaissance.* Chapel Hill: University of North Carolina Press. Pp. xi, 117.

"Trend of Shakespeare Scholarship," *Shakespeare Survey,* 2.107-14.

"Shakespeare as an Elizabethan: Hardin Craig Introduces a Series of Talks on Shakespeare and His World," *The Listener,* 42 (21 July), 99-100.

"An Aspect of Shakespearean Study," *SAB,* 24 (October), 247-57.

Review: Francis A. Yates, *The French Academies of the Sixteenth Century* (1947). *RES,* 25 (July), 263-5.

"Recent Literature of the Renaissance: A Bibliography," *SP,* 46 (April), 205-386.

1950 *A History of English Literature* (by George K. Anderson, Hardin Craig, Louis I. Bredvold, and Joseph Warren Beach). Edited by Hardin Craig. New York: Oxford University Press. Pp. xiii, 697.

"The Literature of the English Renaissance, 1485-1660." In *A History of English Literature,* ed. Hardin Craig. New York: Oxford University Press, pp. 173-342.

"Morality Plays and Elizabethan Drama," *SQ,* 1 (April), 64-72.

Review: H. H. Blanchard (ed.), *Poetry and Prose of the Continental Renaissance in Translation* (1949). *American Historical Review,* 55 (April), 650-51.

1951 *The Complete Works of Shakespeare.* Edited by Hardin Craig. Chicago: Scott, Foresman. Pp. xii, 1338.

"Shakespeare and Elizabethan Psychology: Status of the Subject." In *Shakespeare-Studien: Festschrift für Heinrich Mutschmann,* ed. Walther Fischer and Karl Wentersdorf. Marburg: Elwert, pp. 48-55.

"Motivation in Shakespeare's Choice of Materials," *Shakespeare Survey,* 4.26-34.

1952 *An Introduction to Shakespeare: Eight Plays, Selected Sonnets.* Edited by Hardin Craig. Chicago: Scott, Foresman. Pp. 752.

"A Cutpurse of the Empire: On Shakespeare Cosmology." In *A Tribute to George Coffin Taylor,* ed. William Arnold. Chapel Hill: University of North Carolina Press, pp. 3-16.

"Shakespeare and the Here and Now," *PMLA,* 67 (February), 87-94.

"Woodrow Wilson as an Orator," *Quarterly Journal of Speech,* 38 (April), 145-8.

Review: Ernest A. Strathmann, *Sir Walter Raleigh: A Study in Elizabethan Skepticism* (1951). *JEGP,* 51 (April), 249-50.

Review: G. Wilson Knight, *The Imperial Theme* (3rd ed., 1951). *SQ,* 3 (July), 267-71.

Review: Helen C. White, *The Tudor Books of Private Devotion* (1951). *JEGP,* 51 (October), 596-7.

1953 *The Written Word and Other Essays.* Chapel Hill: University of North Carolina Press. Pp. ix, 90. Includes: "The Written Word," pp. 3-17; "The Vitality of an Old Classic: Lucian and Lucianism," pp. 18-31; "Hamlet and Ophelia," pp. 32-48; "These Juggling Fiends: On the Meaning of *Macbeth,*" pp. 49-61; "Burns and Lowland Scotch," pp. 62-77; "An Ethical Distinction by John Milton," pp. 78-88.

"Review of Shakespearian Scholarship in 1952," *SQ,* 4 (April), 115-24.

Review: Hermann Heuer and others (eds.), *Shakespeare-Jahrbuch,* 84-6 (1950). *MLR,* 48 (January), 67-8.

Review: Douglas Bush, *Classical Influences in Renaissance Literature* (1952). *JEGP,* 52 (April), 255-6.

Review: Jean Robertson (ed.), *Poems by Nicholas Breton* (1952). *JEGP,* 52 (July), 417-18.

1954 Review: Paul H. Kocher, *Science and Religion in Elizabethan England* (1953). *JEGP,* 53 (July), 469-72.

1955 *English Religious Drama of the Middle Ages.* Oxford: Clarendon Press. Pp. viii, 421.

"Walter Clyde Curry and Contemporary Scholarship." In *Essays in Honor of Walter Clyde Curry,* ed. Richmond C. Beatty and Edgar H. Duncan. Nashville: Vanderbilt University Press, pp. 9-22.

"Proof and Probability in the Study of Shakespeare and His Contemporaries," *McNeese Review,* 7 (Spring), 26-38.

1956 "The Dering Version of Shakespeare's *Henry IV,*" *PQ,* 35 (April), 218-19.

Review: M. D. H. Parker, *The Slave of Life: A Study of Shakespeare and the Idea of Justice* (1954). *College English,* 17 (January), 243-4.

1957 *Two Coventry Corpus Christi Plays,* 2nd ed. Early English Text Society, Extra Series, 87. Edited by Hardin Craig. London: Oxford University Press. Pp. xlii, 134.

Review: Robert B. Heilman, *Magic in the Web: Action and Language in Othello* (1956). *Explicator,* 15 (April), Review 4.

1958 "Criticism of Dramatic Texts." In *Studies in Honor of T. W. Baldwin,* ed. Don Cameron Allen. Urbana: University of Illinois Press, pp. 3-8.

1959 "Revised Elizabethan Quartos: An Attempt to Form a Class." In *Studies in the English Renaissance Drama in Honor of Karl Julius Holzknecht,* ed. Josephine W. Bennett, Oscar Cargill, and Vernon Hall. New York University Press, pp. 43-57.

Review: G. Wilson Knight, *The Sovereign Flower* (1958). *SQ,* 10 (Summer), 439-42.

1960 *Woodrow Wilson at Princeton*. Norman: University of Oklahoma Press. Pp. 175.

    New Lamps for Old: A Sequel to The Enchanted Glass. Oxford: Basil Blackwell. Pp. viii, 244.

    "Textual Degeneration of Elizabethan and Stuart Plays: An Examination of Plays in MSS," *Rice Institute Pamphlet*, 46 (January), 71-84.

1961 *A New Look at Shakespeare's Quartos*. Stanford University Press. Pp. iv, 131.

    "From Gorgias to Troilus." In *Studies in Medieval Literature in Honor of Albert C. Baugh*, ed. MacEdward Leach. Philadelphia: University of Pennsylvania Press, pp. 97-107.

    Review: Una Ellis-Fermor, *Shakespeare the Dramatist and Other Papers*, ed. Kenneth Muir (1961). *PQ*, 40 (October), 615-16.

    Review: Mark Eccles, *Shakespeare in Warwickshire* (1961). *Renaissance News*, 14 (Winter), 284-7.

1962 "Ideational Approach to Shakespeare's Plays." In *Studies in English Drama Presented to Baldwin Maxwell*, ed. Charles B. Woods and Curt A. Zimansky. *PQ*, 41 (January), 147-57.

    "The Composition of *King Lear*." In *Renaissance Papers 1961*, ed. George Walton Williams and Peter G. Phialas. Durham: Southeastern Renaissance Conference, pp. 57-61.

INDEX